Basic Physics 1 and 2

David Sang

Series editor
Fred Webber

PUBLISHED BY THE PRESS SYNDICATE OF THE UNIVERSITY OF CAMBRIDGE
The Pitt Building, Trumpington Street, Cambridge CB2 1RP, United Kingdom

CAMBRIDGE UNIVERSITY PRESS
The Edinburgh Building, Cambridge CB2 2RU, United Kingdom
40 West 20th Street, New York, NY 10011–4211, USA
10 Stamford Road, Oakleigh, Melbourne 3166, Australia

First published 1995
Reprinted 1996, 1997

Printed in the United Kingdom at the University Press, Cambridge

A catalogue record for this book is available from the British Library

ISBN 0 521 48502 9 paperback

Designed and produced by Gecko Ltd, Bicester, Oxon

This book is one of a series produced to support individual modules within the Cambridge Modular Sciences scheme. Teachers should note that written examinations will be set on the content of each module as defined in the syllabus. This book is the author's interpretation of the module.

Front cover photograph: A surfer under the crest of a wave in Hawaii, USA; John Callahan/Tony Stone Images

Contents

Introduction

This book covers the requirements of two modules, *Basic Physics 1* and *Basic Physics 2*. The chapters are divided between the two modules as shown in the table. The sequence of chapters within the book is intended to provide a sensible route through the content, if you are studying both modules.

Basic Physics 1	*Basic Physics 2*
1 Motion in a circle	
	2 Gravity
3 Oscillations and vibrations	
4 Superposition of waves	
5 Electrical voltages	
6 Capacitance	
	7 Electric fields
8 Electromagnetism 1	
	9 Electromagnetism 2
10 Electromagnetic induction 1	
	11 Electromagnetic induction 2
12 Phases of matter	
13 Deforming solids	
	14 Ideal gases
	15 Thermodynamics
	16 Thermal energy transfer
17 Quantum physics	
18 Nuclear physics	
19 Radioactivity	

Acknowledgements

1, 18, 23, 25, 28, 36, 40, 43, 48, 54, 56, 62, 69, 76, 129, 133, 138, 142*r*, 164, Andrew Lambert; 6, Erik Viktor/Science Photo Library; 7, 52, 118, 134, Images Colour Library; 12, courtesy of PASCO Scientific; 17, 114*br*, Kim Taylor/Bruce Coleman Ltd; 24, Range/Bettmann/UPI; 26, Robert Harding Picture Library; 27, J.C. Revy/ Science Photo Library; 31, courtesy of David Sang; 39, 41, Tick Ahearn; 64, Alex Bartel/Science Photo Library; 71, Patrice Loiez, CERN/Science Photo Library; 81, Crown Copyright/photo courtesy of National Physical Laboratory; 83, Peter Menzel/ Science Photo Library; 88, Bill Longchore/Science Photo Library; 96, 114*tr*, Philippe Plailly/Science Photo Library; 97, 130, Science and Society Picture Library/The Science Museum; 108, Graham Burns/Life File; 110, Philippe Plailly/ Eurelios/Science Photo Library; 116, Bruno Lucas/ Britstock-IFA; 127, RKS Photography, 130 Purewell, Christchurch, Dorset; 132*a*, Zscharnack/ Britstock-IFA; 132*b*, David Higgs/Tony Stone Worldwide; 136*l*, Alfred Pasieka/Science Photo Library; 136*r*, NASA/Science Photo Library; 137, 142*tl*, Michael Brooke; 139*t*, Tim Garrod/Zul; 141, Sergei Verein/Life File; 142*bl*, Arcam, Pembroke Avenue, Waterbeach, Cambridge; 143, Institut für Angewandte Physik Universität Tübingen, Germany/photo and permission courtesy of Dr Hannes Lichte/by permission of the *Annals of the New York Academy of Sciences*, **4800**, 175–189, 1986; 149, Dept of Physics, Imperial College/Science Photo Library; 154, US Navy/Science Photo Library; 156*bl*, JET/Travel Ink/Life File; 156*br*, David R. Austen/Bruce Coleman Ltd; 161, BSIP/Science Photo Library; 163, N. Feather/Science Photo Library; 165, David Parker/Science Photo Library

Motion in a circle

By the end of this chapter you should be able to:

1. describe how a centripetal force acting at right-angles to the velocity of a moving object gives rise to motion at a steady speed along a circular path (uniform circular motion);
2. describe uniform circular motion in terms of centripetal acceleration,
3. identify forces giving rise to uniform circular motion;
4. recall and use equations for centripetal acceleration and centripetal force:

$$a = \frac{v^2}{r} \qquad F = \frac{mv^2}{r}$$

● **Figure 1.1** Going round in circles at the fairground.

Uniform motion in a circle

In your study of the *Foundation Physics* module, you considered two important aspects of mechanics: **kinematics**, in which the motion of objects is described in terms of displacement, velocity and acceleration; and **dynamics**, in which the motion of objects is explained by Newton's laws of motion, in terms of forces, mass and momentum.

The *Foundation Physics* module considered only objects moving in a straight line. In this chapter, we will extend this study to objects moving along a circular path.

Many objects move in circles *(figure 1.1)*: the hand of a clock as it moves around the clock face; the Earth in its near-circular orbit around the Sun; a child on a merry-go-round in the park; an electron as it orbits the nucleus of a hydrogen atom. In this chapter, we will consider how we can describe this motion (kinematics) and how we can explain it in terms of the forces acting (dynamics).

Steady speed

We will restrict our study to objects that follow circular paths at a steady speed. Speeding up and slowing down are unnecessary complications at this stage.

It is a simple matter to calculate the speed of an orbiting object if we know the length of its orbital path and the time it takes for one orbit *(figure 1.2)*. It is

$$\text{speed} = \frac{\text{circumference of orbit}}{\text{time for one orbit}}$$

If we know the radius of the orbit, then we can work out its circumference (using π, Greek letter pi):

$$\text{circumference of orbit} = 2\pi \times \text{radius of orbit}$$

By rearranging the first of these equations, we can find the time for one orbit if we know speed and circumference.

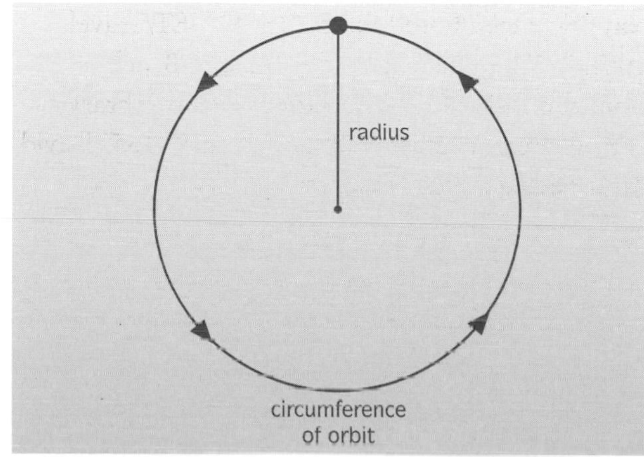

● **Figure 1.2** An object moving round a circular path.

SAQ 1.1

a Each year, the Earth orbits the Sun at an average distance of about 150×10^6 km. Calculate the Earth's speed in its orbit, in $\mathrm{km\,s^{-1}}$.

b The Earth rotates once each day. Its radius is 6400 km. Calculate the speed of rotation of a point on the Earth's equator in $\mathrm{m\,s^{-1}}$.

c A satellite orbits the Earth at a height of 200 km above the Earth's surface. Its speed is $8\,\mathrm{km\,s^{-1}}$. How long does it take for one complete orbit of the Earth? (Radius of Earth = 6400 km.)

Steady speed, changing velocity

So far, we have used the term *speed*. However, if we are to use Newton's laws of motion to explain circular motion, we must go on to consider the *velocity* of an object going round in a circle.

There is an important distinction between speed and velocity: **speed** is a scalar quantity, but **velocity** is a vector quantity, with both magnitude and direction. We need to think about the direction of motion of an orbiting object.

Figure 1.3a shows how we can represent the velocity of an object at various points around its orbit. The arrows are straight (to show the direction of motion at a particular instant). They are drawn as tangents to the circular path. As the object orbits through points A, B, C, etc., its speed remains constant but its direction changes. The arrows representing velocity at these points are collected together in *figure 1.3b*, to show how the direction changes.

Since the direction of velocity v is changing, it follows that v itself (a vector quantity) is changing as the body orbits. Remember, though, that the body's speed is constant.

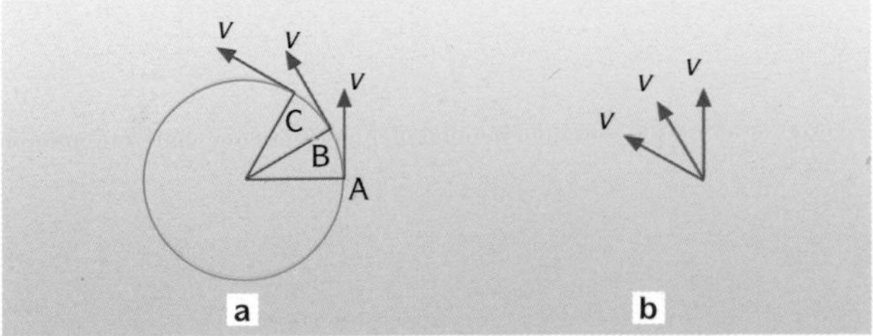

● ***Figure 1.3*** The velocity of an object changes direction as it moves along a circular path.

SAQ 1.2

Why are all the arrows in *figure 1.3a* (or *figure 1.3b*) drawn the same length?

SAQ 1.3

A toy train travels at a steady speed of $0.2\,\mathrm{m\,s^{-1}}$ around a circular track. A and B are two points diametrically opposite to one another on the track *(figure 1.4)*.

a By how much does the train's speed change as it travels from A to B?

b By how much does the train's velocity change as it travels from A to B?

Centripetal forces

When an object's velocity is changing, we say that it is accelerating. In the case of uniform circular motion, the acceleration is rather unusual because, as we have seen, the object's speed does not change but its velocity does. How can an object accelerate, and at the same time have a steady speed?

One way to understand this is to think about what Newton's laws of motion can tell us about this situation.

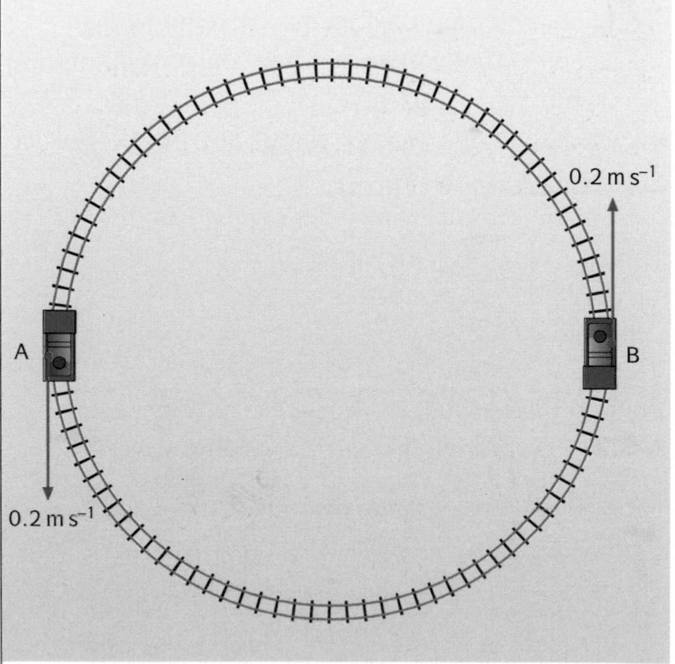

● ***Figure 1.4*** A toy train travelling around a circular track.

Newton's first law

If a body is at rest it will remain at rest, and if it is moving it will continue to move with constant velocity, unless a resultant force acts on it.

In the case of an object moving at steady speed in a circle, we have a body whose velocity is not constant; therefore, there must be a resultant or unbalanced force acting on it.

Now we can think about various situations where objects are going round in a circle, and try to find the force that is acting on them.

Consider a conker on the end of a string. Imagine whirling it in a horizontal circle above your head *(figure 1.5)*. To make it go round in a circle, you have to pull on the string. The pull of the string on the conker is the unbalanced force, which is constantly acting to change its velocity as it orbits your head. If you let go of the string, suddenly there is no tension in the string, and the conker will fly off at a tangent to the circle.

Similarly, the Earth as it orbits the Sun has a constantly changing velocity. Newton's first law says that there must be an unbalanced force acting on it. That force is the gravitational pull of the Sun. If the force disappeared, we would travel off in a straight line towards some terrible fate beyond the Solar System.

Similarly, an electron is held in its orbit of the nucleus of an atom by the force of electrostatic attraction. Electrons are negatively charged, while nuclei are positive, and this results in a force that keeps the electrons orbiting.

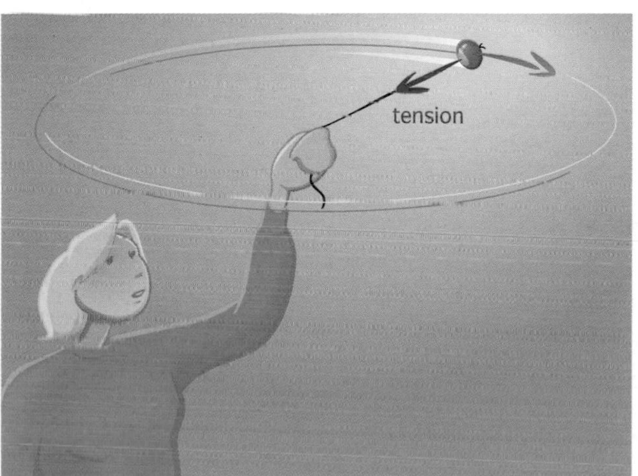

● ***Figure 1.5*** Whirling a conker

In each of these cases, you should be able to see why the direction of the force is as shown in *figure 1.6*. The force on the object is directed towards the centre of the circle. We describe each of these forces as **centripetal** – that is, directed towards the centre.

It is important to note that the word *centripetal* is an adjective. We use it to describe a force that is making something travel along a circular path. It does not tell us what causes this force, which might be gravitational, electrostatic, magnetic, frictional or whatever.

SAQ 1.4

In each of the following cases, say what provides the centripetal force:

a the Moon orbiting the Earth;

b a car going round a bend on a flat, rough road;

c the weight on the end of a swinging pendulum.

SAQ 1.5

A car is travelling along a flat road. Explain why it cannot go around a bend if the road surface is perfectly smooth. What will happen if the driver tries turning the steering wheel?

Centripetal or centrifugal?

The force needed to make an object follow a circular path must be directed towards the centre of the circle. (Think of the tension in the string as you whirl the conker round.) The word *centrifugal* means directed away from the centre of the circle.

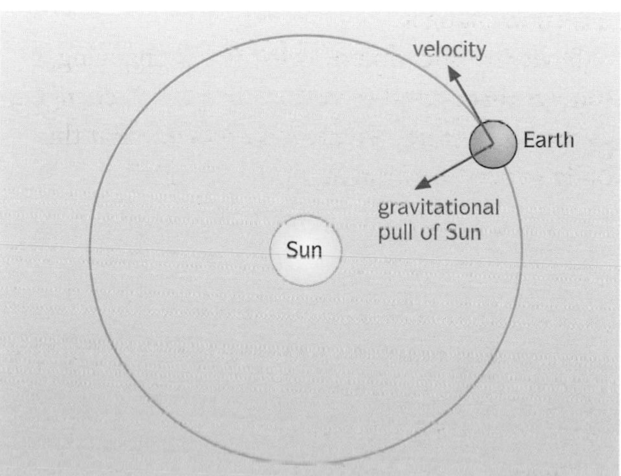

● ***Figure 1.6*** Gravity pulls the Earth towards the Sun.

A force can be centrifugal; for example, the force that you feel the string exerting on your hand is outwards, towards the conker *(figure 1.7)*. We could therefore describe this force as centrifugal. However, we are usually concerned with the resultant force acting on the orbiting object, and this is a centripetal force.

Vector diagrams

Figure 1.8a shows an object travelling along a circular path, at two positions in its orbit. It reaches position B a short time after A. How has its velocity changed between these two positions?

Figure 1.8b shows the two velocity vectors corresponding to A and B. You can see that the object has been pushed so that its velocity has been changed by a small amount, represented by the small arrow that closes the triangle. The direction of this arrow tells us about the direction of the object's acceleration. Notice that it is (more or less) at right-angles to the velocity arrow at A.

You need to know that the velocity is always at a tangent to the circle, while the acceleration is always at right-angles, directed along a radius towards the centre of the circle. Because the acceleration (like the force that causes it) is directed towards the centre of the circle, we can describe it as a centripetal acceleration.

Acceleration at steady speed

Now that we know that the centripetal force and acceleration are always at right-angles to the object's velocity, we can explain why it does not speed up or slow down. If the force is to make the object speed up, it must have a component in the direction of the object's velocity; it must provide a push in the direction in which the object is already travelling. However, here we have a force at 90° to the velocity, so it has no component in the required direction. It acts to pull the object around the circle, without ever making it speed up or slow down.

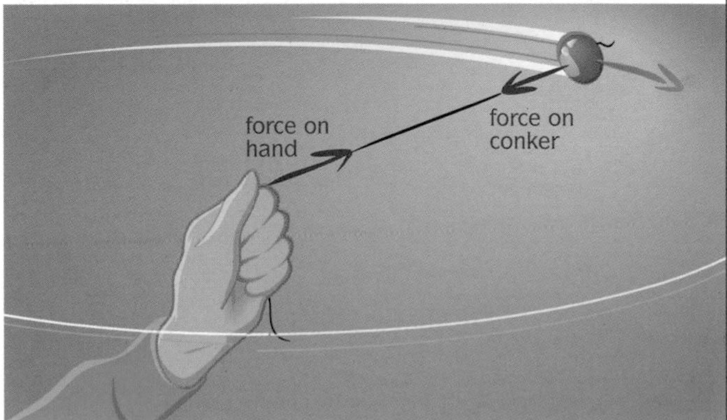

● **Figure 1.7** A centrifugal force and a centripetal force.

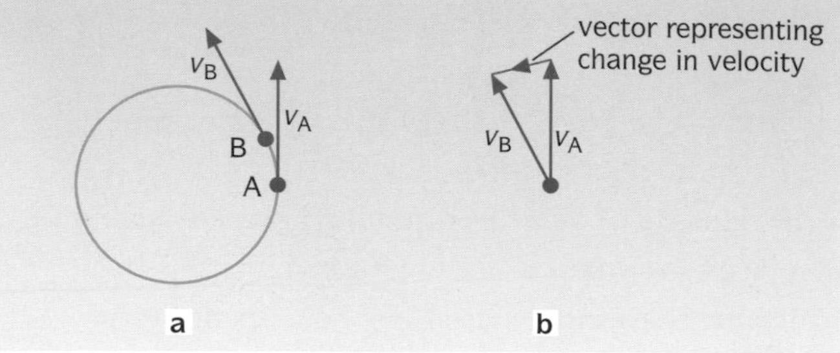

● **Figure 1.8** Changes in the velocity vector.

SAQ 1.6

In uniform circular motion, an object follows a circular path at a steady speed. Describe how each of the following quantities changes as it follows this path: speed, velocity, kinetic energy, momentum, centripetal force, centripetal acceleration. (Refer to both magnitude and direction, as appropriate.)

Calculating force and acceleration

Isaac Newton devised an ingenious 'thought experiment' that allows us to think about circular motion, particularly in connection with objects orbiting the Earth. Consider a large gun on some high point on the Earth's surface, capable of firing objects horizontally. *Figure 1.9* shows what will happen if we fire them at different speeds.

If the object is fired too slowly, gravity will pull it down towards the ground and it will land at some distance from the gun. A faster initial speed results in the object landing further from the gun.

Now, if we try a bit faster than this, the object will travel all the way round the Earth. We have to get just the right speed to do this. As the object is pulled down towards the Earth, the curved surface of the Earth falls away beneath it. The object follows a circular path, constantly falling under gravity but never getting any closer to the surface.

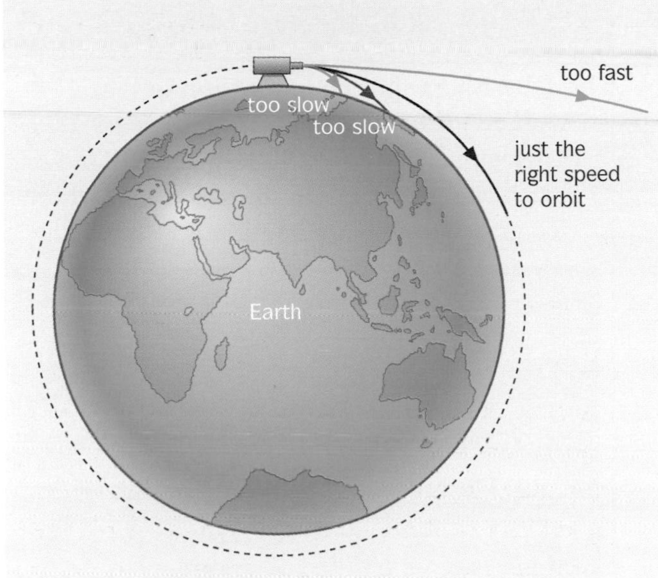

● **Figure 1.9** Newton's 'thought experiment'.

If the object is fired too fast, it travels off into space, and fails to get into a circular orbit. So we can see that there is just one correct speed to achieve a circular orbit under gravity.

An equation for centripetal force

We can think of this another way round. If an object having a particular mass m is to travel in an orbit of radius r and at speed v, there is a particular value of centripetal force F needed to keep it in orbit. The force F must depend on m, v and r. You can investigate the relationship between these quantities in the 'whirling conker' experiment.

Here is the equation for F:

$$\text{centripetal force, } F = \frac{mv^2}{r}$$

If you think about whirling a conker on a string, you should be able to see that the relationships between force, mass and speed are reasonable. A conker of greater mass will require a greater force. To make it move faster will also require a greater force. However, you may not find it obvious that to make it go at the same speed in a bigger circle will require a smaller force, but that is how it behaves.

Newton's second law

Now that we have an equation for centripetal force, we can use Newton's second law of motion to deduce an equation for centripetal acceleration. If we write this law as $a = F/m$, we find

$$\text{centripetal acceleration, } a = \frac{v^2}{r}$$

Remembering that an object accelerates in the direction of the resultant force on it, it follows that both F and a are in the same direction, towards the centre of the circle.

The right speed

We can use the equation for a to calculate the speed that an object must have to orbit the Earth under gravity, as in Newton's thought experiment. Its centripetal acceleration is provided by the acceleration due to the Earth's gravity, i.e. $9.8\,\mathrm{m\,s^{-2}}$ close to the Earth's surface. The radius of its orbit is equal to the Earth's radius, approximately 6400 km. Hence, using $a = v^2/r$, we have

$$9.8\,\mathrm{m\,s^{-1}} = v^2/(6.4 \times 10^6\,\mathrm{m})$$

$$v = \sqrt{9.8 \times 6.4 \times 10^6}\,\mathrm{m\,s^{-1}} = 7920\,\mathrm{m\,s^{-1}}$$

Thus if you were to throw or hit a ball horizontally at almost $8\,\mathrm{km\,s^{-1}}$, it would go into orbit around the Earth, eventually returning to hit you on the back of the head *(figure 1.10)*.

● **Figure 1.10** Don't forget to duck!

SAQ 1.7

How long would it take to orbit the Earth once at this speed?

SAQ 1.8

A stone of mass 0.2 kg is whirled round on the end of a string of length 30 cm. If the string will break when the tension in it exceeds 8 N, what is the greatest speed at which the stone can be whirled without the string breaking?

SUMMARY

- An object moving at a steady speed along a circular path has uniform circular motion.
- It is not in equilibrium; there must be an unbalanced force acting on it.
- Such a force is called a centripetal force, and it acts at right-angles to the object's velocity, towards the centre of the circle.
- The magnitude of the force depends on the object's mass and speed, and the radius of the orbit.
- The object has a centripetal acceleration; its velocity is constantly changing direction, though its speed is steady.

Questions

1 Helen Sharman, the first Briton in space, worked in the Mir space station *(figure 1.11)*. This had a mass of 20 900 kg, and orbited the Earth at an average height of 350 km, where the gravitational acceleration is 8.8 m s^{-2}.

● ***Figure 1.11*** The Mir space station. This is an artist's impression.

Calculate:
a the centripetal force on the satellite;
b the speed at which it orbited;
c the time taken for each orbit;
d the number of times it orbited the Earth each day.
(Radius of Earth = 6400 km.)

2 A stone of mass 0.5 kg is whirled round on the end of a string 0.5 m long. It makes three complete circuits each second. Calculate:
a its speed;
b its centripetal acceleration;
c the tension in the string.

3 Mars orbits the Sun once every 687 days at a distance of 2.3×10^{11} m. The mass of Mars is 6.4×10^{23} kg. Calculate:
a its orbital speed;
b its centripetal acceleration;
c the force exerted on Mars by the Sun.

Gravity

By the end of this chapter you should be able to:

1 describe and use the concept of weight as the effect of a gravitational field on a mass;

2 understand a gravitational field as a field of force and define gravitational field strength as force per unit mass;

3 recall and use Newton's law of gravitation in the form

$$F = -G\frac{m_1 m_2}{r^2};$$

4 derive and use the equation

$$g = -G\frac{m}{r^2}$$

for the gravitational field strength of a point mass;

5 appreciate that, close to the Earth's surface, g is approximately constant and is called the acceleration of free fall;

6 describe an experiment to measure the acceleration of free fall using a freely falling body;

7 define *potential at a point* as the work done in bringing unit mass from infinity to the point;

8 understand and use the relationship between force and potential energy in a uniform gravitational field;

9 use the equation

$$\phi = -G\frac{m}{r}$$

for the potential in the field of a point mass.

● ***Figure 2.1*** Skydivers balance gravity and air resistance.

Gravitational forces and fields

In the last chapter, we considered the motion of objects moving in circular paths, including objects orbiting under the influence of gravity. But what is gravity? How can we describe it, and how can we explain it?

We live our lives with the constant experience of gravity. We know that things fall when we let go of them. We know that we will return to the ground if we jump up in the air. We can live quite happily without thinking about why this is so. Once we start thinking about the force of gravity, which makes things fall, we may come up with some odd ideas.

Young children take it for granted that things fall. They are mystified if you ask them to explain it. They also take it for granted that things stay where they are on the ground; they don't think it necessary to talk about two balanced forces. Surely gravity disappears as soon as something stops falling?

You have probably learnt to show a stationary object with two forces acting on it: the force of gravity (its weight) and the normal force exerted by the ground *(figure 2.2)*. A child does not have this mental picture, but these forces really do exist, as you would discover if you put your fingers underneath a large weight!

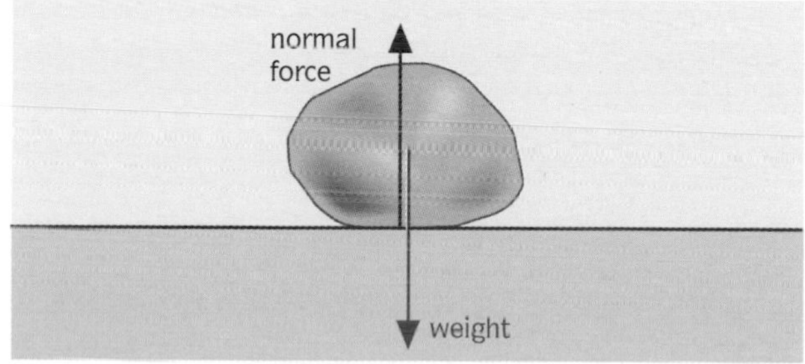

● ***Figure 2.2*** Two balanced forces on a stationary object.

Children learn at school that there is a force called *gravity*, which holds us onto the Earth's surface. So, what causes this gravitational pull of the Earth? Try asking some children. Here are some of the ideas that they may come up with – many adults have similar ideas.

> 'Gravity is made by the Earth spinning. If it stopped spinning, we would all fall off.'
> 'If the Earth spun faster and faster, we would all fall off' *(figure 2.3)*.
> 'Gravity is caused by the Earth's atmosphere pressing down on us.'
> 'If you dropped something on the Moon, it would just float about, because there is no air.'
> 'There is a giant magnet inside the Earth. It attracts us to the Earth.'

Gravity is not caused by the Earth's rotation, but it is true that, if the Earth spun a lot faster, gravity might not be strong enough to hold us on. Nor is gravity caused by the atmosphere. Perhaps this idea comes from seeing astronauts in orbit above the Earth's atmosphere ('in space'), where they appear to be weightless. On the Moon, gravity is weaker than on the Earth, so objects fall more slowly and astronauts can jump higher.

Isaac Newton investigated the question of the Earth's gravity. In particular, he wondered whether the Earth's gravitational pull was confined to the Earth's surface, or whether it extended into space – as far as the Moon. Previously, it had been suggested that the Moon was held in its orbit around the Earth by magnetic attraction. After all, it was known that the Earth was magnetic, and that magnetic forces acted at a distance.

Newton rejected this theory, partly on the grounds that the Sun is very hot, and magnets lose their magnetism when they are heated. Instead, he suggested that it was the mass of a body that caused it to attract other bodies. Objects fall towards the ground because their mass is attracted by the mass of the Earth. The Moon continues in its orbit round the Earth because their two masses attract each other *(figure 2.4)*.

Newton's great achievement was to relate the falling of an apple to the ground to the 'falling' of the Moon as it orbits the Earth.

● ***Figure 2.3*** Hold on to the pole if you don't want to fall off!

A field of force

The influence of the Earth's gravity extends well beyond its surface. The Moon stays in its orbit, 400 000 km away, because of the Earth's pull. The Earth orbits the Sun at a distance of 150 000 000 km because of their attraction for each other. We can picture the Earth's influence by representing it as a field of force. Anywhere in this field, an object that has mass will feel a force attracting it towards the Earth.

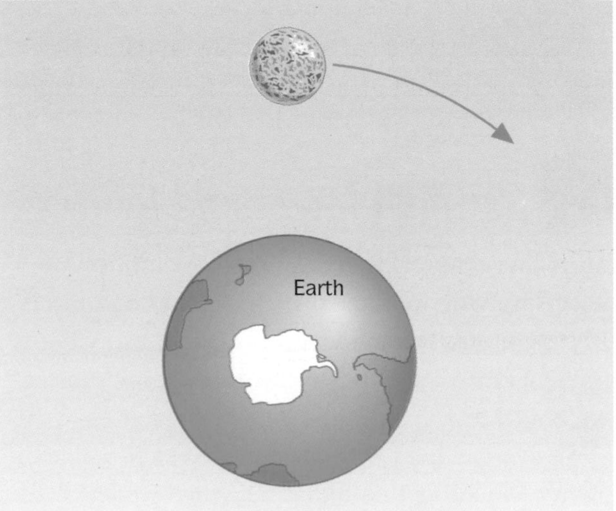

● ***Figure 2.4*** The Moon orbits the Earth under the influence of the Earth's gravity.

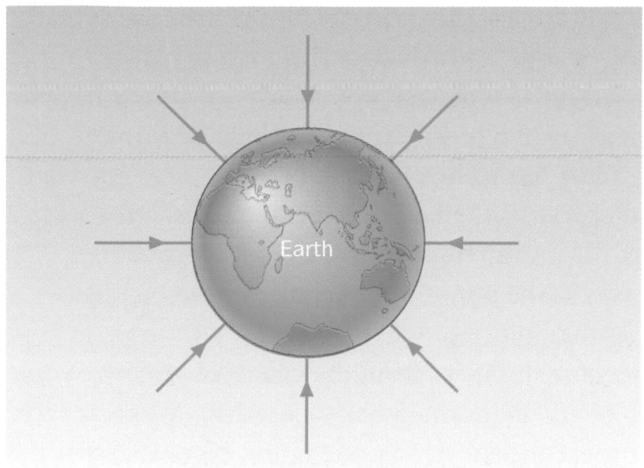

● ***Figure 2.5*** Lines of force represent the Earth's gravitational field.

To make the idea of a field of force seem rather more concrete, we can represent it by drawing lines of force, as shown in *figure 2.5*. (You will be familiar with this from drawings of magnetic fields between bar magnets.) The lines of force tell us two things:

- The arrows on the lines show us the direction of the force on a mass placed in the field.
- The spacing of the lines tells us about the strength of the field – the farther apart they are, the weaker the field.

The drawing of the Earth's field shows that all objects are attracted towards the *centre* of the Earth – even if they are below the surface of the Earth – and that the force gets weaker as you get farther away from the Earth's surface.

The drawing *(figure 2.6)* of the gravitational field inside a building on the Earth's surface shows that the force is directed downwards everywhere in the room, and (because the lines are parallel and evenly spaced) the force is the same at all points in the building. Your weight does not get significantly less when you go upstairs.

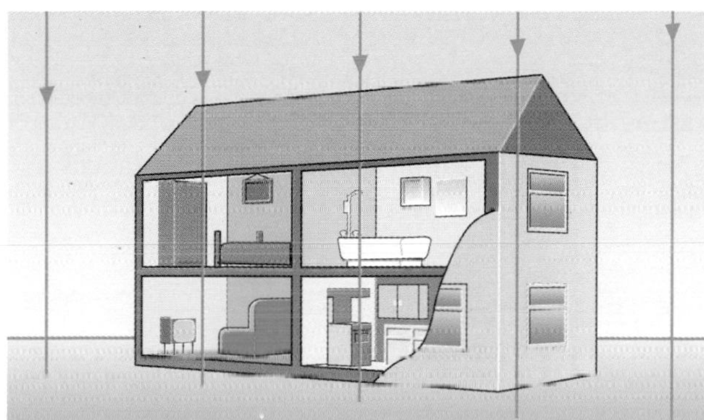

● ***Figure 2.6*** The Earth's gravitational field is uniform on the scale of a building.

We describe the Earth's field as **radial**, since the lines of force *diverge* (spread out) radially from its surface. However, on the scale of a building, the field is **uniform**, since it is equally strong at all points in the building.

Jupiter is a more massive planet than the Earth, and so we would represent its field by showing more closely spaced lines of force.

Newton's law of gravitation

Newton used his ideas about mass and gravity, and his knowledge of magnetic fields, to suggest a **law of gravitation** for two bodies *(figure 2.7)*:

Any two bodies attract each other with a force that is proportional to each of their masses and inversely proportional to the square of the distance between them.

We can write this in a mathematical form (where $\propto$ means 'proportional to'):

$$F \propto \frac{m_1 m_2}{r^2}$$

To make this into an equation, we introduce the gravitational constant G. We also need a minus sign (explained later):

$$F = -G\frac{m_1 m_2}{r^2}$$

In this equation, the symbols have the following meanings: F is the force of attraction of each body on the other, m_1 and m_2 are their masses, r is the

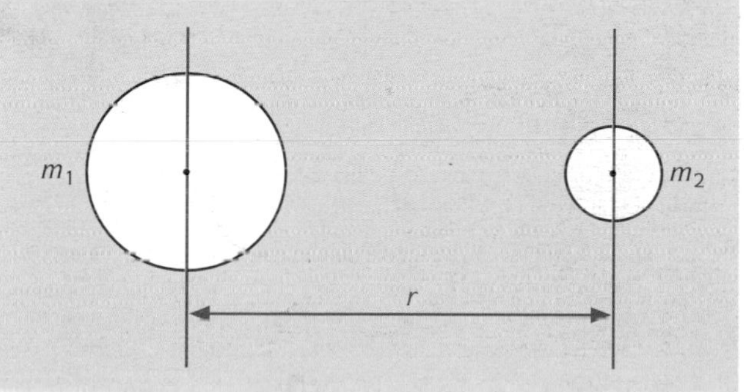

● ***Figure 2.7*** Two bodies separated by distance r.

distance between them, and G is the gravitational constant, with the value $G = 6.67 \times 10^{-11}\,\mathrm{N\,m^2\,kg^{-2}}$.

Let us examine this equation to see why it seems reasonable.

First, each of the two masses is important. Your weight depends on your mass, and on the mass of the planet you happen to be standing on.

Secondly, the further away you are from the planet, the weaker its pull. Twice as far away gives one-quarter of the force. (This can be seen from the diagram of the lines of force (*figure 2.8*). If the distance is doubled, the lines are spread out over four times the area, so their concentration is reduced to one-quarter.) This is called an inverse square law – you may have come across a similar law for radiation such as light or γ-rays (gamma-rays) spreading out from a point source.

The minus sign represents the fact that this is an attractive force. The radial distance r is measured outwards from the attracting body; the force F acts in the opposite direction, and so our sign convention requires that F is negative.

Note that we measure distances from the centre of gravity of one body to the centre of gravity of the other (*figure 2.9*). We treat each body as if its mass was concentrated at one point. Note also that the two bodies attract each other with equal and opposite forces. (This is an example of a pair of equal and opposite forces, as required by Newton's third law of motion.) The Earth pulls on you with a force (your weight) directed towards the centre of the Earth; you attract the Earth with an equal force, directed away from its centre and towards you. Your pull on an object as massive as the Earth has little effect on it. The Sun's pull on the Earth, however, has a very significant effect.

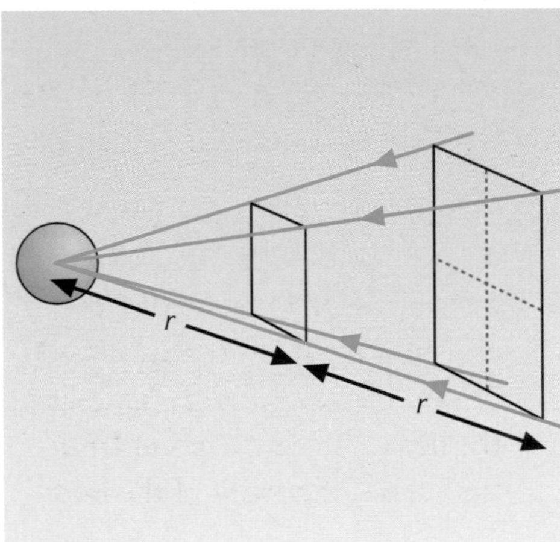

● ***Figure 2.8*** Lines of force are spread out over a greater area at greater distances.

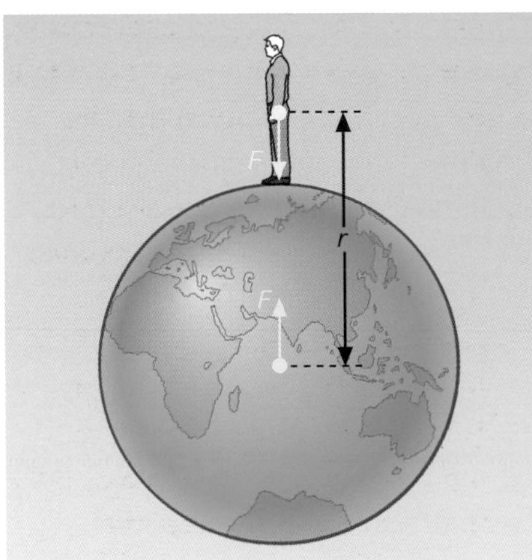

● ***Figure 2.9*** A person and the Earth exert equal and opposite attractions on each other.

SAQ 2.1

Calculate the gravitational force of attraction between two objects each of mass 1 kg, separated by 10 cm.

SAQ 2.2

Estimate the gravitational force of attraction between two people sitting side-by-side on a park bench. How does this force compare with the gravitational force exerted on each of them by the Earth, i.e. their weight?

Gravitational field strength

We can describe how strong a gravitational field is by stating its field strength. We are used to this idea for objects on or near the Earth's surface – the field strength is the familiar quantity g. Its value is approximately $9.8\,\mathrm{m\,s^{-2}}$. The weight of a body of mass m is mg.

To make the meaning of g clearer, we should say that it is approximately $9.8\,\mathrm{N\,kg^{-1}}$. That is, each 1 kg of mass experiences a force of 9.8 N. Gravitational field strength is thus defined by the following equation:

$$g = F/m \qquad \text{or} \qquad F = mg$$

The second arrangement of this equation should be very familiar to you.

Thus gravitational field strength is the answer to the question, 'What force would a 1 kg mass placed at a point in the field

Measuring G – weighing the Earth

The gravitational constant G has a very small value. We only notice the gravitational pull of very massive objects such as the Earth. We don't feel a noticeable gravitational attraction when another person walks past. This means that measuring G is rather difficult – Newton didn't manage it.

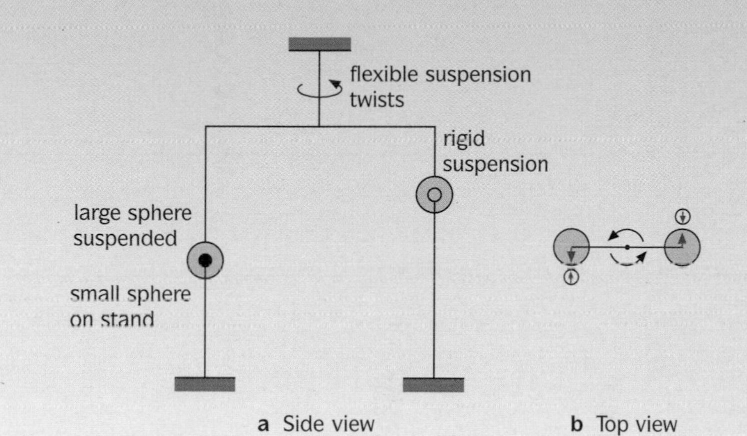

● **Figure 2.10** Cavendish's method for measuring G, using four lead spheres.

Henry Cavendish devised a method for measuring G some decades after Newton's death. The diagrams *(figure 2.10)* show how he did this. Details of Cavendish's lead spheres are as shown below:

Sphere	*Mass*	*Radius*
large	168 kg	152 mm
small	6.22 kg	51 mm

A Calculate the force of attraction between two masses, each of 1 kg, and separated by 10 cm.

B Why does this suggest that Cavendish chose to use lead spheres?

C Calculate the greatest gravitational force that Cavendish's spheres could have exerted on each other.

D Cavendish might have chosen an alternative arrangement, with a single large sphere hanging by a string, and attracted sideways by a single smaller sphere *(figure 2.11)*. Calculate the largest angle θ (theta) that he might have tried to measure.

E Why was Cavendish's method using four spheres better than this alternative arrangement?

F Why did Cavendish have one large sphere hanging lower than the other?

G At the time of Cavendish's experiment, the radius of the Earth was known, but not its mass. Why do you think his experiment was described as 'weighing the Earth'?

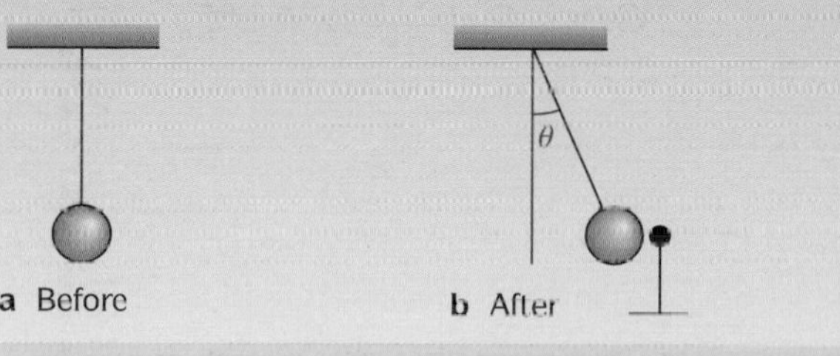

● **Figure 2.11** An alternative method for measuring G.

experience?' Since force is a vector quantity (having both size and direction), it follows that field strength is also a vector. We need to give its direction as well as its magnitude in order to specify it completely.

Now we have two ways of saying what force is exerted on a body of mass m by a second body of mass M:

$$F = mg \quad \text{and} \quad F = -G\frac{Mm}{r^2}$$

(Here we are using M and m as the masses of the large and small bodies respectively.) If we compare these two equations, we can see that

$$mg = -G\frac{Mm}{r^2} \quad \text{or} \quad g = -G\frac{M}{r^2}$$

So the gravitational field strength at a point depends on the mass M of the body causing the field, and the distance r of the point from the centre of gravity of the body.

Measuring g

Gravitational field strength g has units $\mathrm{m\,s^{-2}}$; it is an acceleration. Another name for g is 'acceleration due to gravity'. Any object that falls freely in a gravitational field has this acceleration, approximately $9.8\,\mathrm{m\,s^{-2}}$ near the Earth's surface.

Figure 2.12 shows one method for determining g. When the switch is opened, the ball is released and the timer started. When the ball hits the pad, the timer is stopped. The time of fall t is related to the distance d by

$$d = \tfrac{1}{2}gt^2$$

The distance d is varied, and a graph of t^2 against d is plotted;

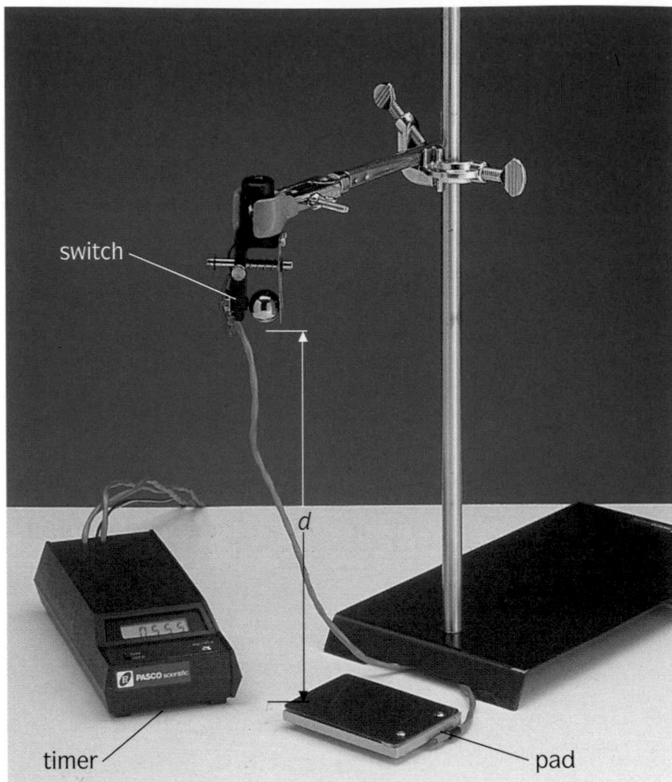

● ***Figure 2.12*** Measuring g by free fall.

g can be found from the gradient:

$$g = \frac{2}{\text{gradient}}$$

An alternative method is shown in *figure 2.13*. A weight with an attached card falls through a light gate. The light beam is broken by the two sections of the card. The computer calculates the speed at which the card is moving as each section passes through; knowing the time interval between these speed measurements, it can then calculate the acceleration. It is worth carrying out both of these experiments, and trying to compare their accuracies. Which method do you consider will give a more accurate value of g?

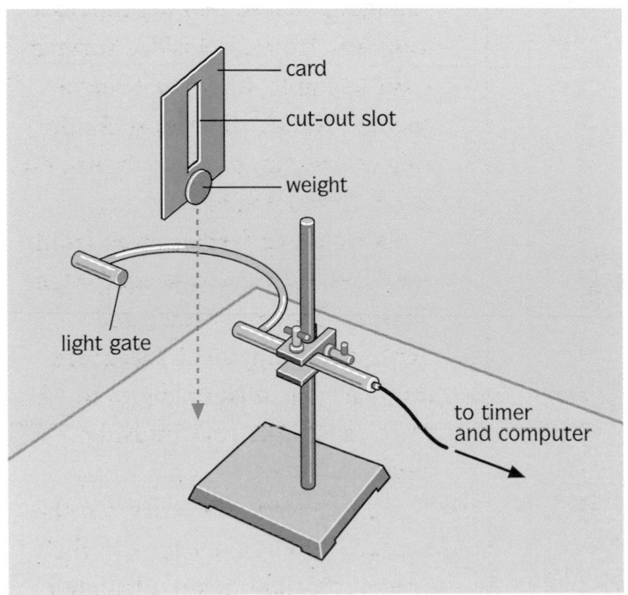

● ***Figure 2.13*** Measuring g using a light gate and timer.

SAQ 2.3

A stone is dropped from rest from the top of a building. It takes 1.56 s to reach the ground, 12.0 m below. Use these values to determine g.

Gravitational energy

If you climb up stairs, you have to do work against the force of gravity. If you lift a heavy object, again you have to do work. You transfer energy to the thing that you lift. The work you do becomes the gravitational potential energy of the raised object. We can calculate this energy, because we know how to calculate work done:

work done = force × distance moved
(in the direction of the force)

The force F needed to raise an object of mass m at a steady speed is equal to its weight, $F = mg$. If we lift it up a height h, the work done against gravity is $mg \times h$. So the gravitational potential energy gained is:

$$E_p = mgh$$

(You might think that the force needed to lift something is greater than its weight. It is true that you need a greater force to start it moving, but then you need only just balance its weight to keep it moving. This is an example of Newton's first law of motion.)

Suppose a person of mass 50 kg climbs a tall building, 20 m high. Their gain in potential energy is

$$\text{potential energy} = 50\,\text{kg} \times 10\,\text{N kg}^{-1} \times 20\,\text{m} = 10\,000\,\text{J}$$

(In fact, they will need a lot more energy than this; the human body is far from 100% efficient in its energy transfers.)

SAQ 2.4

A mountaineer of mass 70 kg eats a chocolate bar. The wrapper states that the bar provides 500 kJ (about 120 kcal) of energy. How high will the mountaineer be able to climb using this energy? Assume she is 10% efficient at converting energy from food to gravitational potential energy.

Gravitational potential

When we described a gravitational field in terms of its strength, we said that g is the force acting on 1 kg at a particular point in the field – the force per unit mass. Now we can describe the energy of objects in a field in the same way. We will think about the energy per unit mass of objects in the field. We call this the gravitational potential ϕ at a point:

$$\text{gravitational potential} = \frac{\text{gravitational potential energy}}{\text{mass}}$$

$$\phi = \frac{E_\text{p}}{m}$$

Since energy is a scalar quantity (as is work done), it follows that potential is also a scalar. It is completely specified when we have said what its size is. It does not have a direction. The idea of gravitational potential energy near the Earth's surface should be familiar to you from your study of the *Foundation Physics* module. The idea of potential may seem a little harder. If you confuse it with field strength, try to remember that potential is related to potential energy; field strength is related to the strength of the force of gravity.

Drawing potential

If you climb a mountain, your potential energy increases as you go up. The gravitational potential at the top of the mountain is greater than at the foot.

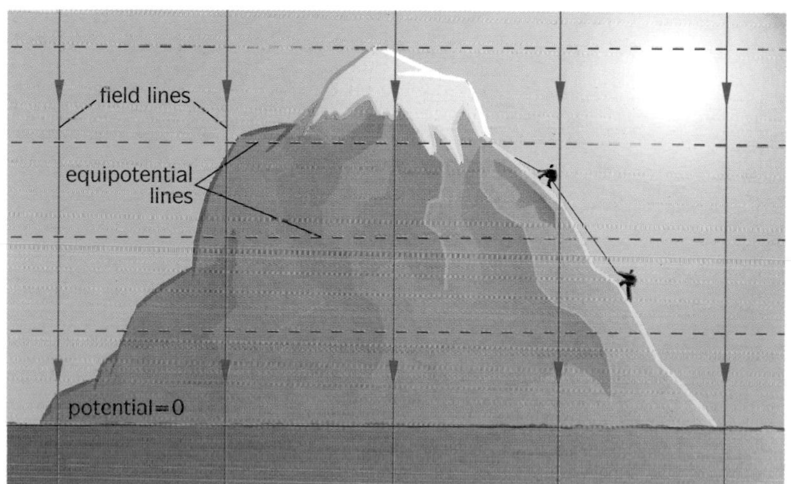

● ***Figure 2.14*** Equipotential lines in a gravitational field.

We can show how gravitational potential increases by drawing equipotential lines onto a diagram of the field lines (lines of force). These are usually drawn at equal intervals of potential *(figure 2.14)*.

Notice that the equipotential lines are always at right-angles to the field lines. If you move horizontally (along an equipotential line), your potential energy does not change. You are not doing any work against gravity. If your movement takes you upwards and you cross equipotential lines, your potential energy increases, as you are doing work against gravity. Notice also that, if we are considering a situation close to the Earth's surface where the field is uniform, we usually take the Earth's surface as the zero of potential energy. Our measurements of height start from the Earth's surface.

Radial fields

Things become more complicated if we are thinking about energy changes when something moves a long way from the Earth's surface – for example, if we are firing a rocket towards the Moon. As the rocket goes up, the Earth's pull on it gets gradually less.

As we move further away from the Earth's surface, the equipotential lines become further and further apart (*figure 2.15*). Since they must be at right-angles to all of the field lines, they must be circles.

How can we now work out the rocket's potential energy? In the previous situation, we calculated the work done against gravity, and

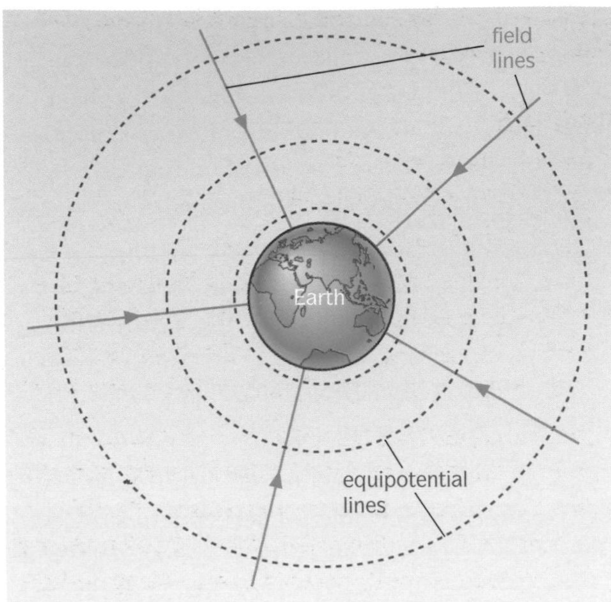

● **Figure 2.15** Equipotential lines around the Earth.

this was easy. We used the force × distance formula, and the force remained constant. For the rocket, the force is not constant, and so we cannot use this simple formula.

Instead, we have to use calculus. (If you are familiar with this branch of mathematics, you may be able to solve this problem for yourself.) The solution is as follows:

$$E_p = -G\frac{Mm}{r}$$

To arrive at this, we have had to make a decision about what we will regard as our zero of potential energy. We could have continued to use sea level (although this would have given a more awkward formula). Instead, we choose to say that a mass has zero gravitational potential energy when it is 'at infinity' – that is, at some point so far from the Earth and any other massive objects that it feels no gravitational force.

Then, to calculate the potential energy of a mass near to the Earth (or anywhere else), we calculate the work done against gravity in bringing the mass from infinity to that point. Since the mass is attracted by the Earth, we do not have to do positive work against gravity to move it; in fact, its potential energy is greater at infinity than anywhere else. It follows that its potential energy is less than zero when it is near the Earth. This explains the minus sign in the equation.

Hence we can arrive at the following definition:

The **gravitational potential** at a point in a field is equal to the work done against gravity in bringing unit mass from infinity to that point.

So $\quad \phi = -G\frac{M}{r}$

It may be easier to understand this by thinking about the flight plan for a rocket trip to the Moon. This is represented in *figure 2.16*. As your rocket climbs away from the Earth's surface, its potential energy increases. At first, the potential increases by $9.8\,\mathrm{J\,kg^{-1}}$ for every metre it rises. However, as the Earth recedes into the distance, the potential increases more and more slowly. If you steer away from the Moon, eventually you will be clear of the Earth's field, and you will have reached a position of zero potential. If you steer towards the Moon, you will eventually reach a point where the Moon's pull is stronger than the Earth's. You will accelerate down towards the Moon's surface (unless you reverse the thrust of your rocket).

We can think of our position on the Earth's surface as being at the bottom of a potential 'hole' or 'well'. The Moon represents a shallower well,

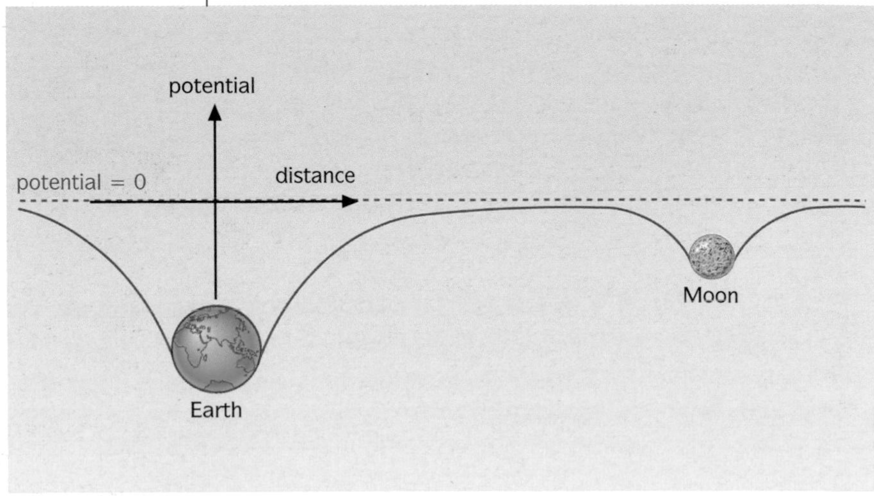

● **Figure 2.16** The Earth and the Moon are in potential 'wells'.

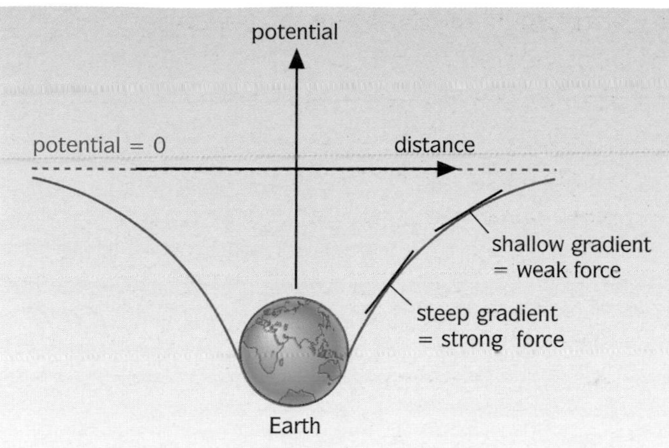

● ***Figure 2.17*** Gravitational force is related to potential gradient.

since it is less massive than the Earth. To get from one to the other, we have to climb out of one potential well and fall into the other. On a diagram like this, the strength of the field is represented by the gradient of the potential graph. This is shown in *figure 2.17*. Where the gradient is steeper, the force is greater.

SAQ 2.5

Radius of Earth = 6400 km
Mass of Earth = 6.0×10^{24} kg
Close to Earth's surface, $g = 9.8\,\text{N kg}^{-1}$

a Imagine that you can throw a stone of mass 1 kg upwards to a height of 100 m. What is its potential energy at this height (relative to the Earth's surface)? How fast must it be moving when it leaves your hand?

b Now imagine that you have invented a catapult which can throw the same stone 1000 km upwards from the Earth's surface. Calculate the potential at the surface of the Earth, and then at a height of 1000 km. By how much has the stone's potential energy changed? How fast must it be moving when it leaves the catapult?

c If you had solved part **b** using the equation $E_p = mgh$, how different would your answer be? Why are the answers different?

A trip to Jupiter!

	Mass/kg	*Radius*/km
Earth	6.0×10^{24}	6400
Moon	7.4×10^{22}	1740
Jupiter	2.0×10^{27}	70000

Suppose that you are bored with rocket flights to the Moon, and have turned your sights on Jupiter instead. You will need enough fuel to take you away from the Earth's gravity, and enough to brake your rocket so that you do not crash-land on Jupiter. Then you will need more fuel for the return journey.

A Calculate the gravitational potential at the Earth's surface.
B Calculate the potential at Jupiter's surface, and the gravitational field strength.
C What problems might you find with carrying enough fuel for this journey? (Use your answer to questions A and B to help you to answer this.)

Fuel	*Energy released on combustion*/MJ kg^{-1}
wood	20
hydrogen	142
methane	55
coal	27

There are a variety of fuels that you might consider. The more energy released per kilogram, the better.

D Why are there no wood-fired rockets in use for space travel?
E How much energy must a fuel provide to take the rocket to the Moon and back?
F Which of the fuels listed above might be suitable for such a trip?
G Would any of them be suitable for a trip to Jupiter and back?

You have calculated the energy needed by an object at the Earth's surface to escape from the Earth's gravity – this is simply equal to the potential at the Earth's surface. Hence you know how much kinetic energy it must have, and hence you can calculate the speed it must have when it leaves the ground using the equation for kinetic energy, $E_k = \frac{1}{2}mv^2$. This speed is called its **escape velocity**.

H Consider the escape velocities for the Earth, the Moon and Jupiter. Which do you expect to be greatest? Check your answer by calculating them.
I What reason does this suggest to you for the fact that the Moon has only a very thin atmosphere?
J Why is there very little hydrogen or helium in the Earth's atmosphere?
K What would you expect to find if you could analyse Jupiter's atmosphere?

SUMMARY

- The force of gravity is an attractive force between any two objects because of their masses.
- We can describe the gravitational effect of an object in terms of a gravitational field around it. The strength of the field at a point is the force exerted on unit mass placed in the field.
- Newton's law gives the force between two masses:

$$F = -G\frac{m_1 m_2}{r^2}$$

- Field strength at distance r from mass m:

$$g = -G\frac{m}{r^2}$$

this describes a radial field.

- On or near the surface of the Earth, the field is uniform: g is approximately constant; its value is equal to the acceleration of free fall.
- An object in a gravitational field has gravitational potential energy. The potential ϕ at a point in the field tells us the potential energy of unit mass placed at the point. It is calculated from the work done in bringing unit mass from infinity (where $\phi = 0$) to the point.
- For a point mass:

$$\phi = -G\frac{m}{r}$$

- Chapter 7 deals with electric fields; there are important parallels between gravitational and electric fields.

Questions

You will need the following data to answer these questions:

	Mass/kg	*Radius*/km	*Distance from Earth*/km
Earth	6.0×10^{24}	6400	
Moon	7.4×10^{22}	1740	3.8×10^5
Sun	2.0×10^{30}	700000	1.5×10^8

1 The value of g is found to be $9.81\,\mathrm{N\,kg^{-1}}$ in the UK, $9.83\,\mathrm{N\,kg^{-1}}$ at the Earth's poles and $9.78\,\mathrm{N\,kg^{-1}}$ at the equator. What does this variation tell you about the shape of the Earth? Would you weigh more at the North Pole or at the equator? Would you be able to measure these differences with an ordinary set of bathroom scales?

2 Mount Everest is approximately 10 km high. How much less would a mountaineer of mass 100 kg (including backpack) weigh at its summit, compared to her weight at the foot? Would this difference be measurable with bathroom scales?

3 Calculate g on the surface of the Moon and on the surface of the Sun. How does this help to explain why the Moon has only a thin atmosphere?

4 Calculate the Earth's field strength at the Moon. What force does the Earth exert on the Moon? What is the Moon's acceleration towards the Earth?

5 Jupiter's mass is 320 times that of the Earth, and its radius is 11.2 times the Earth's. Calculate g on the surface of Jupiter. (Take $g = 9.8\,\mathrm{N\,kg^{-1}}$ on the Earth's surface.)

6 The Moon and the Sun both contribute to the tides on the Earth's oceans. Which has a bigger pull on each kilogram of sea-water, the Sun or the Moon?

7 Astrologers believe that the planets exert an influence on us, particularly at the moment of birth. (They don't necessarily believe that this is an effect of gravity!) Calculate the gravitational force on a 4 kg baby due to Mars (mass of Mars = 6.4×10^{23} kg) when the planet is at its closest to the Earth (100000000 km), and the force on the same baby due to its 50 kg mother at a distance of 0.5 m.

8 There is a point on the line joining the centres of the Earth and the Moon where the gravitational field strength is zero. Is this point closer to the Earth or to the Moon? How far is it from the centre of the Earth?

Oscillations and vibrations

By the end of this chapter you should be able to:

1. describe simple examples of free oscillations;
2. investigate the motion of an oscillator using experimental and graphical methods;
3. understand and use the terms *amplitude*, *frequency*, *period* and *phase difference*;
4. use the relationship

$$\text{period} = \frac{1}{\text{frequency}}$$

5. describe practical examples of damped oscillations, referring to the degree of damping, including critical damping;
6. describe practical examples of forced oscillations and resonance;
7. draw a graph to show how the amplitude of a forced oscillation changes close to the natural frequency of the system, and show how this is affected by damping;
8. give examples of situations where resonance is useful, and where it should be avoided.

● ***Figure 3.1*** The wings of a bird oscillate as it flies.

Free and forced vibrations

A bird in flight flaps its wings up and down *(figure 3.1)*. An aircraft's wings also vibrate up and down; but this is not how it flies. The wings are long and thin, and they vibrate slightly because they are not perfectly rigid. Many other structures vibrate – bridges when traffic flows across, buildings in high winds.

A more specific term than vibration is oscillation. An object **oscillates** when it moves back and forth repeatedly, on either side of some fixed position. If we stop it from oscillating, it returns to the fixed position.

We make use of oscillations in many different ways – for pleasure (a child on a swing), for music (the vibrations of a guitar string), for timing (the movement of a pendulum). Whenever we make a sound, the molecules of the air oscillate back and forth, passing the sound wave along. The atoms of a solid vibrate more and more as the temperature rises.

These examples of oscillations and vibrations may seem very different from one another. In this chapter, we will look at the characteristics that are shared by all oscillations.

Free or forced?

The easiest oscillations to understand are free oscillations. If you pluck a guitar string, it continues to vibrate for some time after you have released it. It vibrates at a particular **frequency** (the number of vibrations per second). This is called its natural frequency of vibration, and it gives rise to the particular note that you hear. Change the length of the string, and you change the natural frequency. In a similar way, the prongs of a tuning fork have a natural frequency of vibration, which you can observe when you strike it on a cork. Every oscillator has a natural frequency of vibration, the frequency with which it vibrates freely after an initial disturbance.

On the other hand, many objects can be forced to vibrate. If you sit on a bus, you may notice that the vibrations from the engine are transmitted to your body, causing you to vibrate with the same frequency. These are not free vibrations of your body; they are forced vibrations. Their frequency is

● ***Figure 3.2*** A ruler with one end free can be stimulated to vibrate.

not the natural frequency of vibration of your body, but the forcing frequency of the bus.

In the same way, you can force a metre ruler to oscillate by waving it up and down; however, its natural frequency of vibration will be much greater than this, as you will discover if you hold one end down on the bench and twang the other end *(figure 3.2)*.

SAQ 3.1

Which of the following are free oscillations, and which are forced: the wing beat of a mosquito; the movement of the pendulum in a grandfather clock; the vibrations of a cymbal after it has been struck; the shaking of a building during an earthquake?

Observing oscillations

Many oscillations are too rapid or too small for us to observe. Our eyes cannot respond rapidly enough if the frequency of oscillation is more than about 5 Hz (five oscillations per second); anything faster than this appears as a blur. In order to see the general characteristics of oscillating systems, we need to find suitable systems that oscillate slowly. Here are three suitable situations to look at.

■ *A mass–spring system*

A trolley, loaded with extra masses, is tethered by identical springs in between two clamps *(figure 3.3)*. Displace the trolley to one side and it will oscillate back and forth along the bench. Listen to the sound of the trolley moving. Where is it moving fastest? What happens to its speed as it reaches the ends of its oscillation? What is happening to the springs as the trolley oscillates?

● ***Figure 3.3*** A trolley tethered between springs will oscillate from side to side.

■ *A long pendulum*

A string, at least 2 m long, hangs from the ceiling with a heavy mass fixed at the end *(figure 3.4)*. Pull the mass some distance to one side, and let go. The pendulum will swing back and forth at its natural frequency of oscillation. Try to note the characteristics of its motion. In what ways is it similar to the motion of the oscillating trolley? In what ways is it different?

■ *A loudspeaker cone*

A signal generator, set to a low frequency (say, 1 Hz), drives a loudspeaker *(figure 3.5)*. You need to be able to see the cone of the loudspeaker. How does this motion compare with that of the pendulum and the mass–spring system? Try using a higher frequency (say, 100 Hz). Use an electronic stroboscope flashing at a similar frequency to show up the movement of the cone. (It may help to paint a white spot on the centre of the cone.) Do you observe the same pattern of movement?

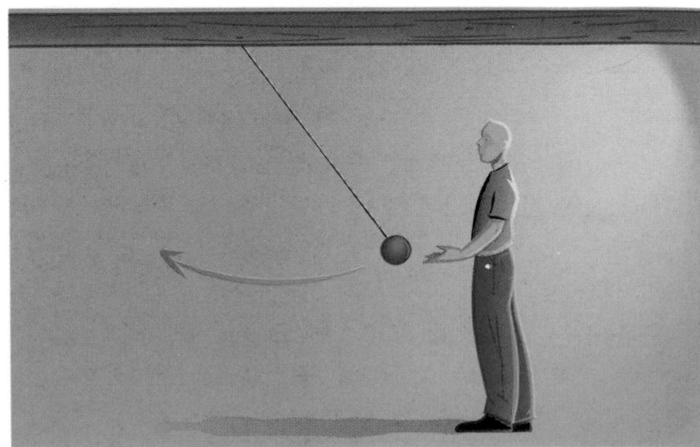

● ***Figure 3.4*** A long pendulum oscillates back and forth.

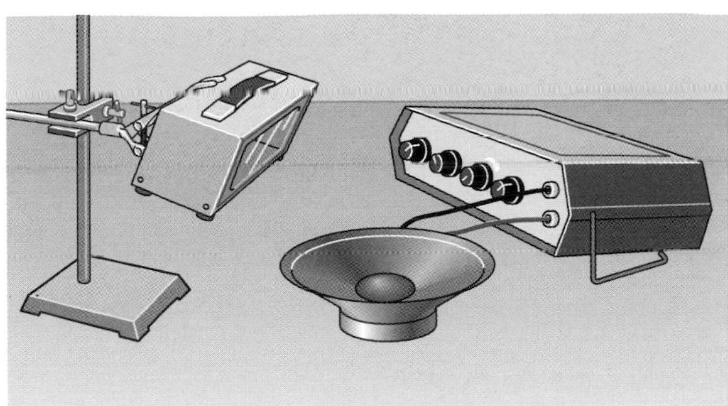

● ***Figure 3.5*** A loudspeaker cone oscillates up and down.

SAQ 3.2

If you could draw a graph to show how the velocity of any of these oscillators changes, what would it look like? Would it be curved like *figure 3.6a*, or saw-toothed like *figure 3.6b*?

Describing oscillations

All of these examples show the same pattern of movement. The trolley speeds up (accelerates) as it moves towards the centre of the oscillation. It is moving fastest at the centre; it slows down again (decelerates) as it moves towards the end of the oscillation. At the extreme position, it stops momentarily, reverses its direction, and accelerates back towards the centre again.

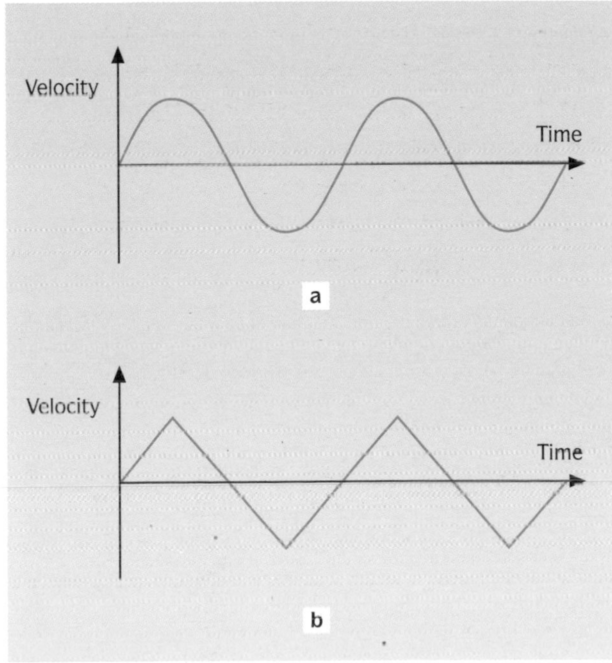

● ***Figure 3.6*** Two possible velocity–time graphs for vibrating objects.

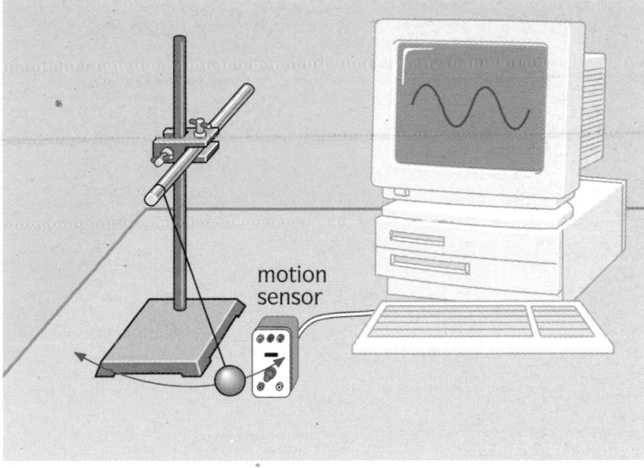

● ***Figure 3.7*** The motion sensor can generate a distance–time graph as the pendulum swings.

This speeding up – slowing down – reversing is the characteristic pattern of free oscillations. You can produce an experimental graph of the motion using a motion sensor connected to a computer (*figure 3.7*). The detector sends out ultrasonic waves, and detects the reflections off the moving pendulum weight.

Graphical analysis

We have looked at some specific examples of oscillating systems. Now we will go on to think about how we can describe and represent oscillating systems in general. You may find it useful to relate these general ideas back to specific examples in order to have a more concrete understanding.

Many oscillating systems can be represented by a displacement–time graph like that shown in *figure 3.8* overleaf. The displacement varies in a smooth way on either side of the midpoint; the shape of this graph is a sine curve, and the motion is sometimes described as sinusoidal.

Notice that the displacement changes between positive and negative values, as the mass moves through the midpoint. The greatest displacement is called the **amplitude** of the oscillation.

The displacement–time graph can also be used to find the period and frequency of the oscillation. The **period** T is the time for one complete oscillation;

note that the oscillating mass must go from one side to the other and back again (or the equivalent). This tells us the number of seconds per oscillation. The **frequency** f is the number of oscillations per second, and so f is the reciprocal of T:

$$\text{frequency} = \frac{1}{\text{period}} \quad \text{or}$$

$$f = \frac{1}{T}$$

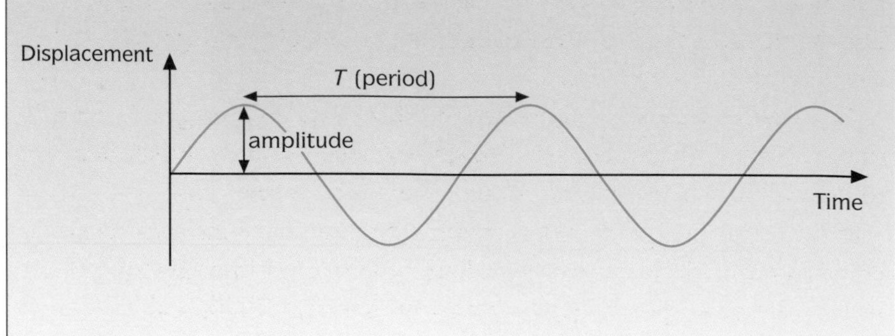

● ***Figure 3.8*** A displacement–time graph to show the meanings of amplitude and period.

SAQ 3.3

From the displacement–time graph shown in *figure 3.9*, deduce the amplitude, period and frequency of the oscillations represented.

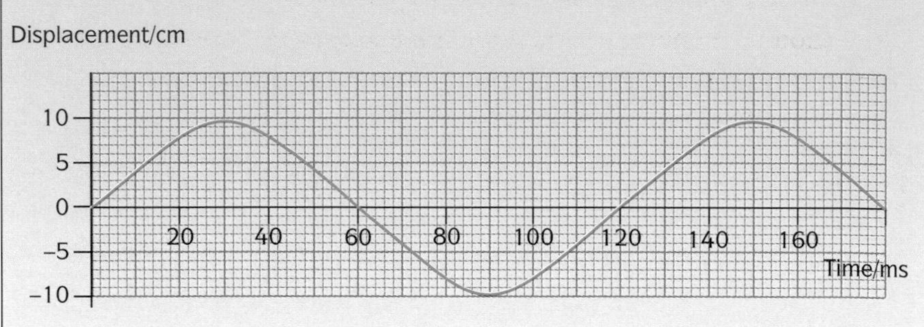

● ***Figure 3.9*** A displacement–time graph for an oscillating body.

Velocity and acceleration

Figure 3.10 shows three related graphs, of displacement, velocity and acceleration against time. These graphs represent the motion of any of the freely oscillating objects we have discussed above. We can deduce the velocity graph from the displacement graph, because velocity is the gradient (slope) of the displacement–time graph. Where the displacement graph is steepest, the velocity is greatest. This corresponds to the points where the displacement is zero, at the midpoint of the oscillations. The velocity is zero where the displacement is maximum, because here the gradient of the displacement graph is zero.

Note that the velocity is positive where the displacement graph is sloping upwards (positive gradient). This corresponds to the

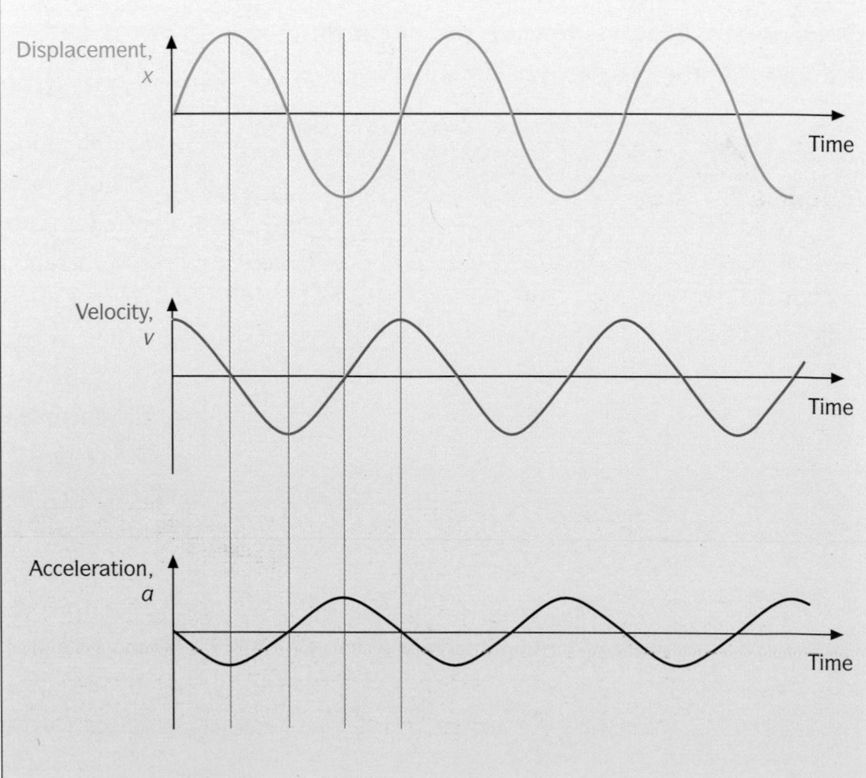

● ***Figure 3.10*** Graphs showing the relationships between displacement, velocity and acceleration for an oscillating body.

half of an oscillation where the mass is moving towards the right. During the other half of the oscillation, the velocity is negative as the mass moves to the left.

In a similar way, we can deduce the acceleration–time graph from the gradient of the velocity–time graph. A steep slope corresponds to greatest acceleration; zero slope means zero acceleration.

It may surprise you to notice that the moving mass has zero acceleration at the midpoint of the oscillation, where it is moving fastest. In fact, the mass speeds up as it approaches the midpoint and it slows down after the midpoint. Hence at the precise midpoint, it is neither speeding up nor slowing down; its acceleration is zero. Its greatest acceleration is at the extreme ends of the oscillation, where its velocity is momentarily zero as it changes direction.

You should be able to see how the three graphs of *figure 3.10* give a description of the motion of an oscillating mass. *Figure 3.11* summarises how displacement, velocity and acceleration change at different points in an oscillation.

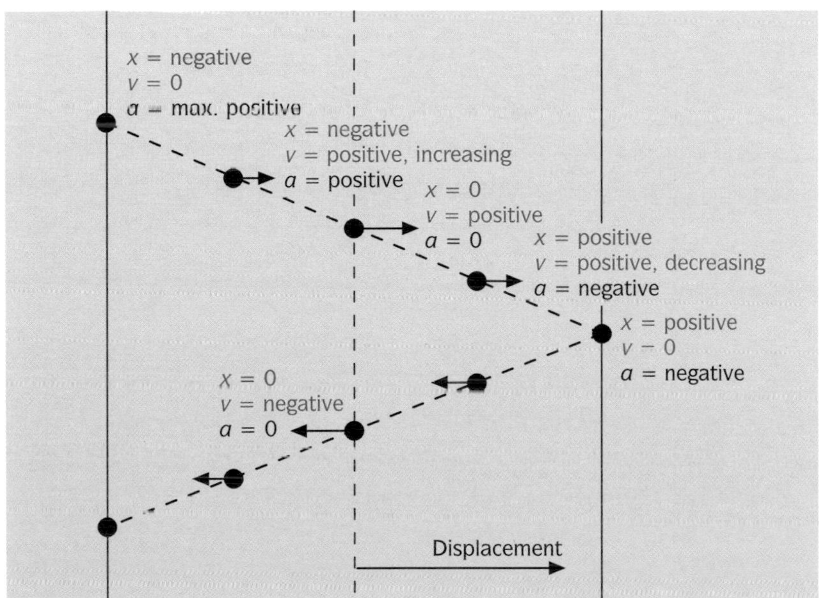

● ***Figure 3.11*** How displacement, velocity and acceleration change during one oscillation.

SAQ 3.4

Figure 3.12 shows the displacement–time graph for an oscillating mass. Use the graph to deduce the following quantities: **a** amplitude, **b** period, **c** frequency, **d** displacement at A, **e** velocity at B, **f** velocity at C.

Acceleration and displacement

If you compare the displacement–time and acceleration–time graphs of *figure 3.10*, you will see that they are very similar to one another. They both have the same shape (a sine curve), but the acceleration graph is inverted relative to the displacement graph. This shape of graph is characteristic of a very important type of oscillatory motion, called **simple harmonic motion** (s.h.m.).

The examples of free oscillations discussed in the first section above are all examples of simple harmonic motion. S.h.m. is very often found in the motion of vibrating structures. It is also found on the microscopic scale,

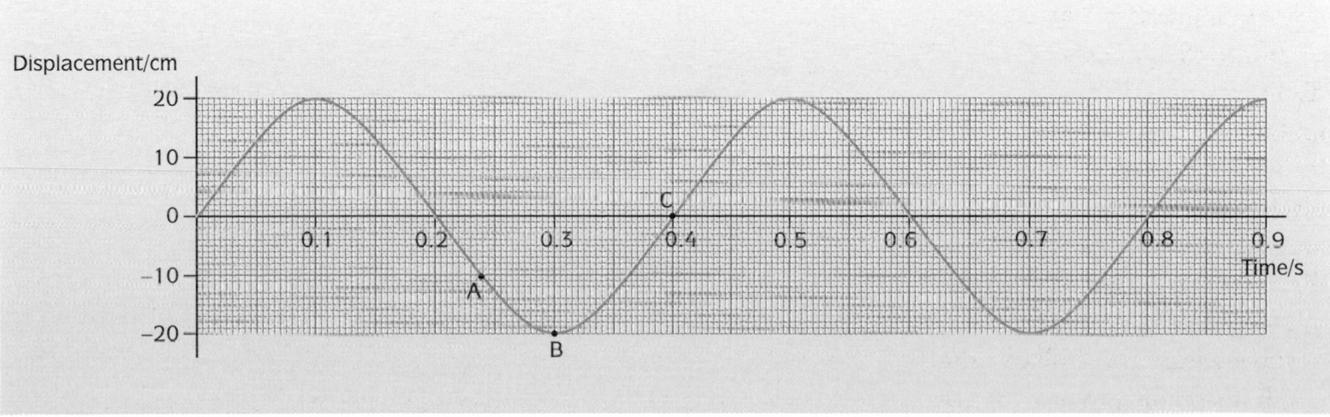

● ***Figure 3.12*** A displacement–time graph.

such as the vibration of atoms in a solid, or the motion of atoms as a sound wave passes through a material.

However, not all oscillations are s.h.m. For example, if you release a marble so that it rolls back and forth in a spherical bowl, its motion will not be strictly simple harmonic. The bowl would have to have a parabolic shape for this to be so.

Phase

The term **phase** describes the point that an oscillating mass has reached within the complete cycle of an oscillation. It is often important to describe the phase difference between two oscillations. The graph of *figure 3.13a* shows two oscillations, which are identical except for their phase. They are out of step with one another; in this example, they are out of phase by one-quarter of a cycle.

SAQ 3.5

a By what fraction of a cycle are the two oscillations represented in *figure 3.13b* out of phase?

b Why would it not make sense to ask the same question about *figure 3.13c*?

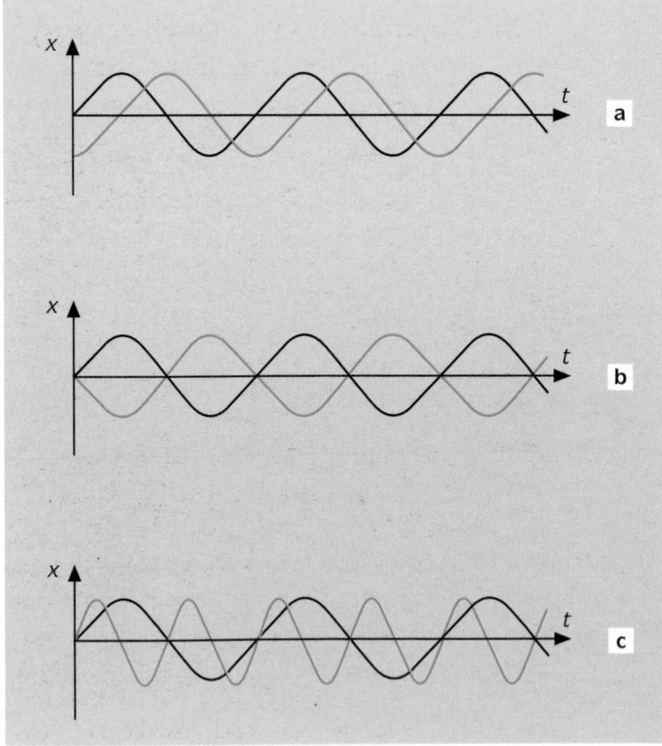

● ***Figure 3.13*** Illustrating the idea of phase difference.

Damped oscillations

In principle, oscillations can go on for ever. In practice, however, the oscillations we observe around us do not. They die out, either rapidly or gradually. A child on a swing knows that the amplitude of their swinging will decline until eventually they come to rest, unless they can put some more energy into the swinging to keep it going.

This happens because of friction. On a swing, there is friction where the swing is attached to the frame, and there is friction with the air. The amplitude of the child's oscillations decreases as the friction transfers energy away from them to their surroundings.

We say that these oscillations are **damped**. Their amplitude decreases according to a particular pattern. This is shown in *figure 3.14*.

The amplitude of damped oscillations does not decrease steadily. It follows an exponential pattern – this is a particular mathematical pattern that arises as follows. At first, the swing moves rapidly. There is a lot of air resistance to overcome, so the swing loses energy quickly, and its amplitude decreases at a high rate. Later, it is moving more slowly. There is less air resistance, and so energy is lost more slowly, and the amplitude decreases at a slower rate. Hence we get the characteristic curved shape, which is the 'envelope' of the graph in *figure 3.14*.

Notice that the frequency of the oscillations does not change as their amplitude decreases. This is a characteristic of simple harmonic motion. The

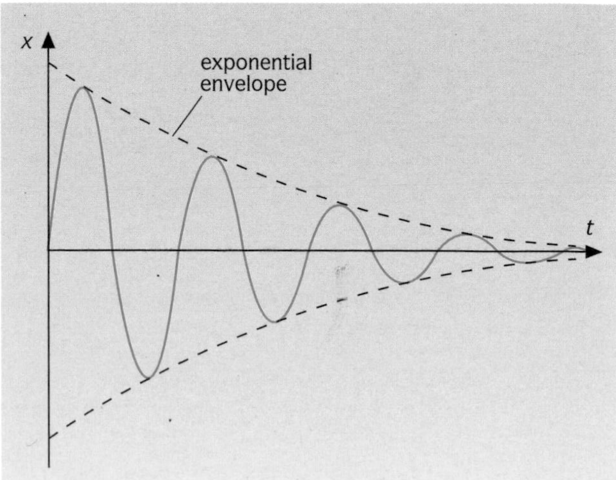

● ***Figure 3.14*** Damped oscillations.

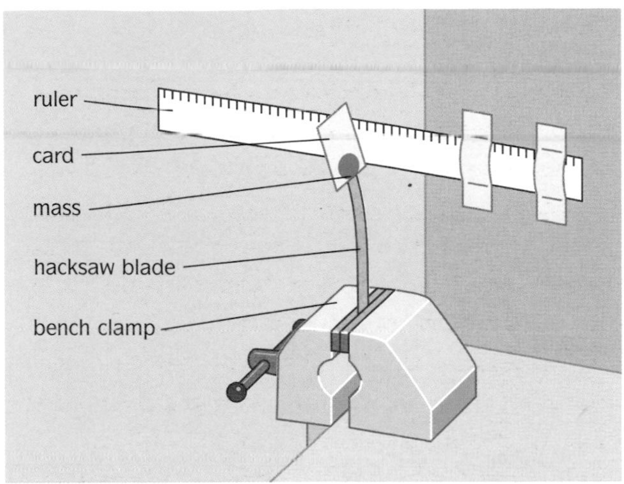

● **Figure 3.15** Damped oscillations with a hacksaw blade.

child may swing back and forth once every two seconds, and this stays the same whether the amplitude is large or small.

Investigating damping

You can investigate the exponential decrease in the amplitude of oscillations using a simple laboratory arrangement *(figure 3.15)*. A hacksaw blade or other springy metal strip is clamped (vertically or horizontally) to the bench. A mass is attached to the free end. This will oscillate freely if you displace it to one side.

A card is attached to the mass so that there is a lot of air resistance as the mass oscillates. The amplitude of the oscillations decreases, and can be measured every five oscillations by judging the position of the blade against a ruler fixed alongside.

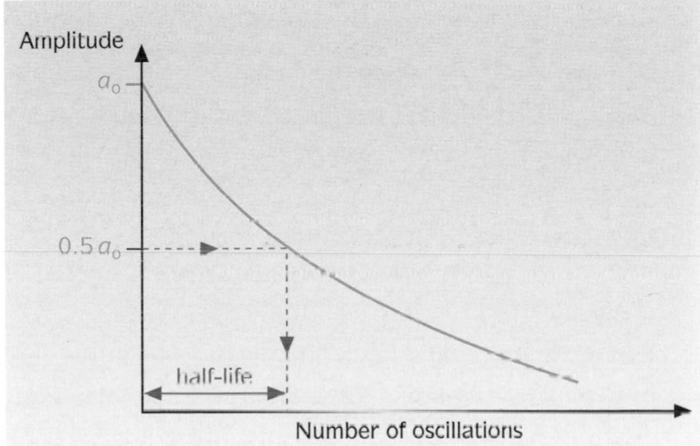

● **Figure 3.16** A typical amplitude–time graph for damped oscillations.

A graph of amplitude against time will show the characteristic exponential decrease. You can find the 'half-life' of this graph by determining the time it takes to decrease to half its initial value *(figure 3.16)*.

By changing the size of the card, it is possible to change the degree of damping, and hence alter the half-life of the graph.

High, low and critical damping

Damping can be very useful if we want to get rid of vibrations. For example, a car has springs *(figure 3.17)*, which make the ride much more comfortable for us when the car goes over a bump. However, we wouldn't want to spend every car journey vibrating up and down as a reminder of the last bump we went over. So the springs are damped by the shock absorbers, and we return rapidly to a smooth ride after every bump.

Figure 3.18 illustrates how oscillations change when the degree of damping is increased. With light damping, the amplitude of the oscillations decreases exponentially over a period of several oscillations. With very heavy damping, there may be no oscillation at all. There is an intermediate level of damping, called **critical damping**, when the oscillating mass returns to rest in the shortest possible time. A car's suspension system is usually adjusted so that the damping is slightly less than critical.

● **Figure 3.17** The springs and shock absorbers in a car suspension system form a damped system.

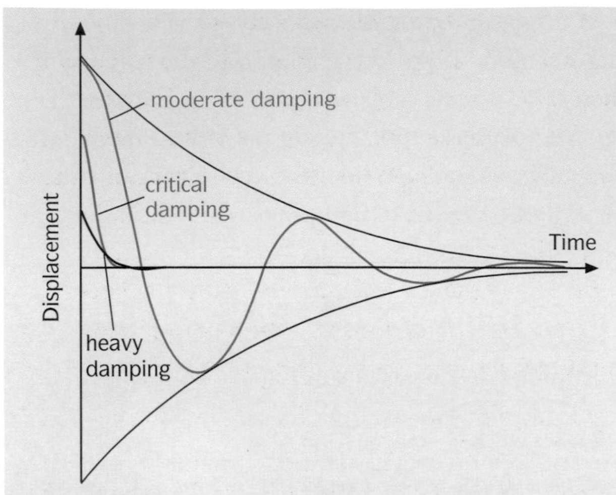

● **Figure 3.18** Different degrees of damping affect the time for which an object oscillates.

Energy and oscillation

To make a mass oscillate, you have to displace it. You do work, and thereby transfer energy to the mass. At the moment when you release the mass, it has potential energy. As it speeds up towards the midpoint of the oscillation, its potential energy decreases and its kinetic energy increases. Then, as it slows down, its kinetic energy decreases again and its potential energy increases. The total amount of energy remains constant.

In any oscillation, there is this regular interchange between potential and kinetic energy. By introducing friction, damping has the effect of removing energy from the system, and the amplitude and maximum speed of the oscillation decrease.

SAQ 3.6

a Sketch graphs to show how you think each of the following quantities would change during the course of a single complete oscillation of an undamped pendulum: kinetic energy; potential energy; total energy.

b How would your graph be different for a critically damped pendulum?

Resonance

Resonance is an important physical phenomenon that can appear in a great many different situations. A tragic example is the Tacoma Narrows bridge disaster *(figure 3.19)*. This suspension bridge in Washington state, USA, collapsed in a mild gale on 1 July 1940. The wind set up oscillating vortices of air around the bridge, which vibrated more and more violently until it broke up under the stress. The bridge had been in use for just four months; engineers learnt a lot about how oscillations can build up when a mechanical structure is subjected to repeated forces.

● **Figure 3.19** The Tacoma Narrows bridge collapsed in 1940, a victim of resonant failure.

You will have observed a much more familiar example of resonance when pushing a small child on a swing; the swing + child has a natural frequency of oscillation; a small push each swing results in the amplitude increasing until the child is swinging high in the air.

Observing resonance

Resonance can be observed with almost any oscillating system. The system is forced to oscillate at a particular frequency; if the forcing frequency happens to match the system's natural frequency of oscillation, the amplitude of the resulting oscillations can build up to become very large.

Barton's pendulums is a demonstration of this *(figure 3.20)*. Several pendulums of different lengths hang from a horizontal string. Each has its own natural frequency of oscillation. The 'driver' pendulum at the end is different; it has a large mass at the end, and its length is equal to that of one of the others. When the driver is set swinging,

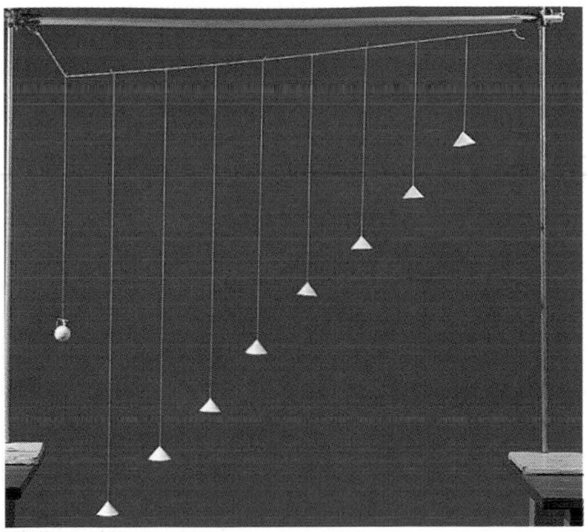

● ***Figure 3.20*** Barton's pendulums.

the others gradually start to move. However, only the pendulum whose length matches that of the driver pendulum builds up a large amplitude.

What is going on here? All the pendulums are coupled together by the suspension. As the driver swings, it moves the suspension, which in turn moves the other pendulums. The matching pendulum is being pushed slightly, once each oscillation, and the amplitude gradually builds up. The other pendulums are being pushed at a frequency that does not match their natural frequency, and the driver has little effect.

In a similar way, if you were to push the child on the swing once every three-quarters of an oscillation, you would soon find that the swing pushed you as often as you pushed it!

You can observe resonance for yourself with a simple mass–spring system. You need a mass on the end of a spring *(figure 3.21)*, chosen so that the mass oscillates up and down with a natural frequency of about 1 Hz. Now hold the top end of the spring and move your hand up and down rapidly, with an amplitude of a centimetre or two. Very little happens. Now move your hand up and down more slowly, close to 1 Hz. You should see the mass oscillating with gradually increasing amplitude. Adjust your movements to the exact frequency of the natural vibrations of the mass and you will see the greatest effect.

● ***Figure 3.21*** Resonance with a mass on a spring.

Defining resonance

For resonance to occur, we must have a system that is capable of oscillating freely. We must also have some way in which the system is forced to oscillate. When the forcing frequency matches the natural frequency of the system, the amplitude of the oscillations grows dramatically.

If the driving frequency does not quite match the natural frequency, the amplitude of the oscillations will increase, but not to the same extent as when perfect resonance is achieved. *Figure 3.22* shows how the amplitude of oscillations depends on the driving frequency in the region close to resonance.

In resonance, energy is transferred from the driver to the resonating system. For example, in the case of the Tacoma Narrows bridge, energy was transferred from the wind to the bridge, causing very large-amplitude oscillations.

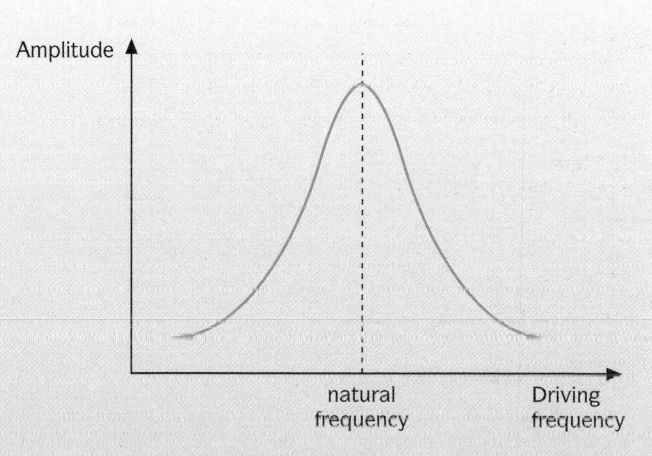

● ***Figure 3.22*** Maximum amplitude is achieved when the driving frequency matches the natural frequency of oscillation.

● **Figure 3.23** Resonance during the Peru earthquake in 1970 caused the collapse of these buildings.

Resonance and damping

During earthquakes, buildings are forced to oscillate by the vibrations of the Earth. Resonance can occur, resulting in serious damage *(figure 3.23)*. In regions of the world where earthquakes happen regularly, buildings may be built on foundations that absorb the energy of the shock waves. In this way, the vibrations are damped and the amplitude of the oscillations cannot reach dangerous levels. This is an expensive business, and so far is restricted to the wealthier parts of the world.

Damping is thus useful if we want to reduce the damaging effects of resonance. *Figure 3.24* shows how damping alters the resonance response curve of *figure 3.22*. Notice that, as the degree of damping is increased, the amplitude of the resonant vibrations decreases. The resonance peak becomes broader. There is also an effect on the frequency at which resonance occurs, which becomes lower.

Using resonance

As we have seen, resonance can be a problem in mechanical systems. However, it can also be useful. For example, many musical instruments rely on resonance – this is discussed further in chapter 4.

Resonance is not confined to mechanical systems. It is made use of in, for example, microwave cooking. The microwaves used have a frequency that matches a natural frequency of vibration of water molecules. The water molecules in the food are forced to vibrate, and they absorb the radiation. The water gets hotter, and the absorbed energy spreads through the food and cooks or heats it.

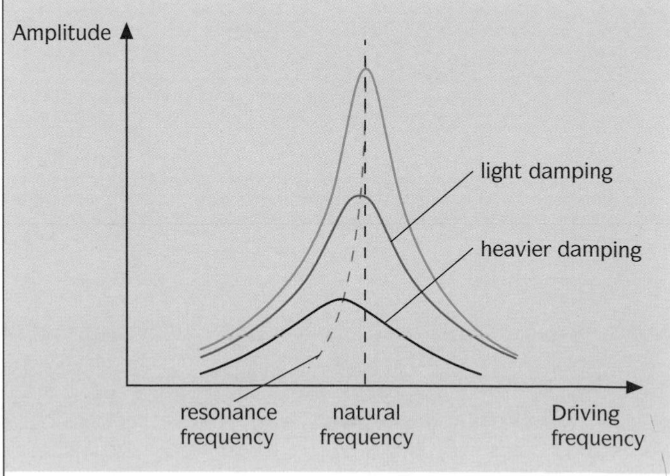

● **Figure 3.24** Damping reduces the amplitude of resonant vibrations.

Magnetic resonance imaging (MRI) is increasingly used in medicine to produce images such as *figure 3.25*, showing aspects of a patient's insides. Radio waves having a range of frequencies are used, and particular frequencies are absorbed by particular atomic nuclei. The frequency absorbed depends on the type of nucleus and on its surroundings. By analysing the absorption of the radio waves, a computer-generated image can be produced. A radio or television set also depends on resonance for its tuning circuitry. The aerial picks up signals of many different frequencies from many transmitters. The tuner can be adjusted to resonate at the frequency of the station we are interested in, and the circuit produces a large-amplitude signal for this frequency only.

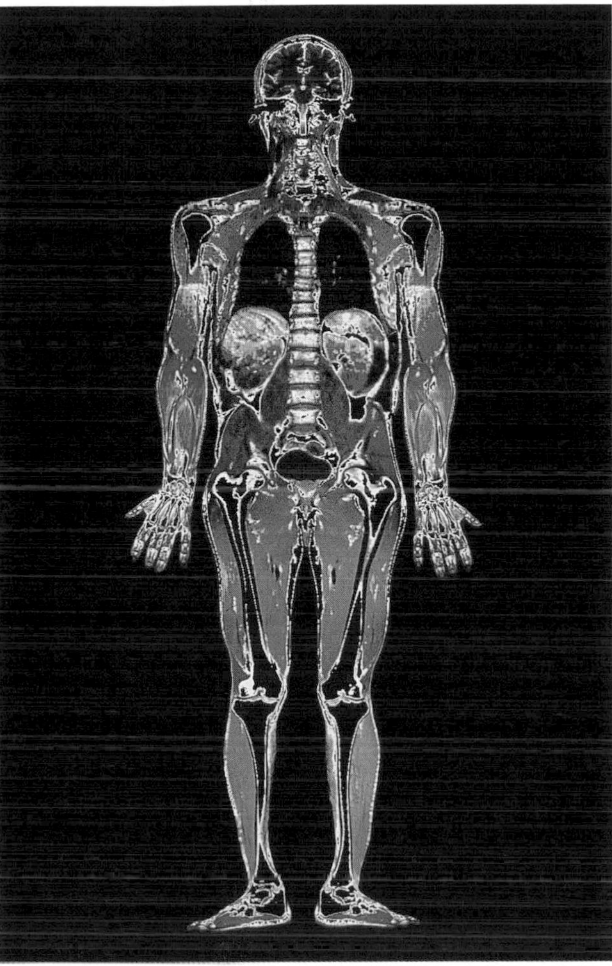

● **Figure 3.25** This magnetic resonance imaging (MRI) picture shows a whole human body. The bones show up with particular clarity.

SAQ 3.7

List three examples of situations where resonance is a problem, and three others where resonance is useful. In each case, say what the oscillating system is, and what forces it to resonate.

SUMMARY

- Many systems, mechanical and otherwise, will oscillate freely when stimulated.
- Some display a particular form of movement called *simple harmonic motion*. For these systems, a graph of displacement against time is a smooth sine curve.
- Damping reduces the amplitude of oscillations.
- When an oscillating system is forced to vibrate close to its natural frequency, the amplitude of vibration increases rapidly; this is resonance. The effect is greatest when the forcing frequency matches the natural frequency.
- Resonance can be a problem, but it can also be very useful.

Superposition of waves

By the end of this chapter you should be able to:

1. explain and use the principle of superposition of waves;
2. understand the term *interference*;
3. describe experiments that demonstrate two-source interference for ripples, light and microwaves;
4. explain the term *coherence*;
5. understand the conditions required for the observation of two-source interference fringes;
6. describe experiments that demonstrate stationary waves for microwaves, stretched strings and air columns;
7. use a graphical method to explain the formation of stationary waves, and identify nodes and antinodes;
8. determine the wavelength of a sound wave using stationary waves;
9. explain the meaning of the term *diffraction*;
10. describe experiments that show diffraction, including diffraction of ripples by wide and narrow gaps.

● ***Figure 4.1*** An electronic synthesiser makes complicated sound waves by mixing together many simpler waves.

The principle of superposition

In the last chapter, we looked at vibrations. When something vibrates, waves are often produced. A vibrating loudspeaker cone produces sound waves in the air. The vibrations of a passing train send shock waves through the ground. In this chapter we are going to look at waves and consider what happens when two or more waves meet.

Describing waves

We will start by seeing how we can represent a wave graphically. *Figure 4.2* shows a wave; here we are representing a wave as an idealised, smooth sinusoidal curve. You may think this is very similar to the way in which we represented vibrations in diagrams such as *figure 3.8*. However, there is a difference. In this graph *(figure 4.2)*, the x axis represents distance, not time. The graph represents a snapshot at one instant in time; a little later, the wave will have moved along a little to the right.

This graph shows how we define two quantities: **amplitude** is the maximum displacement from the midpoint (the fixed position); **wavelength** is the distance between two adjacent wave crests (or troughs, or any other two equivalent points along the wave).

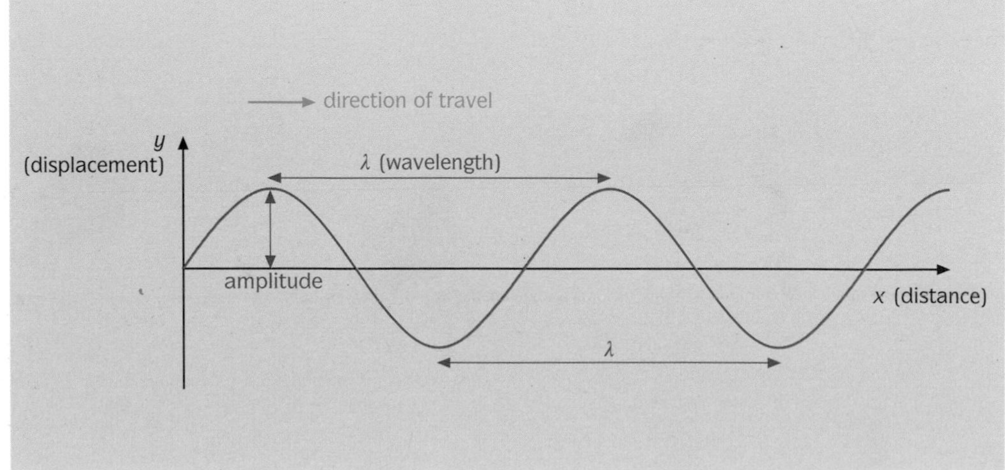

● ***Figure 4.2*** A simple wave, showing the meanings of amplitude and wavelength.

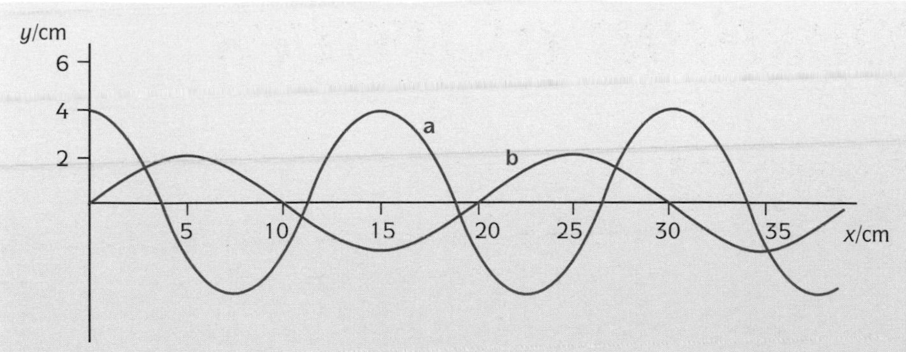

● ***Figure 4.3*** Two waves.

SAQ 4.1

What are the wavelength and amplitude of each of the two waves shown in *figure 4.3*?

Combining waves

So what happens when two waves arrive together at the same place? We can answer this from our everyday experience. What happens when the beams of light waves from two torches cross over? They pass straight through one another. Similarly, sound waves pass through one another, apparently without affecting each other. This is very different from the behaviour of particles; two bullets meeting in mid-air would ricochet off one another in a very un-wave-like way.

The difference between waves and particles is that waves are not made of matter. They are a disturbance, which is much more abstract than particles of matter.

In order to work out the effect of two wave disturbances arriving at a point, we have to see how the two disturbances combine.

The principle of superposition of waves

Figure 4.4 shows two waves (blue and black) of different wavelengths. It also shows the resultant wave (red), which comes from combining these two. How do we find this resultant?

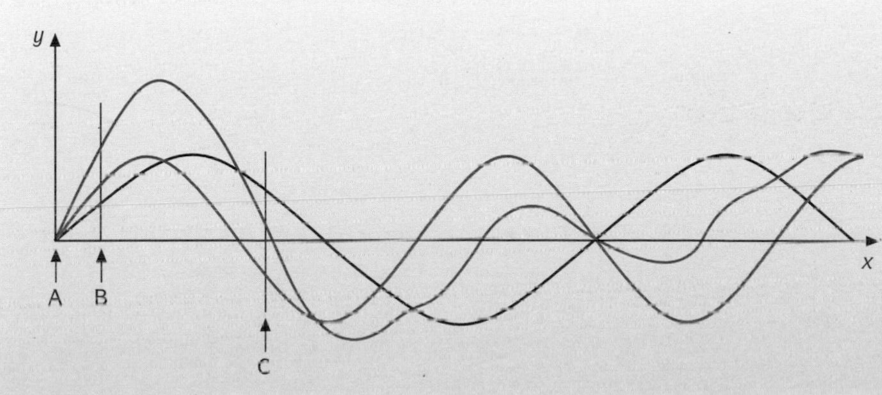

● ***Figure 4.4*** Adding two waves by the principle of superposition.

Consider position A. Here the displacement of both waves is zero, and so the resultant must also be zero.

At position B, both waves have positive displacement, and the resultant displacement is found by adding these together.

At position C, the displacement of one wave is positive while the other is negative. The resultant lies between the two.

We can work our way along the x axis in this way, calculating the resultant effect of the two waves by adding them up at intervals, taking account of their signs (positive or negative). Notice that, for these two waves, the resultant is a rather complex wave with dips and bumps along its length.

The idea that we can find the resultant effect of two waves simply by adding up the displacements at each point along their length is called the **principle of superposition of waves.** It works for all types of waves, and it works for more than two waves.

An electronic synthesiser uses this principle to generate the sounds of different musical instruments. It has electronic circuits that produce sinusoidal signals of different frequencies. By adjusting the controls, you can combine different waves of different frequencies and amplitudes; these waves superpose to give the desired effect (*figure 4.5*).

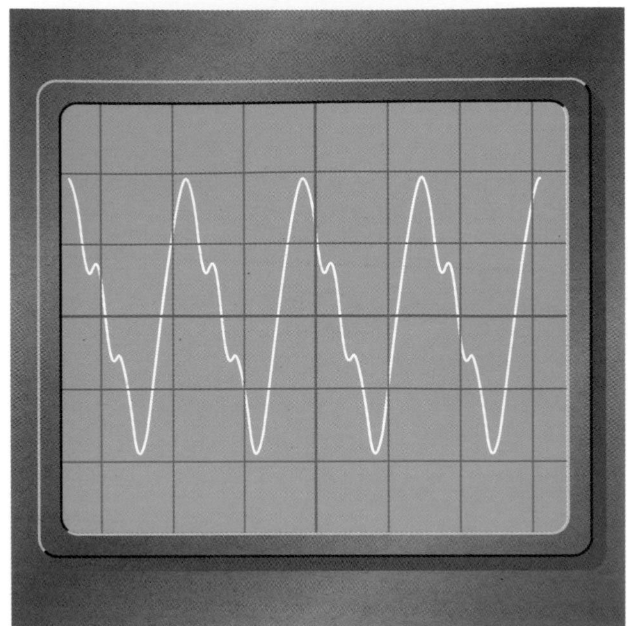

● **Figure 4.5** A waveform generated by adding several together.

SAQ 4.2

On graph paper, draw two 'triangular' waves like those shown in *figure 4.6*. (These are easier to work with than sinusoidal waves.) One should have wavelength 8 cm and amplitude 2 cm; the other wavelength 16 cm and amplitude 3 cm. Use the principle of superposition of waves to determine the resultant displacement at suitable points along the waves, and draw the complete resultant wave.

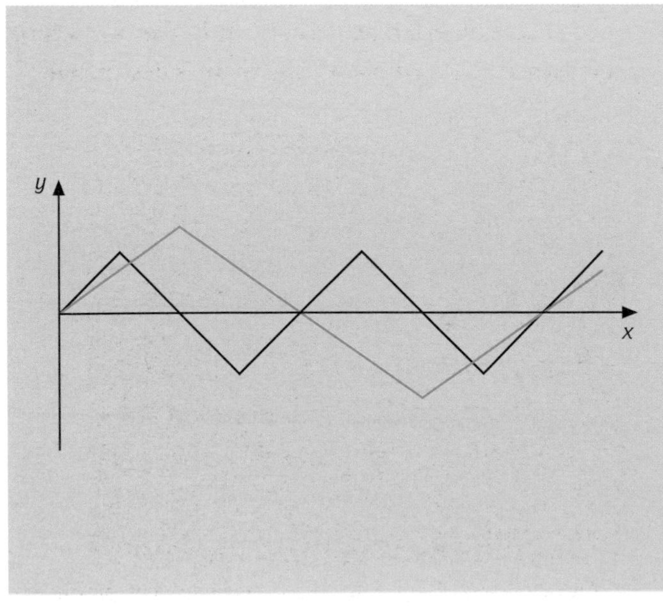

● **Figure 4.6** Two triangular waves.

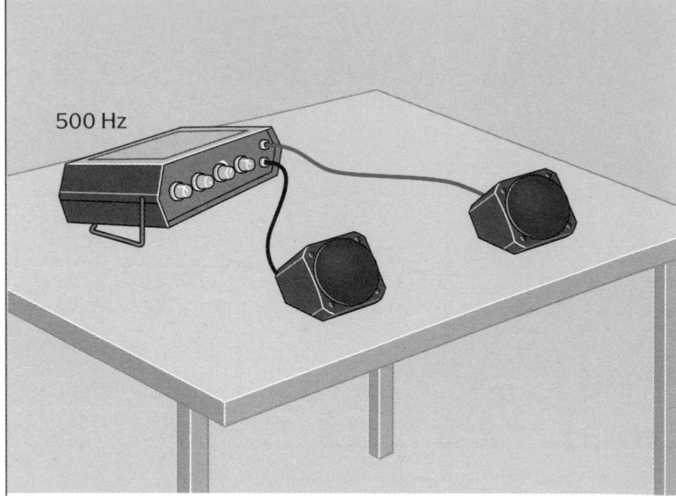

● **Figure 4.7** The sound waves from two loudspeakers combine to give an interference pattern.

Interference

Adding waves of different wavelengths and amplitudes results in complex waveforms. We can find some interesting effects if we consider what happens when two waves having the same wavelength overlap. Again, we will use the principle of superposition to explain what we observe.

A simple experiment shows the effect we are interested in here. Two loudspeakers are connected to a single signal generator *(figure 4.7)*. They each produce sound waves of the same wavelength; if you walk around in the space in front of the loudspeakers, you will observe the resultant effect. A naive view might be that we would hear a sound twice as loud as that from a single loudspeaker. However, this is not what we hear. At some points, the sound is louder than for a single speaker; however, at other points, the sound is much quieter. We are observing the phenomenon known as **interference**.

Explaining interference

Figure 4.8 shows how interference arises. At each point, waves are arriving from the two loudspeakers. At some points, the two waves arrive in step (in phase) with one another *(figure 4.8a)*. The principle of superposition predicts that the resultant wave has twice the amplitude of a single wave, and we hear a louder sound.

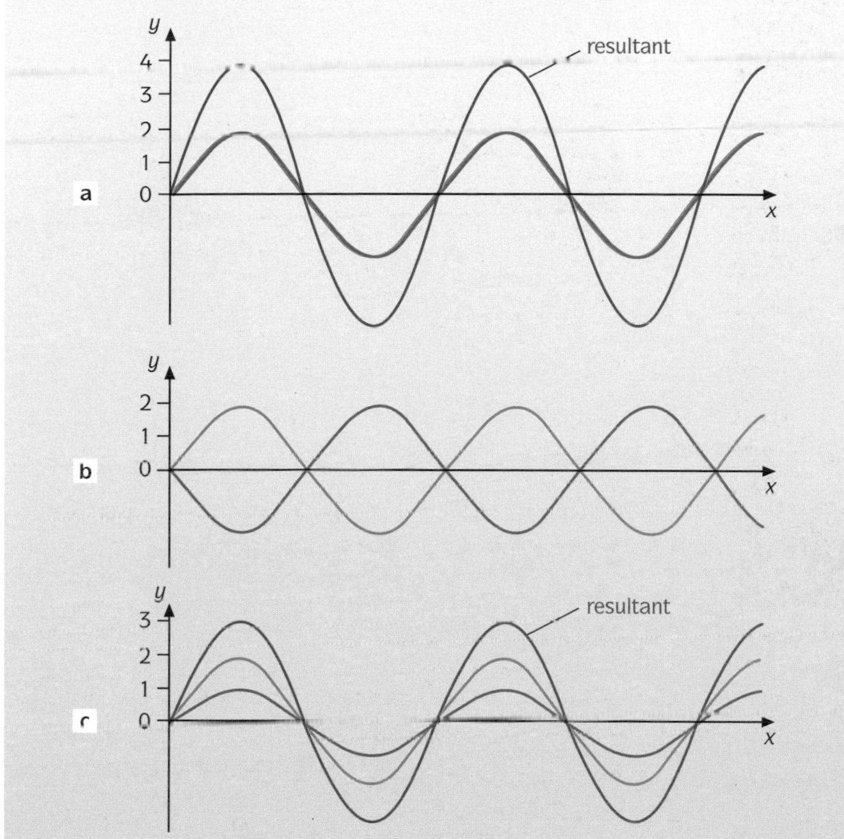

● ***Figure 4.8*** Adding waves by the principle of superposition.

At other points, something different happens. The two waves arrive out of phase with one another *(figure 4.8b)*. There is a cancelling out, and the resultant wave has zero amplitude. At this point, we would expect silence. At other points, the waves are neither perfectly out of step nor perfectly in step, and the resultant wave has an amplitude less than that at the loudest point.

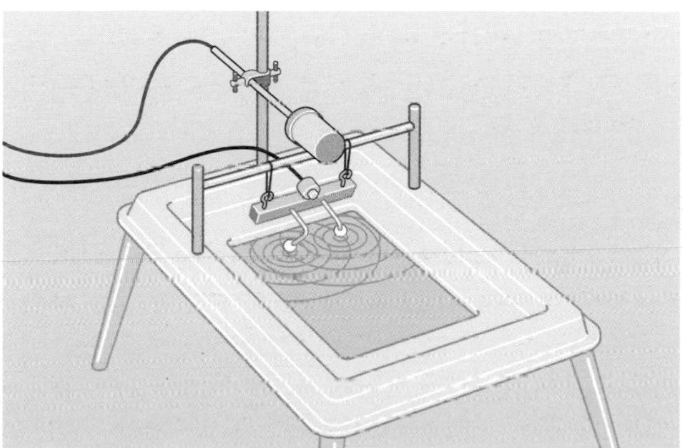

● ***Figure 4.9*** A ripple tank can be used to show how two sets of circular ripples combine.

Where two waves arrive in phase with one another so that they add up, we call this **constructive interference**. Where they cancel out, the effect is known as **destructive interference**.

Where two waves have different amplitudes *(figure 4.8c)*, constructive interference results in a wave whose amplitude is the sum of the two individual amplitudes.

SAQ 4.3

Why must the two loudspeakers be producing sounds of precisely the same frequency in order for us to hear the effects of interference described above?

Observing interference

In a ripple tank

The two dippers in the ripple tank *(figure 4.9)* should be positioned so that they are just touching the surface of the water. When the bar vibrates, each dipper acts as a source of circular ripples spreading outwards. Where these sets of ripples overlap, we observe an interference pattern as shown in *figure 4.10*.

At a position such as A, ripples from the two sources arrive in phase with one another, and constructive interference occurs. At B, the two sets of ripples arrive out of phase, and there is destructive

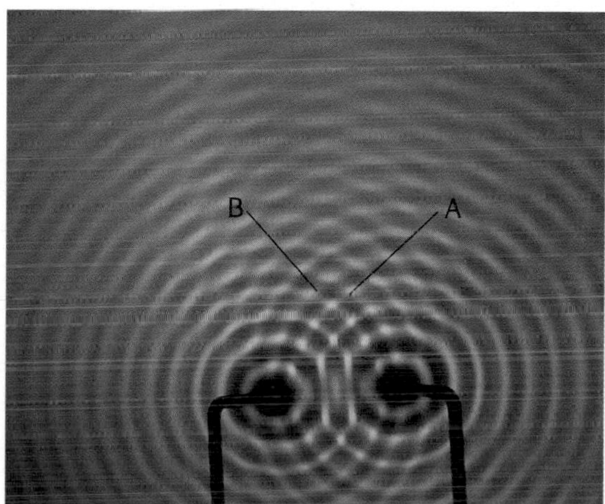

● ***Figure 4.10*** Ripples from two point sources produce an interference pattern.

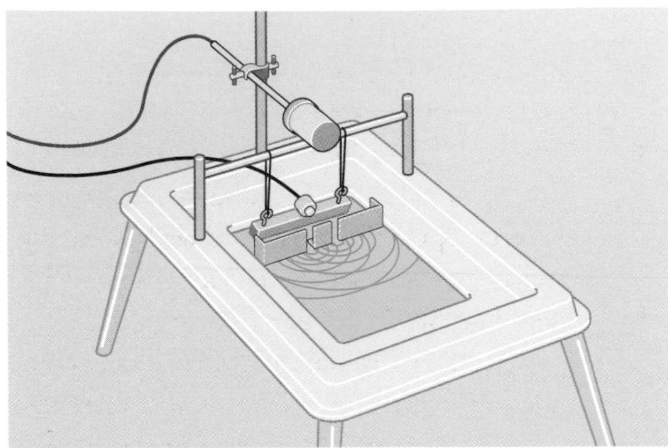

● ***Figure 4.11*** Ripples passing through the two gaps produce an interference pattern in the space beyond.

interference. Although waves are arriving at B, the surface of the water remains approximately flat.

Another way to observe interference in a ripple tank is to use plane waves passing through two gaps in a barrier *(figure 4.11)*. The vibrating bar generates plane (straight) ripples; these emerge through the two gaps in the barrier and spread out into the region beyond. The spreading ripples overlap and an interference pattern results. You should be able to identify points in the diagram where the interference is constructive and where it is destructive.

Interference of light

We can carry out a similar experiment for light. A simple arrangement involves directing the light from a laser through two slits *(figure 4.12)*. The slits are two clear strips in a black slide, separated by a fraction of a millimetre. Where the light falls on the screen, a series of equally spaced dots of light are seen. These are referred to as interference 'fringes', and they are points where light waves from the two slits are arriving in phase with each other, i.e. constructive interference. The dark regions in between are the result of destructive interference.

> **Safety note**
> If you carry out experiments using a **laser**, you should **follow correct safety procedures**. In particular, you should **wear goggles** and **avoid allowing the beam to enter your eye directly**.

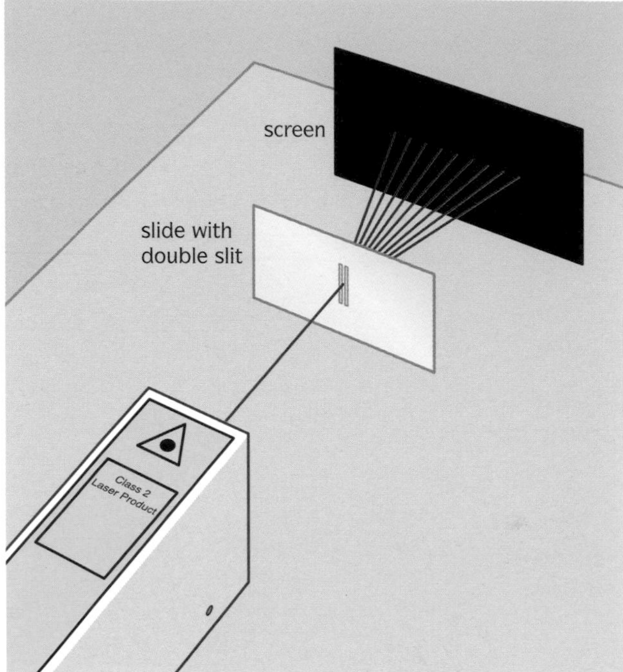

● ***Figure 4.12*** Light beams from the two slits interfere in the space beyond.

These light and dark fringes are the equivalent of the loud and quiet regions that you detected if you investigated the interference pattern of sounds from the two loudspeakers described above. Light fringes correspond to loud, dark fringes to soft or silence.

You can check that light is indeed reaching the screen from both slits as follows. Mark a point on the screen where there is a dark fringe (destructive interference). Now carefully cover up one of the slits so that light from the laser is only passing through one slit. You should find that the pattern of interference fringes disappears. Instead, a broad band of light appears across the screen. The point that was dark is now light. Cover up the other slit instead, and you will see the same effect. You have now shown that light is arriving at the screen from both slits, but at some points (the dark fringes) the two beams of light cancel each other out.

You can achieve similar results with a simple light bulb rather than a laser, but a laser is much more convenient because the light is concentrated into a narrow beam. This famous experiment is called Young's slits, but Young had no laser available to him when he first carried it out in 1801.

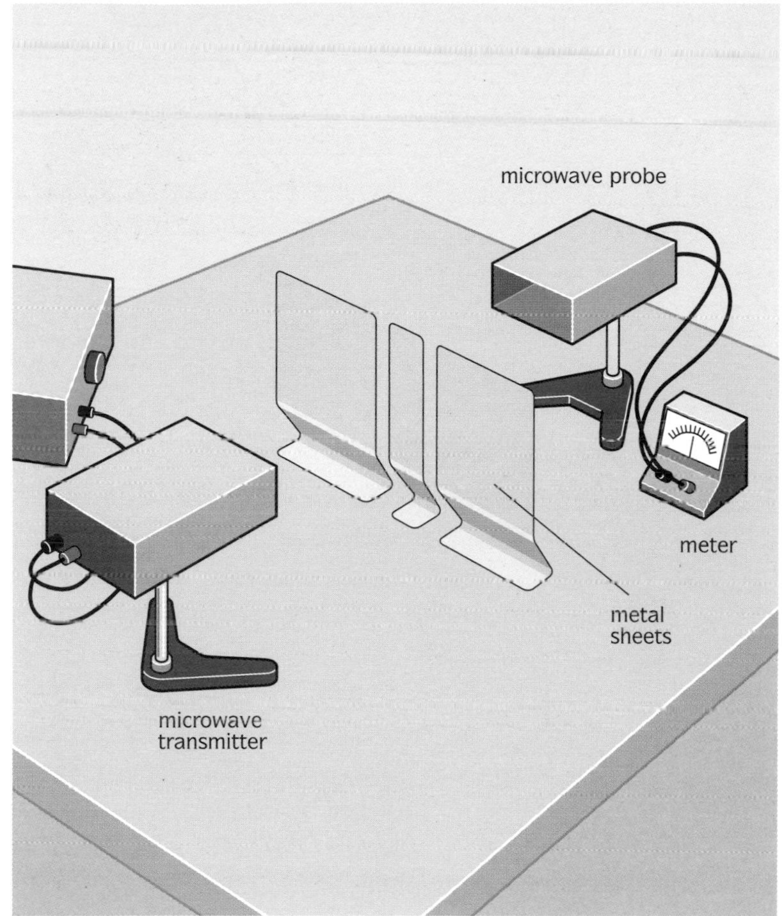

● ***Figure 4.13*** Microwaves can also be used to show interference effects.

Interference of microwaves

Using 2.8 cm wavelength microwave equipment *(figure 4.13)*, you can observe another interference pattern. The microwave transmitter is directed towards the double gap in a metal barrier. The waves spread out into the region beyond, and can be detected using the probe receiver. By moving the probe around, it is possible to detect regions of high intensity (constructive interference) and low intensity (destructive interference). The probe may be connected to a meter, or to an audio amplifier and loudspeaker to give an audible output.

SAQ 4.4

Suppose that the microwave probe is placed at a point of low intensity in the interference pattern. What do you predict will happen if one of the gaps in the barrier is now closed?

Coherence

We are surrounded by wave phenomena – light, sound, infrared radiation and so on. There are waves coming at us from all directions. So why do we not observe interference patterns all the time? Why do we have to go to the lengths of setting up specialised equipment in a laboratory to see these effects?

In fact, we can see interference occurring in everyday life. For example, you may have noticed haloes of light around street lamps on a foggy night. You may have noticed light and dark bands of light if you look at a light through fabric, or with your eyes almost closed. These are interference effects.

However, we usually need specially arranged conditions to see clear interference effects. The reason is this: for constructive interference, we need two sets of waves to be arriving at a point in phase with one another. This condition can be tricky to achieve.

Think about the demonstration with two loudspeakers. If they were connected to different signal generators with slightly different frequencies, they might start off in phase with one another, but they would soon go out of phase *(figure 4.14)*. We would hear loud, then soft, then loud again. The interference pattern would keep shifting around the room.

By connecting the two loudspeakers to the *same* signal generator, we can be sure that the sound waves that they produce are constantly in phase with one another. We say that they act as two **coherent** sources of sound waves (coherent means sticking together).

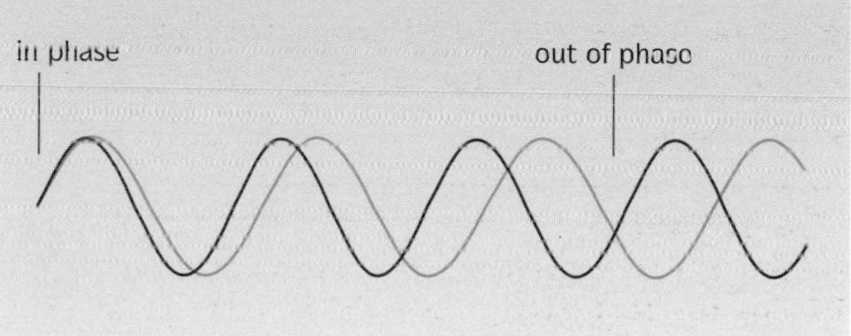

● ***Figure 4.14*** Waves of slightly different wavelengths move in and out of phase with one another.

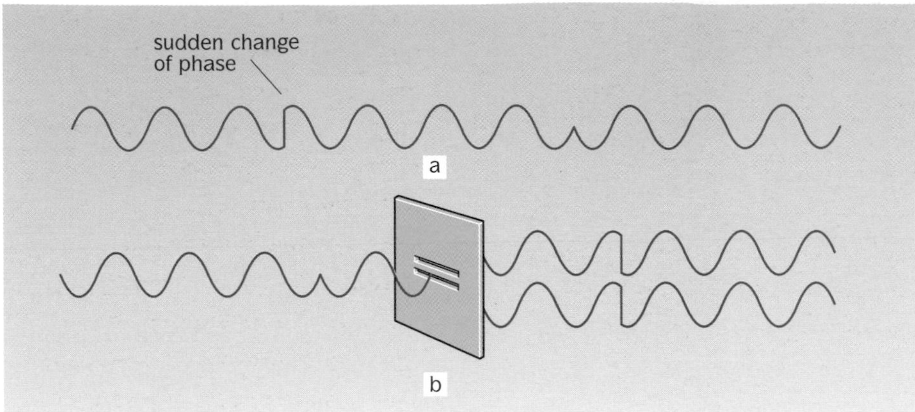

● ***Figure 4.15*** Waves must be coherent if they are to produce a clear interference pattern.

Now think about the laser experiment. Could we have used two lasers producing exactly the same wavelength of light? *Figure 4.15a* represents the light from a laser. We can think of it as being made up of many separate bursts of light. We cannot guarantee that these bursts from two lasers will always be in phase with one another.

This problem is overcome by using a single laser and dividing its light using the two slits *(figure 4.15b)*. The slits act as two coherent sources of light; they are constantly in phase with one another (or there is a constant phase difference between them). If they were not coherent sources, the interference pattern would be constantly changing, far too fast for our eye to detect. We would simply see a uniform band of light, with no bright or dark fringes. From this you should be able to see that, in order to observe interference, we need two coherent sources of waves; that is, they must have the same frequency, and there must be a constant phase difference between them.

SAQ 4.5

Draw sketches to illustrate the following:

a two waves having the same amplitude and in phase with one another;

b two waves having the same amplitude and with a phase difference of one-quarter of a wave between them;

c two waves initially in phase but with slightly different wavelengths.

Use your sketches to explain why two coherent sources of waves are needed to observe interference.

Interference and waves

You are familiar with the idea that sound and light can both be described as waves. Why do we describe them in this way?

True waves are what we observe on water. For physicists, waves are not breakers crashing down on a beach; rather, they are uniform disturbances of water, much more like the small ripples that we see in ripple tanks. We idealise them as waves shaped like the sine curves discussed at the beginning of this chapter. (In practice, it is very difficult to produce such ideal waves on water in the laboratory.)

So what has this to do with sound, light, etc? In this section, we have seen how true waves (ripples) show interference. Interference is a property of waves. We have also seen how sound, light and microwaves also show interference. It follows that we can describe sound, light and microwaves using a wave description.

Waves can show other properties – reflection, refraction, diffraction and polarisation – and we can look for these, too, in the behaviour of light, sound and other phenomena. So rather than saying that light is a wave, it might be better to say that light shows many characteristics of waves, or that we can describe light using a wave model. However, for simplicity, we usually say that light is a wave, and we talk about light waves.

The wave model is one of the fundamental models of physics, and it has been found to apply in many different situations – to sound, to light and other electromagnetic radiation, to the behaviour of electrons in metals, to gravity, and so on.

Stationary waves

The waves we have considered so far in this chapter have been travelling waves; they start from a source and travel outwards. A second important class of waves is stationary waves. These can be observed as follows.

● ***Figure 4.16*** A wave-form helix is used to generate a standing wave pattern.

Use a long spring (a wave-form helix); a long rope or piece of rubber tubing will do instead. Lay it on the floor and fix one end firmly. Wave the other end from side to side so that waves travel along and reflect off the fixed end *(figure 4.16)*. If you adjust the frequency of the waves, you should be able to achieve a pattern like one of those shown in *figure 4.17*. Alter the frequency in order to achieve one of the other patterns.

You should notice that you have to waggle the end of the spring with just the right frequency to get one of these interesting patterns. Faster or slower, and the pattern is no longer established.

Nodes and antinodes

What you have observed is a stationary wave on the spring. There are points along the spring that remain (almost) motionless on the floor, while points on either side are oscillating back and forth. The points that do not move are called **nodes**; points where the spring oscillates with maximum amplitude are **antinodes**. At the same time, it is clear that the wave-shape is not travelling along the spring; hence we call it a **stationary wave.**

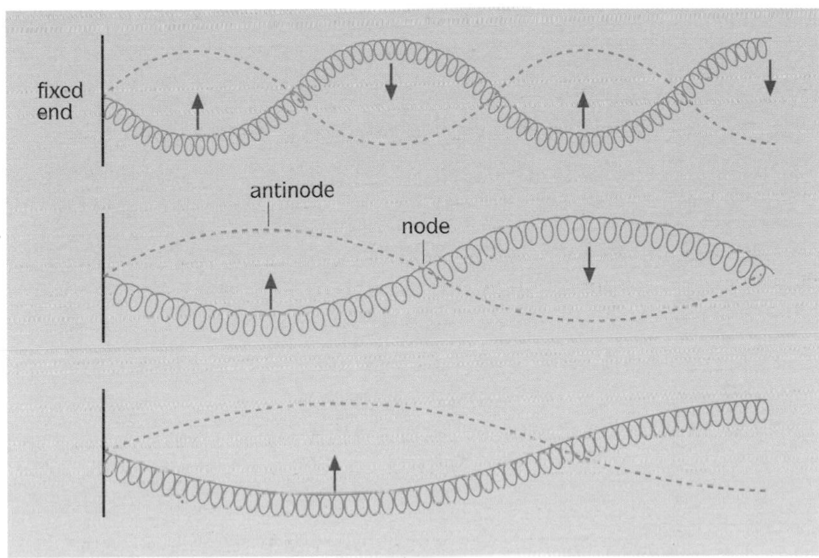

● ***Figure 4.17*** Different standing wave patterns are possible.

We normally represent a stationary wave by drawing the shape of the spring in its two extreme positions *(figure 4.18a)*. The spring appears as a series of loops, separated by nodes. In this diagram, point A is moving downwards. At the same time, point B in the next loop is moving upwards. Hence the sections of spring in adjacent loops are always moving in opposite directions; they are half a cycle out of phase with one another.

If we superimpose the shape of a single wave on a stationary wave pattern *(figure 4.18b)*, we can see that consecutive nodes are separated by half a wavelength (as are consecutive antinodes). Adjacent nodes and antinodes are separated by one-quarter of a wavelength. These are important results, which are useful for determining the wavelengths of different waves.

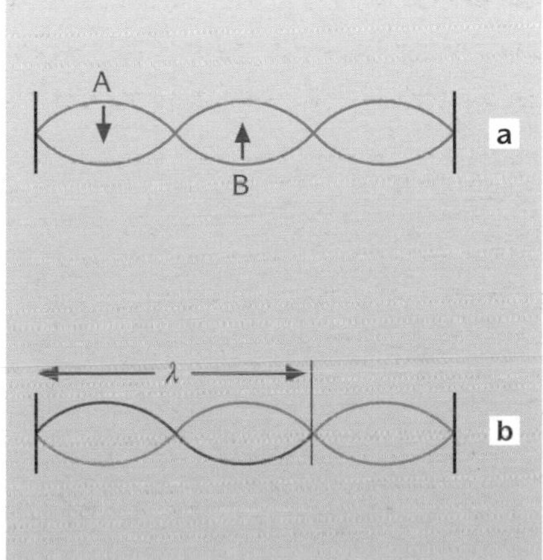

● ***Figure 4.18*** The fixed ends of a string must be nodes in the standing wave pattern.

Observing stationary waves

Stretched strings

A string is attached at one end to a vibration generator, driven by a signal generator *(figure 4.19)*. The other end hangs over a pulley, and weights maintain the tension in the string. When the vibrations are switched on, the string vibrates with small amplitude. However, by adjusting the frequency, it is possible to produce standing waves whose amplitude is several millimetres.

The pulley end of the string is unable to vibrate; this is a node. Similarly, the end attached to the vibrator is only able to move a small amount, and this is also a node. As the frequency is increased, it is possible to observe one loop (one antinode), two loops, three loops and more. By measuring the distance between nodes, it is possible to find the wavelength of the waves on the string.

A flashing stroboscope is useful to reveal the motion of the string at these frequencies, which look blurred to the eye. The frequency of vibration is set so that there are two loops along the string; the frequency of the stroboscope is set so that it almost matches that of the vibrations. Now we can see the string moving 'in slow motion', and it is easy to see the opposite movements of the two adjacent loops *(figure 4.20)*.

This experiment is known as Melde's experiment, and it can be extended to investigate the effects of changing various variables: the length of the string, the tension and the number of loops.

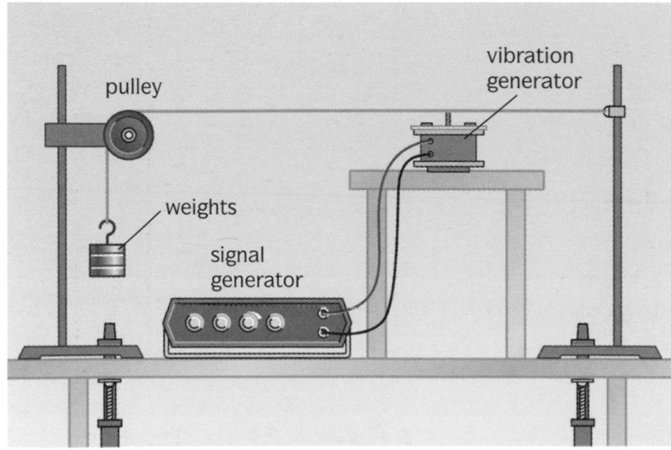

● ***Figure 4.19*** Melde's experiment for investigating standing waves on a string.

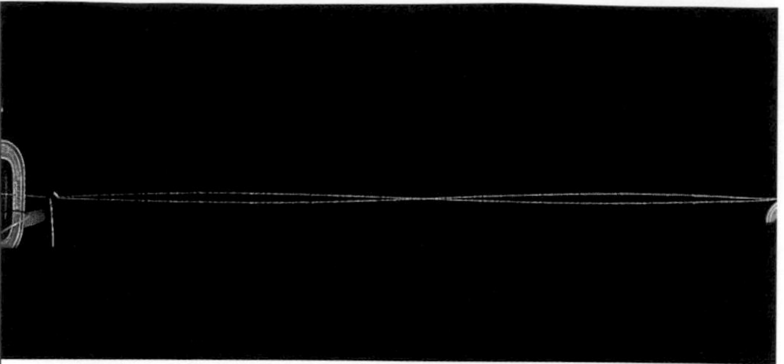

● ***Figure 4.20*** When a standing wave is established, the two halves of the string move in opposite directions.

Microwaves

Start by directing the microwave transmitter at a metal plate, which reflects waves back towards the source *(figure 4.21)*. Move the probe receiver around in the space between the transmitter and the reflector, and you will observe positions of high and low intensity.

SAQ 4.6

a In the above microwave experiment, which positions correspond to nodes, and which are antinodes?

b If the separation of two adjacent points of high intensity is found to be 14 mm, what is the wavelength of the microwaves?

Sound waves in air columns

A glass tube (open at both ends) is clamped so that one end dips into a cylinder of water; by adjusting

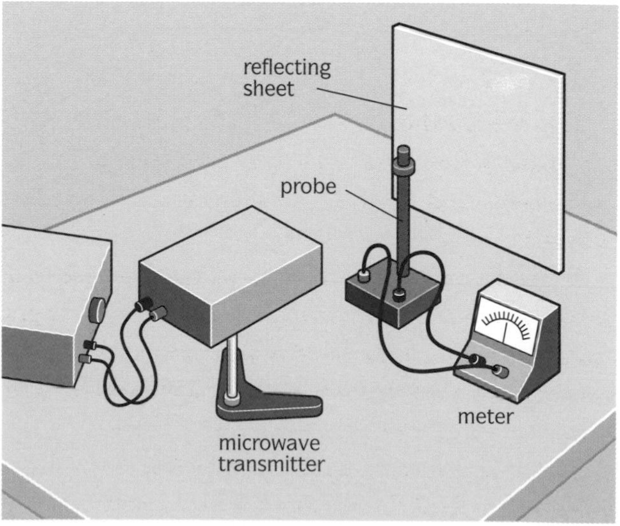

● ***Figure 4.21*** A standing wave is established when microwaves are reflected from the metal sheet.

its height in the clamp, you can change the length of the column of air in the tube *(figure 4.22)*. When you hold a vibrating tuning fork above the open end, the air column may be forced to vibrate, and the note of the tuning fork sounds much louder.

For this to happen, the length of the air column must be just right. The air at the bottom of the tube is unable to vibrate, so this point must be a node. The air at the open end of the tube can vibrate most freely, so this is an antinode. Hence the length of the air column must be one-quarter of a wavelength. (Alternatively, the length of the air column could be set to equal three-quarters of a wavelength – see *figure 4.23*).

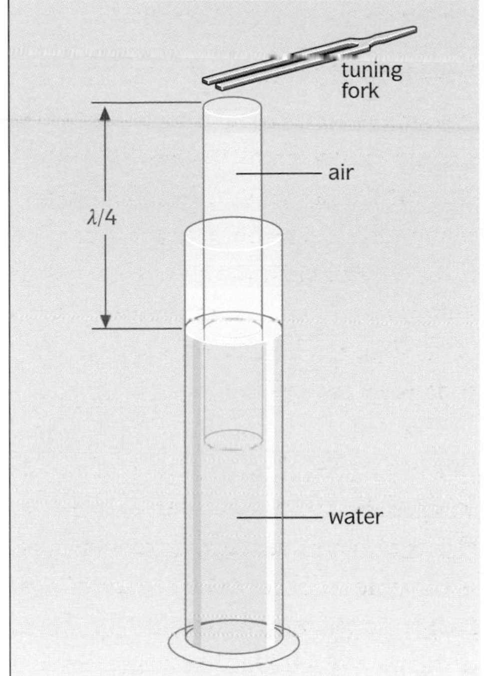

Figure 4.22 A standing wave is established in the air in the tube when the length of the air column is adjusted to the correct length.

Explaining stationary waves

A node is a position where the amplitude of the stationary wave is zero; you might expect this to be the result of destructive interference. Similarly, the amplitude is greatest at an antinode, a result of constructive interference. But how can we have interference here, when we need two sources of waves to observe interference?

The answer is that, in each of the cases described above, we do not have two sources, but we do have two sets of waves. We have the original waves, together with a set of reflected waves. For the stretched string, waves are generated by the vibrator. They travel to the pulley end of the string, where they reflect back. It is interference between the original waves and the reflected waves that results in the establishment of the stationary wave pattern.

For any stationary wave pattern to be established, we need two sets of travelling waves. They must be identical, but travelling in opposite directions.

SAQ 4.7

Explain how two sets of identical but oppositely travelling waves are established in the microwave and air column experiments described above.

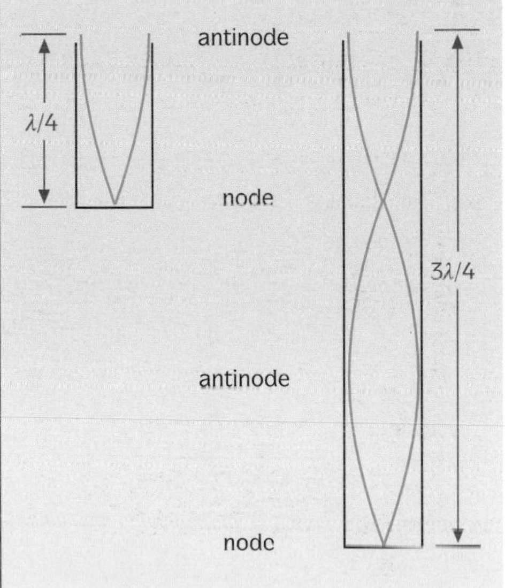

Figure 4.23 Standing wave patterns for air in a tube with one end closed.

Figure 4.24 shows how two sets of travelling waves give rise to a stationary wave. The red waves are travelling to the right, and the blue waves to the left. (The blue waves are a reflection of the red waves.)

In the first diagram, the two waves give rise to a large displacement at A, but they cancel at N. The second diagram shows the situation a short time later. The resultant displacement at A is less than before, and still zero at N. You should be able to follow the sequence of the next two diagrams.

We conclude that, at a point like A, the displacement varies a lot; the amplitude of the resultant wave is greatest here, so this is an antinode. At a point like N, the displacement is always zero, and this is a node.

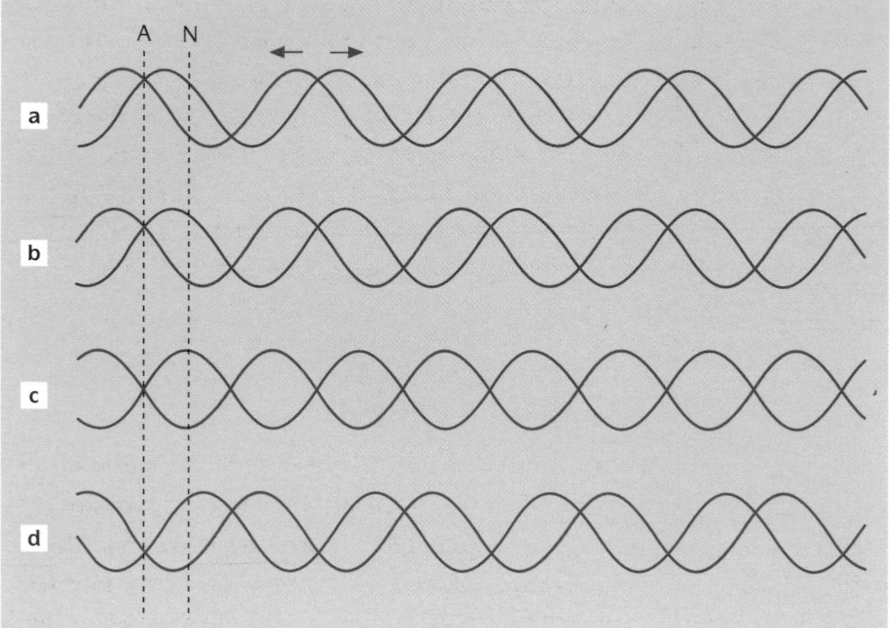

● ***Figure 4.24*** A standing wave is established between the red wave (moving to the right) and the blue wave (moving to the left).

Measuring the wavelength of sound

Since we know that adjacent nodes (or antinodes) of a stationary wave are separated by half a wavelength, we can use this fact to measure wavelengths. For sound, we could use the air column method shown in *figure 4.22*. However, this is not very accurate, since it is found in practice that the antinode is formed a few millimetres above the open end of the tube, and this introduces an inaccuracy into the measurements.

Kundt's dust tube *(figure 4.25)* is better; a loudspeaker sends sound waves along the inside of a tube. They reflect off the closed end. When a stationary wave is established, the dust at the antinodes vibrates violently. It tends to accumulate at the nodes, where the movement of the air is least. Hence the positions of the nodes and antinodes can be clearly seen.

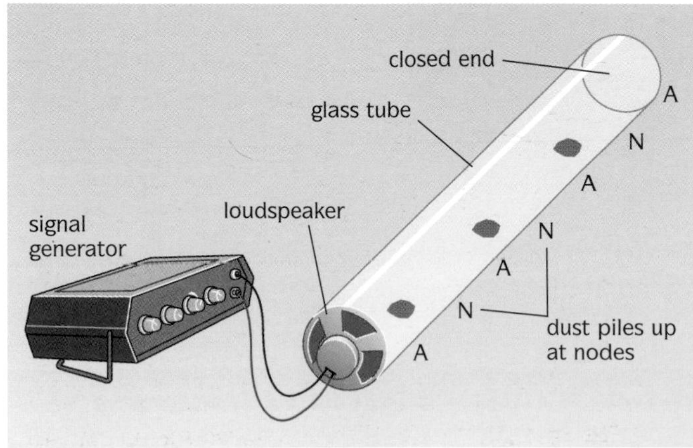

● ***Figure 4.25*** Kundt's dust tube.

An alternative method is shown in *figure 4.26*; this is the same arrangement as used for microwaves. The loudspeaker produces sound waves, and these are reflected from the vertical board. The microphone detects the stationary sound wave in the space between the speaker and the board, and its output is displayed on the oscilloscope. It is simplest to turn off the timebase of the oscilloscope, so that the spot no longer moves across the screen. The spot moves up and down the screen, and the height of the vertical trace gives a measure of the intensity of the sound.

By moving the microphone along the line between the speaker and the board, it is easy to detect nodes and antinodes. For maximum accuracy, we do not measure the separation of adjacent nodes; rather, it is best to measure across several nodes.

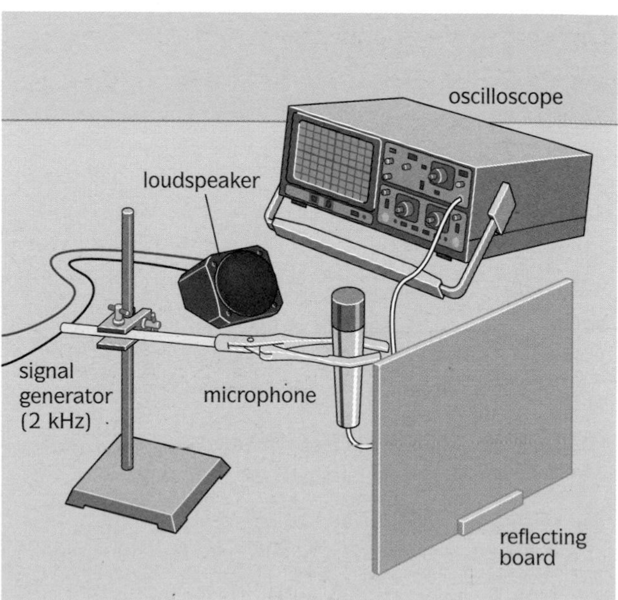

● ***Figure 4.26*** A standing sound wave is established between the loudspeaker and the board.

SAQ 4.8

a Suggest why it is easier to determine accurately the position of nodes rather than antinodes.

b Explain why it is better to measure across several nodes.

SAQ 4.9

For sound waves of frequency 2500 Hz, it is found that two nodes are separated by 20.0 cm, with three antinodes between them. What is the wavelength of these sound waves? Use the equation $v = f\lambda$ to determine the speed of sound in air.

Stationary waves and resonance

The production of different notes by musical instruments often depends on the establishment of stationary waves *(figure 4.27)*. For a stringed instrument such as a guitar, the two ends of a string are fixed, so nodes must be established at these points. When the string is plucked half-way along its length, it vibrates with an antinode at its midpoint.

Similarly, the air column inside a wind instrument is caused to vibrate by blowing, and the note that is heard depends on a standing wave being established. By changing the length of the air column, as in a trombone, the note can be changed. Alternatively, holes can be uncovered so that the air can vibrate more freely, giving a different pattern of nodes and antinodes.

In practice, the sounds that are produced are made up of several different stationary waves having different patterns of nodes and antinodes. The musician's skill is in stimulating the string or air column to produce a desired mixture of frequencies.

In a sense, this is a form of resonance; the string or air column is forced to vibrate. It has its own natural frequency of vibration, and the note of this frequency therefore sounds loudest. The air column experiment described above is often called a resonance tube.

● ***Figure 4.27*** When a guitar string is plucked, the vibrations continue for some time afterwards.

Diffraction of waves

As discussed above, interference is a property of waves. Two waves can arrive together at a point to give a resultant effect of zero; they have cancelled each other out, and we call this destructive interference. This is not a property we would expect to find for particles of matter. Two particles cannot cancel each other out in the way that two waves can.

Thus we can say that, if we can observe interference, we must be dealing with waves. Now we are going on to consider diffraction, another wave phenomenon.

Diffraction of ripples in water

Since water waves are our standard form of waves, we should start with these. A ripple tank can be used to show diffraction; plane waves are generated using a vibrating bar, and they then arrive at a gap in a barrier *(figure 4.28)*. Where the ripples strike the barrier, they are reflected back. Where they arrive at the gap, however, they pass through

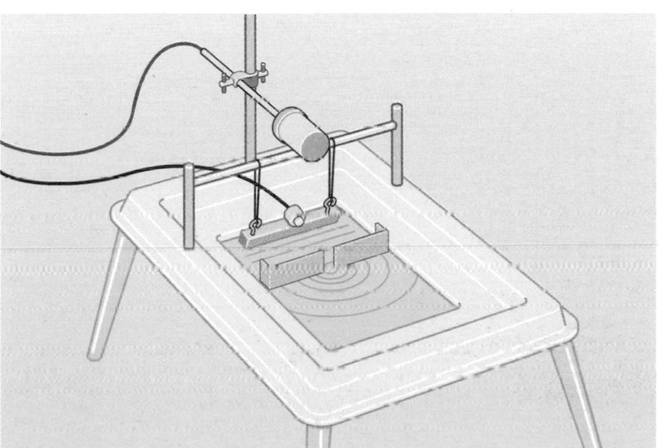

● ***Figure 4.28*** Ripples, initially straight, spread out into the space beyond the gap in the barrier.

and spread out into the space beyond. It is this spreading out of waves as they travel through a gap (or past the edge of a barrier) that is called **diffraction**.

The extent to which ripples are diffracted depends on the width of the gap. This is illustrated in *figure 4.29*. The lines in this diagram represent wave fronts. It is as if we are looking down on the ripples from above, and drawing lines to represent the tops of the ripples at some instant in time.

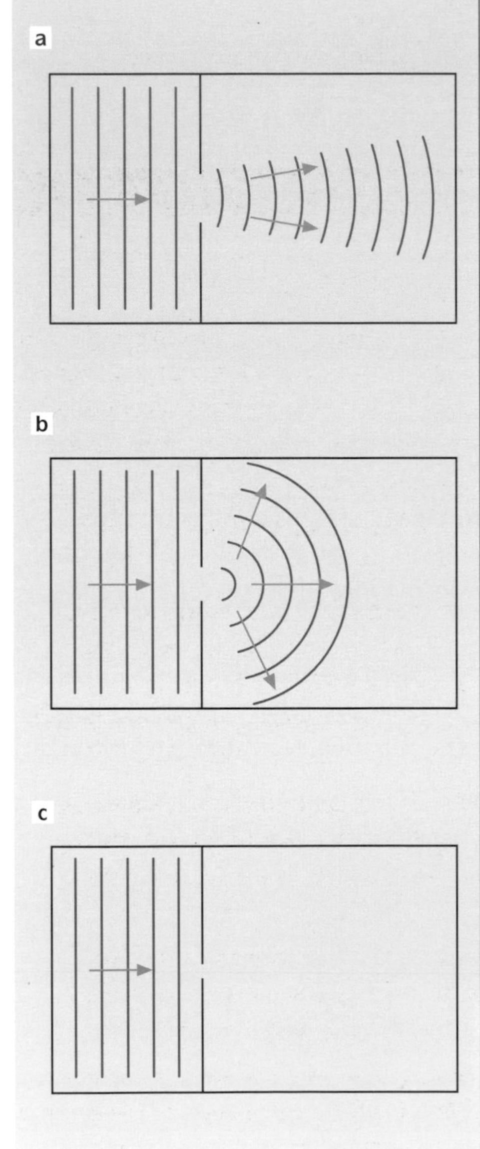

● ***Figure 4.29*** The extent to which ripples spread out depends on the relationship between their wavelength and the width of the gap.

When the width of the gap is large compared to the wavelength of the ripples, the diffraction effect is small. As the gap becomes narrower, the effect becomes more pronounced. It is greatest when the width of the gap is equal to the wavelength of the ripples.

If the gap becomes smaller still, it becomes increasingly difficult for any of the ripples to get through at all, and we see very little disturbance beyond the barrier.

Diffraction of other waves

Diffraction effects are greatest when waves pass through a gap with a width equal to their wavelength. This is useful in explaining why we can observe diffraction readily for some waves but not for others. For example, sound waves in the audible range have wavelengths from a few millimetres to a few metres. Thus we might expect to observe diffraction effects for sound in our environment. Sounds, for example, diffract as they pass through doorways. The width of a doorway is comparable to the wavelength of a sound, and so a noise in one room spreads out into the next room.

Visible light has much shorter wavelengths, so it is not diffracted noticeably by doorways. However, we can observe diffraction when we pass light through a narrow gap, for example through a narrow slit. When laser light is directed onto a slit whose width is similar to the wavelength of the light, it spreads out into the space beyond to form a smear on the screen *(figure 4.30)*. An adjustable slit allows you to see the effect of gradually narrowing the gap.

Note that we made use of diffraction in the Young's double-slit experiment discussed above on page 32. If light did not diffract when it passed through the slits, there would not be two sets of light waves overlapping to produce the fringes that we observe.

Cars need external radio aerials because radio waves have wavelengths longer than the size of the windows, so they cannot diffract into the car. If you try listening to a radio in a train without an external aerial, you will find that FM signals can be picked up weakly (their wavelength is about 3 m), but AM signals, with longer wavelengths, cannot get in at all.

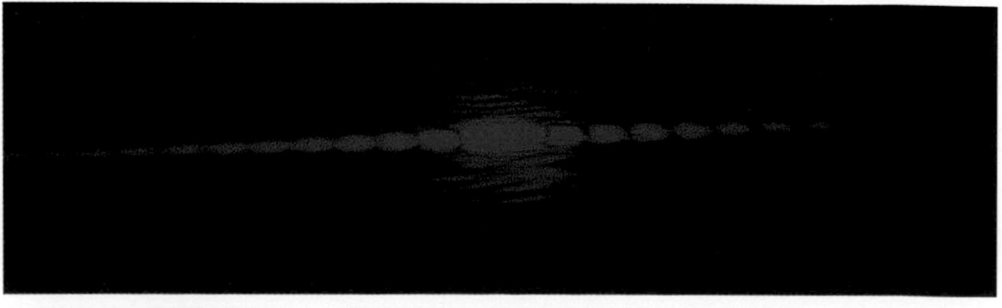

● ***Figure 4.30*** Light is diffracted as it passes through a slit.

SAQ 4.10

A microwave oven *(figure 4.31)* uses microwaves whose wavelength is 12.5 cm. The front door of the oven is made of glass with a metal grid inside; the gaps in the grid are a few millimetres across. Explain how this design allows us to see the food inside the oven, while the microwaves are not allowed to escape into the kitchen (where they might cook us).

Explaining diffraction

Diffraction is another wave effect that can be explained by the principle of superposition. We have to think about what happens when a plane ripple reaches a gap in a barrier *(figure 4.32)*. Each point on the surface of the water in the gap is moving up and down. Each of these moving points acts as a source of new ripples spreading out into the space beyond the barrier. Now we have a lot of new ripples, and we can use the principle of superposition to find their resultant effect. Without trying to calculate the effect of an infinite number of ripples, we can say that in some directions the ripples add together (constructive interference), while in other directions there is cancelling out. Hence an interference pattern appears beyond the barrier.

● ***Figure 4.31*** A microwave oven has a metal grid in the door to keep microwaves in and let light out.

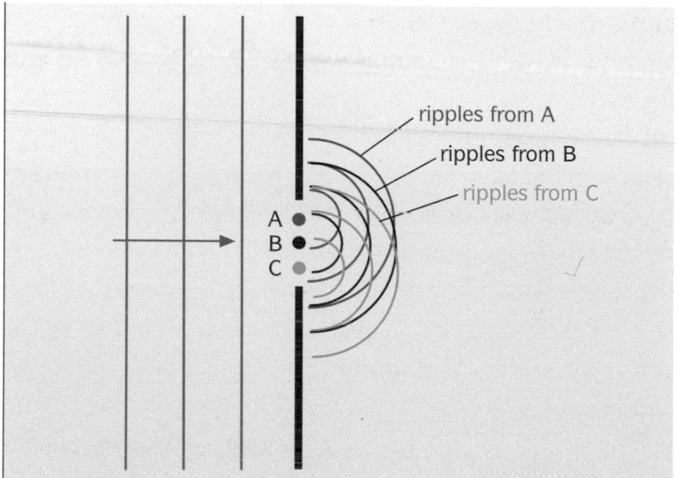

● ***Figure 4.32*** Ripples from all points across the gap contribute to the pattern in the space beyond.

SUMMARY

- Waves are a periodic disturbance by which energy is transferred from place to place.
- When two or more waves coincide, we can deduce their net effect using the principle of superposition of waves. The resultant disturbance at a point is found by adding up the separate disturbances of the individual waves.
- Interference, stationary waves and diffraction are all wave phenomena that can be explained using this principle.
- Interference can be observed when waves from two coherent sources overlap. Constructive interference occurs where waves arrive in phase; destructive interference occurs when they are out of phase by half a cycle.
- Stationary waves are established when two identical waves travelling in opposite directions meet. Usually this happens when one wave is a reflection of the other.
- A stationary wave has a characteristic pattern of nodes (no disturbance) and antinodes (maximum disturbance).
- Diffraction happens when waves arrive at a gap in a barrier, and spread into the space beyond. The effect is greatest when the width of the gap is equal to the wavelength of the waves.

Electrical voltages

By the end of this chapter you should be able to:

1 define *electromotive force* (e.m.f.) as the energy transferred by a source in driving unit charge round a complete circuit;

2 understand the distinction between e.m.f. and potential difference (p.d.);

3 understand the consequences of the internal resistance of a source of e.m.f. for external circuits;

4 understand how a potential divider is used as a source of variable p.d.

Electromotive force and potential difference

In your studies of science, you will often have used a voltmeter to measure voltages. You may think of a voltage simply as something measured by a voltmeter. In everyday life, the word is used in a casual way – 'A big voltage can go through you and kill you.' In this chapter, we will consider a bit more carefully just what we mean by voltage in relation to electric circuits.

Look at the simple circuit in *figure 5.1*. The three voltmeters are measuring three voltages: 12 V across the power supply, and 8 V and 4 V across the two resistors. You will not be surprised to see that the voltage across the power supply is equal to the sum of the voltages across the resistors. However, it is important to realise that the 12 V measured across the power supply is a different kind of voltage from the other two voltages. To see why, we need to think about the flow of current around the circuit.

From your study of electricity in the *Foundation Physics* module, you will know that current is the flow of electric charge around a circuit. *Figure 5.2* shows the same circuit as in *figure 5.1*, but here we are looking at the movement of one coulomb (1 C) of charge round the circuit. Energy is transferred to the charge by the power supply. It flows round the circuit, transferring some of its energy to the first resistor, and the rest to the second resistor.

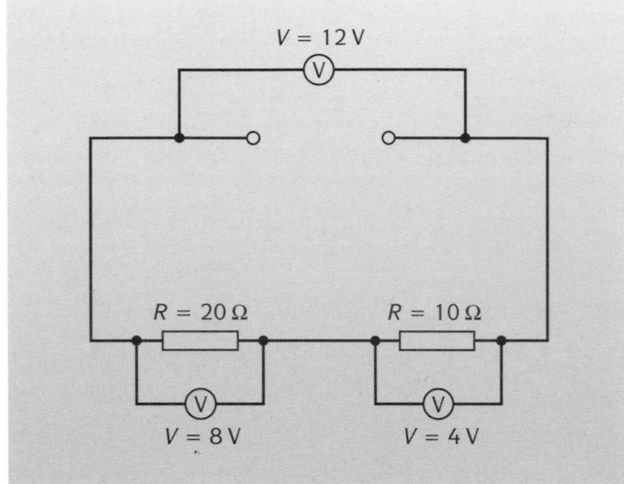

● ***Figure 5.1***

The voltages measured by the voltmeters tell us about these energy transfers. We distinguish between a voltage where the charge is losing energy (potential difference, V) and a voltage where energy is being transferred to the charge (electromotive force, $\mathcal{E}$). Thus the voltage across the power supply is an **electromotive force** or e.m.f., while the voltage across each resistor is a **potential difference** or p.d.

Electromotive force is not a very helpful name, since e.m.f. is a voltage (measured in volts), not a force (which would be measured in newtons).

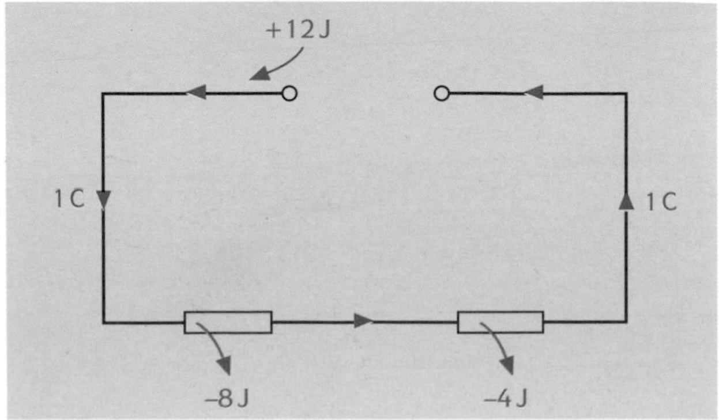

● ***Figure 5.2*** Energy transfers around a circuit.

However, the name should remind you that an e.m.f. is a voltage that supplies the energy to push a charge around a circuit.

Voltage and energy

In the *Foundation Physics* module, you learnt the relationship between potential difference and energy transferred. When a charge Q moves through a potential difference V, it transfers energy W. These quantities are related by

$$W = QV \qquad \text{or} \qquad V = W/Q$$

It is perhaps simplest to remember this by recalling that a volt is a joule per coulomb, $1\,\text{V} = 1\,\text{J}\,\text{C}^{-1}$. In other words, when 1 C of charge moves through a p.d. of 1 V, it transfers 1 J of energy. When 1 C moves through 5 V, it transfers 5 J, and so on.

Electromotive force $\mathcal{E}$ is defined in the same way. The energy W transferred to a charge Q by an e.m.f. $\mathcal{E}$ is given by

$$W = Q\mathcal{E} \qquad \text{or} \qquad \mathcal{E} = W/Q$$

Sources of e.m.f. *(figure 5.3)* are often labelled with their e.m.f. For example, a 1.5 V cell transfers 1.5 J of energy to each coulomb of charge that it pushes around a circuit. A 12 V power supply supplies 12 J to each coulomb, and the 230 V mains transfers 230 J to each 1 C of charge.

SAQ 5.1

How much energy is transferred to 1 C of charge by a 6 V battery, and by a 5 kV high-voltage supply?

● **Figure 5.3** Some sources of e.m.f.

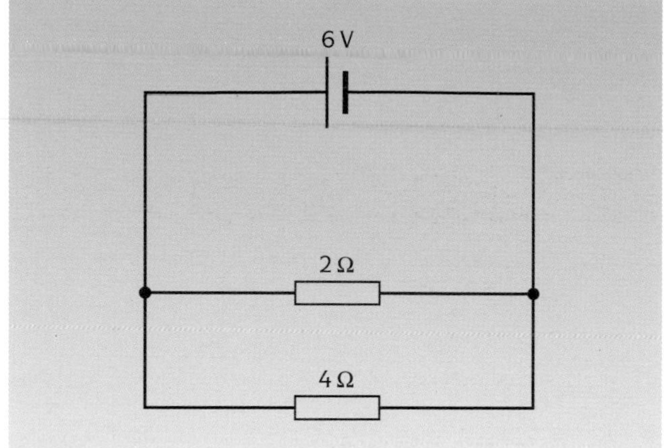

● **Figure 5.4**

SAQ 5.2

A 12 V battery drives a current of 2 A round a circuit for a minute (1 min). How much charge flows around the circuit in this time? How much energy is transferred to the charge? What power is supplied by the battery?

SAQ 5.3

Describe the energy transfers that occur in 1 s in the circuit shown in *figure 5.4*.

Internal resistance

You will be familiar with the idea that, when you use a power supply or other source of e.m.f., you cannot assume that it is providing you with the exact voltage that its controls suggest. You need to measure the voltage to be sure of its value. There are two reasons for this. First, the supply may not be made to a high degree of precision, batteries become flat, and so on. However, there is a second, more important, reason for measuring the voltage of the supply to be sure of its value. Experiments show that the supply voltage depends on the circuit of which it is part. In particular, the voltage of a supply decreases if it is required to supply more current.

Figure 5.5 shows a circuit you can use to investigate this effect, and a schematic graph of how the voltage might decrease as the current supplied increases.

Why does this happen? It is an inevitable feature of any source of e.m.f. To understand why, we

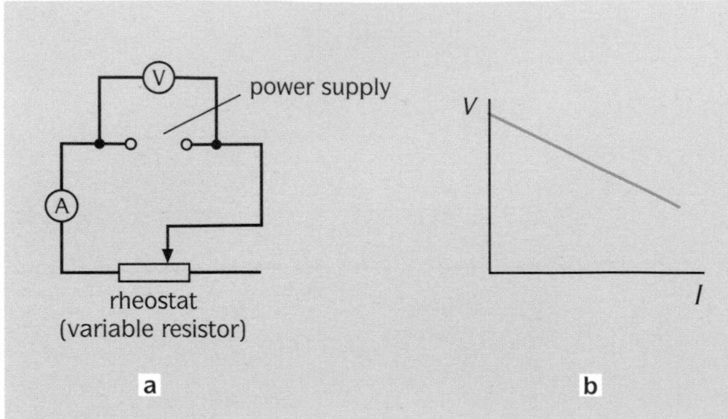

● ***Figure 5.5***

a A circuit for determining the e.m.f. and internal resistance of a supply;

b typical form of results.

need to think more carefully about how electric charge flows around a circuit. The important point is to look at what happens to charge flowing though the power supply.

In *figure 5.6*, you can see that charge is flowing through the resistor *R*, and transferring energy to it. Here the charge is flowing from positive to negative. Now, we also have to imagine that the charge flows through the power supply. As it flows through, energy is transferred from the supply to the charge. (Notice that, in the supply, the charge is flowing from negative to positive.) The e.m.f. of the supply tells us the energy transferred to each 1 C of charge.

Now we must think about the insides of the power supply. There are wires inside a power supply. Alternatively, the charge may have to flow through the chemical electrolytes and electrodes that make up a cell. Wires and chemicals have electrical resistance, and some of the energy of the charge is transferred to this. When the charge has travelled through the source of e.m.f., it has gained a lot of energy, but it has also lost some of what it gained.

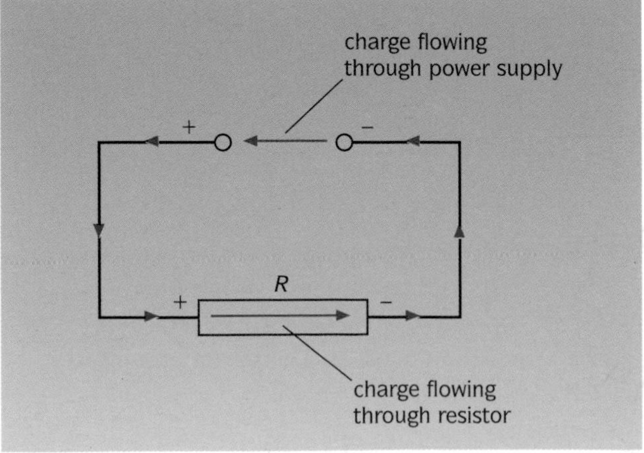

● ***Figure 5.6*** The flow of current around a circuit.

The resistance within a source of e.m.f. is called its **internal resistance**, *r*. It can often help to solve problems if we show it explicitly in circuit diagrams *(figure 5.7)*. Here, we are representing a cell as if it were a 'perfect' cell of e.m.f. $\mathcal{E}$, together with a separate resistor *r*. The circle enclosing $\mathcal{E}$ and *r* represents the fact that these two are, in fact, a single component.

Now we can work out the current that flows when this cell is connected to an external resistor *R*. You can see that *R* and *r* are in series with each other, because the current *I* flows first through one and then through the other. Their combined resistance is thus $R + r$, and we can write

$$\mathcal{E} = I(R+r) \qquad \text{or} \qquad \mathcal{E} = IR + Ir$$

We cannot measure $\mathcal{E}$ directly, because we can only connect a voltmeter across the whole cell, including its internal resistance *r*. If we connect a voltmeter across the cell, we will measure its terminal p.d., *V*, given by

$$V = IR$$

This will be less than the e.m.f. $\mathcal{E}$ by an amount Ir, called the **lost volts**. If we combine these two equations, we get

$$V = \mathcal{E} - Ir$$

or terminal p.d. = e.m.f. − lost volts

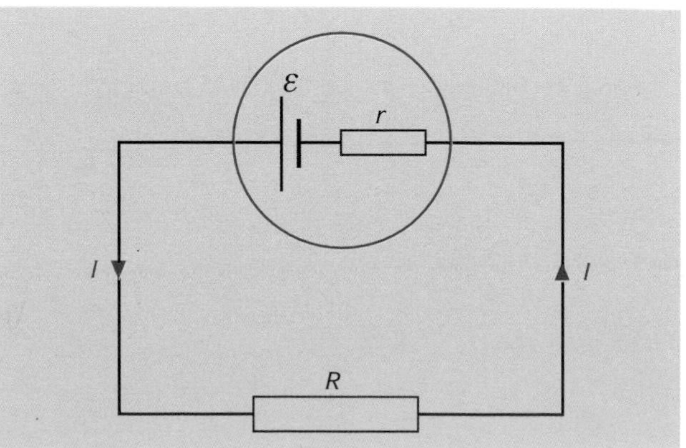

● ***Figure 5.7*** It can be helpful to show the internal resistance of a supply explicitly in a circuit diagram.

The lost volts tell us the energy transferred to the internal resistance of the supply. If you short circuit a battery with a piece of wire, a big current will flow, and you may feel the battery getting warm as energy is transferred within it. This is also why you may damage a power supply by trying to make it supply a larger current than it is designed to give.

SAQ 5.4

A battery of e.m.f. 5 V and internal resistance 2 Ω is connected to an 8 Ω resistor. Draw a circuit diagram, and calculate the current that flows around the circuit.

SAQ 5.5

Calculate the current flowing in each circuit in *figure 5.8*. Calculate also the terminal p.d. and the lost volts for each cell.

SAQ 5.6

Four identical cells, each of e.m.f. 1.5 V and internal resistance 0.1 Ω, are connected in series. What current will this combination of cells drive through a bulb of resistance 2.0 Ω?

Measuring electromotive force and internal resistance

You can get a good idea of the e.m.f. of a supply by connecting a digital voltmeter across it. A digital voltmeter has a high resistance (usually at least one million ohms, 1 MΩ), so only a tiny current will flow through it. The lost volts will then only be a tiny fraction of the e.m.f. If you want to measure r as well as $\mathcal{E}$, you need to use a circuit like that shown in *figure 5.5*. When the variable resistor is altered, the current in the circuit changes, and measurements can be recorded of I and V. The internal resistance r can be found from a graph of V against I (*figure 5.9*).

[Compare the equation $V = \mathcal{E} - Ir$ with the equation of a straight line $y = mx + c$. By plotting V on the y axis and I on the x axis, a straight line should result. The intercept on the y axis is $\mathcal{E}$, and the gradient is $-r$. In practice, you may find that the graph is curved. This is because r changes as more current flows – we cannot simply describe the internal resistance as if there were an extra resistor inside the power supply.]

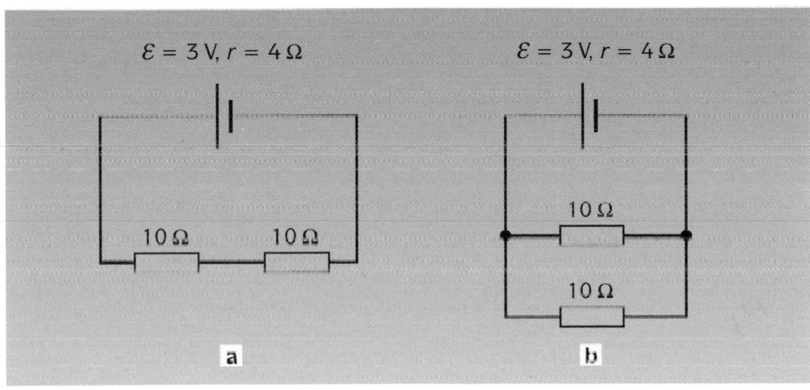

● **Figure 5.8**

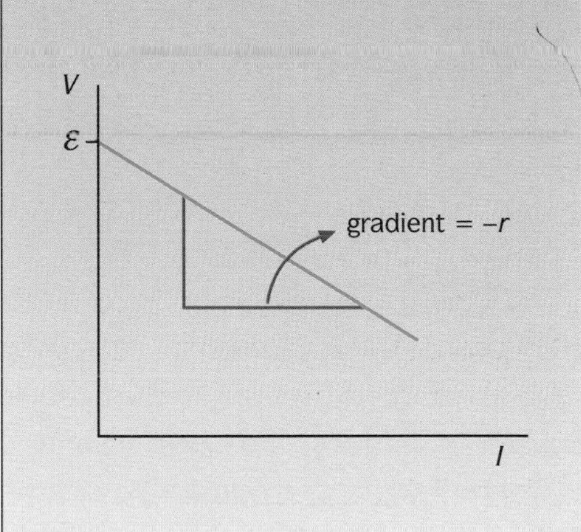

● **Figure 5.9** $\mathcal{E}$ and r can be found from this graph.

The power supply shown in *figure 5.3* has a small graph to indicate to the user how much its terminal p.d. decreases as the current increases.

SAQ 5.7

The voltage supplied by a battery is found to be 3.0 V when measured with a high-resistance voltmeter. When the battery is connected to a 10 Ω resistor, its terminal p.d. drops to 2.8 V. What is its internal resistance?

SAQ 5.8

The results of an experiment to determine $\mathcal{E}$ and r for a power supply are shown below. Plot a suitable graph and use it to find $\mathcal{E}$ and r.

V/V	1.43	1.33	1.18	1.10	0.98
I/A	0.10	0.30	0.60	0.75	1.00

The effects of internal resistance

You should now be clear about the need to measure the voltage of any source of e.m.f., rather than simply believing the voltage that it claims to supply. The more current it supplies, the more its terminal p.d. will decrease.

An example of this can be seen if a driver tries to start a car with the headlamps on. The starter motor requires a large current from the battery, the battery's terminal p.d. drops, and the headlamps dim.

To get an efficient transfer of energy from a source of e.m.f. to an external resistor, the internal resistance should be small compared to the external resistance ($r \ll R$).

SAQ 5.9

A car battery has an e.m.f. of 12 V and an internal resistance of 0.04 Ω. The starter motor draws a current of 100 A. What is the terminal p.d. of the battery when the starter motor is in operation? If the headlamps are rated at 12 V, 36 W, what is their resistance? To what value will their power output decrease when the starter motor is in operation?

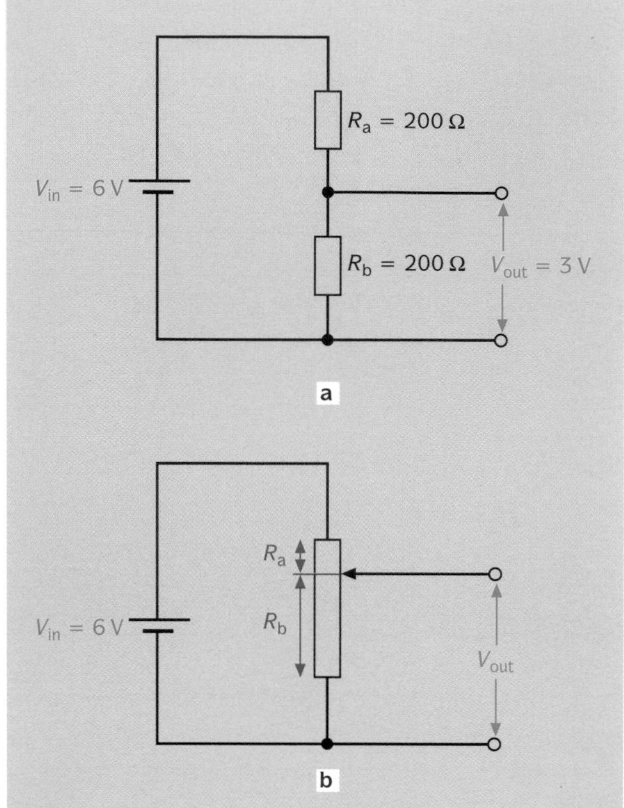

● **Figure 5.10** Two potential dividers.

Potential dividers

How can we get 3 V from a 6 V battery? Sometimes we want to use only part of the voltage of a supply. To do this, we use an arrangement of resistors called a potential divider.

Figure 5.10 shows two potential dividers, each connected across a 6 V battery. The first, **a**, consists of two equal resistors R_a and R_b. The voltage across R_b is half of the 6 V of the battery. The second potential divider, **b**, is more useful. It consists of a single variable resistor. By moving the sliding contact, we can achieve any value of V_{out} between 0 V (slider at the bottom) and 6 V (slider at the top).

V_{out} depends on the relative values of R_a and R_b. You can calculate the value of V_{out} using

$$V_{out} = V_{in} \frac{R_b}{R_a + R_b}$$

Potential dividers in use

Potential dividers are often used in electronic circuits. They are useful when a sensor is connected to a processing circuit, as in *figure 5.11*. Here, a thermistor is being used to detect temperature, perhaps the temperature of a fish tank. If the temperature rises, the resistance of the thermistor decreases and the voltage V_{out} increases. By changing the variable resistor R_b, you can control the range over which V_{out} varies. This would allow you to set the temperature at which a heater operates, for example.

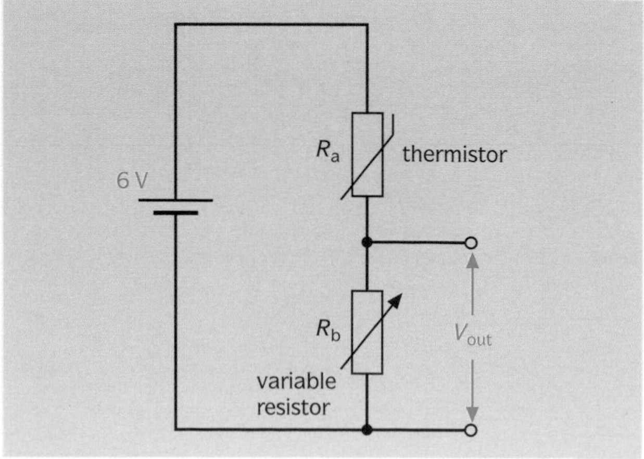

● **Figure 5.11**

Potential dividers are especially useful in circuits where voltages are important, but only small currents are flowing. If large currents are involved, then you should notice that some current must flow through both R_a and R_b. This will result in a waste of power in these resistors.

SAQ 5.10

Over what range will V_{out} vary in *figure 5.12* as the variable resistor R_b is adjusted over its full range from 0 Ω to 50 Ω?

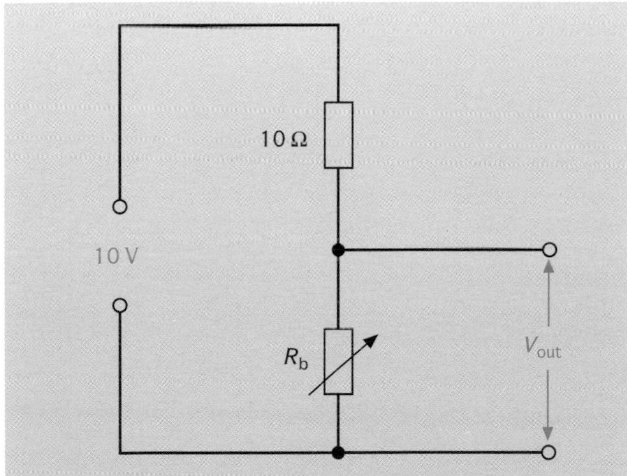

● **Figure 5.12**

SAQ 5.11

The light-dependent resistor (LDR) in *figure 5.13* has a resistance of 300 Ω in full sunlight, and 1 MΩ in darkness. What values will V_{out} have in these conditions?

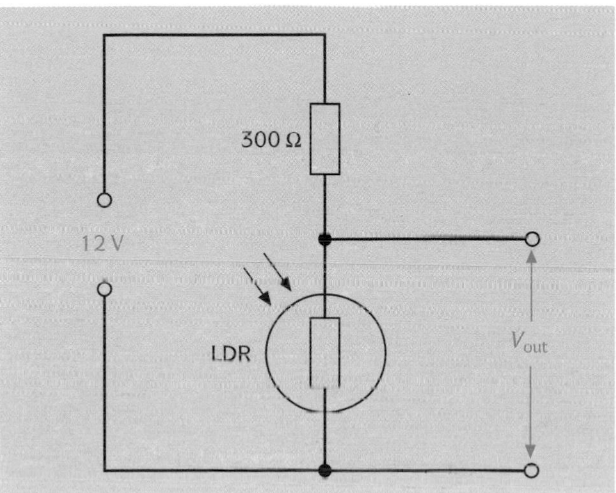

● **Figure 5.13**

SUMMARY

- A voltage is needed to push an electric current around a circuit.
- The voltage provided by a battery or power supply is an electromotive force (e.m.f.).
- Electric charge is given energy by the e.m.f. of the supply; it loses energy as it passes through the potential difference (p.d.) across components in the circuit.
- Any voltage is a measure of the energy transferred per unit charge; a volt is a joule per coulomb.
- Because a source of e.m.f. has internal resistance, this must be included in calculations of current and voltage.
- A potential divider uses two resistors or a variable resistor to provide a variable source of p.d.

Capacitance

By the end of this chapter you should be able to:

1 understand the function of capacitors in simple circuits;

2 define *capacitance* (from $C = Q/V$) and the *farad*;

3 use $W = \frac{1}{2}CV^2$ to calculate the energy stored in a capacitor.

Using capacitors

Capacitors are components used in many electrical and electronic circuits. They store electrical charge (and energy), and this means they have many valuable applications. For example, capacitors are used in computers; they are charged up in normal use, and then they gradually discharge if there is a power failure, so that the computer will operate long enough to save valuable data. The photograph *(figure 6.1)* shows the variety of sizes and shapes of capacitors.

All capacitors have two leads, connected to two metal plates where the charge is stored. Between the plates is an insulating material called the dielectric. *Figure 6.2* shows a schematic version of the construction of a capacitor; in practice, many have a spiral 'Swiss-roll' form.

To charge up a capacitor, it must be connected to a voltage. This pushes positive charge onto one plate; positive charge is then repelled from the opposite plate, leaving it negatively charged. Note that there is a flow of positive charge (a current) all the way round the circuit until the capacitor is charged up to the supply voltage V *(figure 6.3)*.

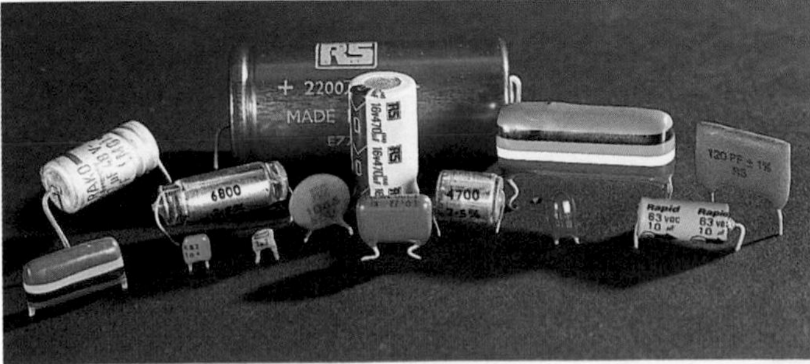

● ***Figure 6.1*** A variety of capacitors.

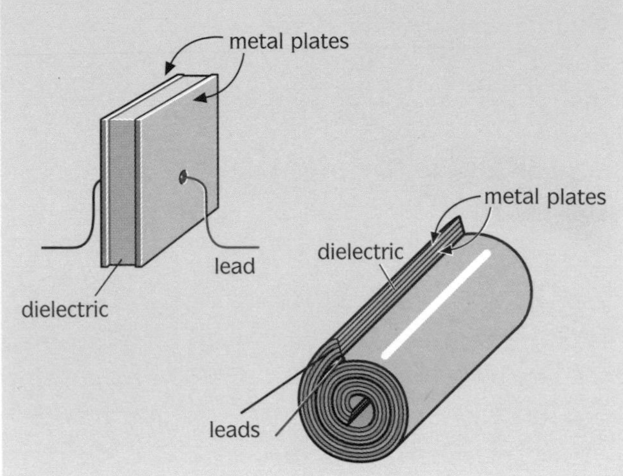

● ***Figure 6.2*** The construction of typical capacitors.

If one plate of the capacitor stores charge $+Q$, then the other stores an equal and opposite charge $-Q$. We say that the charge stored is Q. To make the capacitor store more charge, we would have to use a higher voltage. If we connect the leads of the charged capacitor together, the charge $+Q$ flows round to cancel out the $-Q$, and the capacitor is now discharged.

You can observe a capacitor discharging as follows: Connect the two leads of a capacitor to the terminals of a battery. Disconnect, and then reconnect the leads to a light-emitting diode

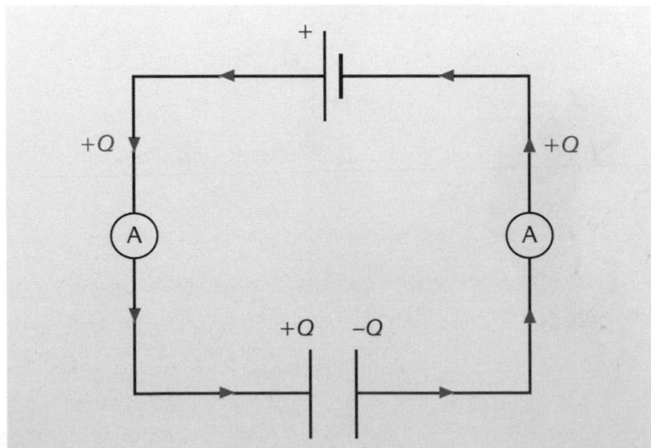

● ***Figure 6.3*** The flow of charge when a capacitor is charged up.

(LED). It is best to have a protective resistor in series with the LED. The LED will glow as the capacitor discharges. This may last for some time, as only a small current will flow through the high resistance of the LED.

[Note: The convention is that current is the flow of positive charge. In many situations, such as in metals, it is free electrons that flow. Electrons are negatively charged; the current flows in the opposite direction to the electrons – see *figure* 6.4.]

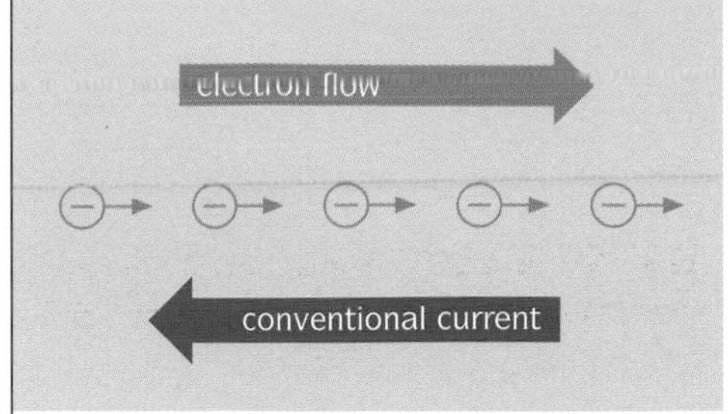

● ***Figure 6.4*** A flow of electrons to the right constitutes a conventional current to the left.

The meaning of capacitance

Look at some capacitors. They are marked with the value of their capacitance; as you might expect, capacitors of greater volume have greater capacitance. What do these numbers mean? Capacitance tells us about how good a capacitor is at storing charge. Since the amount of charge stored (Q) also depends on the voltage V used to charge up the capacitor, we have to take this into account. The equation that defines capacitance C is

$$C = Q/V \qquad \text{or} \qquad Q = CV$$

From the first form of this equation, you can see that the capacitance of a capacitor is the amount of charge stored for each volt used to charge it up.

The second form shows that the charge stored is proportional to two things: the capacitance C of the capacitor and the voltage (double the voltage stores double the charge).

Units of capacitance

The unit of capacitance is the **farad**, F. From the equation that defines capacitance, you can see that this must be the same as the units of charge (coulombs, C) divided by volts (V):

$$1\,\text{F} = 1\,\text{C}\,\text{V}^{-1}$$

In practice, a farad is a large unit. Few capacitors are big enough to store 1 C when charged up to 1 V. If you look at some capacitors, you will see their values marked in pF or μF (μ is Greek mu; sometimes manufacturers write uF or MFD):

$$1\,\text{pF} = 10^{-12}\,\text{F} \qquad 1\,\mu\text{F} = 10^{-6}\,\text{F}$$

Other markings on capacitors

Many capacitors are marked with their highest safe working voltage. If you exceed this value, then charge may leak across between the plates, and the dielectric will cease to be an insulator.

Some capacitors (electrolytic ones) must be connected correctly in a circuit. They have an indication to show which end must be connected to the positive of the supply. Failure to connect correctly will damage the capacitor, and can be dangerous.

SAQ 6.1

How much charge is stored by a 200 μF capacitor charged up to 15 V? Give your answer in microcoulombs (μC) and in coulombs (C).

SAQ 6.2

What is the capacitance of a capacitor that stores 0.001 C of charge when charged to 500 V? Give your answer in farads (F), microfarads (μF) and picofarads (pF).

SAQ 6.3

What is the average current that flows when a 50 μF capacitor is charged to 10 V in 0.01 s?

Measuring capacitance

In order to determine the capacitance of a capacitor, you need to find out how much charge it stores at a particular voltage. (Remember that capacitance is the charge stored per volt.) One way to measure charge is to measure the current flowing into the capacitor as it charges up, and the time for which the current flows.

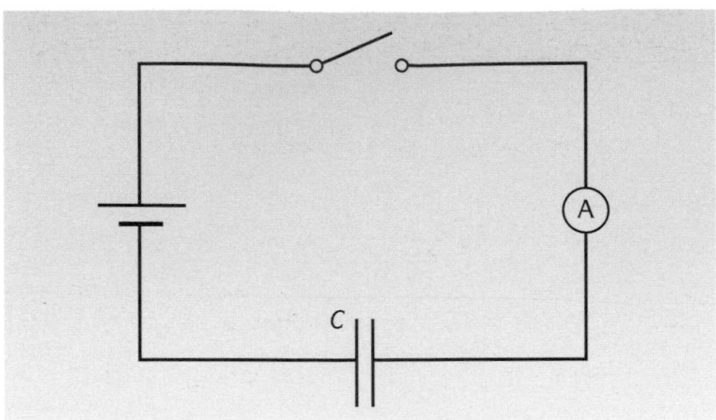

● **Figure 6.5**

Figure 6.5 shows a suitable circuit for this. Because the current changes – it decreases gradually – it is necessary to record the current at regular intervals of time. This results in a graph like that in *figure 6.6*. The charge stored by the capacitor is the area under the graph. This is found by counting squares, or by cutting out and weighing the required area.

Note that this method is only suitable for fairly large values of capacitance, say, 100 μF or more; small capacitors store only a small amount of charge, so the current that flows when they discharge is correspondingly small.

SAQ 6.4

A student charges up a capacitor C through a resistor, and records the current I flowing at intervals of 10 s. The results are shown below. The voltage across the capacitor after 60 s was 8.5 V. Plot a suitable graph, and use it to estimate the value of C.

I/μA	200	142	102	75	51	37	27
t/s	0	10	20	30	40	50	60

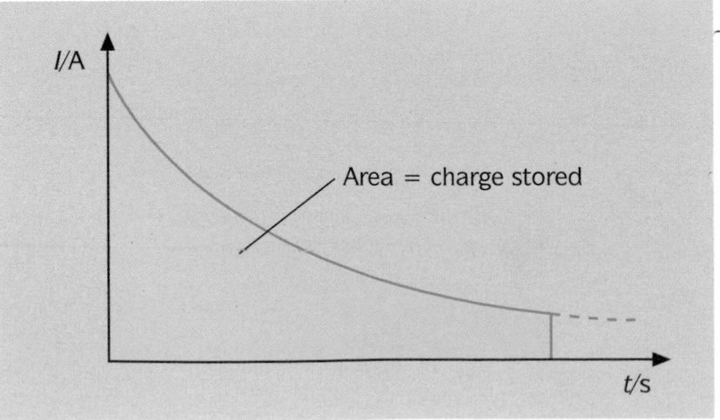

● **Figure 6.6** The area under a current–time graph represents the charge stored by a capacitor.

Energy stored in a capacitor

When you charge a capacitor, you use a power supply to push electric charge onto its plates. The charge has been pushed to a voltage higher than zero volts, so it has been given energy. You recover this energy when you discharge the capacitor.

If you charge up a large capacitor (1000 μF or more) to 6 V, disconnect it from the supply, and then connect it across a 6 V lamp, you can see the energy as it is released from the capacitor. The lamp will flash briefly. Clearly, such a capacitor does not store much energy when it is charged.

The energy W that a capacitor stores depends on two things: its capacitance C and the potential difference to which it is charged, V. There is an equation that shows how W depends on C and V:

$$W = \tfrac{1}{2}CV^2$$

Suppose we charge a 2000 μF capacitor to a p.d. of 10 V. How much energy is stored? Using $W = \frac{1}{2}CV^2$ we obtain $W = \frac{1}{2} \times 2000 \times 10^{-6} \times 10^2 = 0.1\,\text{J}$. This is a small amount of energy – compare it with the energy stored by a rechargeable battery, typically of the order of 10 000 J. A charged capacitor will not do to keep a personal stereo running for any length of time. Because W depends on V^2, it follows that doubling the charging voltage means that four times as much energy is stored. (This comes about because, when you double the voltage, not only is twice as much charge stored, but it is stored at twice the voltage.)

Investigating energy stored

If you have a sensitive joulemeter (capable of measuring millijoules, mJ), you can investigate the equation for energy stored. A suitable circuit is shown in *figure 6.7*.

The capacitor is charged up when the switch connects it to the power supply. When the switch is altered, the capacitor discharges through the joulemeter. (It is important to wait for the capacitor to discharge completely.) The joulemeter will indicate the amount of energy released.

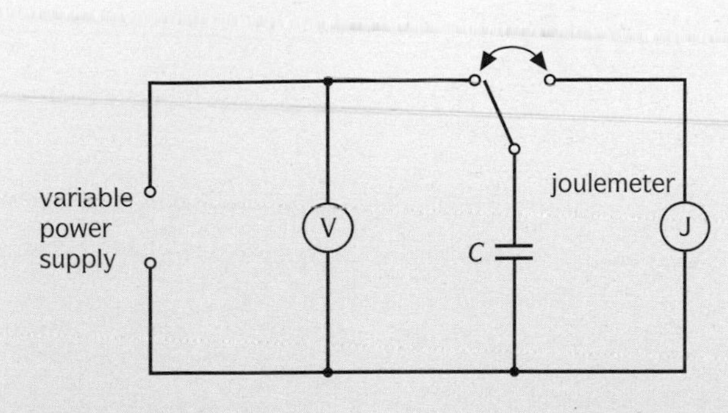

● ***Figure 6.7*** With the switch to the left, the capacitor charges up; to the right, it discharges through the joulemeter.

By using capacitors with different values of C, and by changing the charging voltage V, you can investigate how the energy stored W depends on C and V.

SAQ 6.5

Calculate the energy stored in each of the following cases:

a a 5000 μF capacitor charged to 5 V;

b a 5000 pF capacitor charged to 5 V;

c a 200 μF capacitor charged to 230 V.

SAQ 6.6

Which stores more charge, a 100 μF capacitor charged to 200 V or a 200 μF capacitor charged to 100 V? Which stores more energy? (You may be able to answer this question simply by considering the equations $Q = CV$ and $W = \frac{1}{2}CV^2$, rather than performing detailed calculations.)

SAQ 6.7

A 10 000 μF capacitor is charged to 12 V, and then connected across a lamp rated at 12 V, 36 W.

a How much energy is stored by the capacitor?

b For how long could this amount of energy keep the lamp fully lit?

SUMMARY

- Capacitors are constructed from two metal sheets ('plates'), separated by an insulating material, the dielectric.
- Capacitors store charge, proportional to the p.d. between the plates. Capacitance is the charge stored per unit of p.d.; a farad is a coulomb per volt.
- Capacitors store energy; the energy stored, W, at voltage V is $\frac{1}{2}CV^2$.

Electric fields

By the end of this chapter you should be able to:

1 describe an electric field as a field of force, having field strength equal to the force per unit charge;

2 represent an electric field by field lines;

3 use Coulomb's law

$$F = \frac{Q_1 Q_2}{4\pi\varepsilon_0 d^2}$$

for the force between two point charges in a vacuum or in the air;

4 calculate field strength, the force on a charge and potential energy in a uniform field and in a spherical field;

5 describe the effect of a uniform field on the motion of a charged particle;

6 define *potential at a point*, and relate field strength to potential gradient;

7 recognise the analogy between electric and gravitational fields.

Attraction and repulsion

You will already know a bit about electric (or electrostatic) fields, from your experience of static electricity in everyday life, and from your studies in science. In this chapter, you will learn how we can make these ideas more formal.

● ***Figure 7.1*** Lightning flashes, dramatic evidence of natural electric fields.

This chapter follows a parallel course to our exploration of ideas about gravity in chapter 2. We will look at how electric forces are caused, and how we can represent their effects in terms of electric fields. Then we will find mathematical ways of calculating electric forces and field strengths. The last section deals with the ideas of energy and potential in electric fields.

Static electricity can be useful – it is important in the process of photocopying, in dust precipitation to clean up industrial emissions, and in crop-spraying, among many other applications. It can also be a nuisance. Who hasn't experienced a shock, perhaps when getting out of a car or when touching a door handle? Static electric charge has built up and gives us a shock when it discharges.

We explain these effects in terms of electric charge. Simple observations in the laboratory give us the following picture:

- Objects are usually electrically neutral (uncharged), but they may become electrically charged, for example when one material is rubbed against another.
- There are two types of charge, which we call positive and negative.
- Opposite types of charge attract one another; like charges repel *(figure 7.2)*.
- A charged object may also be able to attract an uncharged one; this is called electrostatic induction.

These observations are macroscopic; that is, they are descriptions of phenomena that we can

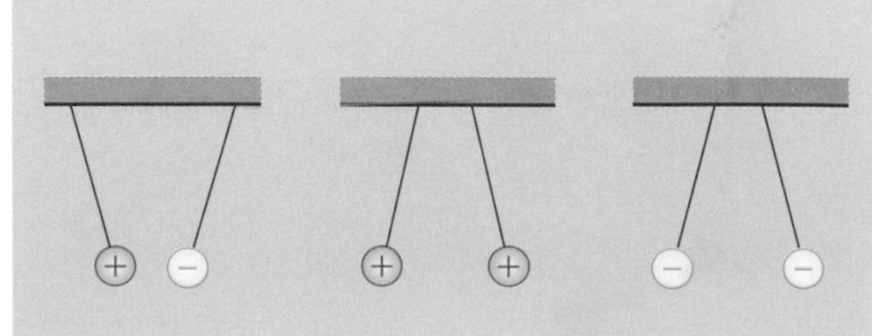

● ***Figure 7.2*** Attraction and repulsion between electric charges.

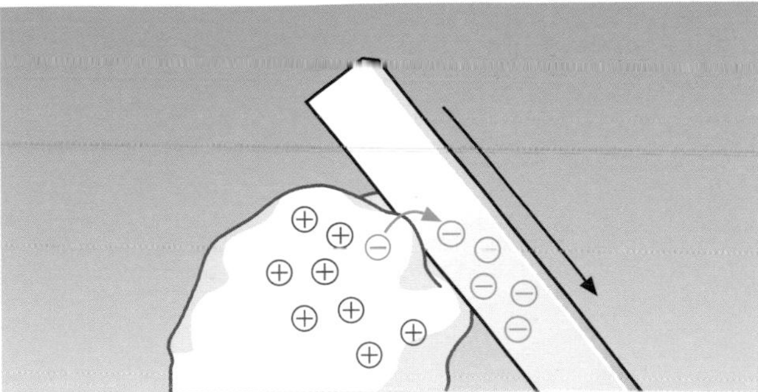

● ***Figure 7.3*** The force of friction can transfer electrons from one material to another.

observe in the laboratory, without having to consider what is happening on the microscopic scale, at the level of particles such as atoms and electrons. However, we can give a more subtle explanation if we consider the microscopic picture of static electricity.

Matter is made up of three types of particles: electrons (which have negative charge), protons (positive) and neutrons (neutral). An uncharged object has equal numbers of protons and electrons, whose charges therefore cancel out.

When one material is rubbed against another, there is a force of friction between them, and electrons may be rubbed off one material onto the other *(figure 7.3)*. The material that has gained electrons is now negatively charged, and the other material is positively charged.

If a positively charged object is brought close to an uncharged one, the electrons in the second object may be attracted; we observe this as a force of attraction between the two objects. (This is electrostatic induction.)

Note that it is usually electrons that are involved in moving within a material, or from one material to another. This is because electrons, which are on the outside of atoms, are less strongly held within a material than protons; they may be free to move about within a material (like the conduction electrons in a metal), or they may be relatively weakly bound within atoms.

Investigating electric fields

If you rub a strip of plastic so that it becomes charged, and then hold it close to your hair, you feel your hair being pulled upwards *(figure 7.4)*.

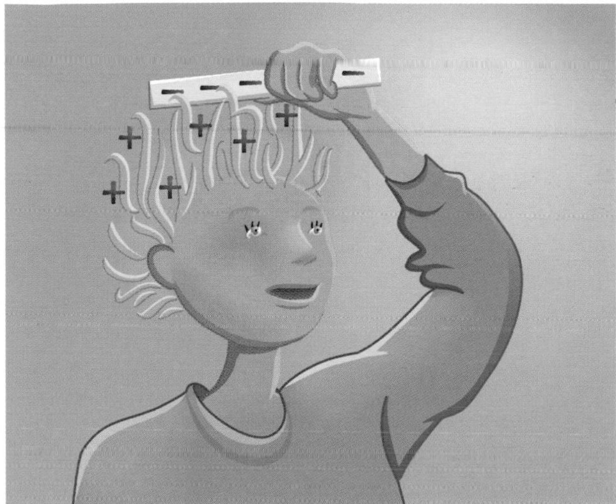

● ***Figure 7.4*** A hair-raising experience.

The influence of the charged plastic spreads into the space around it; we say that there is an electric field around the charge. In order to produce an electric field, we need unbalanced charges (as with the charged plastic). In order to observe the field, we need to put something in it that will respond to the field (as your hair responded). There are two simple ways in which you can do this in the laboratory.

The first uses a charged strip of gold foil, attached to an insulating handle *(figure 7.5)*. The second uses grains of a material such as semolina; these line up in an electric field, rather like the way in which iron filings line up in a magnetic field *(figure 7.6)*.

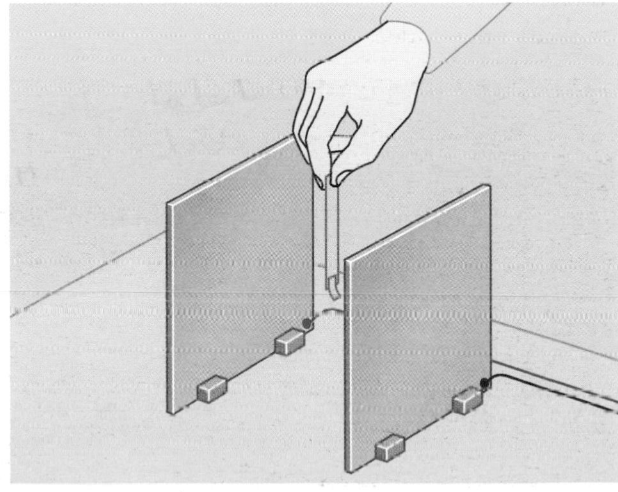

● ***Figure 7.5*** Investigating the electric field between two charged metal plates.

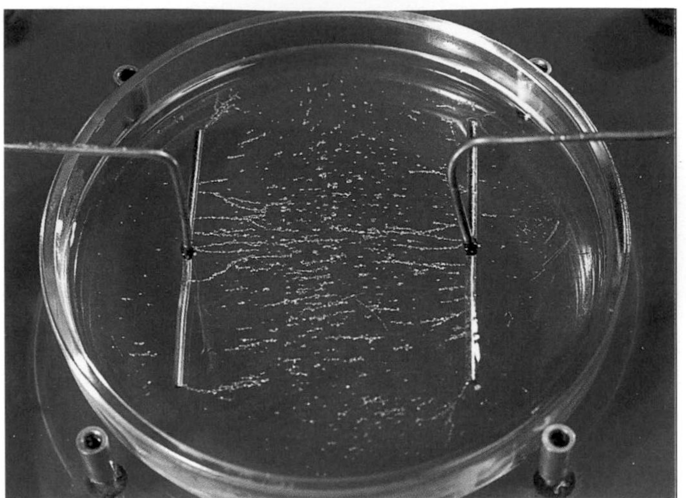

● **Figure 7.6** Apparatus showing uniform electric field.

Representing electric fields

We can draw electric fields in much the same way that we can draw gravitational and magnetic fields, by showing lines of force. The three most important shapes are shown in *figure 7.7*.

As with gravitational fields, this representation tells us two things about the field: its direction (from the direction of the lines), and how strong it is (from their separation). The arrows go from positive to negative; they tell us the direction of the force on a positive charge in the field.

A uniform field has the same strength at all points. This is like the field found, for example, between the parallel plates of a charged capacitor.

A radial field spreads outwards in all directions, for example from a point charge or from a charged sphere.

We can draw electric fields for other arrangements. Note the symbol for earth, which is assumed to be uncharged (i.e. at zero volts).

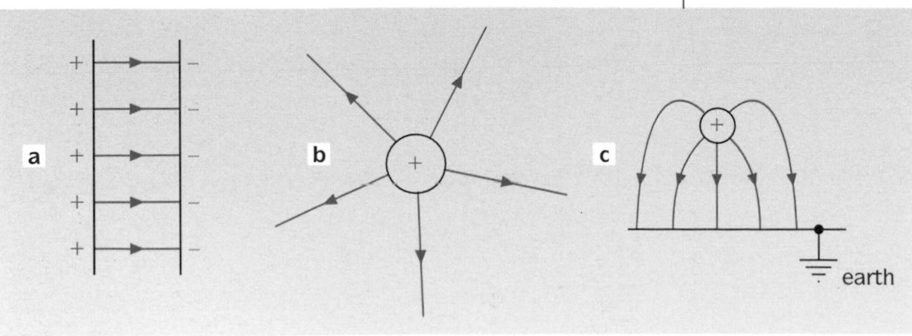

● **Figure 7.7** Lines of force representing **a** a uniform field, **b** a radial field, and **c** the field of a positive charge close to earth.

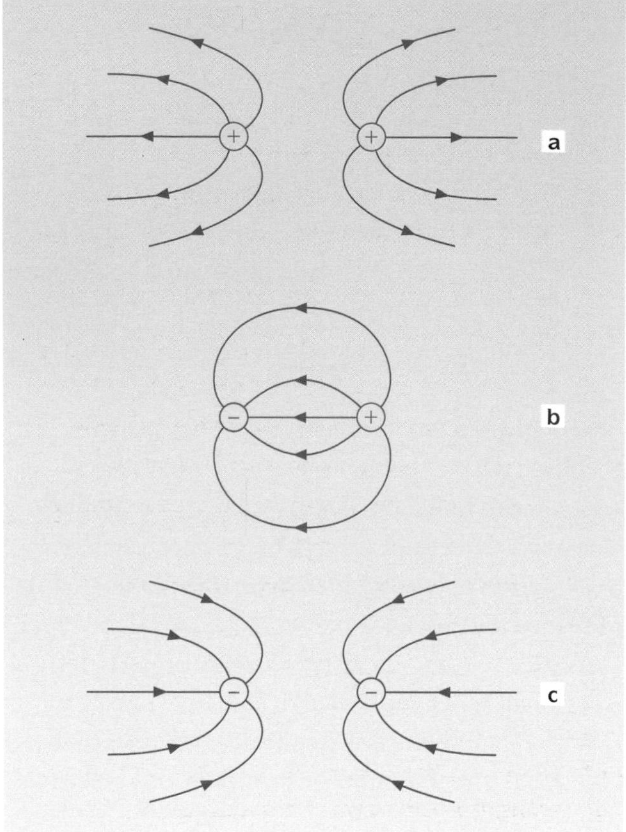

● **Figure 7.8** Electric fields between charges.

SAQ 7.1

Which of the three diagrams in *figure 7.8* represents two positive charges repelling each other? Which represents two negative charges? Which represents two opposite charges?

SAQ 7.2

Many molecules are described as polar; that is, they have regions that are positively or negatively charged, though they are neutral overall. Draw a diagram to show how you would expect sausage-shaped polar molecules like those shown in *figure 7.9* to arrange themselves in a solid.

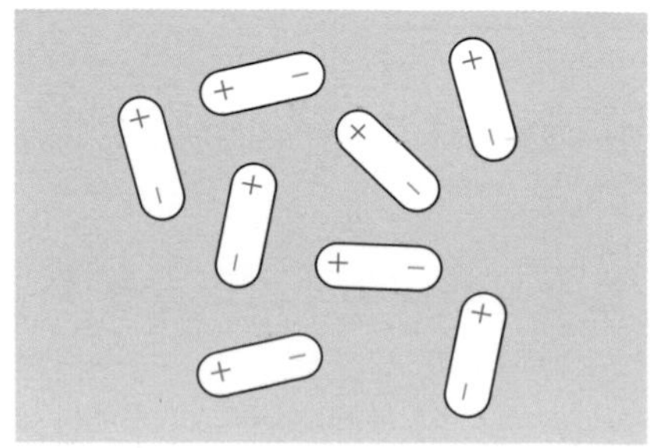

● **Figure 7.9** Polar molecules.

Electric field strength

For a gravitational field, we defined its strength at a point as being the force exerted on a kilogram mass placed at that point. Similarly, for electric fields, we can define electric field strength E as follows: the **electric field strength** at a point is the force per unit charge exerted on a positive charge placed at the point.

So to define electric field strength, we imagine putting a positive test charge in the field and measuring the electric force that it feels *(figure 7.10)*. (If you have used a charged gold leaf to investigate a field, this illustrates the principle of testing the field with a charge.)

From this definition, we can write an equation for E:

$$E = \frac{F}{Q}$$

You should be able to see that the unit of electric field strength is the newton per coulomb ($\mathrm{N\,C^{-1}}$).

The strength of a uniform field

You can set up a uniform field between two parallel metal plates by connecting them to the terminals of a high-voltage power supply *(figure 7.11)*. The strength of the field between them depends on two factors:

- The higher the voltage V between them, the stronger the field.
- The greater their separation d, the weaker the field.

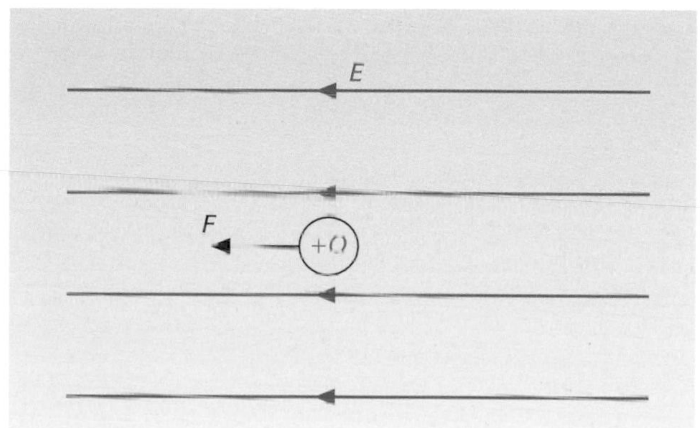

● ***Figure 7.10*** A field of strength E exerts force F on charge Q.

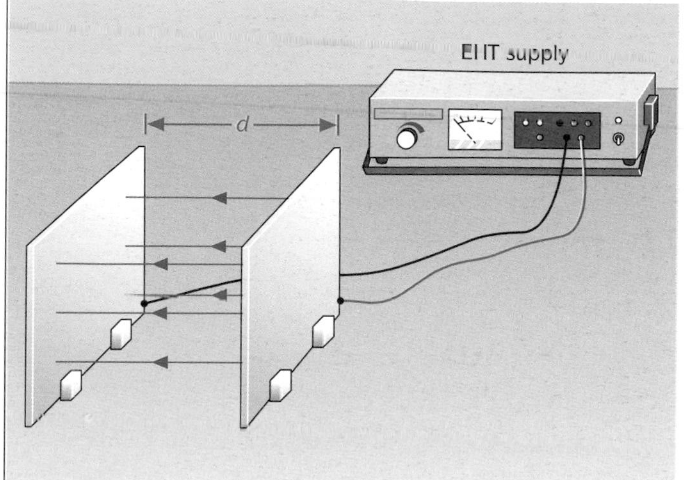

● ***Figure 7.11*** A uniform field exists between two parallel charged plates.

These can be combined to give an equation for E:

$$E = -\frac{V}{d}$$

(Note the minus sign. This is necessary because, in *figure 7.11*, the voltage V increases towards the right while the force F acts towards the left. V and F are in opposite directions.)

From this equation, you can see that we could have given the units of electric field strength as volts per metre ($\mathrm{V\,m^{-1}}$).

$$1\,\mathrm{V\,m^{-1}} = 1\,\mathrm{N\,C^{-1}}$$

SAQ 7.3

Figure 7.12 shows an arrangement of parallel plates, each connected to a different voltage. The electric field lines are shown between the first pair. Copy and complete the diagram.

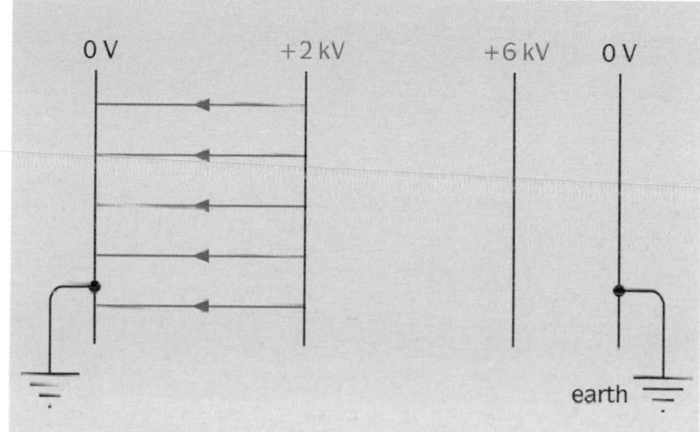

● ***Figure 7.12***

SAQ 7.4

Air is usually a good insulator. However, a spark can jump through dry air when the electric field strength is greater than about $40\,000\,\mathrm{V\,cm^{-1}}$. This is called electrical breakdown.

a A Van de Graaff generator *(figure 7.13)* is found to be able to make sparks jump across a 4 cm gap. What is the voltage produced by the generator?

b The highest voltage reached by the live wire of a conventional mains supply is 325 V. How close would you have to get to a live wire to get a shock from it?

c Estimate the voltage of a thunder-cloud from which lightning strikes the ground 100 m below.

Force on a charge

Now we can calculate the force F on a charge Q in the uniform field between two parallel plates. We have to combine the general equation for field strength $E = F/Q$ with the equation for the strength of a uniform field $E = -V/d$. This gives

$$F = QE = -\frac{QV}{d}$$

For an electron with charge $-e$, this becomes:

$$F = \frac{eV}{d}$$

Figure 7.14 shows a situation where this force is important. A beam of electrons is entering the space between two charged parallel plates. How will the beam move?

We have to think about the force on a single electron. In the diagram, the upper plate is

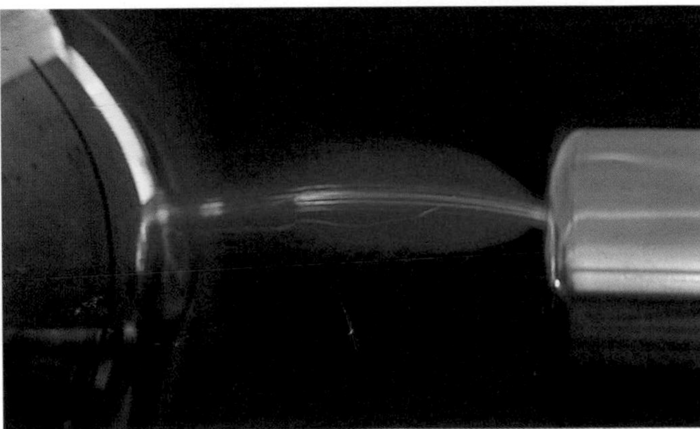

● **Figure 7.13** A Van de Graaff generator produces voltages sufficient to cause sparks in air.

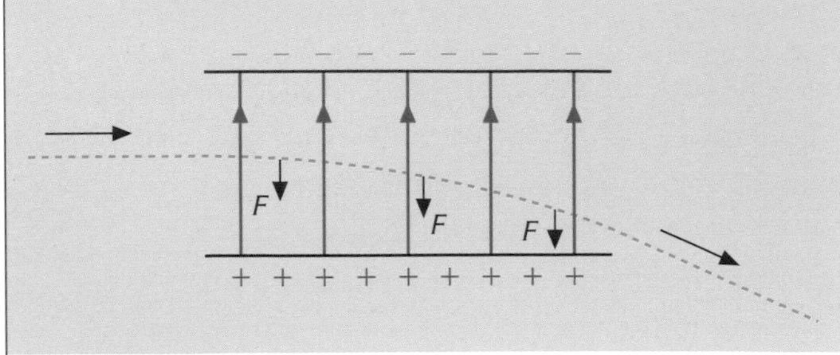

● **Figure 7.14** The parabolic path of a moving electron in a uniform electric field.

negative relative to the lower plate, and so the electron is pushed downwards. (You can think of this simply as the negatively charged electron being attracted by the positive plate, and repelled by the negative plate.)

If the electron was stationary, it would accelerate directly downwards. However, in this example, the electron is moving to the right. Its horizontal velocity will be unaffected by the force; however, as it moves sideways, it will also accelerate downwards. It will follow a curved path, as shown. This curve is a parabola.

Note that the force on the electron is the same at all points between the plates, and it is always in the same direction (downwards, in this example).

[This situation is equivalent to a ball being thrown horizontally in the Earth's uniform gravitational field, *(figure 7.15)*. It continues to move at a steady speed horizontally, but at the same time it accelerates downwards. The result is the familiar curved trajectory shown. For the electron described above, the force of gravity is tiny, negligible compared to the electric force on it.]

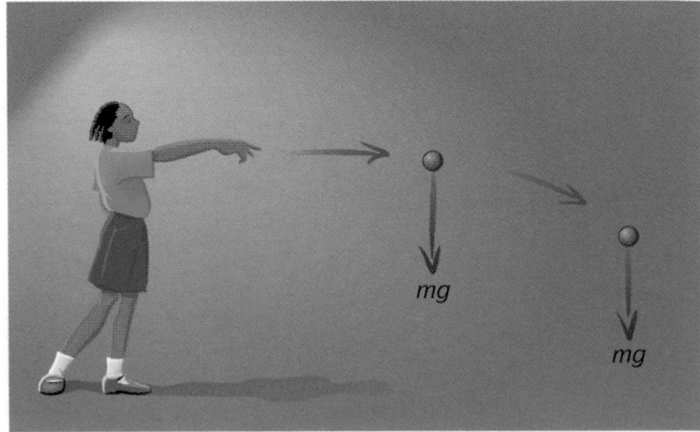

● **Figure 7.15** A ball, thrown in the uniform gravitational field of the Earth, follows a parabolic path.

SAQ 7.5

A particle of charge +2 C is placed between two parallel plates, 10 cm apart, and with a potential difference of 5 kV between them. Calculate the field strength between the plates, and the force exerted on the charge.

SAQ 7.6

We are used to experiencing accelerations that are usually less than $10\,\mathrm{m\,s^{-2}}$. For example, when we fall, our acceleration is about $9.8\,\mathrm{m\,s^{-2}}$. When a car turns a corner sharply at speed, its acceleration is unlikely to be more than $5\,\mathrm{m\,s^{-2}}$. However, if you were an electron, you would be used to experiencing much greater accelerations than this.

Calculate the acceleration of an electron (charge $-e = -1.6\times10^{-19}$ C, mass $m_e = 9.11\times10^{-31}$ kg) in a television tube where the electric field strength is $50\,000\,\mathrm{V\,cm^{-1}}$.

SAQ 7.7

a Explain how the electric force on a charged particle could be used to separate a beam of electrons and positrons into two separate beams. (Positrons are positively charged electrons, produced in radioactive decay.)

b Explain how this effect could be used to identify different ions that have different masses and charges.

Coulomb's law

Charles Coulomb was a French physicist. In 1785 he proposed a law that describes the force that one charged particle exerts on another. This law, as you might expect, is remarkably similar to Newton's law of gravitation. **Coulomb's law** says that:

Any two charged particles exert a force on each other that is proportional to each of their charges and inversely proportional to the square of the distance between them.

We can write this in a mathematical form:

$$F = \frac{Q_1 Q_2}{4\pi\varepsilon_0 d^2}$$

In this equation, the symbols have the following meanings (see *figure 7.17*): F is the force of each body on the other, Q_1 and Q_2 are their charges and d is the distance between them. The constant of

● ***Figure 7.17*** The variables involved in Coulomb's law.

Measuring *e*

The charge e of an electron is very small (-1.6×10^{-19} C) and difficult to measure. The American physicist Robert Millikan devised an ingenious way to do it. He used tiny droplets of oil, charged by friction, and suspended in a uniform electric field *(figure 7.16)*.

If a particular droplet was stationary, he knew that the electric force acting on it upwards was equal to the force of gravity acting downwards on it. (He managed to find the weight of these tiny droplets by measuring their terminal velocity as they fell through the air, another ingenious part of his technique.)

Study the diagram, and use the information it contains to help you answer the questions that follow.

A The upper plate in the diagram is connected to the positive terminal of the supply. What does this tell you about the sign of the charge on the droplet?

B What is the electric field strength between the two plates?

C What is the weight of the droplet?

D What is the electric force acting on it when it is stationary?

E What is the charge on the droplet? What is the significance of this value?

F In Millikan's experiment, he included a source of β-radiation (β is Greek beta). (This kind of radiation is simply electrons.) When an oil droplet was irradiated, it was suddenly observed to start moving upwards. What explanation can you give for this?

G What new value of voltage between the plates would you now expect to hold it stationary?

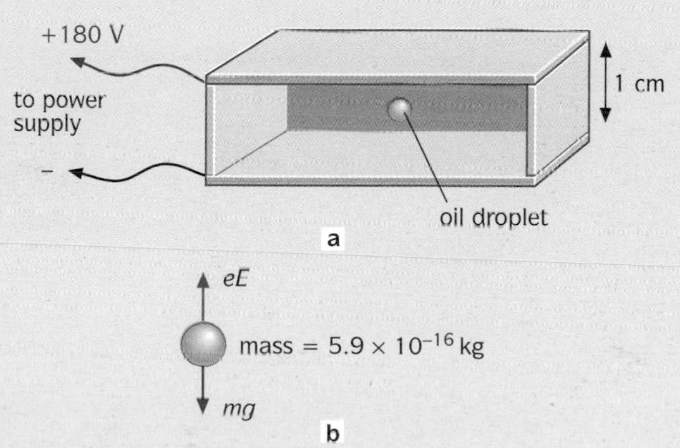

● ***Figure 7.16*** Millikan's oil-drop experiment to determine the charge of an electron.

proportionality is written as $1/(4\pi\varepsilon_0)$, where ε_0 is known as the **permittivity of free space** – a measure of how easy it is for an electric field to pass through space (ε is the Greek letter epsilon).

Since the value of ε_0 is approximately $8.85 \times 10^{-12}\,\mathrm{F\,m^{-1}}$, it follows that, numerically, $1/(4\pi\varepsilon_0) = 9 \times 10^9$ (approximately), and we can write Coulomb's law as

$$F = \frac{9 \times 10^9 \times Q_1 Q_2}{d^2}$$

Following your earlier study of Newton's law of gravitation, you should not be surprised by this relationship. The force depends on each of the properties producing it (in this case, the charges), and it is an inverse square law – if the particles are twice as far apart, the force is a quarter of its previous value *(figure 7.18)*.

Note that we measure the distance between two charged spheres from the centre of one to the centre of the other – they behave as if their charge was all concentrated at the centre, even though it is probably uniformly spread over the surface.

Note also that, if we have a positive and a negative charge, then the force F is negative. We interpret this as an attraction. Positive forces, as between two like charges, are repulsive. In gravity, we only have attraction.

Investigating Coulomb's law

It is quite tricky to investigate the force between charged particles, because charge tends to leak away into the air during the course of any experiment. Also, the amount of charge we can investigate is difficult to measure, and usually small, giving rise to small forces.

Figure 7.19 shows one way of doing this. As one charged sphere is lowered down towards the other, their separation decreases and so the force increases, giving an increased reading on the balance.

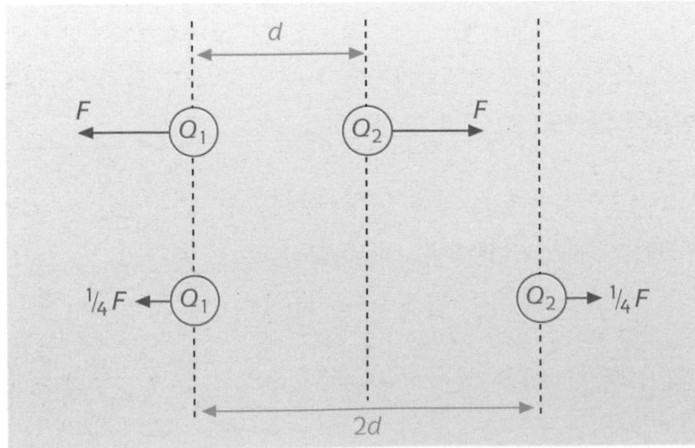

● ***Figure 7.18*** Double the separation results in one-quarter of the force.

Field strength in a radial field

Field strength E is defined by the equation $E = F/Q$. So to find the field strength near a point charge (or outside a charged sphere), we have to picture a positive test charge placed in the field, and work out the force per coulomb on it. We can find this from Coulomb's law, with the second charge $= +1\,\mathrm{C}$.

$$E = \frac{Q}{4\pi\varepsilon_0 d^2}$$

This tells us the field strength E at distance d from a charge Q.

You will need the data below to answer the self-assessment questions.

	Charge	*Mass*
electron	$-1.6 \times 10^{-19}\,\mathrm{C}$	$9.11 \times 10^{-31}\,\mathrm{kg}$
proton	$+1.6 \times 10^{-19}\,\mathrm{C}$	$1.67 \times 10^{-27}\,\mathrm{kg}$

$\varepsilon_0 = 8.85 \times 10^{-12}\,\mathrm{F\,m^{-1}}$
$G = 6.67 \times 10^{-11}\,\mathrm{N\,m^2\,kg^{-2}}$

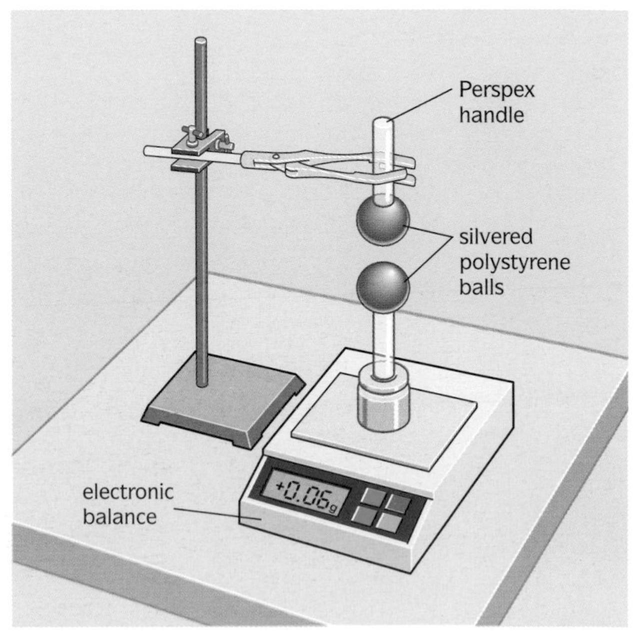

● ***Figure 7.19*** Investigating Coulomb's law.

SAQ 7.8

Two protons in the nucleus of an atom are separated by 10^{-15} m. Calculate the force of electrostatic repulsion between them, and the force of gravitational attraction between them. Is gravity enough to balance the electric repulsion tending to separate them? What does this suggest to you about the forces between protons in a nucleus?

SAQ 7.9

An iron atom has a nucleus that contains 26 protons (and a lot of neutrons). Its electrons orbit at a typical distance of 10^{-10} m. Calculate the attractive force exerted by the nucleus on a single electron at this distance.

The nucleus of an iron atom has a diameter of 4.9×10^{-15} m. Calculate the field strength where the electrons are, and at the surface of the nucleus.

SAQ 7.10

A Van de Graaff generator produces sparks when the field strength at its surface is $40\,000\,\mathrm{V\,cm^{-1}}$. If the diameter of the sphere is 40 cm, what is the charge on it?

Electric potential

When we discussed gravitational potential (page 13), we started from the idea of potential energy. The potential at a point is then the potential energy of unit mass at the point. We will approach the idea of electrical potential in the same way. However, you may be relieved to know that you already know something about the idea of electrical potential, because you already know about voltage and potential difference. This section shows how we formalise the idea of voltage, and why we use the expression 'potential difference' for some kinds of voltage.

Electric potential energy

When an electric charge moves through an electric field, its potential energy changes. Think about this concrete example: if you want to move one positive charge closer to another positive charge, you have to push it *(figure 7.20)*. This is simply because there is a force of repulsion between the charges. You have to do work in order to move one charge closer to the other.

In the process of doing work, energy is transferred from you to the charge that you are pushing. Its potential energy increases.

If you let go of the charge, it will move away from the repelling charge. This is analogous to lifting up a mass; it gains gravitational potential energy as you lift it, and it falls if you let go.

● Figure 7.20 Work must be done to push one positive charge towards another.

Energy changes in a uniform field

We can also think about moving a positive charge in a uniform electric field between two charged parallel plates. If we move the charge towards the positive plate, we have to do work. The potential energy of the charge is therefore increasing. If we move it towards the negative plate, its potential energy is decreasing *(figure 7.21)*.

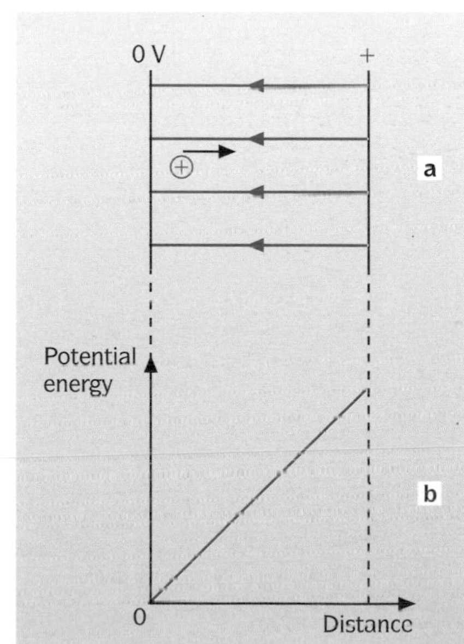

● Figure 7.21 Electrostatic potential energy changes in a uniform field.

Since the force is the same at all points in a uniform field, it follows that the energy of the charge increases steadily as we push it from one plate to the other. The graph of potential energy against distance is a straight line.

We can calculate the change in potential energy of a charge Q as it is moved from one plate to the other very simply. The potential difference (voltage) between the plates tells us the energy change per coulomb in moving from one plate to the other. (Recall from chapter 5 that one volt is one joule per coulomb.) Hence, for charge Q, the work done in moving it from one plate to the other is

$$W = QV$$

We can rearrange this equation as

$$V = \frac{W}{Q}$$

This is really how voltage V is defined. It is the energy per unit charge at a point in an electric field. By analogy with gravitational potential, we call this the electric potential at a point. Now you should be able to see that what we regard as the familiar idea of voltage should more correctly be referred to as electric potential. The difference in voltage between two points is the potential difference (p.d.) between them.

As with gravitational fields, we have to say where we consider a charge to have zero potential energy – we must define the zero of potential.

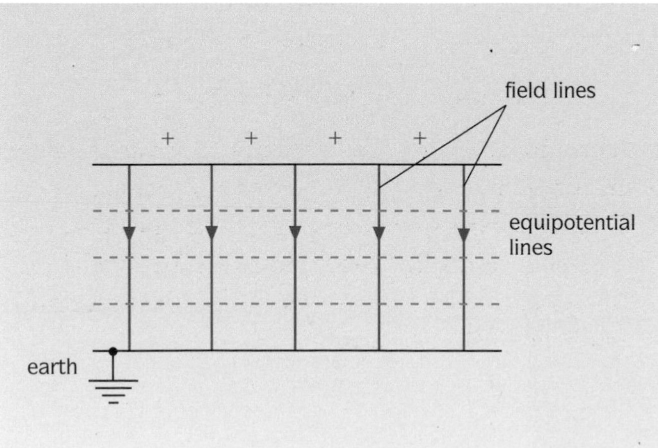

● ***Figure 7.22*** Equipotential lines in a uniform electric field.

Usually, in a laboratory situation, we define the earth as being at a potential of zero volts. If we draw two parallel charged plates arranged horizontally, with the lower one earthed *(figure 7.22)*, you can see immediately how similar this is to our idea of gravitational fields. The diagram also shows how we can include equipotential lines in a representation of an electric field.

We can extend the idea of electric potential to measurements in electric circuits. In *figure 7.23*, the power supply provides a potential difference of 10 V. The value of the potential at various points is shown. You can see that the middle resistor has a potential difference across it of (8 − 2) V = 6 V.

Energy in a radial field

Imagine again pushing a small positive test charge towards a large positive charge. At first, the repulsive force is weak, and you have only to do a small amount of work. As you get closer, however, the force increases (Coulomb's law), and you have to work harder and harder.

The potential energy of the test charge increases as you push it. It increases more and more rapidly the closer you get to the repelling charge. This is shown by the graph in *figure 7.24*. We can write an equation for the potential V at a distance d from a charge Q:

$$V = -\frac{Q}{4\pi\varepsilon_0 d}$$

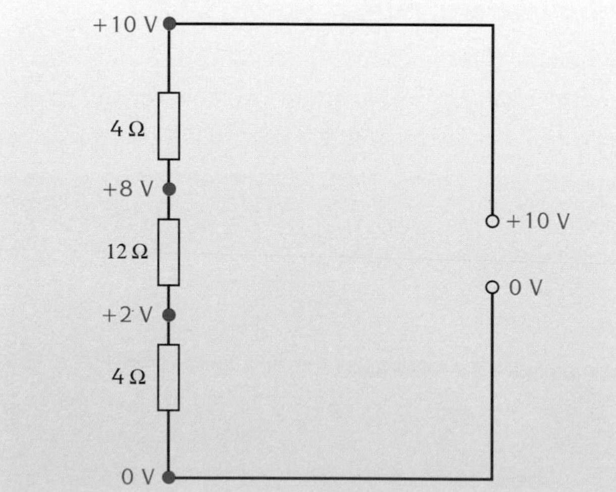

● ***Figure 7.23*** Changes in potential around an electric circuit.

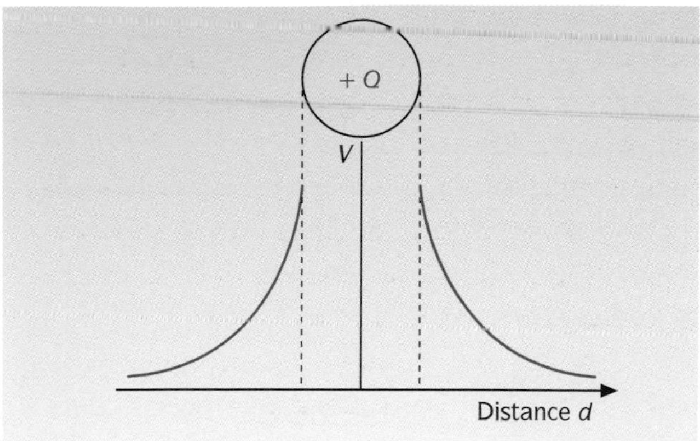

● ***Figure 7.24*** The potential decreases according to an inverse law near a charged sphere.

(This comes from the calculus process of integration, applied to the Coulomb's law equation.) You should be able to see how this relationship parallels the equivalent formula for gravitational potential in a radial field:

$$\phi = -G\frac{M}{r}$$

We can show these same ideas by drawing field lines and equipotential lines. The equipotentials get closer together as we get closer to the charge *(figure 7.25)*.

To arrive at the result above, we must again define our zero of potential. Again, we say that a charge has zero potential when it is at infinity (some place where it is beyond the influence of any other charges). If we move towards a positive charge, the potential is positive. If we move towards a negative charge, the potential is negative.

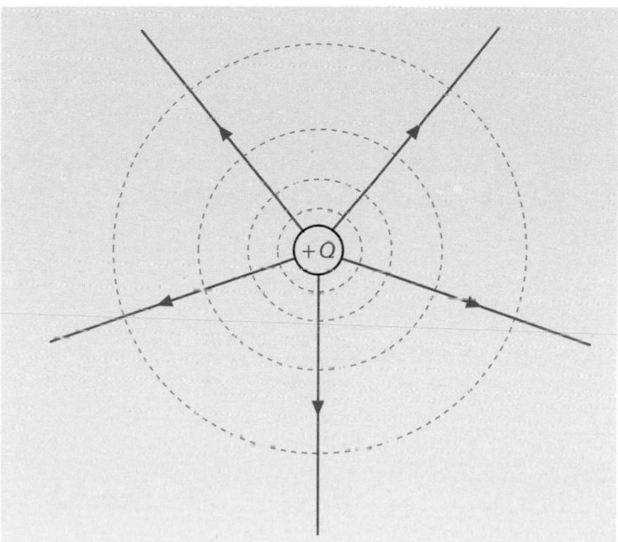

● ***Figure 7.25*** Equipotential lines near a positively charged sphere.

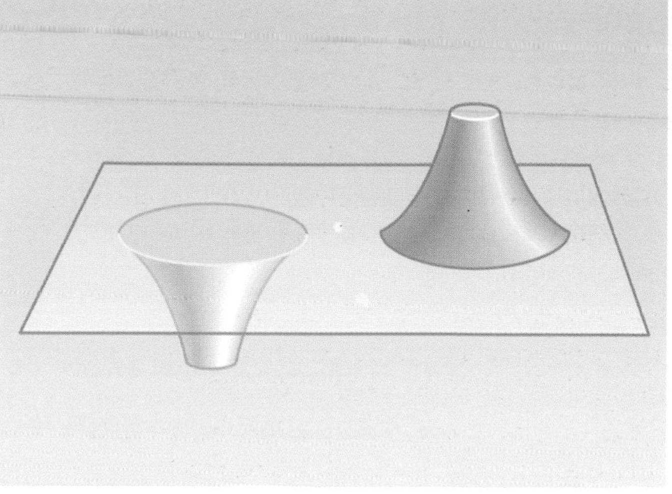

● ***Figure 7.26*** A 'potential well' and a 'potential hill'.

This allows us to give a strict definition of electric potential:

The **electric potential** at a point is equal to the work done per unit charge in moving a positive charge from infinity to that point.

Field strength and potential gradient

We can picture electric potential in the same way that we thought about gravitational potential. A negative charge attracts a positive test charge, so we can regard it as a potential 'well'. A positive charge is the opposite, a 'hill' *(figure 7.26)*. The strength of the field is shown by the slope (gradient) of the sides of the hill or well:

field strength = − potential gradient

The minus sign is needed because, if we are going up a potential hill, the force on us is pushing us back down the slope, in the opposite direction.

This relationship applies to all electric fields. You can see that, for a uniform field, the potential gradient is V/d, and hence

$$E = -\frac{V}{d}$$

This is the relationship quoted without proof in the earlier section (page 55).

Sorting out ideas

There are several related quantities that can easily be confused when thinking about electric fields, and several formulae that are also related. It is important to know which ideas apply to all fields, and which apply only to radial fields, or only to uniform fields. A summary of all this is now given:

■ *All electric fields*

force F — field strength $E = \frac{F}{Q}$

potential energy W — potential $V = \frac{W}{Q}$

field strength = − potential gradient

■ *Units*

F/N — E/N C^{-1} or V m^{-1}

W/J — V/V or J C^{-1}

■ *Uniform fields*

$F = \frac{QV}{d}$ — $E = -\frac{V}{d}$

$W = QV$ — $V = V$

■ *Radial fields*

$F = \frac{Q_1Q_2}{4\pi\varepsilon_0 d^2}$ — $E = \frac{Q}{4\pi\varepsilon_0 d^2}$

$W = -\frac{Q_1Q_2}{4\pi\varepsilon_0 d}$ — $V = -\frac{Q}{4\pi\varepsilon_0 d}$

Comprehension

The drawing in *figure 7.27* shows a thunder-cloud above the Earth. The electric field it creates is shown by the lines of force.

Many tall buildings have lightning conductors. These help to conduct away any lightning that strikes the building. They also help to discharge thunder-clouds without lightning striking.

If you have a Van de Graaff generator running so that sparks ('lightning') are jumping to a nearby earthed sphere, you can simulate the effect of a lightning conductor. Bring up the sharp point of a pin towards the dome of the generator *(figure 7.28)*; the sparks will stop. A very small current is flowing through the air to the pin and through you to earth. Remove the pin and the sparks start again.

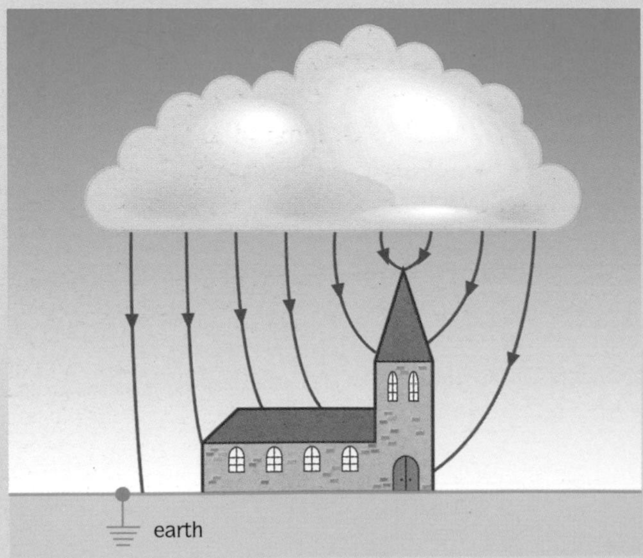

● ***Figure 7.27*** The electric field below a thunder-cloud.

● ***Figure 7.28*** The effect of a sharp point in an electric field.

A Copy the diagram of the thunder-cloud, and add equipotential lines. (Remember that they are always at right-angles to the field lines.)

B Where is the electric field strongest? Explain your answer by referring to the field lines, and by referring to the equipotential lines.

C Where is lightning more likely to strike?

D Draw a diagram to show why the sharp pin prevents the generator from sparking.

SUMMARY

- An electric field is a field of force, and can be represented by field lines.
- The strength of the field is the force acting on unit charge placed at a point in the field.
- The potential at a point is the work done in bringing unit charge from infinity to the point.
- In a uniform field (e.g. between two parallel charged plates) the force on a charge is the same at all points; the strength of the field is given by $E = -V/d$.
- A point charge gives rise to a spherical field: field strength $E = Q/(4\pi\varepsilon_0 d^2)$ and potential $V = Q/(4\pi\varepsilon_0 d)$.
- These relationships are derived from Coulomb's law for the force between two charged particles: $F = Q_1Q_2/(4\pi\varepsilon_0 d^2)$.
- Field strength is numerically equal to the potential gradient at a point.

Questions

1 a What would be the electrical potential energy of a charge of +1 C placed at each of the points A, B, C, D in the diagram in *figure 7.29*?

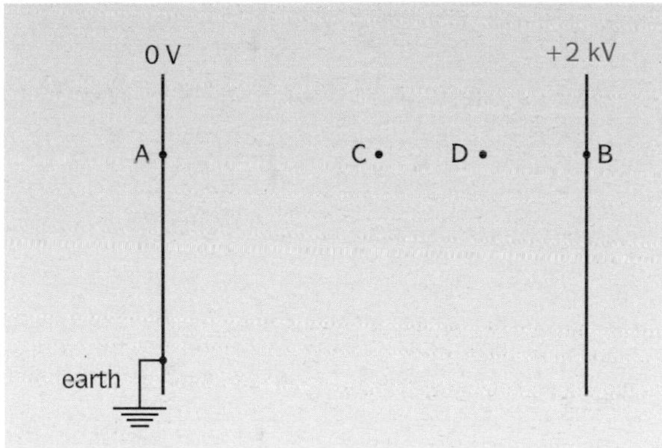

● ***Figure 7.29*** A uniform field.

b What would the potential energy of a +2 C charge be at each of these points? (C is half-way between A and B; D is half-way between C and D.)

2 A Van de Graaff generator has a dome of radius 10 cm. It is charged up to a potential of 100 000 V (100 kV). How much charge does it store? What is the potential at a distance of 10 cm from the dome?

3 A field strength of about 40 000 V cm^{-1} is needed for air to break down. Any field strength greater than this will result in the air becoming conducting and charge leaking away.

a What is the greatest voltage to which a 20 cm radius Van de Graaff generator dome can be raised without breakdown occurring?

b To achieve a higher voltage, would the dome need to be larger or smaller?

4 a How much work would be done in moving a +1 C charge along the following paths shown in *figure 7.30*: from E to H; from E to F; from F to G; from H to E?

How would your answers differ for

b a −1 C charge

c a +2 C charge?

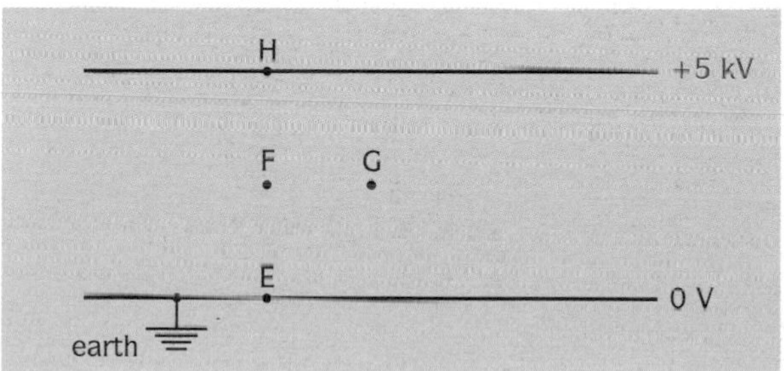

● ***Figure 7.30*** A uniform field.

Electromagnetism 1

By the end of this chapter you should be able to:

1 describe a magnetic field as a field of force, produced by a permanent magnet or an electric current;
2 represent a magnetic field by field lines;
3 appreciate that a force acts on a current-carrying conductor that crosses a magnetic field;
4 predict the direction of the force using Fleming's left-hand rule;
5 predict the direction of the force on a moving charge in a magnetic field;
6 sketch flux patterns for currents in a long straight wire, a flat circular coil and a long solenoid, and describe the effect of a ferrous core on the field of a long solenoid;
7 describe the principle of electromagnets and appreciate their uses.

Magnetic fields

Magnets are fascinating things. Our everyday experience is that we need to touch something if we want to make it move. The attraction and repulsion between the poles of magnets is an example of 'action at a distance', and appears almost magical.

● ***Figure 8.1*** This train is supported at a precise distance above the track by computer-controlled electromagnets.

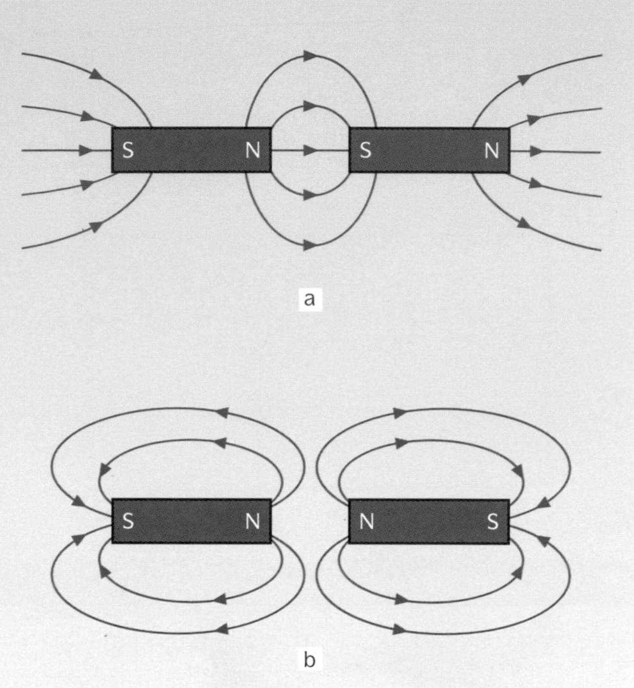

● ***Figure 8.2*** Magnetic field patterns for two bar magnets, **a** attracting and **b** repelling.

In this chapter, we will look at magnetic forces and fields, how they arise, and how they interact.

You can make a magnetic field in two ways: using a permanent magnet, or using an electric current. You should be familiar with the magnetic field patterns of bar magnets *(figure 8.2)*. These can be shown up using iron filings or plotting compasses.

We represent magnetic fields, like gravitational and electric fields, by drawing lines of force. These show the direction of the force that a magnetic north pole would feel at any point in the field. They come out of north poles and go into south poles. The field is strongest where the lines are closest together.

An electromagnet makes use of the magnetic field created by an electric current *(figure 8.3)*. A coil is used because this concentrates the magnetic field. One end becomes a north pole (field lines emerging), while the other end is the south pole. Another name for a coil like this is a solenoid.

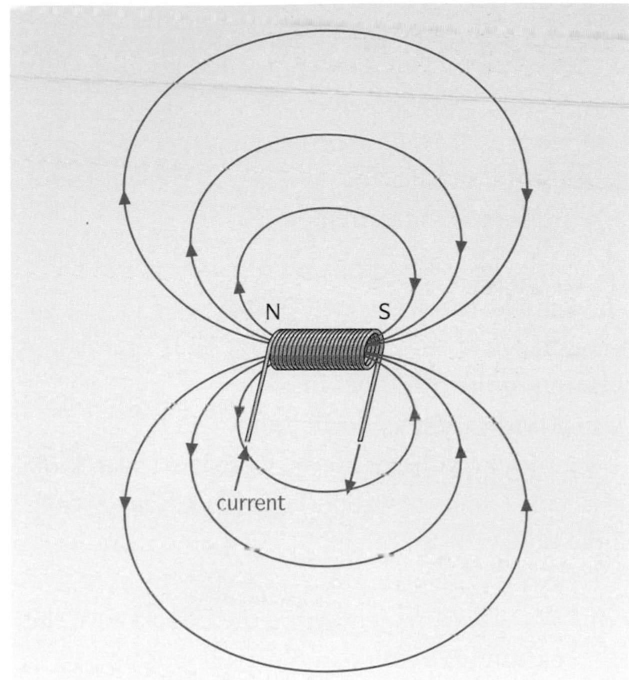

● ***Figure 8.3*** The magnetic field pattern of a current-carrying coil (a solenoid).

If we unravel an electromagnet, we get a weaker field. This too can be investigated using iron filings or compasses. The field lines shown in *figure 8.4* are circular, around the wire. Further away from the wire, the field lines are drawn further apart, representing the weaker field at this distance. Reversing the current reverses the direction of the field.

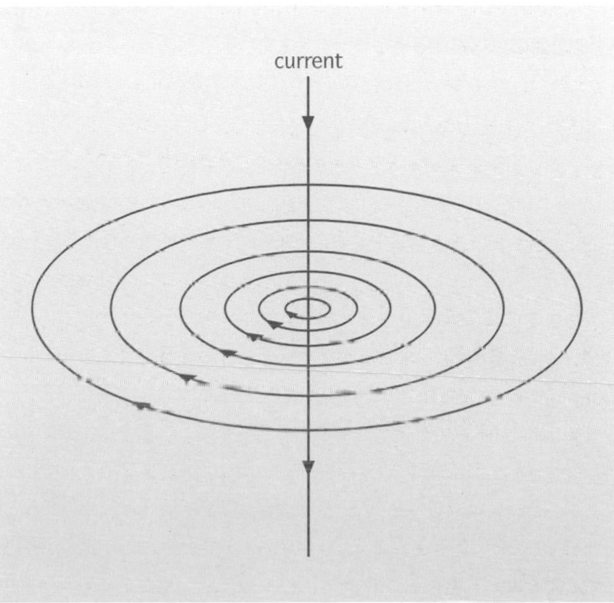

● ***Figure 8.4*** The magnetic field pattern around a current flowing in a wire.

There is really no fundamental difference between these two ways of creating magnetic fields. In a permanent magnet, the field is generated by the movement of electrons. Each electron represents a tiny current as it circulates around within its atom, and this current sets up a magnetic field. In a ferrous material such as iron, the weak fields due to all the electrons combine together to make a strong field, which spreads out into the space beyond the magnet.

Electromagnets

An electromagnet is a device that is designed to make best use of the magnetic effect of a current. Electromagnets form the basis of many types of electric motors, relay switches, generators and transformers. Because electric current can be switched on and off easily, and reversed at high speed, they have a great advantage in these applications over permanent magnets.

Many electromagnets make use of the way in which ferrous materials such as iron behave in a magnetic field. A soft iron core inside the electromagnet greatly increases the strength of the field (*figure 8.5*). Soft iron must be used; hard steel would retain some of its magnetism when the current switched off, and energy is wasted in reversing the field in a hard magnetic material.

A flat coil of wire produces a similar form of magnetic field when a current flows through it. From *figure 8.6*, you can see that it is as if a solenoid had been squashed flat. Field lines pass through the middle of the coil and form loops around the wire.

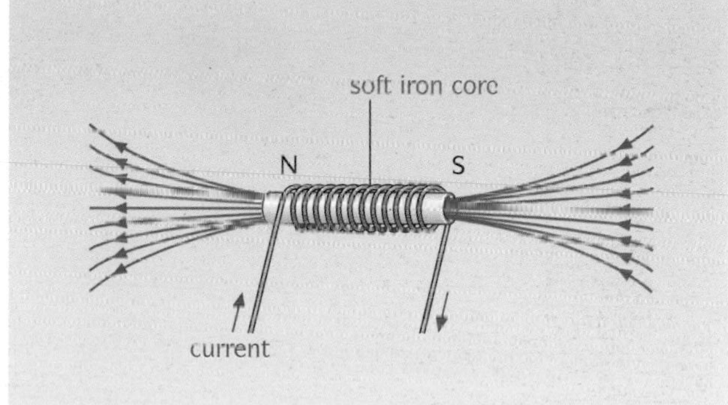

● ***Figure 8.5*** A soft iron core greatly increases the strength of the field inside a coil.

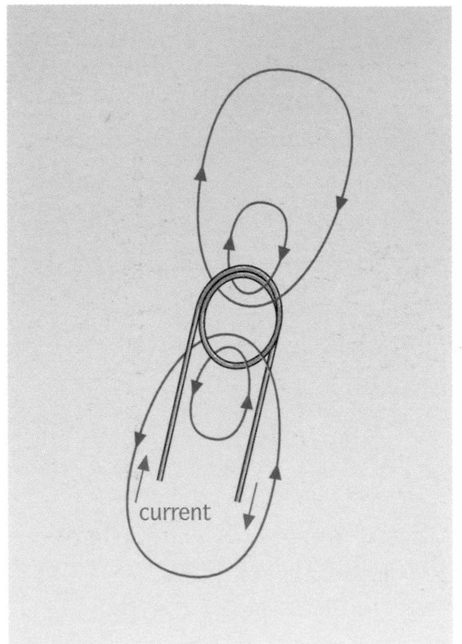

● ***Figure 8.6*** The magnetic field pattern around a flat coil.

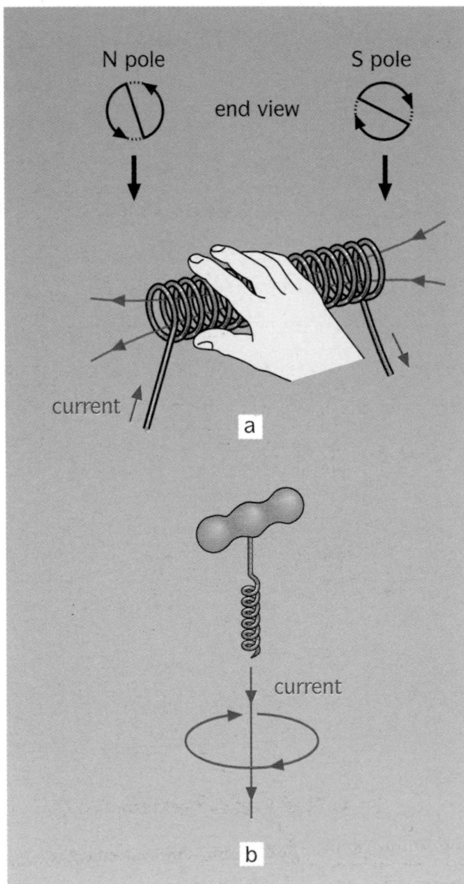

● ***Figure 8.7*** Two rules for determining the direction of a magnetic field, **a** inside a solenoid and **b** around a current-carrying wire.

Field direction

The idea that field lines emerge from north poles and go into south poles is simply a convention. Even the most powerful microscope will not allow you to see the arrows on the field lines!

Figure 8.7 shows some useful rules for remembering the direction of the magnetic field produced by a current:

- The right-hand grip rule gives the direction of field lines in an electromagnet. Imagine gripping the coil, so that your fingers go around it following the direction of the current. Your thumb now points in the direction of the field lines inside the coil, i.e. it points towards the electromagnet's north pole.
- Another way to identify the poles of an electromagnet is to look at it end on, and decide which way round the current is flowing. The diagrams show how you can remember that clockwise is a south pole, anticlockwise is a north pole.
- The corkscrew rule is a way of remembering the direction of the field lines around a current-carrying wire. Imagine pushing a corkscrew into a cork, and turning it. The direction in which you push is the direction of the current, and the field lines go round in the direction in which you are turning the corkscrew.

SAQ 8.1

Sketch the magnetic field pattern around a long straight wire carrying an electric current. Now, alongside this first sketch, draw a second to show the field pattern if the current flowing was doubled and its direction reversed.

Investigation

Use a Magnaprobe to investigate the magnetic field in each of the situations shown in *figure 8.8*. (A Magnaprobe is a small bar magnet suspended so that it can tilt in any direction to show the magnetic field – a kind of three-dimensional plotting compass.)

In each case, draw a diagram to show your prediction of the shape of the magnetic field, before you do the experiment.

Devise a way to tell where the field is strong and where it is weak. (You might use the Magnaprobe, or a plotting compass, or some other means. Your method might involve making use of the Earth's magnetic field, or another bar magnet, or you may devise some other method entirely.)

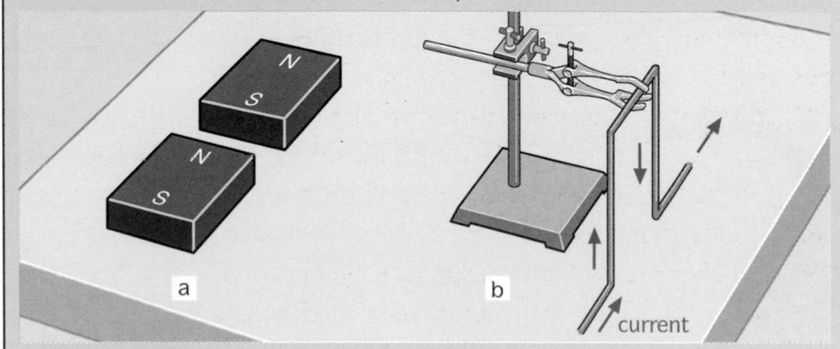

● ***Figure 8.8*** **a** Two bar magnets. **b** A current flowing in a stiff wire.

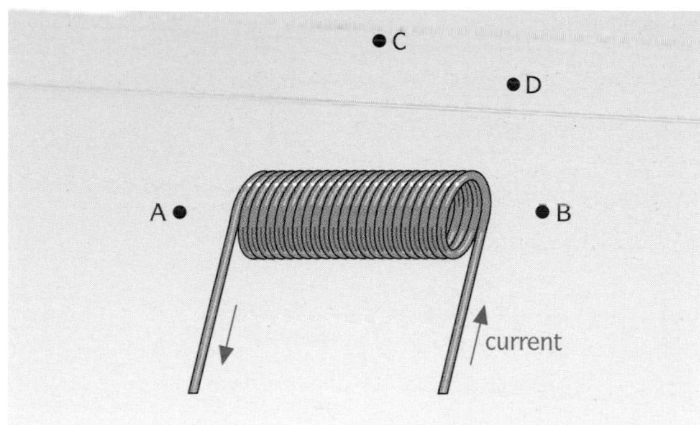

● ***Figure 8.9*** A current carrying solenoid.

SAQ 8.2

Copy the diagram in *figure 8.9*, and label the N and S poles of the electromagnet. Show on the diagram the direction in which the needle of a plotting compass would point at each of the positions A, B, C and D.

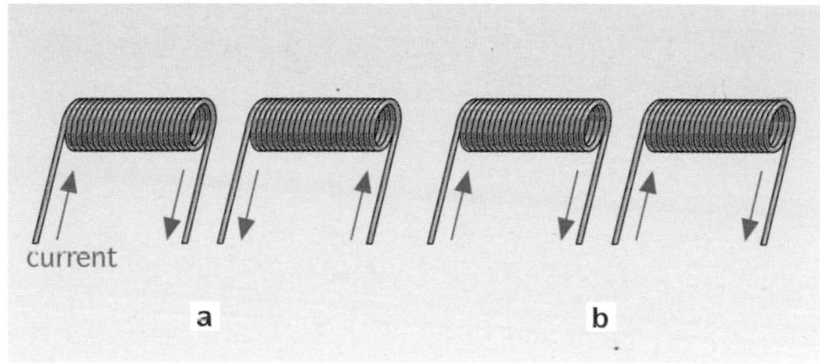

● ***Figure 8.10*** Two pairs of solenoids.

SAQ 8.3

Which of the pairs of electromagnets shown in *figure 8.10* will attract one another, and which will repel?

Magnetic force

Because an electric current is surrounded by a magnetic field, it will interact with any other magnetic field. The simplest situation is shown in *figure 8.11*.

The magnets create a fairly uniform magnetic field. The rod has a current flowing through it. As soon as the current is switched on, the rod starts to roll, showing that a force is acting on it.

We use **Fleming's left-hand rule** to predict the direction of the force. There are three things here, all of which are mutually at right-angles to each other – the magnetic field, the current in the rod,

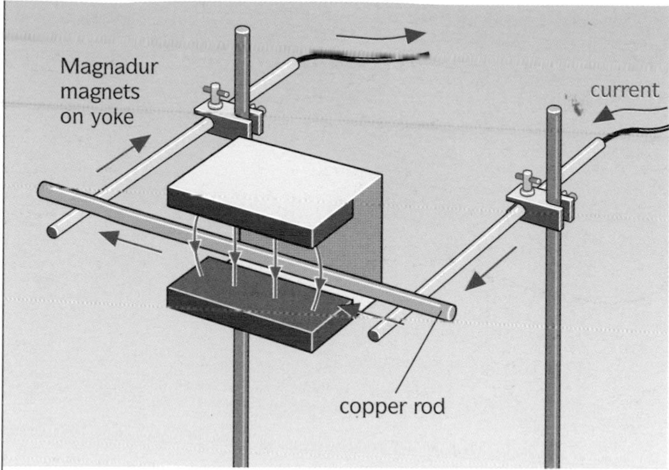

● ***Figure 8.11*** The copper rod is free to roll along the two horizontal steel 'rails'.

and the force on the rod. These can be represented by holding the thumb and first two fingers of your left hand so that they are mutually at right-angles (*figure 8.12*). Your fingers then represent:

- thuMb – Motion
- First finger – Field
- seCond finger – Current

You should practise using your left hand to check that the rule correctly predicts these directions.

The production of this force is known as the motor effect, because this force is used in electric motors. In a simple motor, a current flowing in a coil produces a magnetic field; this field interacts with a second field produced by a permanent magnet.

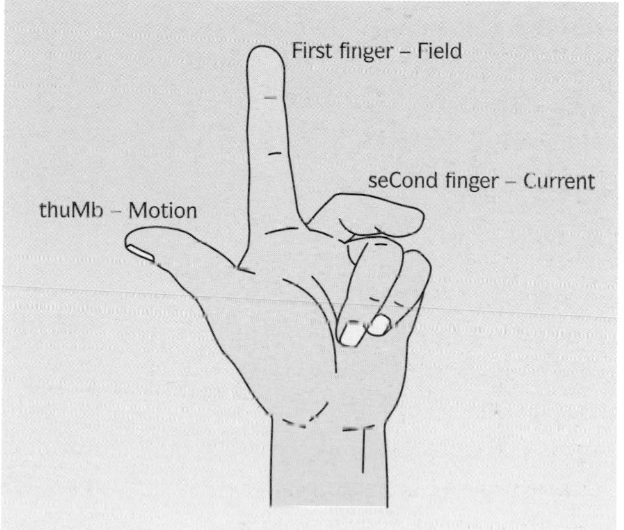

● ***Figure 8.12*** Fleming's left-hand rule.

We can explain this force by thinking about the magnetic fields in this situation. The first field is due to the permanent magnets; the second is due to the current flowing through the rod. These fields combine to produce the force on the rod.

Figure 8.13a shows a perspective view; in practice, it is easier to draw a two-dimensional view, as shown in *figure 8.13b*. Note the symbols that are used to mean that the current is flowing at right-angles to the paper, in to or out of the diagram.

SAQ 8.4

Figure 8.14 shows three examples of conductors in magnetic fields. For each example, decide whether there will be a magnetic force on the conductor. If there is a force, in what direction will it act?

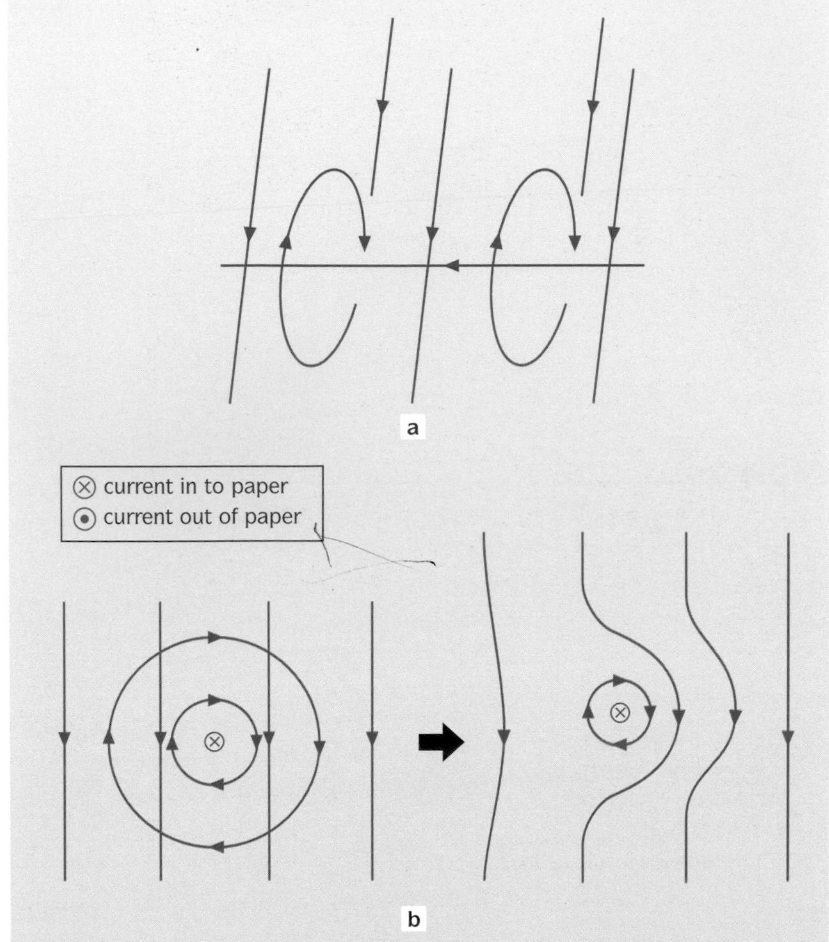

● ***Figure 8.13*** A current flowing in a straight wire produces a magnetic field that interacts with an external field.

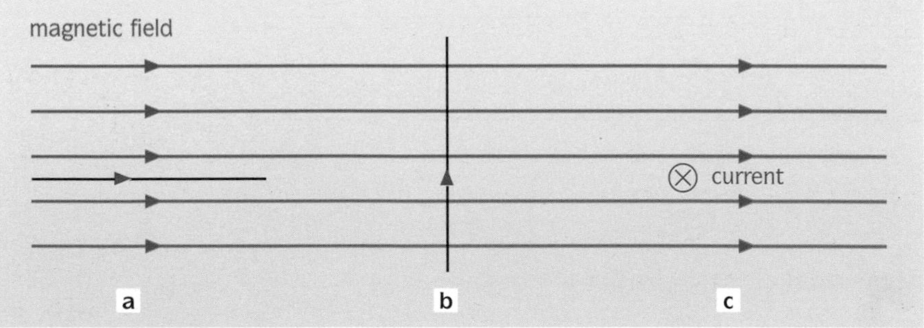

● ***Figure 8.14*** Three conductors in a magnetic field.

Moving particles

The world of atomic physics is populated by a great variety of particles – electrons, protons, neutrons, positrons, and more. Many of these particles are electrically charged, and their motion is influenced by electric and magnetic fields. Indeed, we use this fact to help us to distinguish one particle from another.

You can use your knowledge of how charged particles and electric currents are affected by fields to interpret diagrams of moving particles. You must bear in mind that electric current is the flow of positive charge. When electrons are moving, the conventional current is regarded as flowing in the opposite direction.

Observing the force

Electron beam tubes *(figure 8.15)* can be used to demonstrate the magnetic force on a moving charge. A beam of electrons is produced by an 'electron gun', and magnets or electromagnets can be used to apply a magnetic field.

You can use such an arrangement to observe the effect of changing the strength and direction of the field, and the effect of

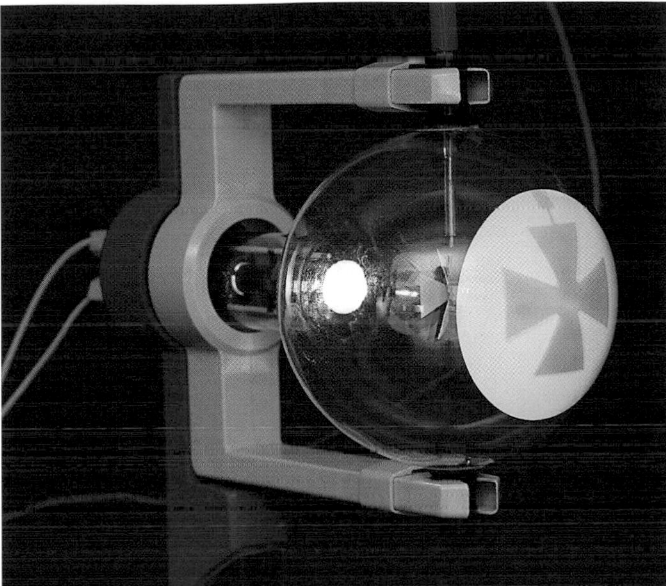

● **Figure 8.15** An electron beam tube.

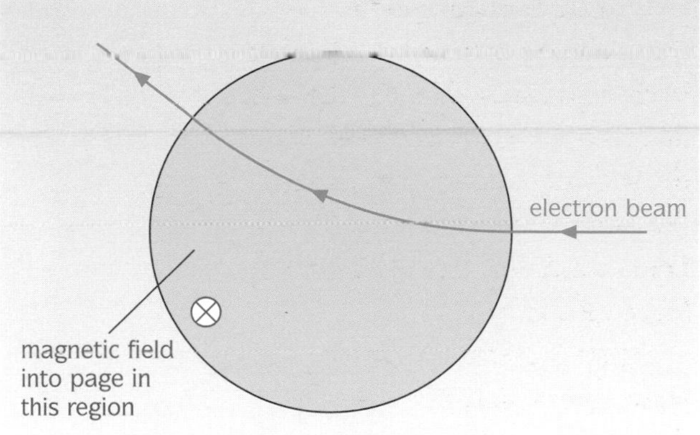

● **Figure 8.16** A beam of electrons is deflected as it crosses a magnetic field. The magnetic field into the page is represented by the blue cross in the circle.

reversing the field. Note that you can seriously damage a television set by bringing a magnet close to the screen.

If you are able to observe a beam of electrons like this, you should find that the force on the electrons moving through the magnetic field can be correctly predicted using Fleming's left-hand rule. In *figure 8.16*, a beam of electrons is moving from right to left, into a region where a magnetic field is directed into the page. Since electrons are negatively charged, they represent a conventional current (flow of positive charge) from left to right. Fleming's left-hand rule predicts that the force on the electrons will be upwards, and the beam will be deflected up the page.

It is this force that gives rise to the motor effect. The electrons in a wire experience a force when they flow across a magnetic field, and they transfer the force to the wire itself.

Using electron beams

Televisions, oscilloscopes and computer monitors all make use of beams of electrons. Electrons are moved about using magnetic and electric fields, and the result can be a rapidly-changing image on the screen.

The picture in *figure 8.17* shows the construction of a typical tube. The electron gun has a heated cathode. The positively charged anode attracts electrons from the cathode, and they pass through the anode to form a narrow beam in the space beyond. The direction of the beam can be changed using an electric field between two plates (as shown in *figure 8.17*), or a magnetic field created by electromagnetic coils.

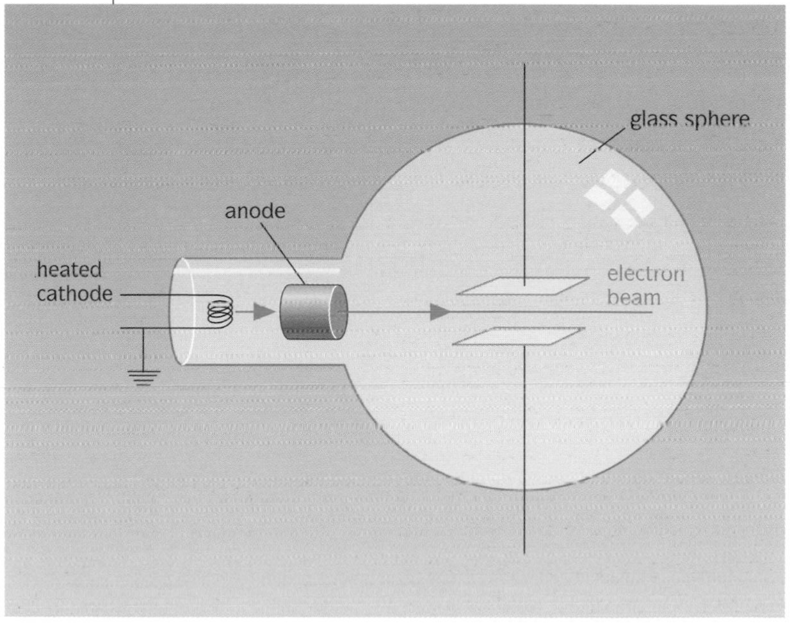

● **Figure 8.17** The construction of an electron beam tube.

SAQ 8.5

In the diagram in *figure 8.18*, particles from a radioactive source are passing through a magnetic field. Which tracks are those of α-particles (alpha particles, + charge), β-particles (beta particles, – charge) and γ-rays (gamma-rays, no charge)?

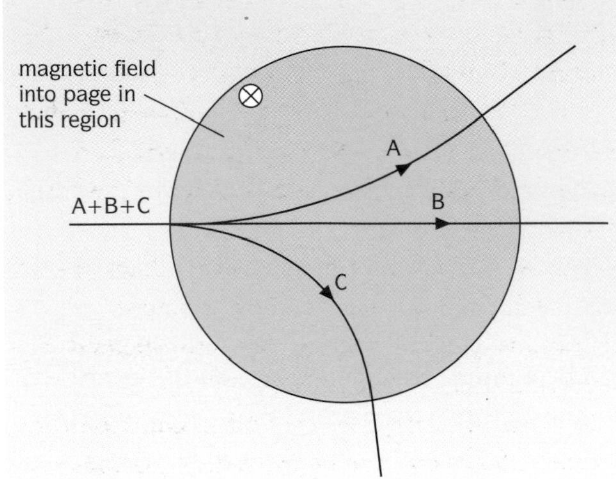

● ***Figure 8.18*** Three types of radiation passing through a magnetic field.

SUMMARY

- Magnetic fields are produced by permanent magnets and by electric currents. We can represent them by lines of force.
- The field of a current in a wire can be strengthened by forming it into a coil, and by adding a ferrous core. This is the principle of electromagnets.
- When a current flows across a magnetic field, there is an interaction between the two fields.
- The direction of the resulting force is given by Fleming's left-hand rule. The same rule gives the direction of the force on a moving charge in a magnetic field.

Electromagnetism 2

By the end of this chapter you should be able to:

1. recall and use $F = BIl \sin\theta$ for the force on a current-carrying conductor in a magnetic field;
2. define magnetic flux density and the tesla;
3. understand how this force can be used to measure flux density using a current balance;
4. understand how to use a Hall probe to measure flux density;
5. recall and use $F = BQv \sin\theta$ for the force on a charge moving in a magnetic field;
6. use appropriate equations for the flux density in flat coils and solenoids, and near a long straight wire;
7. explain the forces between two current-carrying conductors, derive an expression for these forces and predict their directions;
8. explain how these forces lead to a definition of the ampere.

Magnetic flux

A useful way to think about a magnetic field is in terms of magnetic flux. The word 'flux' means something that flows, and we picture magnetic flux flowing out of the north pole of a magnet and travelling round to the south pole. The lines of force can then be called flux lines, and they show the direction in which this imaginary fluid is flowing.

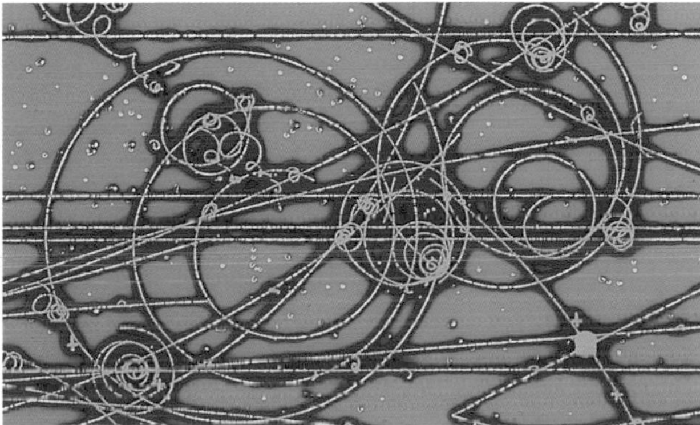

● ***Figure 9.1*** Here, beams of electrons lose energy and are deflected by a magnetic field so that they follow a spiral path.

The strength of a magnetic field depends on how concentrated the flux is. Where there is a lot of flux flowing, the field is strong. To be more precise, we think of the **magnetic flux density**: the amount of flux flowing through unit area at a point in the field. *Figure 9.2* shows two points in the field of a bar magnet, one where the magnetic field strength (flux density) is high, and another where it is low.

The symbol used for flux density is B, and its unit is the tesla (T). We will look at precise definitions of these when we have investigated magnetic forces in more detail.

You may have expected to find an equation for magnetic force comparable with the equations for electric and gravitational forces (Coulomb's law and Newton's law). We could write an equation for the force exerted by one magnetic pole M_1 on another, M_2. We would expect it to be of the form:

$$F = \text{constant} \times \frac{M_1 M_2}{r^2}$$

where r is the distance between the poles. In fact, it is possible to derive a whole theory of magnetism

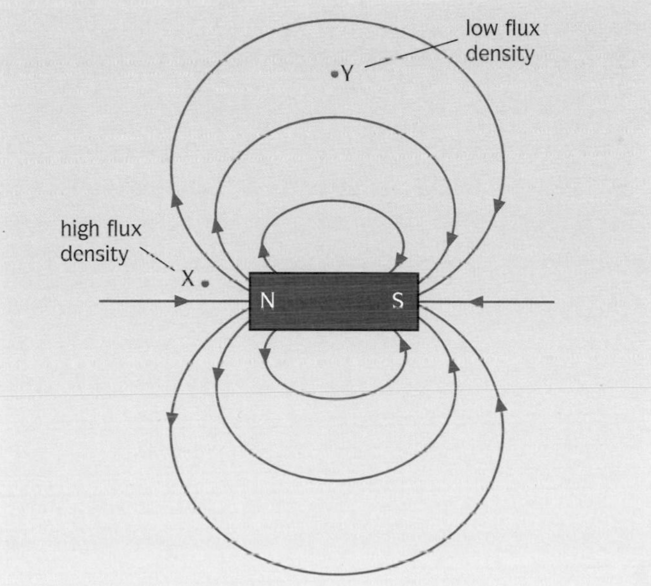

● ***Figure 9.2*** Magnetic flux density B is high where lines of force are close together.

based on such an equation. However, this is not the convention accepted by physicists today. The reason is that we cannot have two isolated north poles, in the way that we can have two positive charges. Every bar magnet or electromagnet has a north pole *and* a south pole, and this complicates the situation. Indeed, we can think of a south pole as being simply a north pole viewed from the other end. (It is like trying to imagine a battery with only a positive terminal.)

Scientists have put considerable effort into searching for particles that have just one magnetic pole (magnetic monopoles). If such particles do exist, they would be very awkward to deal with in the laboratory. You can imagine what would happen if you took the lid off a box of them!

Measuring magnetic force

In order to say how strong a magnetic field is, we will look at the force it can exert on an electric current. A device called a current balance can be used in experiments to investigate the force on a current-carrying conductor in a magnetic field. *Figure 9.3* shows a simple version of a current balance. A current flows through the wire frame; the magnetic field pushes the frame downwards.

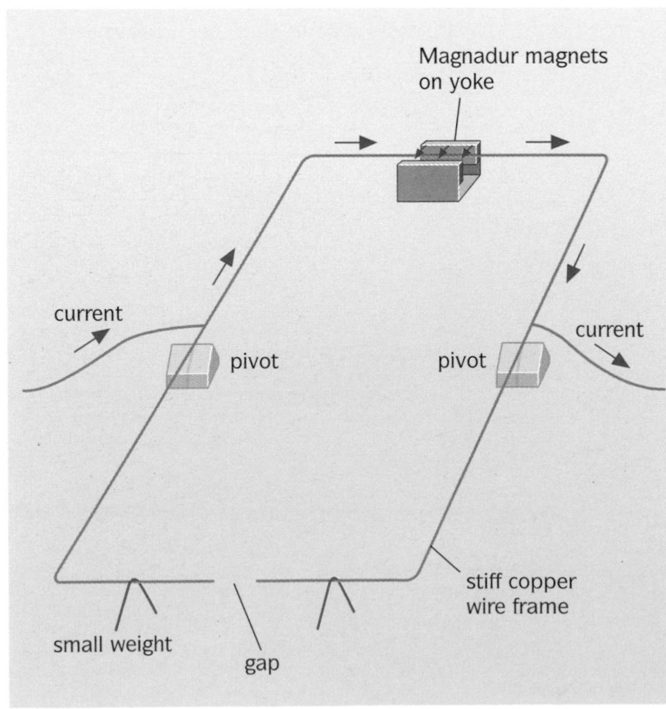

● ***Figure 9.3*** A laboratory current balance.

By adding small weights to the other side of the frame, you can restore it to a balanced position. The magnetic force must be equal to the restoring weight.

With this arrangement, you can investigate the factors that affect the size of the force F. As you might guess, F depends on:

- the magnetic field strength (flux density) B;
- the current I;
- the length l of the conductor in the magnetic field.

It is not unreasonable to suppose that the force will be greater in a stronger field, if the current is greater, and if there is a greater length of conductor in the field. In fact, F is proportional to each of these quantities. We can write an equation to sum this up:

$$F = BIl$$

(The force on a current in a field is sometimes known as 'the BIl force'.)

We should have written this as a proportionality, $F \propto BIl$. However, we use this equation to define magnetic flux density. The correct way to think of this is as follows:

When a current I flows through a conductor of length l in a magnetic field, it feels a force F. The stronger the field, the greater the force. We say that the strength of the field B is given by

$$B = \frac{F}{Il}$$

A magnetic field has a strength of one tesla (1 T) if it exerts a force of 1 N on a conductor of length 1 m, carrying a current of 1 A at right-angles to the field.

Thus the equation $B = F/Il$ defines the quantity **magnetic field strength** (flux density) B, and its unit, the tesla:

$$1\,\mathrm{T} = 1\,\mathrm{N\,A^{-1}\,m^{-1}}$$

Currents crossing fields

We explained the force on a current-carrying conductor in a field in terms of the interaction of the two magnetic fields: the field due to the

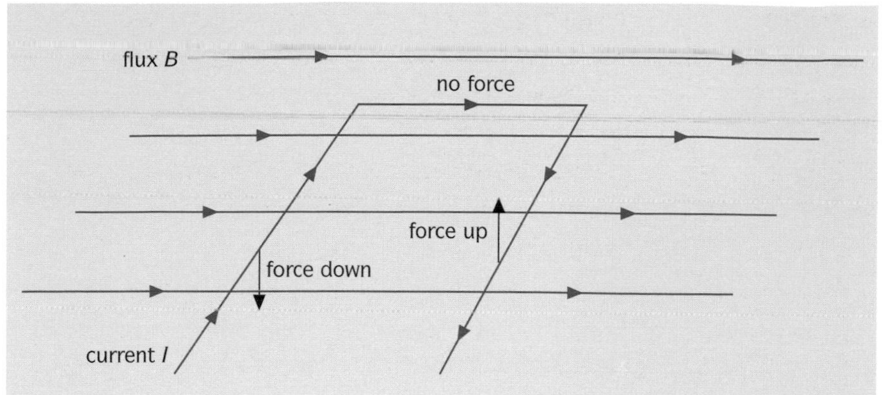

● ***Figure 9.4*** The force on a current crossing a magnetic field.

current, and the external field. Here is another, more abstract, way of thinking of this:

Whenever an electric current flows so that it cuts across lines of magnetic flux *(figure 9.4)*, a force is exerted on the current. We imagine that it is the cutting across of flux by current that creates the force.

This is a useful idea, because it saves us thinking about the field due to the current. In the diagram, we can see that there is only a force when the current cuts across the flux. Where the current flows parallel to the flux, there is no force, since no flux is cut.

Now we must consider the situation where the current cuts across a magnetic field at an angle other than a right-angle. In *figure 9.5*, the force gets weaker as the conductor is moved round from OA (angle $\theta = 90°$) to OB, OC and finally to OD (no force, angle $\theta = 0°$). To calculate the force, we need to find the component of the current that is flowing across the field. This is $I \sin\theta$, and so the $F = BIl$ equation becomes

$$F = BIl \sin\theta.$$

This force is very important – it is the basis of electric motors. A current flows through a coil of wire in a magnetic field, and the resulting forces turn the coil.

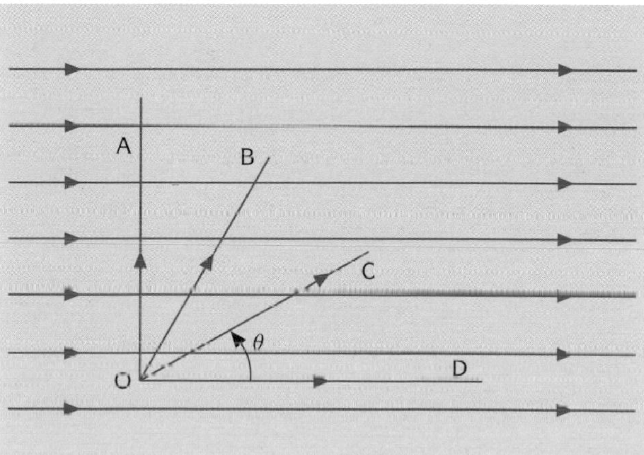

● ***Figure 9.5*** The force on a current depends on the angle it makes with the magnetic flux.

Let us now look at an example. An electric motor has a loop of wire with the dimensions shown in *figure 9.6*. The loop is in a magnetic field of flux density 0.1 T, and a current of 2 A flows through it. Calculate the torque (moment) that acts on the loop in the position shown.

Using the equation $F = BIl$, $B = 0.1\,\text{T}$, $I = 2\,\text{A}$ and $l = 0.05\,\text{m}$, we can calculate the force on one side of the loop as $F = 0.1\,\text{T} \times 2\,\text{A} \times 0.05\,\text{m} = 0.01\,\text{N}$.

The two forces on opposite sides of the loop are equal and anti-parallel; in other words, they form a couple. From the *Foundation Physics* module, you should recall that the torque (moment) of a couple is equal to the magnitude of one of the forces times the perpendicular distance between them. The two sides of the loop are separated by 0.1 m, so the

$$\begin{aligned} \text{torque} &= \text{force} \times \text{separation} \\ &= 0.01\,\text{N} \times 0.1\,\text{m} = 0.001\,\text{N m} \end{aligned}$$

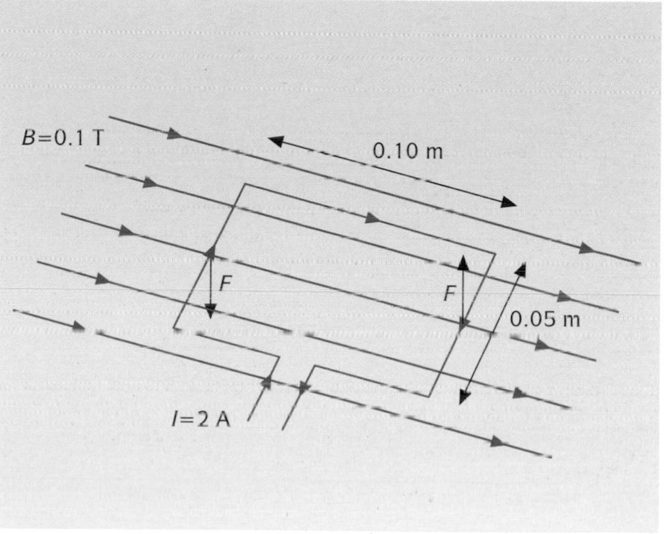

● ***Figure 9.6*** Current flowing in a small loop.

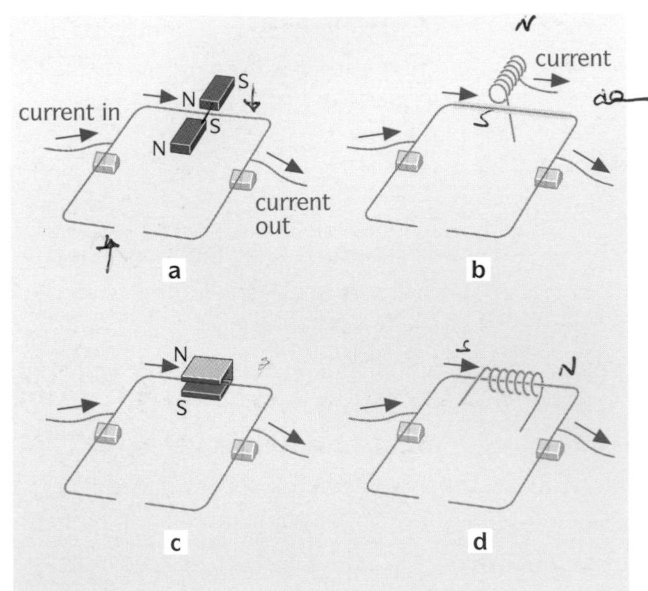

● ***Figure 9.7*** Four current balances.

SAQ 9.1

In the examples shown in the diagrams in *figure 9.7*, which current balances will tilt? Will the side carrying the current tilt upwards or downwards?

SAQ 9.2

A current balance can be used to measure the strength of a magnetic field. In the example shown in *figure 9.8*, a current of 0.5A is flowing, and a student finds that a counterweight of mass 0.02g is needed to restore balance. The section of the conductor in the field is 5cm long. What is the flux density of the field?

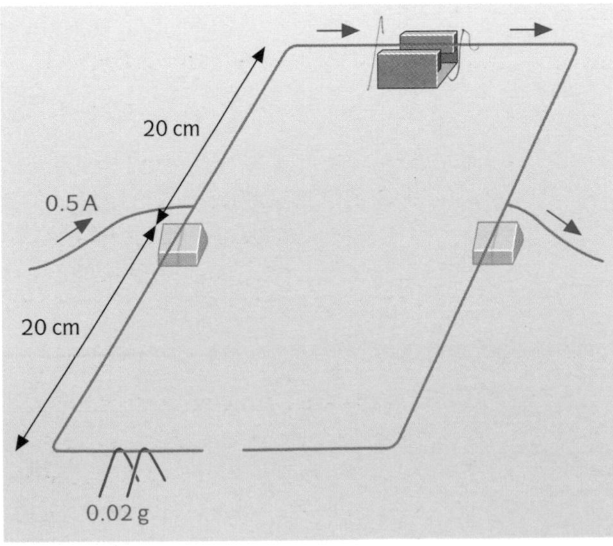

● ***Figure 9.8*** A current balance.

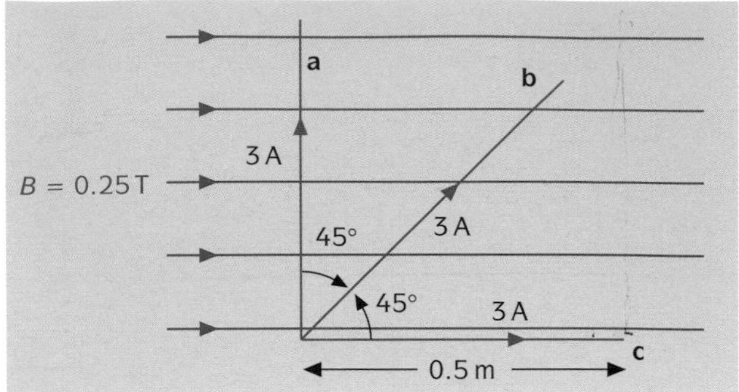

● ***Figure 9.9*** Three currents crossing a magnetic field.

SAQ 9.3

The force on a current in a field depends on its direction relative to the field. What force will be exerted on each of the currents shown in *figure 9.9*, and in what direction will it act?

SAQ 9.4

The coil of an electric motor is made up of 200 turns of wire carrying a current of 1A. The coil is square, with sides of length 20cm, and it is in a magnetic field of flux density 0.05T.

a What is the greatest force exerted on the side of the coil?

b In what position must the coil be for this force to have its greatest turning effect?

c List **four** ways in which the motor could be made more powerful.

The magnetic force on a moving charge

Any moving charge constitutes an electric current. It creates a magnetic field around itself, and this can interact with an external magnetic field – this is the origin of the motor effect (page 67).

We can make an intelligent guess about the factors that determine the size of the force on a moving charge in a magnetic field *(figure 9.10)*. It will depend on:

- the strength of the magnetic field (flux density), B;
- the charge on the particle, Q;
- the speed with which it is moving, v.

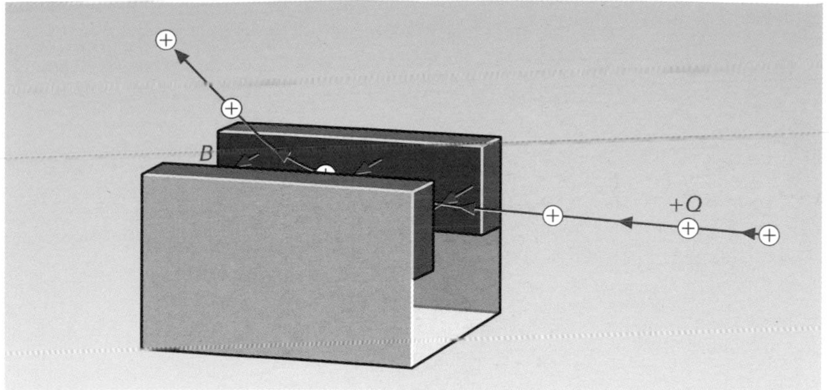

● **Figure 9.10** The path of a charged particle is curved in a magnetic field.

In the same way that we guessed the equation $F = BIl$, we can guess the equation for the force on a charge moving in a direction at right-angles to the magnetic field:

$$F = BQv$$

If the particle is moving at an angle θ to the magnetic field, this equation becomes

$$F = BQv \sin \theta$$

We can show that the two equations $F = BIl$ and $F = BQv$ are consistent with one another, as follows. Since current I is the rate of flow of charge, we can write $I = Q/t$. Substituting in $F = BIl$ gives

$$F = BQl/t$$

Now, l/t is the speed v of the moving particle, and so we can write

$$F = BQv$$

For an electron, whose charge is $-e$, the force on it is

$$F = -Bev$$

(The force on a moving charge is sometimes called 'the *Bev* force', and it is really no different from the *BIl* force.)

It is important to note that the force F is always at right-angles to the particle's velocity v, and its direction can be found using the left-hand rule *(figure 9.11)*. Because F is perpendicular to v, a particle moving in a magnetic field will travel along a circular path. We can describe F as a centripetal force, because it is always directed towards the centre of the circle.

SAQ 9.5

A beam of electrons, moving at $10^6 \, \mathrm{m\,s^{-1}}$, is directed through a magnetic field of flux density 0.5T. Calculate the force on each electron if **a** the beam is at right-angles to the magnetic flux, and **b** if it is at an angle of 45° to the flux.

(Note: magnitude of electron charge $e = 1.6 \times 10^{-19}$C.)

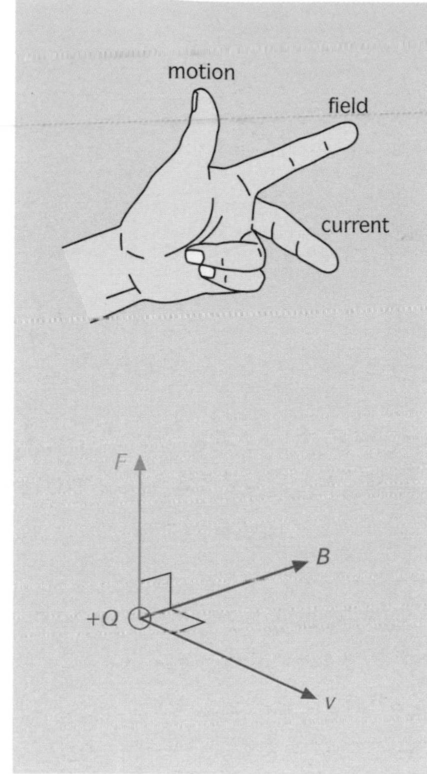

● **Figure 9.11** Fleming's left-hand rule, applied to a moving positive charge.

SAQ 9.6

An electron beam in a vacuum tube is directed at right-angles to a magnetic field, so that it travels along a circular path. Predict the effect on the size and shape of the path that would be produced by each of the following changes:

a Increasing the magnetic field.

b Reversing the magnetic field.

c Slowing down the electrons.

d Tilting the beam, so that the electrons have a component of velocity along the magnetic field.

SAQ 9.7

Positrons are particles identical to electrons, except that their charge is positive ($+e$). Suggest how a magnetic field could be used to separate a mixed beam of positrons and electrons.

Investigation

A deflection tube *(figure 9.12)* is designed to show a beam of electrons passing through a combination of electric and magnetic fields. By adjusting the strengths of the fields, you can balance the two forces on the electrons, and the beam will remain horizontal.

To find the speed of the electrons emerging from the anode, you need to know the cathode–anode voltage, V_{ca}. An individual electron has charge $-e$, and an amount of work $e \times V_{ca}$ is done on it in accelerating it from the cathode to the anode. This is its kinetic energy:

$$eV_{ca} = \tfrac{1}{2}m_e v^2$$

If the electron beam remains straight, it follows that the electric and magnetic forces on each electron are balanced:

$$eV/d = Bev$$

where V/d is the electric field strength between the two deflection plates.

Combining these two equations (to eliminate v) gives

$$\frac{e}{m_e} = \frac{V^2}{2V_{ca}B^2d^2}$$

If you can measure the voltages V and V_{ca}, the flux density B and the plate separation d, you can now find the charge:mass ratio of an individual electron. Since we know the electron charge $-e = -1.6\times10^{-19}$C, you can also use this experiment to find the electron mass m_e.

In this experiment, there are three variables that you might consider changing. Draw up a plan showing the following points:

- What factors will you vary?
- How will you vary them in a systematic way?
- What will you measure?
- How will you record and process your results?
- What patterns will you expect to see in your results?

Carry out the investigation, and use your results to find values for e/m_e and m_e.

[Note: The magnetic field is provided by two coils, called Helmholtz coils *(figure 9.13)*, which give a very uniform field in the space between them. Each coil has N turns and they are separated by a distance r, which is equal to the radius of the coil. To find the strength of the magnetic field, you need to measure the current I flowing through them. Then the flux density B is given by $B = 9.05\times10^{-7}\times NI/r$.]

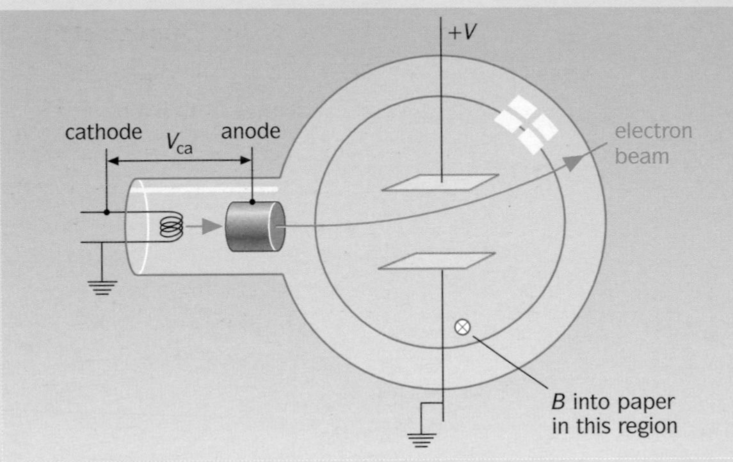

● **Figure 9.12** The path of an electron beam in a deflection tube.

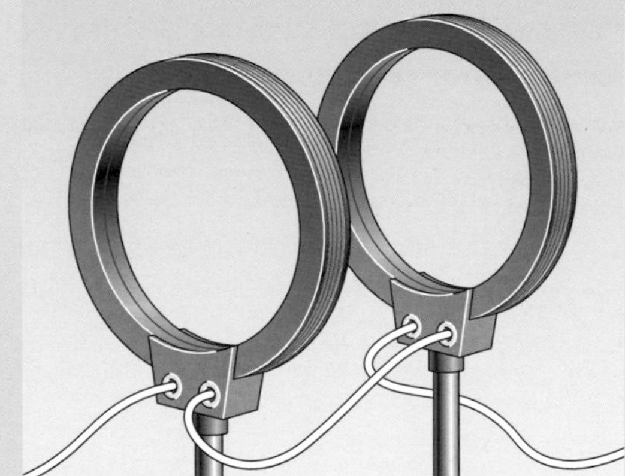

● **Figure 9.13** A pair of Helmholtz coils is used to give a uniform magnetic field.

Measuring magnetic flux density

The simplest device for measuring magnetic flux density B is a Hall probe *(figure 9.14)*. When the probe is held so that the field lines are passing at right-angles through the flat face of the probe, the meter gives a reading of the value of B. Some instruments are calibrated so that they give readings in microteslas (μT) or milliteslas (mT). Others are not calibrated, so you must either calibrate them, or use them to obtain relative measurements of B.

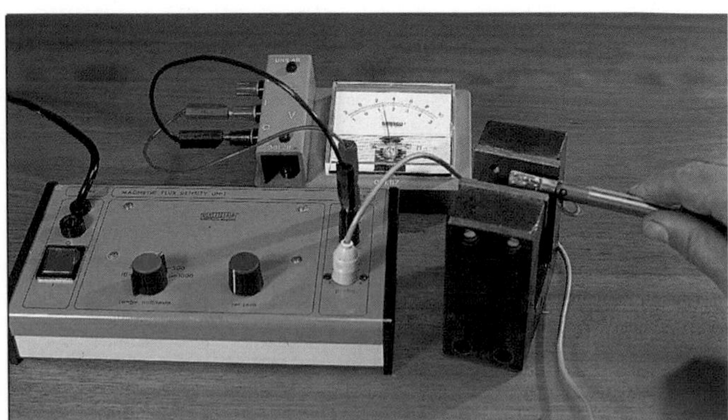

● **Figure 9.14** A Hall probe can be used to measure the flux density of a magnetic field.

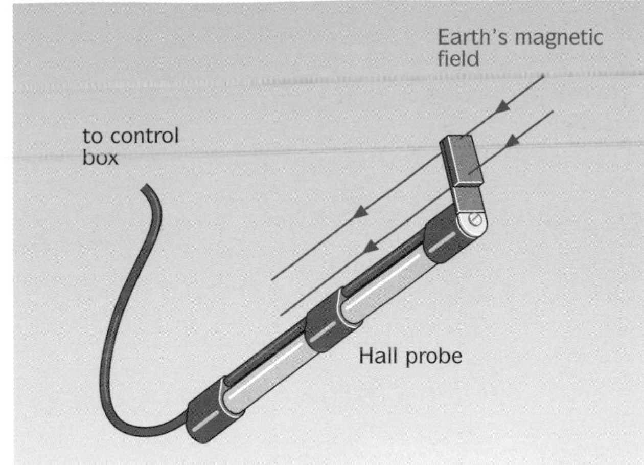

● ***Figure 9.15*** Using a Hall probe to measure the flux density of the Earth's magnetic field.

A Hall probe is sensitive enough to measure the Earth's magnetic flux density. The probe is first held so that the Earth's field lines are passing directly through it *(figure 9.15)*. It is then rapidly rotated so that the field lines are passing through the probe in the opposite direction. The change in the reading of the meter is twice the Earth's flux density.

If the probe is not held in the correct orientation, the reading on the meter will be reduced.

How a Hall probe works

The probe is a slice of semiconductor *(figure 9.16)*. This material is used because the electrons move much faster in a semiconductor than in a metal for a given current, and so the effect is much greater. A small current flows through the probe, from one end to the other. When a magnetic field is applied, the electrons are pushed sideways by the *Bev* force, so that they accumulate along one side of the probe. This is detected as a small voltage across the probe. The control box amplifies the voltage, and it is displayed by the meter.

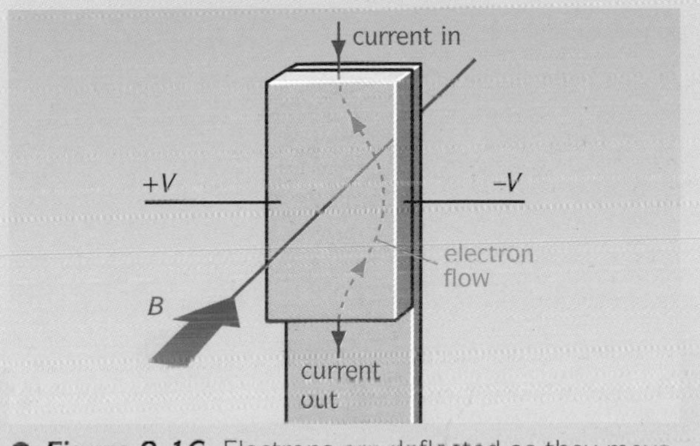

● ***Figure 9.16*** Electrons are deflected as they move through the Hall probe.

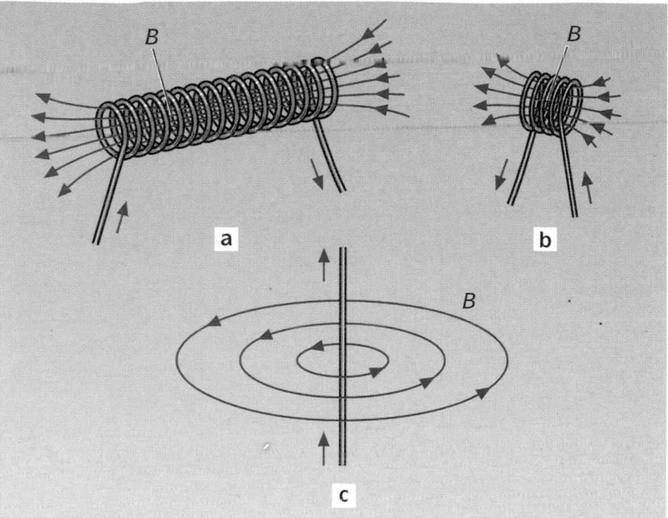

● ***Figure 9.17*** Magnetic flux produced by a current flowing in **a** a long solenoid, **b** a flat circular coil and **c** a long straight wire.

Calculating B

There are three useful equations for calculating the magnetic flux density produced by a current in the three important situations shown in *figure 9.17*; these are given below. In each of these equations, I = current and μ_0 = a constant, the permeability of free space. In the SI system of units, this has the exact value $4\pi \times 10^{-7}\,\mathrm{H\,m^{-1}}$.

- At the centre of a long solenoid:

$$B = \mu_0 \frac{NI}{l}$$

where N = number of turns, l = length of solenoid, or

$$B = \mu_0 nI$$

where $n = N/l$ = number of turns per metre.

- At the centre of a flat circular coil:

$$B = \mu_0 \frac{NI}{2r}$$

where N = number of turns, r = radius of coil.

- Near a long straight wire:

$$B = \mu_0 \frac{I}{2\pi d}$$

where d = distance from wire.

If you look at these equations, you will see that they all have a similar form. B is proportional to the current flowing, and to the number of turns of the coil. B is also inversely proportional to some measure of length. This should not surprise you too much; for example, if you are further from a current-carrying wire, the flux density is bound to be less.

SAQ 9.8

Calculate the flux density at a distance of 10 cm from a long straight wire carrying a current of 5 A. How does this value compare with the Earth's magnetic flux density (approximately 5×10^{-5} T)?

SAQ 9.9

Calculate the flux density at the centre of a flat coil, diameter 10 cm, consisting of 20 turns of wire carrying a current of 2 A.

SAQ 9.10

A long solenoid is made by closely winding wire of thickness 0.5 mm, so that adjacent turns of wire are touching. What will be the value of the flux density at the centre of the solenoid when a current of 3 A flows?

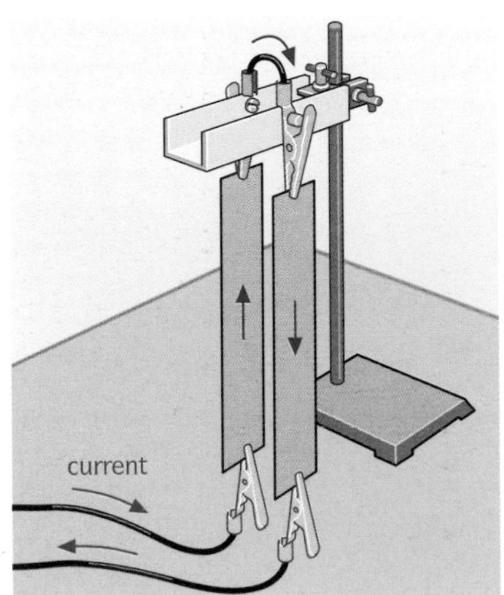

● ***Figure 9.18*** Current flowing through two aluminium foil strips.

Investigation

Use a Hall probe to investigate the equations for B given above.

- *Solenoid*
  Investigate B along the axis of a solenoid. Try varying the current. Use different solenoids with different numbers of turns per metre (different values of n) and different cross-sectional areas.
- *Coil*
  Vary the number of turns, the diameter and the current.
- *Straight wire*
  Vary the current and the distance from the wire. Rotate the probe to determine the shape of the magnetic field.

SAQ 9.11

Why is the flux density at the open end of a solenoid equal to half that at the centre of the solenoid?

Forces between currents

Any electric current has a magnetic field around it. If we have two currents, each will have its own magnetic field, and we might expect these to interact. You can observe the attraction and repulsion between two currents using the equipment shown in *figure 9.18*.

Two long thin strips of aluminium foil are mounted so that they are parallel and a small distance apart. By connecting them in series with a power supply, you can make a current flow through first one and then the other. By changing the connections, you can make the current flow first in the same direction through both strips (parallel currents) and then in opposite directions (anti-parallel currents).

If you try this out, you will observe the strips of foil either bending towards each other or away from each other. (Foil is used because it is much more flexible than wire.)

You should find that parallel currents attract one another, while anti-parallel currents repel. This may seem surprising, since we are used to opposite charges attracting, and opposite magnetic poles attracting. Now we have found that opposite currents repel one another.

Explaining the forces

There are two ways to understand the origin of these forces. In the first, we draw the magnetic fields around two current-carrying wires (*figure 9.19*). The first part of the diagram shows two unlike (anti-parallel) currents, one flowing into the page, the other flowing out of the page. Their magnetic fields circle round, and in the space between the wires there is an extra-strong field. We imagine the field lines squashed together, and the result is that they push the

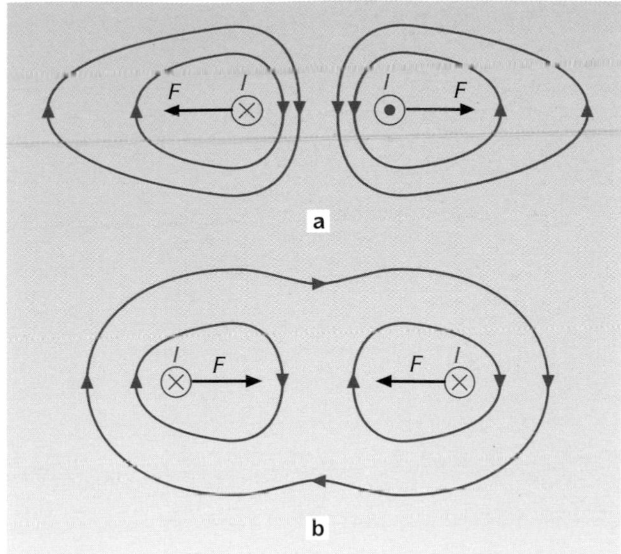

● **Figure 9.19** The forces on parallel currents.

wires apart. The diagram also shows the resultant field, and the repulsive forces on the two wires.

The second part of *figure 9.19* shows the same idea, but for two like (parallel) currents. In the space between the two wires, the magnetic fields cancel out. The wires are pushed together.

The other way to explain the forces between currents is to use the idea of the motor effect. *Figure 9.20* again shows two like currents, I_1 and I_2, but this time we only consider the magnetic field of one of them. The second current is flowing across the magnetic field of the first one; from the diagram, you can see that B is at right-angles to I_2. Hence there will be a force on I_2 (the BIl force),

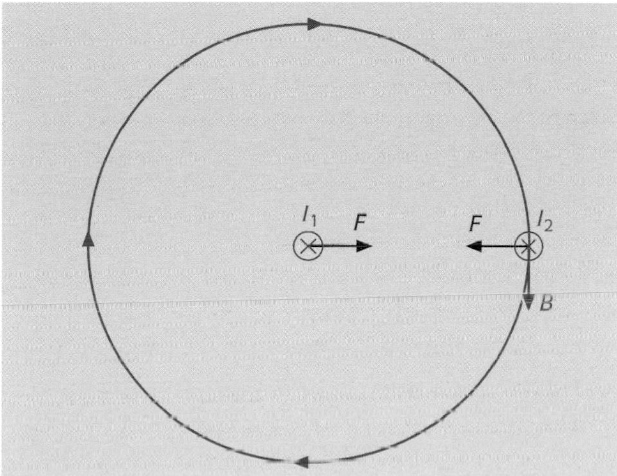

● **Figure 9.20** Explaining the force between two currents.

and we can find its direction using Fleming's left-hand rule. The arrow shows the direction of the force, which is towards I_1. Similarly, there will be a BIl force on I_1, directed towards I_2.

Calculating the forces

Because we know about the flux density near a current, and we know about the BIl force, we can calculate the force that one current exerts on another.

In *figure 9.21*, two wires are shown. They are each of length l, and they are separated by d metres. They carry currents I_1 and I_2. We calculate the force on wire 2 in two steps. First we find the flux density B at wire 2 due to I_1:

$$B = \mu_0 I_1/(2\pi d)$$

Now we can find the force F on wire 2:

$$F = BI_2 l = \mu_0 I_1 I_2 l/(2\pi d)$$

It is more usual to express this as the force per unit length, F/l, which acts on the wire:

$$\frac{F}{l} = \mu_0 \frac{I_1 I_2}{2\pi d}$$

We shall now do a worked example. Two long straight parallel wires are fixed 2 cm apart. Currents of 2 A and 5 A flow through the two wires respectively. What is the force per unit length

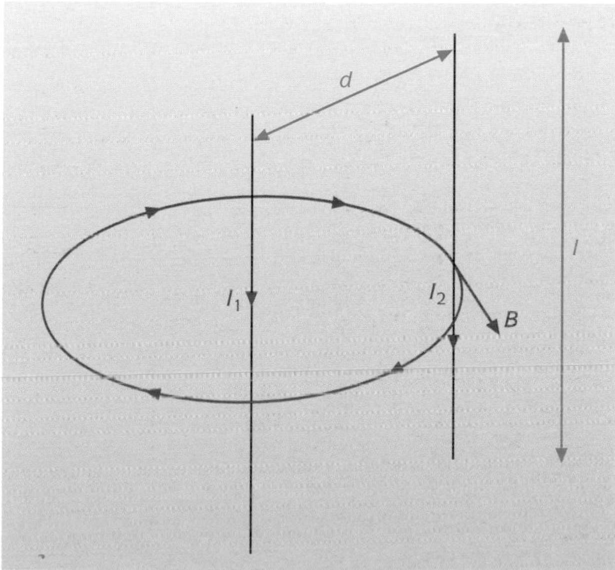

● **Figure 9.21** Calculating the force between two currents.

acting on each wire?

We have $\mu_0 = 4\pi \times 10^{-7}\,\mathrm{H\,m^{-1}}$, $I_1 = 2\,\mathrm{A}$, $I_2 = 5\,\mathrm{A}$, $d = 0.02\,\mathrm{m}$. Hence

$$F/l = \mu_0 I_1 I_2/2\pi d = 4\pi \times 10^{-7}\,\mathrm{H\,m^{-1}} \times 2\,\mathrm{A} \times 5\,\mathrm{A}/(2\pi \times 0.02\,\mathrm{m}) = 10^{-4}\,\mathrm{N\,m^{-1}}$$

So a force of 10^{-4} N acts on each metre of wire. This is a small force, even for reasonably large currents separated by a small distance. This explains why we use flexible strips of foil to observe the effect.

SAQ 9.12

The flex of an electric heater is 2 m long. It contains a live wire and a neutral wire, each carrying the same current of 8 A, but in opposite directions. If the wires are separated by 5 mm, what force will each exert on the other? Will they attract or repel each other?

SAQ 9.13

Two long parallel wires carry parallel currents. Wire 1 carries 1 A, and wire 2 carries 100 A. Which force is greater, the force on wire 2 due to the current in wire 1, or the force on wire 1 due to the current in wire 2? Justify your answer.

SAQ 9.14

Two flat circular coils of wire are set up side by side, as shown in *figure 9.22*. They are connected in series so that the same current flows around each, and in the same direction. Will the coils attract or repel one another? Explain your answer first by describing the coils as electromagnets, and secondly by considering the forces between parallel currents. What will happen if both currents are reversed?

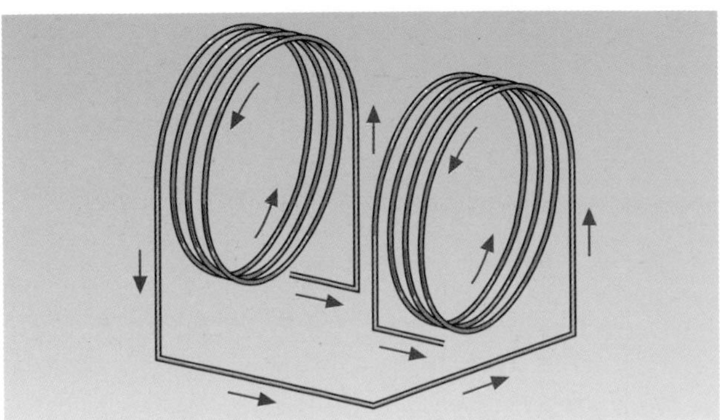

● ***Figure 9.22*** Two coils carrying the same current.

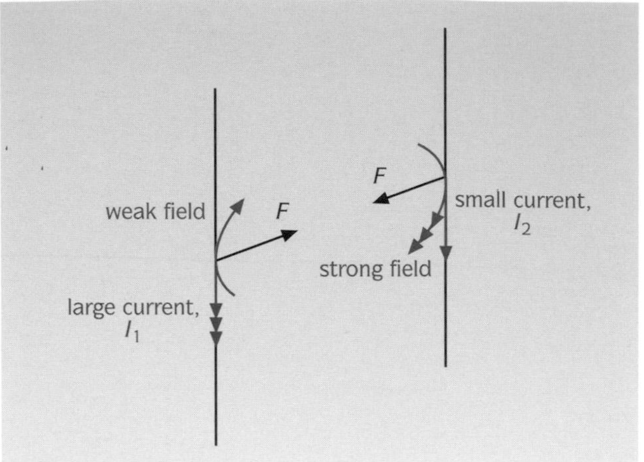

● ***Figure 9.23*** Two currents of different magnitudes are attracted by equal, opposite forces.

Magnitudes of forces

If a big current flows parallel to a small current, which will feel the greater force? *Figure 9.23* shows this situation. Will wire 2 feel a bigger force, because it is in the strong field due to current 1? Will wire 1 feel the bigger force, because a big current feels a big *BIl* force? We can answer this by considering the expression for F/l:

$$\frac{F}{l} = \mu_0 \frac{I_1 I_2}{2\pi d}$$

We can see that F/l depends on both I_1 and I_2. It doesn't matter which current we consider to be I_1 and which I_2, we get the same answer for F/l. The big current is sitting in a weak field due to the small current, and the small current is sitting in a strong field due to the big current. The resulting force is the same. You may have come to this conclusion in your answer to SAQ 9.13 above.

Figure 9.24a shows the correct answer, a pair of equal and opposite forces. These are a pair of forces, which can be thought of as 'action and reaction' in Newton's third law of motion. They are equal in magnitude, but opposite in direction. They are both of the same type (electromagnetic), and they act on different bodies (the two wires).

As usual with Newton's third law, it can help to think about the consequences if these forces were not equal and opposite. This is shown in *figure 9.24b*. One wire feels a bigger force than the other.

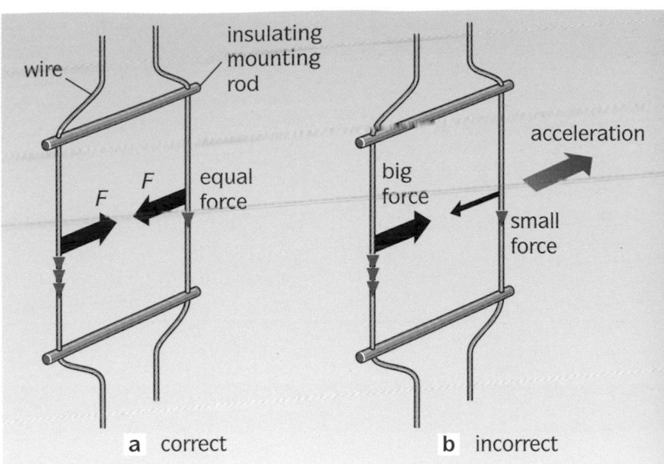

● **Figure 9.24** The attractive forces are an action–reaction pair.

● **Figure 9.25** This current balance at the National Physical Laboratory is used to calibrate meters to a high degree of accuracy.

We could fix these two wires into a spacecraft, switch on the currents, and the unbalanced force would accelerate us rapidly into space. If we used superconducting wires, we would need no energy at all to keep accelerating!

Defining the ampere

The force between two currents gives us an unambiguous way of defining the unit of current, the ampere. We picture two long wires, each carrying a current of 1 A. They are separated by 1 m. What is the force between them?

Using $F/l = \mu_0 I_1 I_2 / 2\pi d$, it follows that $F/l = 4\pi \times 10^{-7}\,\mathrm{H\,m^{-1}} \times 1\,\mathrm{A} \times 1\,\mathrm{A}/2\pi \times 1\,\mathrm{m}$ $= 2 \times 10^{-7}\,\mathrm{N\,m^{-1}}$. Hence the force between two currents, each of 1 A, flowing in two long straight parallel wires 1 m apart is 2×10^{-7} N per metre of their length. This means that, by measuring the force between two currents, we can find their sizes.

In practice, this type of measurement is made using an elaborate form of current balance, such as the one shown in *figure 9.25*. By defining the ampere in this way, it is possible for scientists in different laboratories in different countries to be sure that they all mean the same thing when they talk about currents in amperes.

The ampere is defined in terms of the force (in newtons) between two wires. Newtons are defined in terms of kilograms, metres and seconds, three of the base units of the SI system. The ampere is a fourth base unit, and allows us to relate electrical units to the other units of the SI system.

The chart *(figure 9.26)* shows how, having defined the ampere, we can go on to define other electrical units in terms of the base units. For example, the equation $F = BIl$ shows how the tesla is related to the ampere:

$$B = \frac{F}{Il} \quad \text{so} \quad 1\,\mathrm{T} = 1\,\mathrm{N\,A^{-1}\,m^{-1}}$$

SAQ 9.15

How are the following units related to the base units (m, kg, s, A) of the SI system: coulomb C, volt V, farad F, tesla T?

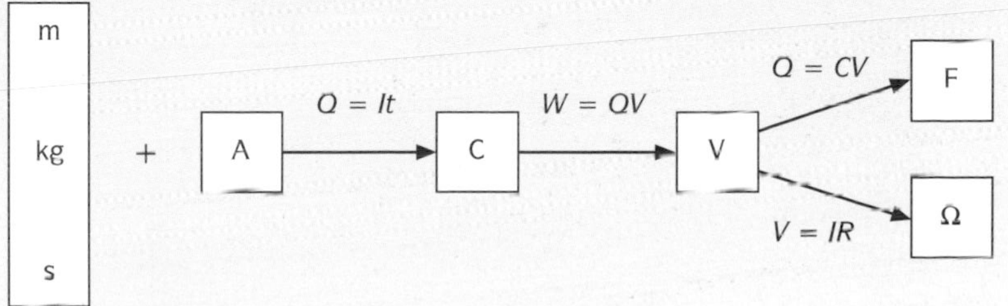

● **Figure 9.26** Relationships between units in the SI system.

SUMMARY

- We describe the strength of a magnetic field in terms of magnetic flux density.
- We measure the flux density of a field using a Hall probe, or using a current balance.
- The force on a current-carrying conductor in a magnetic field is given by $F = BIl \sin\theta$; this arises from the force on the moving charges within the conductor, given by $F = BQv \sin\theta$.
- We can calculate the flux density near a coil or wire.
- There is a force between two parallel currents, and this is used as the basis of the definition of the ampere.

Questions

1 Use your knowledge of the forces on charged particles to work out where the electron beam will strike the screen in the tube shown in *figure 9.27*. Break the problem into small steps as follows.

Note: electron charge $-e = -1.6 \times 10^{-19}$ C; electron mass $m_e = 9.11 \times 10^{-31}$ kg.

- **a** Electrons are attracted from the cathode to the anode by the potential difference between them. Calculate the kinetic energy gained by an electron as it accelerates from the cathode to the anode, and use this value to calculate the speed of the electron.
- **b** In this tube, the electron beam is deflected by the electric field between two parallel plates. Calculate the strength of the field, and the force on a single electron.
- **c** The horizontal component of the electron's velocity is not affected by the electric field. Why is this? Calculate the time the electron takes to travel through the space between the plates.
- **d** The electrons are accelerated upwards by the electric force on them. Calculate their acceleration, and use your answer to deduce the upward component of the electron's velocity as it emerges from the space between the plates.
- **e** From your knowledge of the components of the electron's velocity, calculate the angle ϕ.
- **f** Calculate how far up the screen the beam will strike.
- **g** Explain how your answer would differ if the anode–cathode voltage was increased, and if the voltage between the deflecting plates was increased.
- **h** The beam can be restored to its horizontal path if a magnetic field is applied in the region between the two parallel plates. Calculate the flux density B needed to do this. In what direction must the magnetic field act?

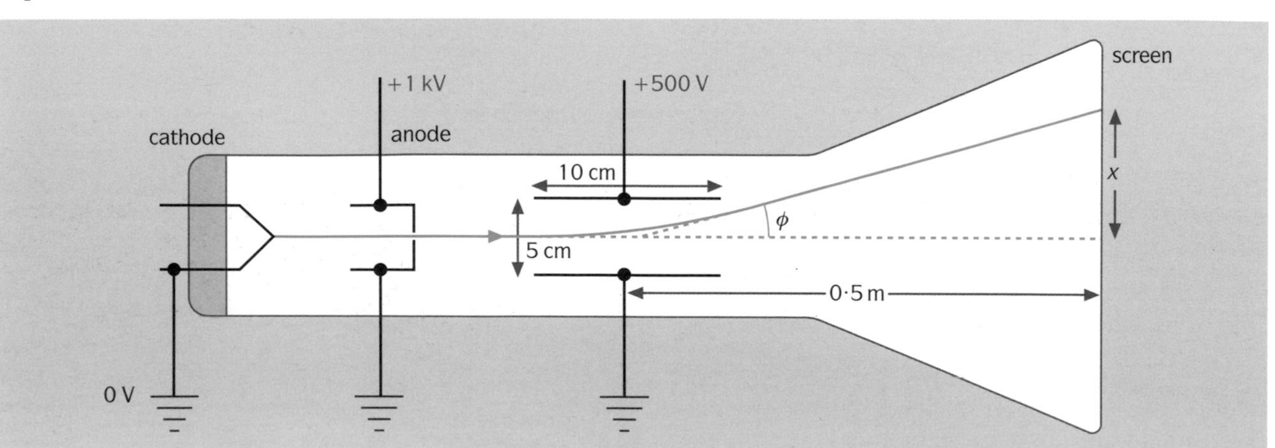

● ***Figure 9.27*** A cathode-ray tube.

Electromagnetic induction 1

By the end of this chapter you should be able to:

1 understand qualitatively the meaning of *magnetic flux* and *magnetic flux linkage*;

2 describe and interpret experiments that demonstrate the relationship between the magnitude and direction of an induced e.m.f. and the change of flux linkage producing the e.m.f.

Generating electricity

Most of the electricity we use is generated by electromagnetic induction. This process goes on in the generators at work in power stations and, on a much smaller scale, in bicycle dynamos. It is the process whereby electricity and magnetism combine to induce or generate a current or voltage.

Here are some simple experiments in which you can observe some of the features of electromagnetic induction. In each case, try to predict what you will observe before you try the experiment.

● **Figure 10.1** These giant wind turbines drive generators, which use electromagnetic induction to produce electricity.

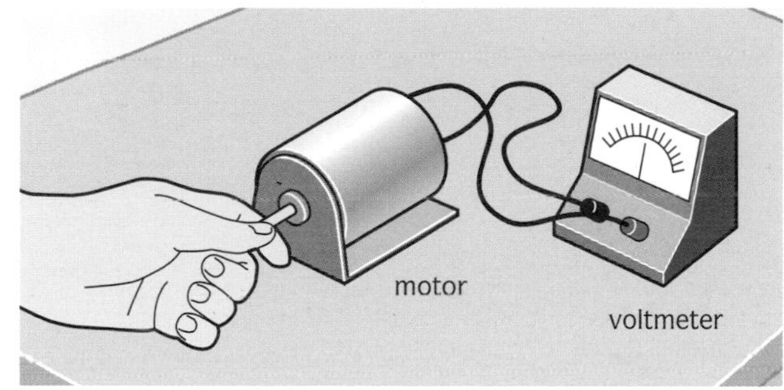

● **Figure 10.2** A motor works in reverse as a generator.

■ *Experiment 1*

Connect a small electric motor to a moving-coil voltmeter *(figure 10.2)*. Spin the shaft of the motor and observe the deflection of the meter. What happens when you spin the motor more slowly? What happens when you stop?

Usually, we connect a motor to the voltage provided by a power supply, and it turns. In this experiment, you have turned the motor and it generates a voltage. A generator is like a motor working in reverse.

■ *Experiment 2*

Connect a solenoid to a sensitive microammeter, such as a light beam galvanometer *(figure 10.3)*. Move a bar magnet in towards the coil. Hold it still, and then remove it. How does the deflection on the meter change? Try different speeds, and the other pole of the magnet. Try weak and strong magnets.

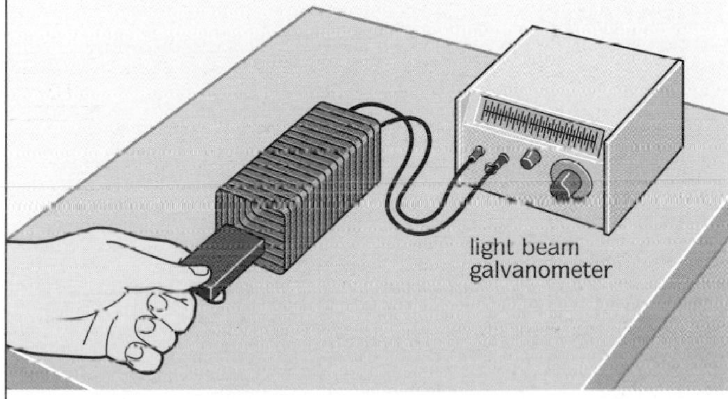

● **Figure 10.3** A moving magnet near a coil generates a small current.

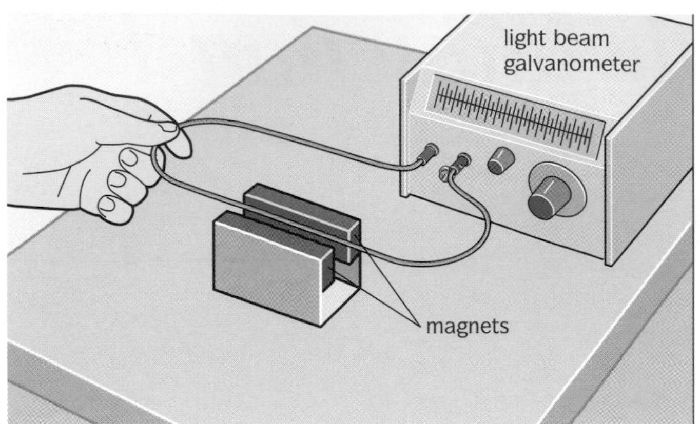

● ***Figure 10.4*** Investigating the current induced when a wire moves through a magnetic field.

With the same equipment, move the coil towards the magnet and observe the deflection of the meter.

■ *Experiment 3*
Connect a long wire to the sensitive meter. Move the middle section up and down between the poles of a horseshoe magnet *(figure 10.4)*. Double up the wire so that twice as much passes through the magnetic field. What happens to the meter reading? How can you form the wire into a loop to give twice the deflection on the meter?

In all these experiments, you have seen an electric current generated or induced. In each case, there is a magnetic field and a conductor. When you move the magnet or the conductor, the induced current flows. When you stop, the current stops.

Explaining electromagnetic induction

Magnetic flux

You have seen that relative movement of a conductor and a magnetic field induces a current to flow in the conductor, if the conductor is part of a complete circuit. (In the experiments above, the meter was used to complete the circuit.) Now we need to think about how to explain these observations, using what we know about magnetic fields.

Start by thinking about a simple bar magnet. It creates a magnetic field in the space around it. We represent this field by lines of force *(figure 10.5)*. It can help to think of these as lines of magnetic flux. 'Flux' means something that flows, and we picture magnetic flux flowing out of the north pole of the magnet, round to the south pole.

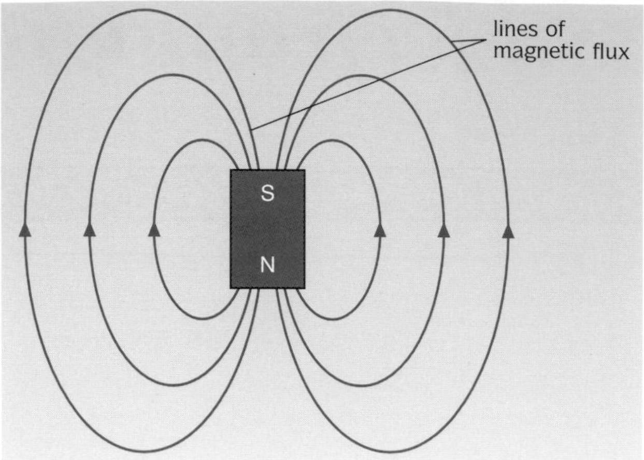

● ***Figure 10.5*** Magnetic flux around a permanent bar magnet.

(The idea of flux is very useful, particularly to electrical engineers, who often trace the flow of magnetic flux around a magnetic circuit, just as we can trace the flow of electric current around an electric circuit.)

Now think about what happens when a wire is moved into the magnetic field *(figure 10.6)*. As it moves, it cuts across the magnetic flux. Remove the wire from the field, and again it must cut across the flux, but in the opposite direction.

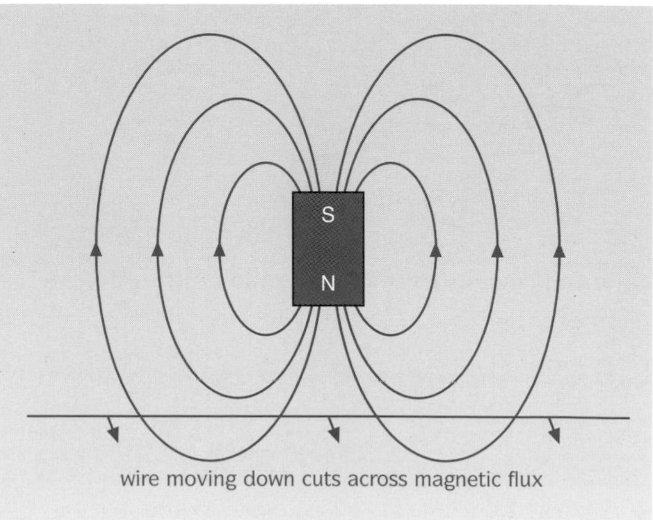

● ***Figure 10.6*** Inducing a current by moving a conductor through a magnetic field.

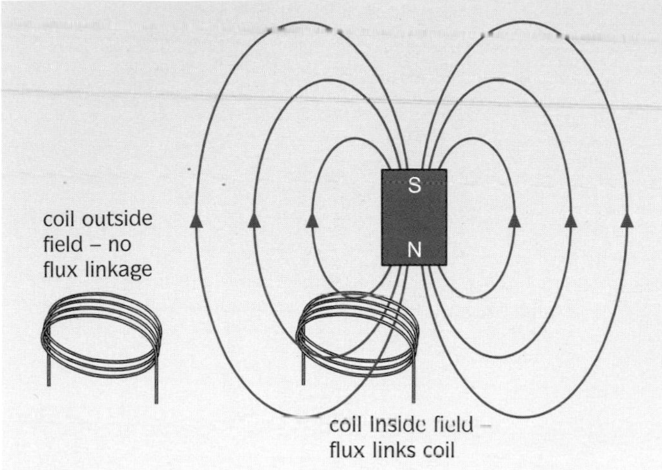

● ***Figure 10.7*** The flux linking a coil changes as it is moved in to and out of a magnetic field.

We think of this cutting of flux by a conductor as the effect that gives rise to an induced current flowing in the conductor. It doesn't matter whether the conductor is moved through the field, or the magnet is moved past the conductor, the result is the same – an induced current flows.

The effect is magnified if we use a coil of wire. Each bit of wire cuts across the magnetic flux, and so each contributes to the induced current. For a coil of N turns, the effect is N times greater than for a single turn of wire.

Another way to think of this is to talk about the flux that 'links' the coil *(figure 10.7)*. When the coil is outside the field, no flux links it. When it is inside the field, flux links it by flowing through it. Moving the coil in to or out of the field changes the flux linkage, and this induces a current.

Current direction

How can we predict the direction in which an induced current will flow? For the motor effect in chapter 8, we used Fleming's left-hand rule. Electromagnetic induction is like the mirror image of the motor effect. Instead of a current flowing across a magnetic field and movement resulting, we have movement of a conductor across a magnetic field, and a current results. So you should not be too surprised to find that we use the mirror image of the left-hand rule: **Fleming's right-hand rule.**

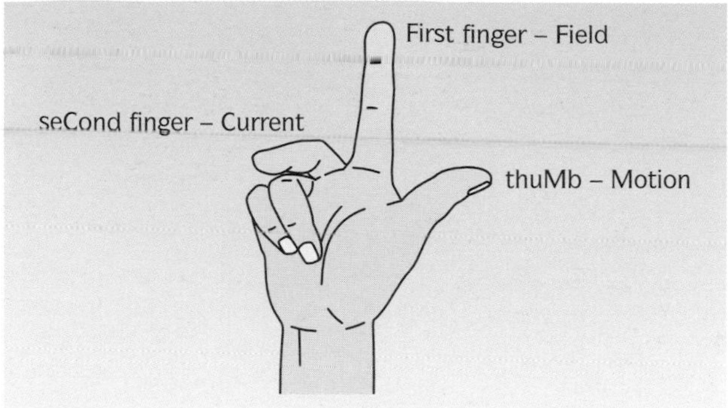

● ***Figure 10.8*** Fleming's right-hand rule.

The three fingers represent the same things again *(figure 10.8)*:

- thuMb – Motion
- First finger – Field
- seCond finger – Current

In the example shown in *figure 10.9*, the conductor is being moved downwards across the magnetic flux, which is flowing as shown, from north to south. The induced current flows in the conductor as shown. Check this with your own right hand. You should also check that reversing the movement or the field will result in the current flowing in the opposite direction.

Induced e.m.f.

Because a conductor is not always part of a complete circuit, the induced current cannot always flow all the way round a circuit. Instead, positive charge will accumulate at one end of the conductor, leaving the other end negatively charged. We have created a voltage between the ends of the conductor.

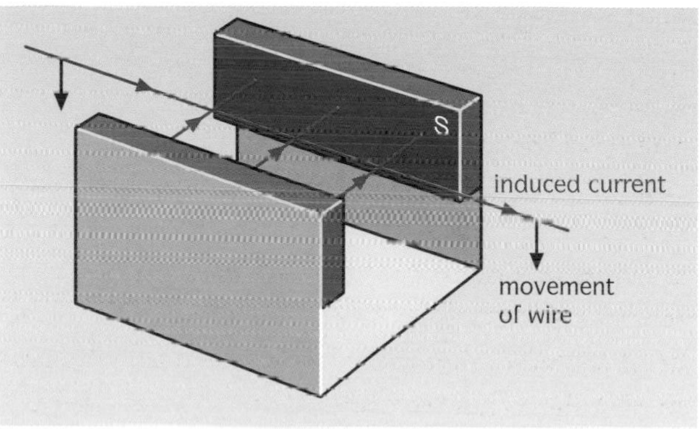

● ***Figure 10.9*** Deducing the direction of the induced current.

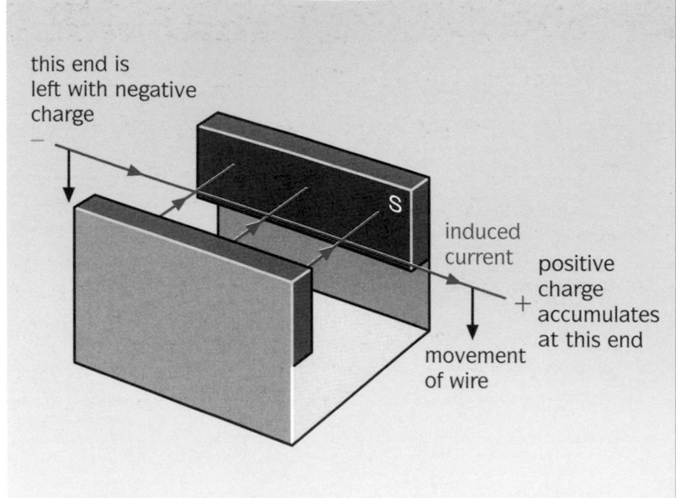

● ***Figure 10.10*** A voltage is induced across the ends of the conductor.

Is this voltage a potential difference or an e.m.f.? (Recall the distinction between these two types of voltage, which was discussed in chapter 5.)

Since we could connect the ends of the conductor so that it made a current flow through some other component, such as a lamp, which would light up, it must be an e.m.f. – a source of electrical energy. *Figure 10.10* shows how the induced current gives rise to an induced e.m.f. Notice that, within the conductor, current flows from negative to positive, in the same way that it does inside a battery or any other source of e.m.f.

From the three experiments in the above section, you should see that the size of the induced e.m.f. depends on several factors.

For a *straight wire*:

- the strength of the magnetic field;
- the length of the wire;
- the speed of movement of the wire.

For a *coil of wire*:

- the strength of the magnetic field;
- the area of the coil;
- the number of turns of wire;
- the rate at which the coil turns in the field.

You should be able to see that, for the coil, all of these factors contribute to the rate at which the flux linking the coil changes.

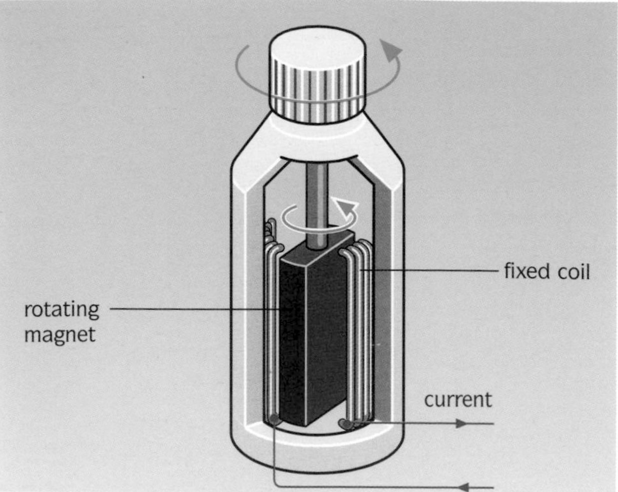

● ***Figure 10.11*** In a bicycle dynamo, a permanent magnet rotates inside a fixed coil of wire.

SAQ 10.1

Use the idea of magnetic flux to explain how a bicycle dynamo *(figure 10.11)* generates electricity.

SAQ 10.2

Use the idea of magnetic flux linkage to explain why, when a magnet is moved into a coil, the e.m.f. induced depends on the strength of the magnet and the speed at which it is moved.

SAQ 10.3

The coil in *figure 10.12* is rotating in a uniform magnetic field. In which direction will the induced current flow in side AB, and in side CD? Which terminal, X or Y, will become positive?

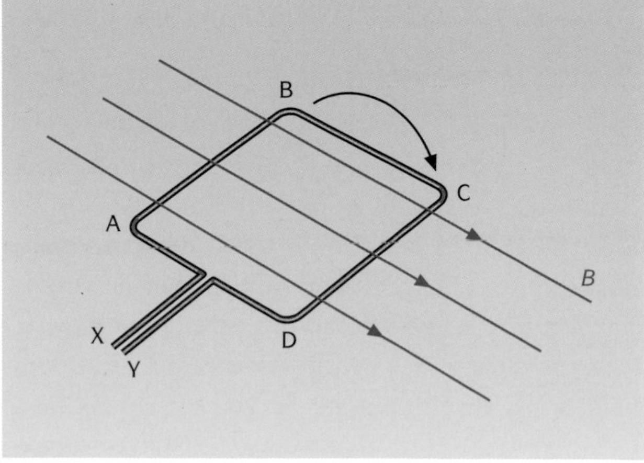

● ***Figure 10.12*** A coil rotates in a magnetic field.

SAQ 10.4

When an aircraft flies from east to west, its wings are an electrical conductor cutting across the Earth's magnetic flux. In the Northern Hemisphere, which wingtip will become positively charged? Why will this wingtip be negative in the Southern Hemisphere?

SAQ 10.5

In an experiment to investigate the factors that affect the magnitude of an induced e.m.f., a student moves a wire back and forth between two magnets, as shown in *figure 10.13*. Explain why the e.m.f. generated in this way is much smaller than if the wire is moved up and down in the field.

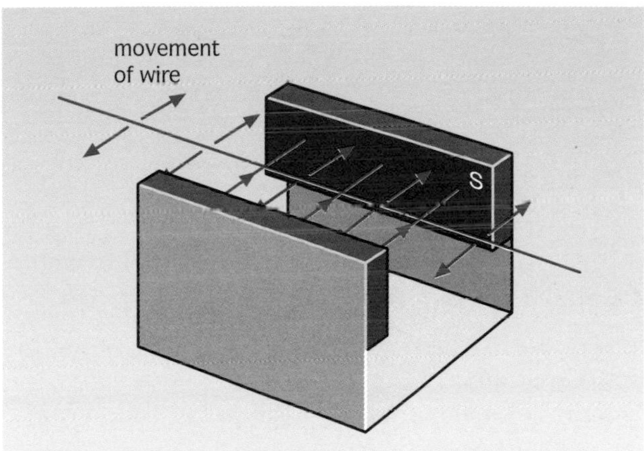

● ***Figure 10.13*** A wire is moved horizontally in a horizontal magnetic field.

SAQ 10.6

In the type of generator found in a power station, a large electromagnet is made to rotate inside a fixed coil. An e.m.f. of 25 kV is generated; this is an alternating voltage of frequency 50 Hz. What factors do you think would affect the magnitude of the e.m.f.? What factor determines the frequency?

SUMMARY

- We picture a magnetic field in terms of magnetic flux.
- The flux passing through a coil is the flux linkage.
- When the flux linking a coil changes, or when a conductor is moved so that it cuts across magnetic flux, an e.m.f. is induced across the conductor.
- This e.m.f. depends on the rate at which flux is cut.
- The direction in which any induced current flows is given by Fleming's right-hand rule.

Electromagnetic induction 2

By the end of this chapter you should be able to:

1. define *magnetic flux*, Φ, *magnetic flux linkage* and the *weber*;
2. recall and use $\Phi = BA$;
3. recall and use Faraday's and Lenz's laws of electromagnetic induction;
4. describe and explain simple examples of electromagnetic induction.

Magnetic flux

In chapter 10, we looked at the ideas of electromagnetic induction in a qualitative way. In this chapter, we will see how to calculate the value of the induced e.m.f., and look at a general way of determining its direction.

In chapter 9, we saw how magnetic flux density B is defined from the equation $F = BIl$. Now we can go on to define magnetic flux as a quantity.

We can think of **flux density** as a measure of how closely spaced the lines of magnetic flux are; in other words, how concentrated they are as they pass through a particular area – the amount of flux per square metre. Now we can say that the total amount of flux Φ (Φ is the Greek capital letter phi)

● **Figure 11.1** The generators of this power station produce electricity at an induced e.m.f. of 25 kV.

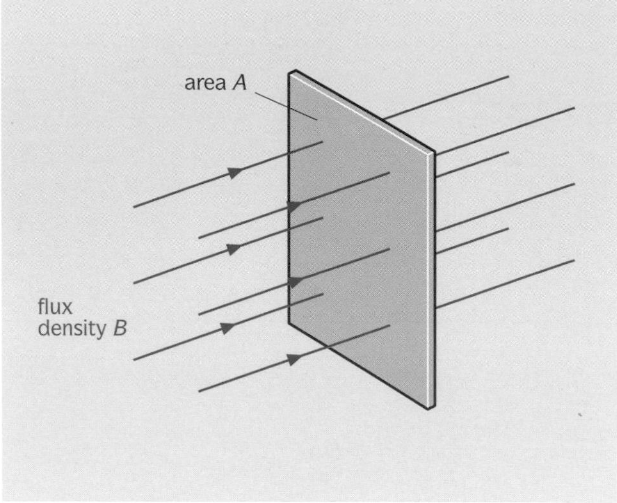

● **Figure 11.2** Defining flux Φ.

is equal to the flux density B multiplied by the area A through which it is flowing *(figure 11.2)*. So

$$\Phi = BA \qquad \text{or} \qquad B = \Phi/A$$

The unit of magnetic flux is the weber, Wb. From the second form of the equation, we can see how teslas and webers are related:

$$1\,\text{T} = 1\,\text{Wb}\,\text{m}^{-2}$$

That is, one tesla is one weber of flux passing through one square metre.

Similarly, for a coil having N turns, we can define the magnetic flux linking the coil:

$$\text{flux linkage } \Phi = BAN$$

We shall now do two worked examples.

1 The magnetic flux density through the centre of a solenoid of cross-sectional area $5\,\text{cm}^2$ is $0.01\,\text{T}$. How much flux passes through the solenoid?

We have $B = 0.01\,\text{T}$ and $A = 5\,\text{cm}^2 = 5\times10^{-4}\,\text{m}^2$. Hence $\Phi = BA = 0.01\,\text{T} \times 5\times10^{-4}\,\text{m}^2 = 5\times10^{-6}\,\text{Wb}$.

2 How much flux links a coil of area $0.1\,\text{m}^2$ and having 250 turns *(figure 11.3)*, when it is placed at right-angles to a uniform magnetic field of flux density $2\times10^{-3}\,\text{T}$?

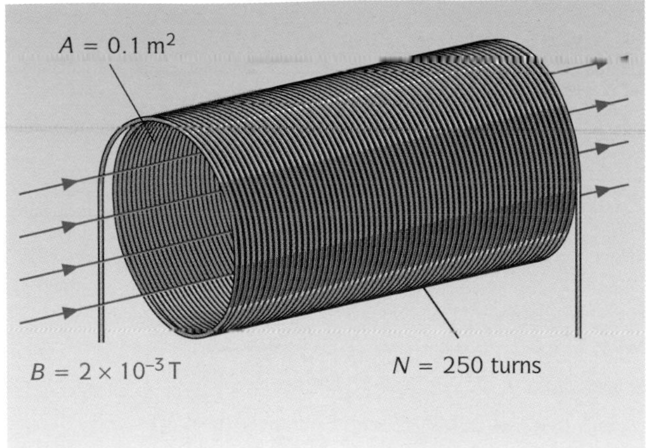

● ***Figure 11.3*** Magnetic flux linking a coil.

We have $B = 2\times10^{-3}$ T, $A = 0.1\,\text{m}^2$ and $N = 250$ turns.
Hence $\Phi = BAN = 2\times10^{-3}\,\text{T} \times 0.1\,\text{m}^2 \times 250 = 0.05\,\text{Wb}$.

(In answering SAQs 11.1 to 11.4, you may have to recall some of the expressions for B that were introduced in chapter 9. You will also need the permeability of free space, $\mu_0 = 4\pi\times10^{-7}\,\text{H}\,\text{m}^{-1}$.)

SAQ 11.1

A bar magnet produces a flux density of 0.15 T at the surface of its N pole. If the pole measures 1 cm × 1.5 cm, how much flux does this pole produce?

SAQ 11.2

In the British Isles, the vertical component of the Earth's magnetic field has a flux density of 5.0×10^{-5} T. If the area of the British Isles is $2.9\times10^{11}\,\text{m}^2$, how much magnetic flux passes through?

SAQ 11.3

A solenoid is wound on a tubular former of diameter 5.0 cm and length 25 cm *(figure 11.4)*. If there are 200 turns of wire and a current of 2 A is made to flow through it, what is the flux density at the centre of the coil? How much flux passes through the coil?

SAQ 11.4

A rectangular coil, 5 cm × 7.5 cm, and having 120 turns, sits in a magnetic field of flux density 1.2 T. Calculate the flux that links the coil.

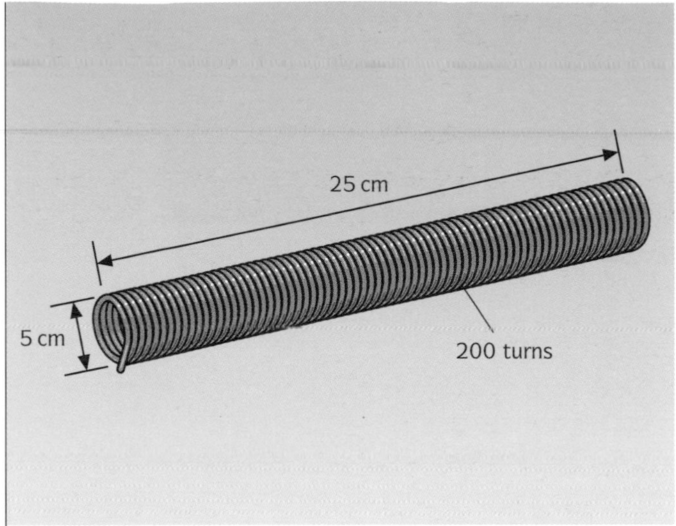

● ***Figure 11.4***

Faraday's law

In chapter 10, we saw that electromagnetic induction occurs whenever a conductor cuts across lines of magnetic flux – for example, when a coil is rotated in a magnetic field so that the flux linking the coil changes. The value of the induced e.m.f. depends on the rate at which flux is cut.

Faraday's law of electromagnetic induction is a quantitative statement of this. It says:

The magnitude of the induced e.m.f. in a conductor is proportional to the rate at which magnetic flux is cut by the conductor.

We can write this in mathematical symbols, relating the e.m.f. $\mathcal{E}$ to the rate at which flux Φ is cut, $\mathrm{d}\Phi/\mathrm{d}t$:

$$\mathcal{E} \propto \frac{\mathrm{d}\Phi}{\mathrm{d}t}$$

In the SI system of units, the constant of proportionality in this relationship is -1, which gives us a simple equation to use to calculate $\mathcal{E}$:

$$\mathcal{E} = -\frac{\mathrm{d}\Phi}{\mathrm{d}t}$$

In words, this equation says that the induced e.m.f. is equal to the rate at which magnetic flux is cut. (The reason for the minus sign, which represents Lenz's law, will be dealt with in the next section.)

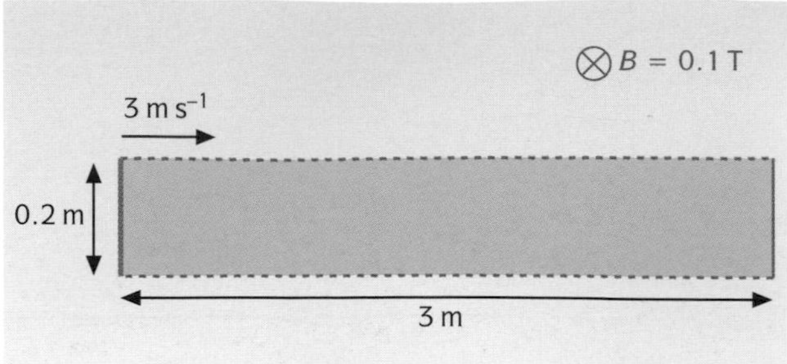

● ***Figure 11.5*** A moving conductor cuts across magnetic flux.

For a coil having *N* turns of wire, the e.m.f. will be *N* times greater than for a single turn:

$$\mathcal{E} = -N \frac{d\Phi}{dt}$$

Thus the e.m.f. induced in a coil is equal in magnitude to the rate of change of the flux linking the coil.

We shall now do two worked examples.

1 A straight wire of length 0.2 m moves at a steady speed of $3\,\mathrm{m\,s^{-1}}$ across a magnetic field of flux density 0.1 T. What will be the e.m.f. induced across the ends of the wire?

To determine the e.m.f. $\mathcal{E}$, we need to find the rate at which the wire is cutting flux; in other words, how much flux it cuts each second. *Figure 11.5* shows that, in 1 s, the wire travels 3 m, and so the area *A* of flux that it cuts is $3\,\mathrm{m} \times 0.2\,\mathrm{m} = 0.6\,\mathrm{m^2}$.

Hence $A = 0.6\,\mathrm{m^2}$ and $B = 0.1\,\mathrm{T}$. So the amount of flux Φ cut in this time is $\Phi = BA = 0.1\,\mathrm{T} \times 0.6\,\mathrm{m^2} = 0.06\,\mathrm{Wb}$.

This is the amount of flux cut in 1 s, i.e. the rate at which flux is cut. By Faraday's law, this is equal to the induced e.m.f. Hence $\mathcal{E} = 0.06\,\mathrm{V}$.

2 (This example shows one way in which the flux density of a magnetic field can be measured – *figure 11.6*.) A coil of wire having 2500 turns and of area $1\,\mathrm{cm^2}$ is placed between the poles of a magnet so that the magnetic flux passes perpendicularly through the coil. The flux density of the field is 0.5 T. The coil is pulled rapidly out of the field in a time of 0.1 s. What e.m.f. is induced across the ends of the coil?

When the coil is pulled from the field, the flux linking it falls to zero. We have to calculate the flux linking the coil when it is in the field.

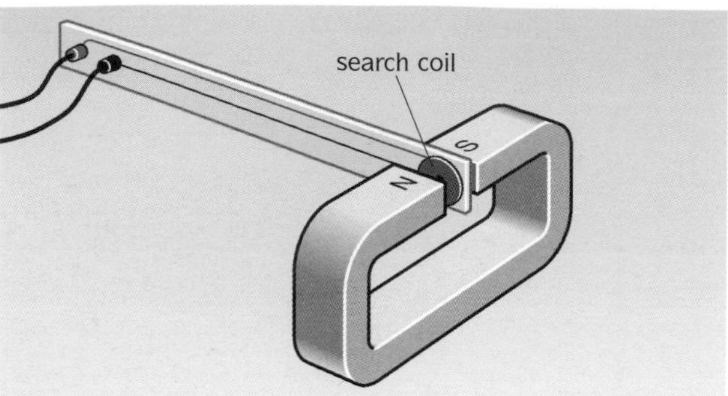

● ***Figure 11.6*** A search coil can be moved in to and out of a magnetic field to detect magnetic flux.

$$\Phi = BAN = 0.5\,\mathrm{T} \times 1\times10^{-4}\,\mathrm{m^2} \times 2500$$
$$= 0.125\,\mathrm{Wb}$$

Since the flux linkage falls from this value to zero in 0.1 s, we can calculate the rate of change of flux linkage, which is equal to the induced e.m.f.:

$$\mathcal{E} = -d\Phi/dt = 0.125\,\mathrm{Wb} / 0.1\,\mathrm{s} = 1.25\,\mathrm{V}$$

(Note that, in this example, we have assumed that the flux linking the coil falls steadily to zero during the time interval of 0.1 s. Our answer is thus the average value of the e.m.f.)

SAQ 11.5

A wire of length 10 cm is moved through a distance of 2 cm in a direction at right-angles to its length in the space between the poles of a magnet, where the flux density is 1.5 T. If this takes 0.5 s, calculate the average e.m.f. induced in the wire.

SAQ 11.6

An aircraft of wingspan 40 m flies horizontally at a speed of $300\,\mathrm{m\,s^{-1}}$ in an area where the vertical component of the Earth's magnetic field is $5\times10^{-5}\,\mathrm{T}$. Calculate the e.m.f. generated between the aircraft's wingtips.

SAQ 11.7

Figure 11.7 shows a small coil of wire, having 2000 turns and of area $1\,\mathrm{cm^2}$, placed between the poles of a powerful magnet. The ends of the coil are connected to a voltmeter. The coil is then pulled out of the magnetic field, and the voltmeter records an average e.m.f. of 0.4 V over a time interval of 0.2 s. What is the flux density between the poles of the magnet?

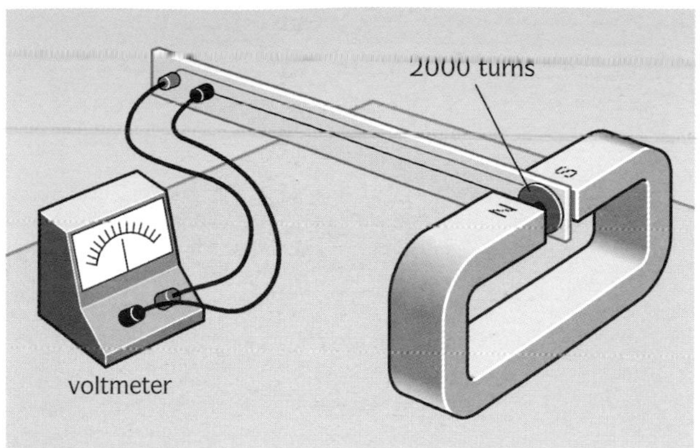

● *Figure 11.7* Using a search coil to measure flux.

Lenz's law

We use Faraday's law to calculate the magnitude of an induced e.m.f. Now we can go on to think about the direction of the e.m.f.; in other words, which end of a wire or coil moving in a magnetic field becomes positive, and which becomes negative?

In chapter 10, we saw that Fleming's right-hand rule gives the direction of an induced current. This is a particular case of a more general law, Lenz's law, which will be explained in this section. First, we will see how the motor effect and the dynamo effect are related to each other.

The origin of electromagnetic induction

So far, we have not given an explanation of electromagnetic induction. You have seen, from the experiments at the beginning of chapter 10, that it does occur, and you know the factors that affect it. But why does an induced current flow?

Figure 11.8 gives an explanation. A straight wire XY is being pushed downwards through a horizontal magnetic field *B*. Now, think about the free electrons in the wire. They are moving downwards, so they are in effect an electric current. Of course, because electrons are negatively charged, the conventional current is flowing upwards.

We now have a current flowing across a magnetic field, and the motor effect will therefore come into play. Using Fleming's left-hand rule, we can find the direction of the force on the electrons. The diagram shows that the electrons will be pushed in the direction from X to Y. So a current has been induced to flow in the wire; its direction is from Y to X.

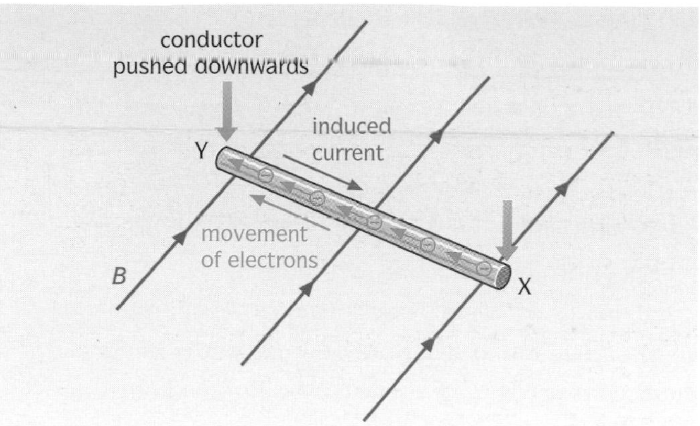

● *Figure 11.8* Showing the direction of induced current flow.

Now we can check that Fleming's right-hand rule gives the correct directions for motion, field and current, which it indeed does.

So, to summarise, an induced current flows because the electrons are pushed by the motor effect. Electromagnetic induction is simply a consequence of the motor effect.

Positive and negative

In *figure 11.8*, electrons are found to accumulate at Y. This end of the wire is thus the negative end of the e.m.f., and X is positive. If the wire was connected to an external circuit, electrons would flow out of Y, round the circuit, and back into X. *Figure 11.9* shows how the moving wire is equivalent to a cell (or any other source of e.m.f.).

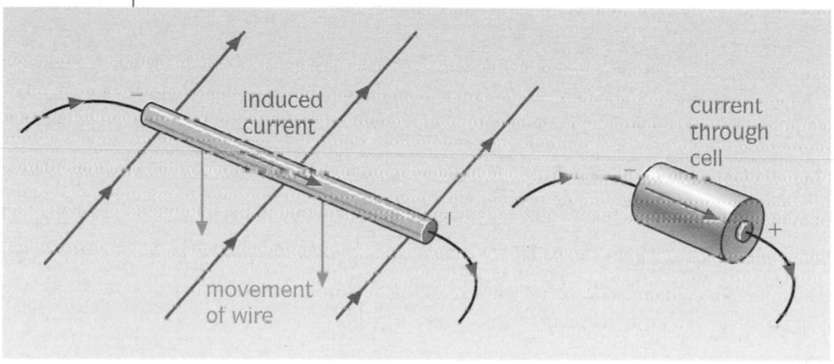

● *Figure 11.9* A moving conductor in a magnetic field is a source of e.m.f., equivalent to a cell.

Forces and movement

Electromagnetic induction is how we generate most of our electricity. We turn a coil in a magnetic field, and the mechanical energy we put in is transferred to electrical energy. By thinking about these energy transfers, we can deduce the direction in which an induced current will flow.

Figure 11.10 shows one of the experiments from chapter 10. The north pole of a magnet is being pushed towards a coil of wire. An induced current flows in the coil, but which way round does it flow? The diagram shows the two possibilities.

When the current flows in the coil, it becomes an electromagnet. One end becomes the N pole, the other the S pole. In *figure 11.10a*, the current flows so that the end nearest the approaching N pole becomes a S pole. These poles will attract one another, and you could let go of the magnet and it would be dragged into the coil. The magnet would accelerate into the coil, the induced current would increase further, and the force of attraction between the two would also escalate.

In this situation, we would be putting no energy into the system, but the magnet would be gaining kinetic energy, and the current would be gaining electrical energy. A nice trick if you could do it, but against the principle of conservation of energy!

It follows that *figure 11.10b* must show the correct situation. As the magnet is pushed towards the coil, the induced current flows so that the end of the coil nearest the magnet becomes a N pole. The two poles repel one another, and you have to do work to push the magnet into the coil. The energy transferred by your work is transferred to electrical energy of the current.

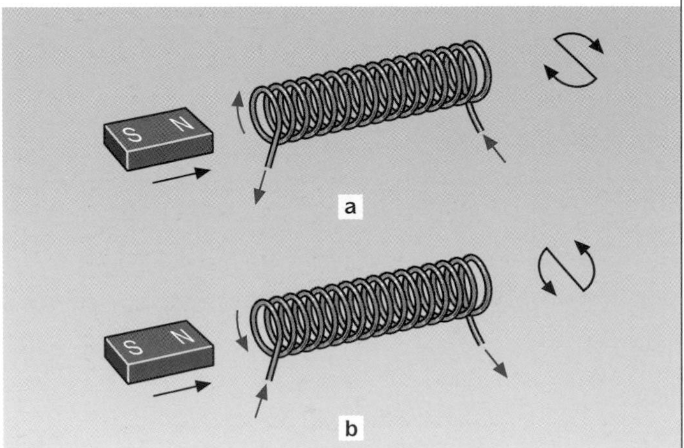

● ***Figure 11.10*** Moving a magnet towards a coil: which way does the induced current flow?

SAQ 11.8

Use these ideas to explain what happens if **a** you stop pushing the magnet towards the coil, and **b** you pull the magnet away from the coil.

Figure 11.11 shows how we can apply the same thinking to a straight wire being moved through a magnetic field. An induced current flows in the wire, but in which direction? Since this is a case of a current flowing across a magnetic field, a force will act on it (the motor effect), and we can use the left-hand rule to deduce its direction.

First we will consider what happens if the induced current flows in the wrong direction. This is shown in *figure 11.11a*. The left-hand rule shows that the force that results would be in the direction in which we are trying to move the wire. The wire would thus be accelerated, the current would increase, and again we would be getting both kinetic and electrical energy for no energy input.

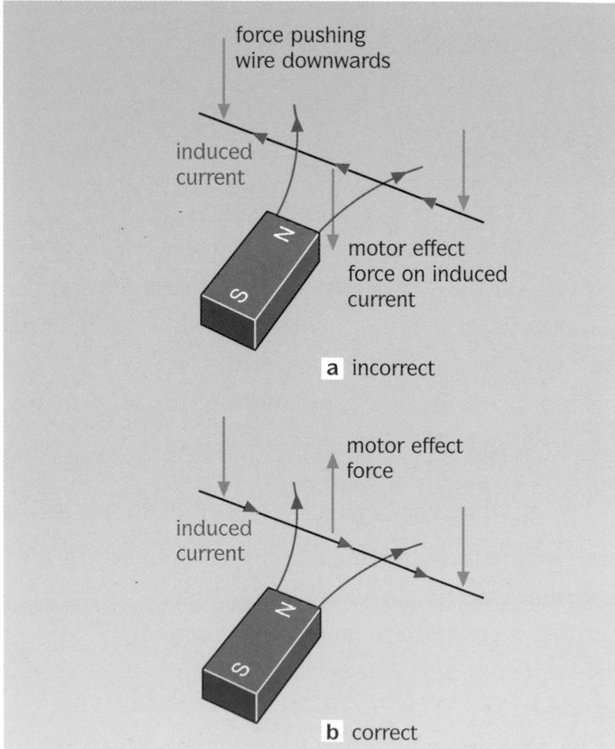

● ***Figure 11.11*** Moving a conductor through a magnetic field: which way does the induced current flow?

The induced current must flow as in *figure 11.11b*. The force that acts on it due to the motor effect pushes against you as you try to move the wire through the field. You have to do work to move the wire, and hence to generate electricity.

SAQ 11.9

Draw a diagram to show the directions of the induced current and of the opposing force if you now try to move the wire upwards through the magnetic field.

A general law

Lenz's law summarises this general principle. Induced currents flow in such a way that they always produce a force that opposes the motion that is being used to produce them. If they flowed the opposite way, we would be getting energy for nothing. Here is a statement of **Lenz's law:**

Any induced current will flow (or an induced e.m.f. will be established) in a direction so as to oppose the change that is producing it.

The idea of this opposition to change is encapsulated in the minus sign in the equation for Faraday's law:

$$\mathcal{E} = -\frac{d\Phi}{dt}$$

SAQ 11.10

A bar magnet is dropped vertically downwards through a long solenoid, which is connected to an oscilloscope (*figure 11.12*). The oscilloscope trace shows how the e.m.f. induced in the coil varies as the magnet accelerates downwards.

a Explain why an e.m.f. is induced in the coil as the magnet enters it (section AB of the trace).

b Explain why no e.m.f. is induced while the magnet is entirely inside the coil (section BC).

c Explain why section CD shows a negative trace, why the peak e.m.f. is greater over this section, and why CD represents a shorter time interval than AB.

SAQ 11.11

You can turn a bicycle dynamo by hand, and cause the lamps to light up. Use the idea of Lenz's law to explain why it is easier to turn the dynamo when the lamps are switched off than when they are on.

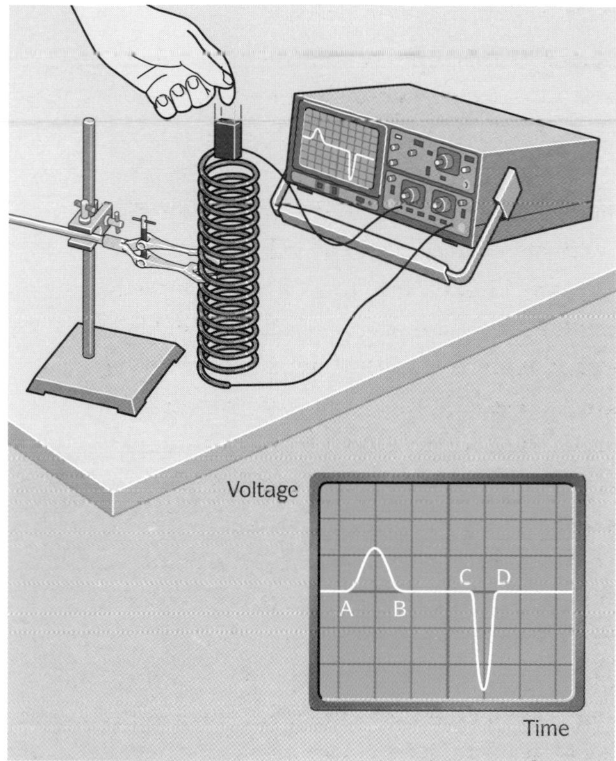

● ***Figure 11.12*** **a** A bar magnet falls through a long coil. **b** The oscilloscope trace shows how the induced voltage varies with time.

Using electromagnetic induction

An induced e.m.f. can be generated in a variety of ways. What they all have in common is that a conductor is cutting across magnetic flux. (In some cases, the conductor moves; in others, the flux moves.)

We can generate electricity by spinning a coil in a magnetic field. This is equivalent to using an electric motor backwards. *Figure 11.13* shows such a coil in several different orientations as it spins.

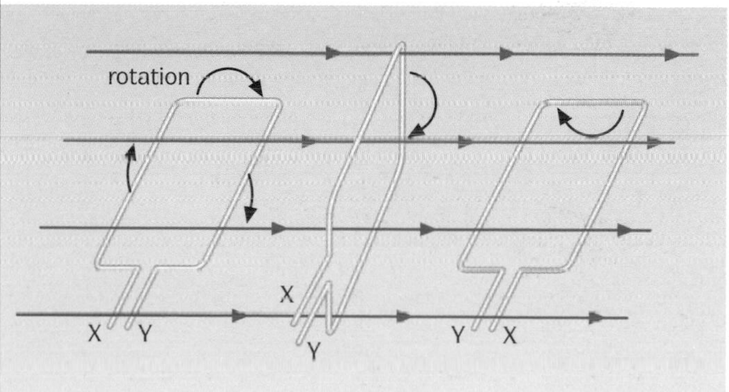

● ***Figure 11.13*** A coil rotating in a magnetic field.

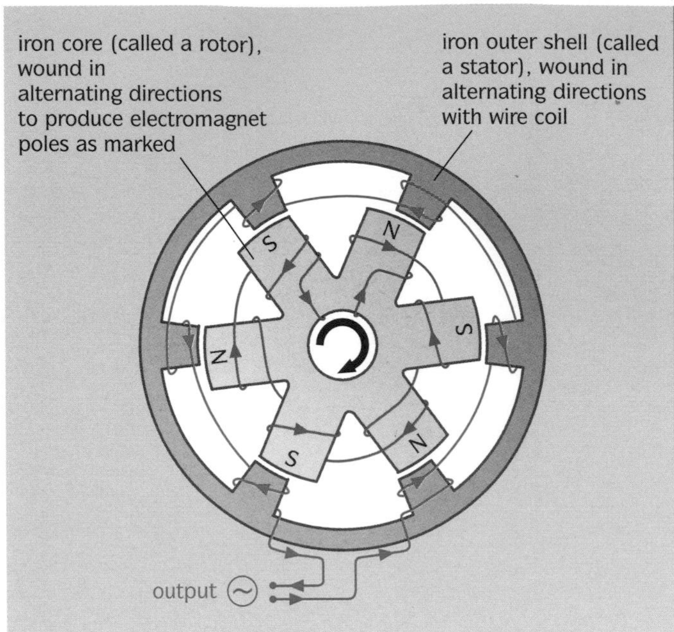

● ***Figure 11.14*** In a generator, an electromagnet rotates inside a coil.

Notice that the coil is cutting flux rapidly when it is horizontal – one side is cutting down through the flux, the other is cutting upwards. In this position, we get a large induced e.m.f. When the coil is vertical, it is travelling along the lines of flux. No flux is being cut, and so the induced e.m.f. is zero.

Hence, for a coil like this we get a varying e.m.f. – this is how alternating current is generated. In practice, it is simpler to keep the large coil fixed and spin an electromagnet inside it *(figure 11.14)*. A bicycle dynamo is similar, but in this case a permanent magnet is made to spin inside a fixed coil. This makes for a very robust device.

Another use of electromagnetic induction is in transformers. An alternating current in the primary coil produces a varying magnetic field in the core *(figure 11.15)*. The secondary coil is also wound round this core, so the flux linking the secondary coil is constantly changing. Hence a varying e.m.f. is induced across the secondary.

SAQ 11.12

Explain why, if a transformer is connected to a steady (d.c.) supply, no e.m.f. is induced across the secondary coil.

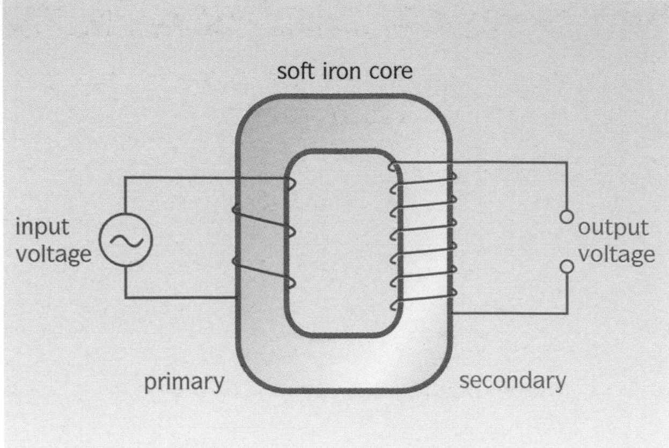

● ***Figure 11.15*** A transformer consists of two coils linked by an iron core.

SAQ 11.13

Figure 11.16 represents a coil of wire ABCD being rotated in a uniform horizontal magnetic field. Copy and complete the diagram to show the direction of the induced current flowing in the coil, and the directions of the forces on sides AB and CD that oppose the rotation of the coil.

SAQ 11.14

Does a bicycle dynamo generate alternating or direct current? Justify your answer.

SAQ 11.15

The peak e.m.f. induced in a rotating coil in a magnetic field depends on four factors: magnetic flux density B, area of the coil A, number of turns N and rate of rotation ω. Use the ideas of Faraday's and Lenz's laws to explain why the e.m.f. should be proportional to each of these quantities.

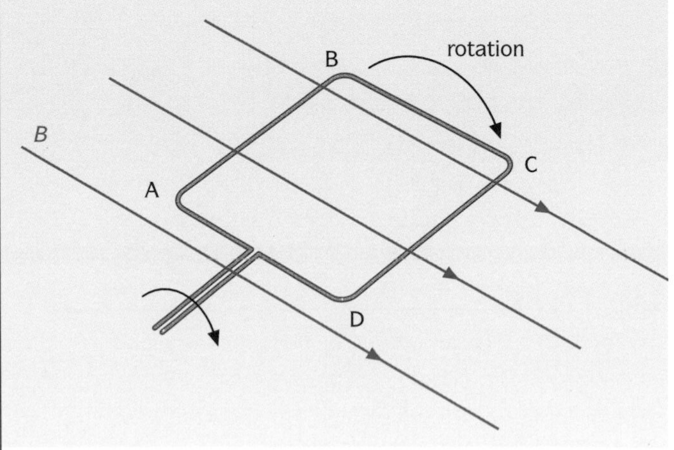

● ***Figure 11.16*** A coil rotating in a magnetic field.

SUMMARY

- In a magnetic field of flux density B, the flux passing through an area A is given by $\Phi = BA$.
- The flux passing through a coil is called the flux linkage.
- Flux is measured in webers.
- When a conductor moves so that it cuts across magnetic flux, or when the flux linking a coil changes, an e.m.f. is induced across the conductor.
- The e.m.f. is proportional to the rate at which flux is cut (Faraday's law) and the induced current flows so as to oppose the change producing it.
- Electromagnetic induction is used in many ways, including dynamos, generators and transformers.

Phases of matter

By the end of this chapter you should be able to:

1 define the terms *density* and *pressure*;

2 relate the differences in structures and densities of solids, liquids and gases to the spacing, ordering and motion of molecules;

3 describe a simple kinetic model for solids, liquids and gases;

4 describe an experiment that demonstrates Brownian motion, and appreciate the evidence this gives for the movement of molecules in gases;

5 use the kinetic model to explain the pressure exerted by gases;

6 derive and use the equation for pressure in a fluid, $p = \rho g h$;

7 understand the origin of the upthrust acting on a body in a fluid;

8 distinguish between the processes of melting, boiling and evaporation;

9 define *specific heat capacity* and use the equation $\Delta Q = mc\Delta\theta$;

10 define *specific latent heat* and use the equation $\Delta Q = mL$;

11 describe and explain the cooling that accompanies evaporation both in terms of specific latent heat and in terms of the escape of high-energy molecules.

● ***Figure 12.1*** This image, made using a scanning tunnelling microscope, shows atoms of gold (orange) on a graphite surface (green).

A particle model

In science, we use models. We try to explain many different phenomena using a few simple models – for example, the *wave model* is used to explain sound, light, the behaviour of electrons in metals, the energy levels of electrons in atoms and so on. In this chapter, we are going to look at the *particle model* of matter in order to see some of the different aspects of the behaviour of matter that it can explain.

Macroscopic and microscopic

We live in a macroscopic world. '*Macro*' means large, and our large-scale world includes rocks, trees, buildings, people and other animals, the atmosphere, planets and so on. We can simplify this complex world by focussing on particular materials – metals, stone, plastic, water, air. We can make measurements of many macroscopic properties of these materials – density, temperature, strength, viscosity, elasticity, pressure. However, in science, we are always looking for underlying explanations.

You will be familiar with a microscopic description of matter as being made up of particles. '*Micro*' means small, and these tiny particles may be atoms or ions or molecules. By developing a simple picture of the way in which these particles behave, we can arrive at explanations of many of the macroscopic properties of matter listed above.

There is a great deal of satisfaction for a scientist in the way in which a simple microscopic model can explain a very diverse range of macroscopic phenomena. Nowadays we have techniques for showing up the particles from which matter is made, at least at the level of atoms and molecules. But bear in mind that many of these ideas were developed long before there was any possibility of 'seeing' atoms. In fact, until recently, a textbook like this might well have said that, because atoms are so small, there was no hope of ever seeing an individual atom. Inventions like the scanning

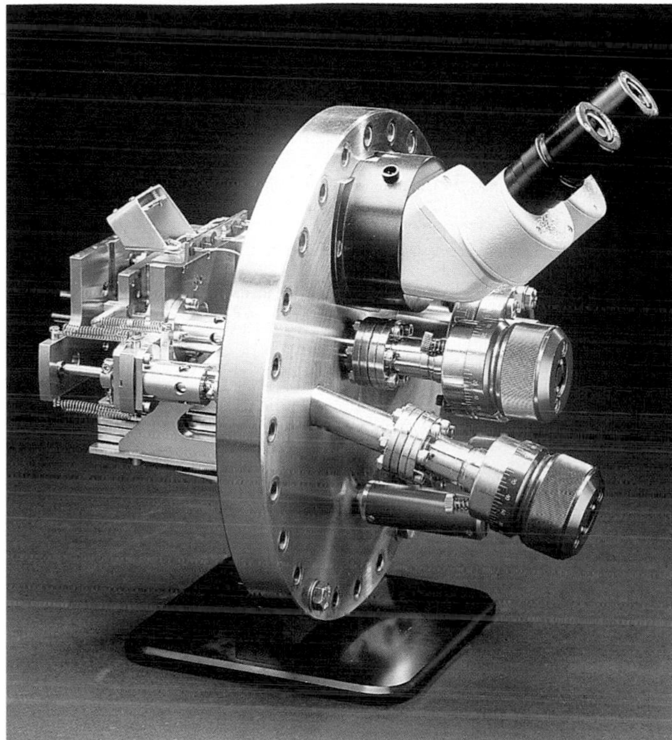

● ***Figure 12.2*** This scanning tunnelling microscope is capable of showing details of the arrangement of atoms on a scale as small as 10^{-10} m.

tunnelling microscope *(figure 12.2)* have changed all this.

The kinetic model

The model that we are going to use to describe matter is based on the following assumptions:

- Matter is made up of tiny particles.
- These particles tend to attract one another.
- The particles tend to move about.

(The word '*kinetic*' means moving.)

For simplicity, we picture the particles as small, hard spheres. *Figure 12.3* shows the three states of matter, solid, liquid and gas, as represented by this model. We describe the differences between these three states in terms of three criteria:

- The *spacing* of the particles – how far apart are they, on average?
- The *ordering* of the particles – are they arranged in an orderly or a random way?
- The *motion* of the particles – are they moving quickly, slowly or not at all?

You should be familiar with the idea that, as a material changes from solid to liquid to gas, there is a change from close spacing to greater spacing, from order to disorder, and from restricted motion to free, fast motion.

SAQ 12.1

Figure 12.3 illustrates how the kinetic model represents solids, liquids and gases. (These diagrams are two-dimensional representations only.) Explain how the diagrams represent the differences in spacing, ordering and motion of particles between the three states of matter.

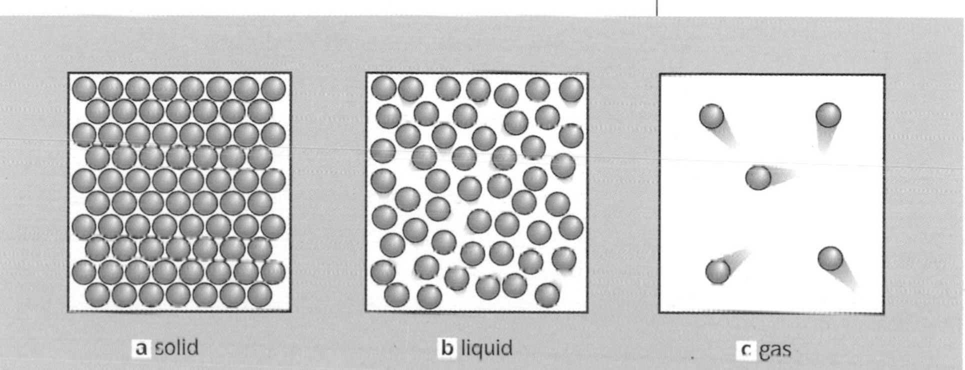

● ***Figure 12.3*** Typical arrangements of atoms in **a** a solid, **b** a liquid and **c** a gas.

Density

Density is a macroscopic property of matter; it is something we can measure and use without having to think about microscopic particles. It tells us about how concentrated the matter is:

$$\text{density} = \frac{\text{mass}}{\text{volume}}$$

$$\rho = \frac{M}{V}$$

(The symbol used here for density, ρ, is the Greek letter rho.)

The standard unit for density in the SI system is kg m^{-3}; you may also find values quoted in g cm^{-3}. It is useful to remember that

Material		Density, ρ/kg m^{-3}
Metals	osmium	22480
	gold	19300
	silver	10500
	copper	8960
	aluminium	2700
Other solids	concrete	2200
	glass	2500–4500
	Perspex	1190
	ice	920
	rubber	920
	wood	200–1200
Liquids	mercury	13600
	bromine	3100
	water	1000
	ethanol	790
	ether	740
Gases	chlorine	3.21
	carbon dioxide	1.98
	oxygen	1.43
	air	1.29
	nitrogen	1.25
	water vapour	0.80 at 0°C
	steam	0.58 at 100°C
	helium	0.18
	hydrogen	0.09

● ***Table 12.1*** Densities of various materials

these units are related by:

$$1000\,\text{kg}\,\text{m}^{-3} = 1\,\text{g}\,\text{cm}^{-3}$$

and that the density of water is approximately $1000\,\text{kg}\,\text{m}^{-3}$.

Table 12.1 gives some more values. (Notice that the density of a gas depends on its temperature and pressure. The values in the table are given at standard temperature and pressure (STP), which are temperature = 0°C, pressure = 101325 Pa.)

SAQ 12.2

a Which are more dense, in general, metals or non-metals?

b Show that the density of air is consistent with the suggestion that air is a mixture of oxygen (21% approximately) and nitrogen (79% approximately).

c Draw a diagram to represent the particles of some water at 0°C with water vapour above it at the same temperature.

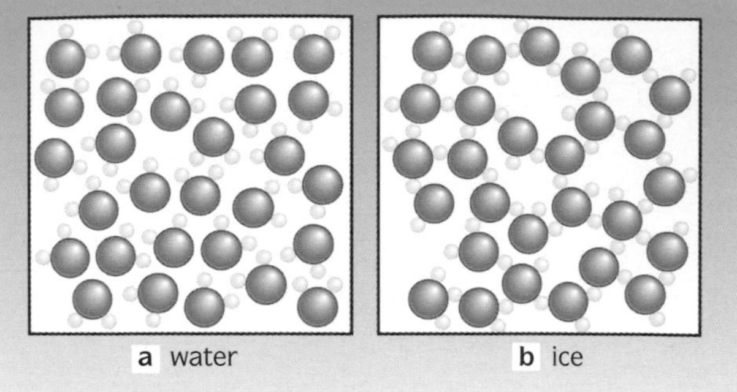

● ***Figure 12.4*** The molecules of water occupy less space **a** as a liquid than **b** as a solid.

Modifying the model

The kinetic model we have described so far is very useful, but it cannot explain everything. It often has to be modified to explain particular observations. The change in density of ice when it melts is a case in point.

Our model suggests that, when a solid melts, the particles from which it is made become slightly more disordered and further apart on average. We would thus expect a liquid to be less dense than the corresponding solid. This is generally the case, but there are exceptions. Ice is less dense than water, for example, and iron also expands when it freezes.

We have to modify the model. For water, we picture the particles as being some shape other than spherical (*figure 12.4*). When liquid water becomes solid ice, the particles pack in such a way that there is more empty space, and so the solid is less dense than the liquid.

Gases

We picture the particles that make up a gas as being fast-moving. They bounce off the walls of their container (and off each other) as they travel around at high speed. But how do we know that these particles are moving like this?

It is much harder to find ways of visualising the particles of a gas than those of a solid, simply because they are moving about in such a disordered way, and because most of a gas is empty space. However, the movement of gas particles was investigated as long ago as the 1820s, by an English botanist, Robert Brown. He was investigating the motion of pollen grains; it is easier in the laboratory to look at the movement of smoke grains.

Observing Brownian motion

The oxygen and nitrogen molecules that make up the air are far too small to see; they are much smaller than the wavelength of light. So we have to look at something bigger, and see the effect of the air molecules. In this experiment *(figure 12.5)*, the smoke cell contains air into which a small amount of smoke has been introduced. The cell is lit from the side, and the microscope is used to view the smoke grains.

The smoke grains show up as tiny specks of reflected light, but they are too small to see any detail of their shape. What is noticeable is the way they move. If you can concentrate on a single grain, you will see that it follows a somewhat jerky and erratic path. This is a consequence of the grain suffering repeated collisions with air molecules. Since the air molecules are much smaller than the smoke grain, we can deduce that they must be moving much faster than the smoke grain if they are to affect it in this way.

[Note that you may observe that all of the smoke grains in your field of view have a tendency to travel in one particular direction. This is a consequence of convection currents in the air. Also, you may have to adjust the focus of the microscope to keep track of an individual grain, as it moves up or down in the cell.]

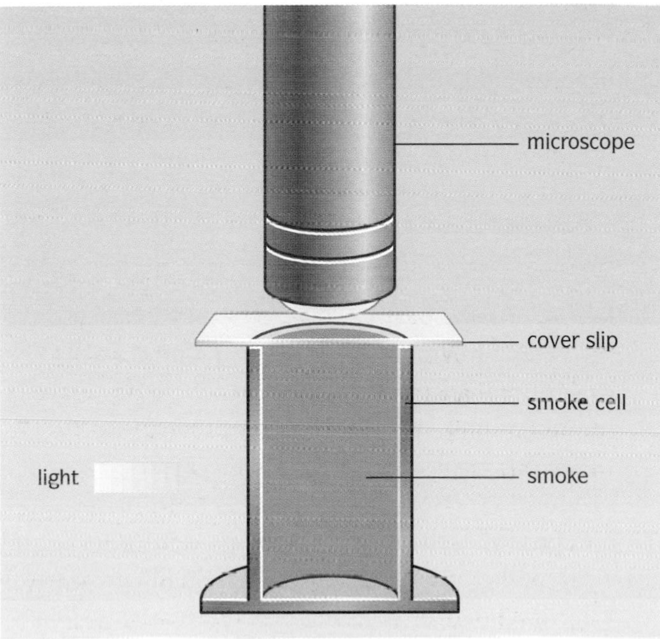

● ***Figure 12.5*** Experimental arrangement for observing Brownian motion.

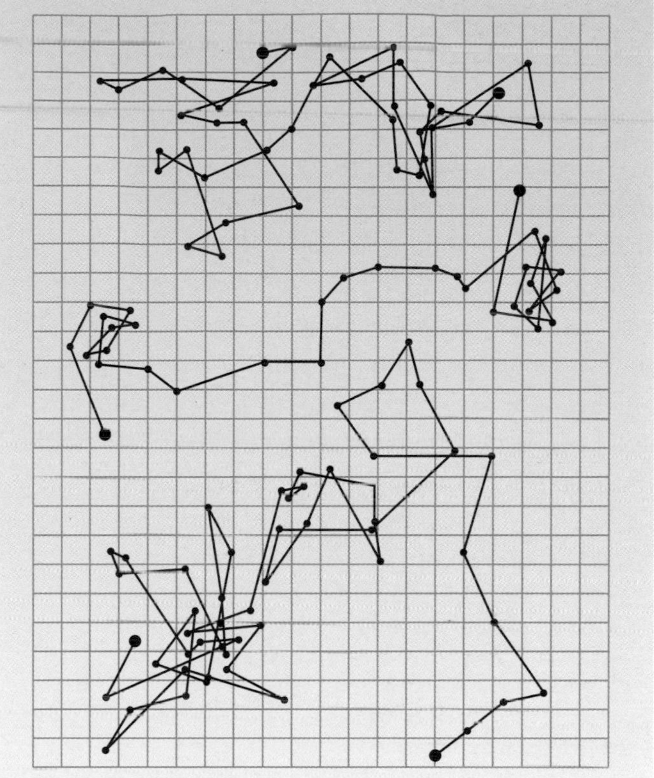

● ***Figure 12.6*** Brownian motion of a particle, as drawn by the French scientist Perrin.

Figure 12.6 shows the sort of path followed by a particle showing Brownian motion. In fact, this is from a paper by the French physicist Jean Perrin, published in 1911. He was looking at the movement of a pollen grain suspended in water. He recorded its position every 30 s; the grid spacing is approximately 3 μm. From this he could deduce the average speed of the grain, and hence work out details of the movement of water molecules.

SAQ 12.3

Consider a smoke grain, mass M and speed V. It is constantly buffeted by air molecules, mass m and speed v. It is reasonable to assume that the smoke grain will have kinetic energy approximately equal to the kinetic energy of a single air molecule (KE = $\frac{1}{2}mv^2$). Show that, since $M \gg m$ (M is much greater than m), it follows that the air molecules must be moving much faster than the smoke grain ($v \gg V$).

Fast molecules

For air at standard temperature and pressure, the average speed of the molecules is about $400\,\mathrm{m\,s^{-1}}$. At any moment, some are moving faster than this, and others more slowly. If we could follow the movement of a single air molecule, we would find that, some of the time, its speed was greater than this average; at other times it would be less. The velocity of an individual molecule changes every time it collides with anything else.

This value for molecular speed is reasonable. It is comparable to (but greater than) the speed of sound in air (approximately $330\,\mathrm{m\,s^{-1}}$ at STP). If the molecules were moving much faster than this, they would be approaching escape velocity (chapter 2), and the atmosphere would have escaped from the Earth's gravitational field long ago.

Pressure

A gas exerts pressure on any surface with which it comes into contact. Pressure is a macroscopic property, defined as follows: the **pressure** on a surface is the force exerted per unit area of the surface.

$$p = \frac{F}{A}$$

(p = pressure, F = force, A = area). The unit of pressure is the pascal, Pa.

$$1\,\mathrm{Pa} = 1\,\mathrm{N\,m^{-2}}$$

The pressure of the atmosphere at sea level is approximately 100 000 Pa. The surface area of a typical person is $2\,\mathrm{m^2}$. Hence the force exerted on them by the atmosphere is 200 000 N. This is approximately the weight of 200 000 apples! Fortunately, our insides press outwards with an equal and opposite force, so we do not collapse under the influence of this large force.

SAQ 12.4

A box of dimensions 10 cm × 20 cm × 50 cm contains air at a pressure of 100 000 Pa. Calculate the force exerted on each face of the box.

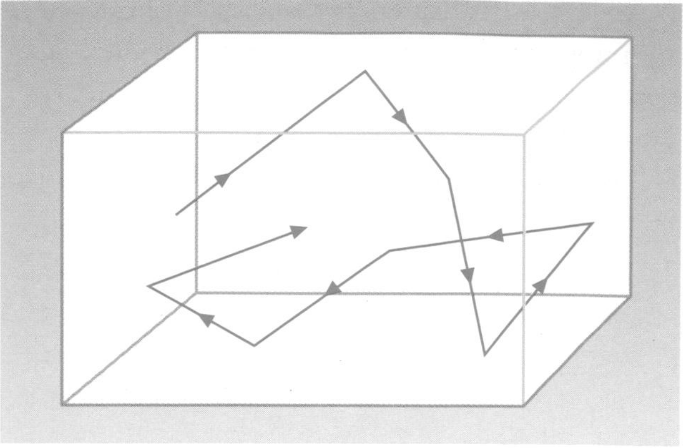

● ***Figure 12.7*** The path of a single molecule in an otherwise empty box.

Explaining pressure

We can explain the macroscopic phenomenon of pressure by thinking about the behaviour of the microscopic particles that make up the atmosphere. *Figure 12.7* shows the movement of a single molecule of the air in a box. It bounces around inside, colliding with the various surfaces of the box. At each collision, it exerts a small force on the box. The pressure on the box is a result of the forces exerted by the vast number of molecules in the box.

Of course, because of the great difference in scale between ourselves and the air molecules that are constantly battering us, we do not observe a multiplicity of tiny forces. Instead, the pressure of the atmosphere is a constant effect, which we do not notice under normal circumstances.

Pressure in fluids

We spend most of our lives on the surface of the Earth, with many kilometres of atmosphere above us. We are living at the bottom of a layer of air, and this air presses down on us. The force it exerts on the ground, and on us, is simply its weight.

We can experience a similar but more pronounced effect if we go to the bottom of another fluid, the sea. If we descend into the sea in a submarine, the pressure gets gradually greater. There is a danger of being crushed by the weight of water above, and submarines have to be designed to withstand great forces.

We can work out an expression for the pressure on a surface by thinking about the weight of fluid pressing down on it.

Consider a tank containing fluid of density ρ to a depth h. The area of the base of the tank is A (see *figure 12.8*). We will calculate the weight of the fluid pressing down on the base, and then find the pressure that results:

volume of fluid = area of base × depth = Ah
mass of fluid = density × volume = ρAh
weight of fluid = mass × g = ρAhg

This is the force exerted on the base. Therefore

pressure on base = force/area = $\rho Ahg/A = \rho hg$

This is usually written as

$$p = \rho gh$$

Note that this expression for pressure is independent of the area of the base. It does not matter what shape the container has *(figure 12.9)*, the pressure at a depth h is the same. Note also that this pressure acts equally in all directions. If we think of the microscopic picture of pressure as the result of many tiny forces due to molecules bouncing off the surfaces of the container, you will see that all surfaces experience the pressure *(figure 12.10)*.

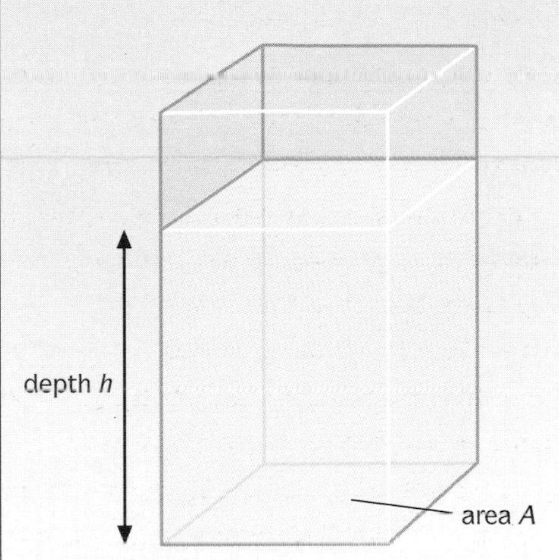

● ***Figure 12.8*** The pressure of a fluid on the base of a container is due to the weight of the fluid.

● ***Figure 12.9*** Pressure at depth h is independent of the shape of the container.

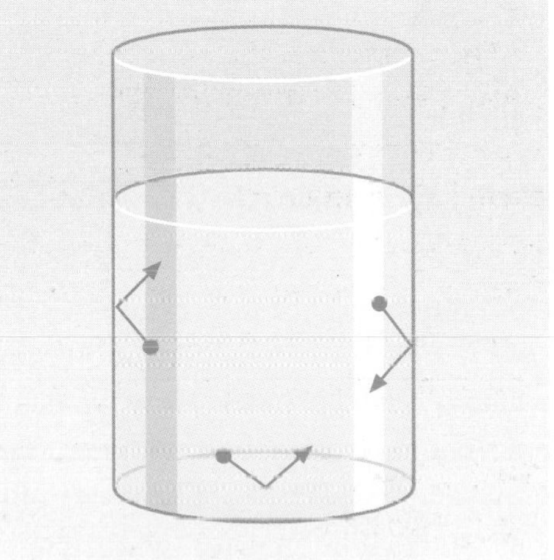

● ***Figure 12.10*** A fluid exerts pressure in all directions.

SAQ 12.5

a The atmosphere has density $1.29\,\mathrm{kg\,m^{-3}}$ at sea level, where the pressure is approximately 100 000 Pa. Use these values to deduce an approximate value for the height of the atmosphere.

b The atmosphere becomes less dense the higher you go. Therefore, is your answer to part **a** an underestimate or an overestimate?

c Mount Everest is approximately 9 km high. Explain why mountaineers climbing to this height often take oxygen with them.

SAQ 12.6

A swimming pool is 0.75 m deep at the shallow end and 2.3 m deep at the deep end. Calculate the pressure on the bottom of the pool at each end. (Density of water = $1000\,\mathrm{kg\,m^{-3}}$.)

Upthrust

If you have ever tried to sit on the bottom at the deep end of a swimming pool, you will know that it is not easy. It helps to breathe out and propel yourself downwards with your hands. The water pushes you back towards the surface with quite a significant force.

The upwards force that the water exerts on you is called the **upthrust**. This is the same force as that which keeps ships afloat and hot air balloons aloft.

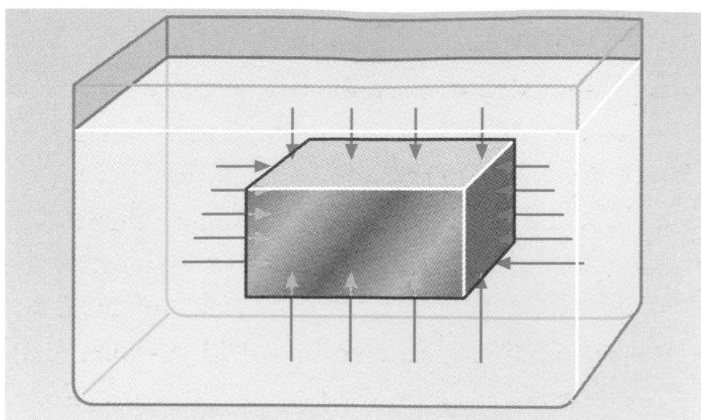

● ***Figure 12.11*** Since pressure increases with depth, there is a greater force on the bottom of the object than on the top; this is the origin of upthrust. The lengths of the arrows represent the sizes of the forces.

Upthrust comes about because there is a difference in pressure at different levels in a fluid. *Figure 12.11* shows how the pressure varies over the surface of a submerged box. Notice that the horizontal forces cancel each other out. The upward force on the bottom of the box is greater than the downward force on the top. Hence there is a resultant upthrust on the box. We can find the upthrust by finding the difference in pressures on the two surfaces. We have

pressure on top surface $= \rho g h_1$
force F_1 on top surface $= A\rho g h_1$
pressure on lower surface $= \rho g h_2$
force F_2 on lower surface $= A\rho g h_2$

So

$$\text{upthrust} = F_2 - F_1 = A\rho g(h_2 - h_1)$$

Since $A(h_2 - h_1)$ = volume of box, you should be able to see that the upthrust is thus equal to the weight of water displaced. This is **Archimedes' principle.**

The microscopic view

So far, we have considered how upthrust originates from the difference in pressure at different depths. This is a macroscopic description, since pressure is a macroscopic quantity. Now we need to think of a microscopic explanation, in terms of the movement of particles. The water molecules are constantly colliding with the surfaces of the box shown in *figure 12.11*. Why is the force resulting from the collisions greater on the lower surface than on the upper surface? The reason is that the molecules at a greater depth are moving faster. If a molecule moves towards the surface, it gains gravitational potential energy and hence must lose kinetic energy – it moves more slowly. Slower molecules have a smaller effect when they collide with the surfaces of the box.

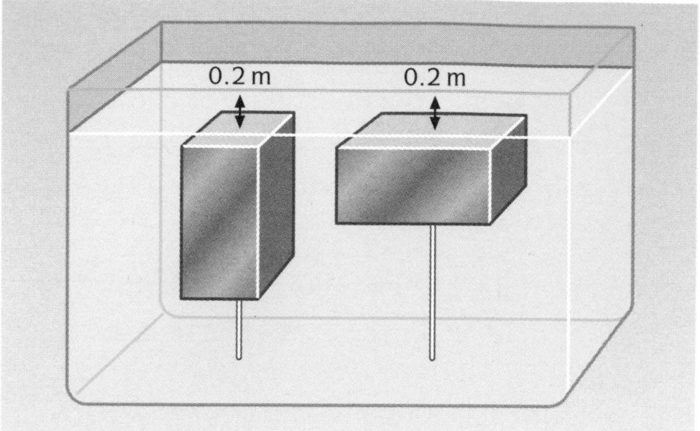

● ***Figure 12.12*** Two identical objects experience the same upthrust.

SAQ 12.7

Figure 12.12 shows two identical boxes, each 0.5 m × 0.5 m × 1 m, suspended 0.2 m below the surface of some water. By calculating the forces on the upper and lower surfaces of each box, show that the upthrust on each is the same. (Density of water $\rho = 1000\,\text{kg}\,\text{m}^{-3}$, acceleration due to gravity $g = 9.8\,\text{m}\,\text{s}^{-2}$.)

Changes of state

Many solid materials, when heated, undergo a change of state. They first become a liquid, and then a gas. Some materials change directly from the solid state into a gas. (Some solids dissociate into simpler substances when heated, but we are not concerned here with such chemical changes.)

Figure 12.13 represents these changes of state at the molecular level. We will consider first what happens when a solid melts. The particles of the solid gain enough energy to break some of the bonds with their neighbours; they adopt a more disordered arrangement, and usually their average spacing increases. The particles are more free to move around within the bulk of the material. The solid has melted.

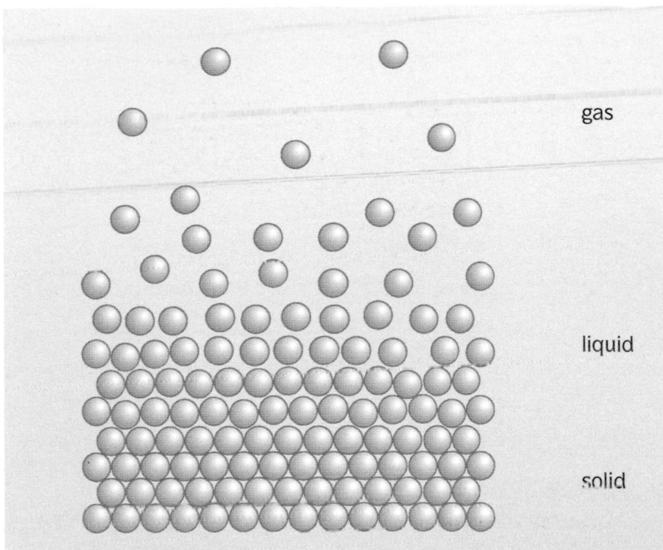

● ***Figure 12.13*** Changes of state.

As the liquid is heated further, the particles become more disordered, further apart and faster moving. Eventually, at the boiling point, the particles have sufficient energy to break free from their neighbours. They are now much farther apart, moving rapidly about in a disordered state. The liquid has boiled to become a gas.

When a liquid boils at atmospheric pressure, its volume increases by a factor of about 1000. In the liquid state, the molecules were closely packed; now they are occupying 1000 times as much space. It follows that about 99.9% of the volume of a gas is empty space. If the diameter of a single molecule is d, it follows that the average separation of molecules in the gas is $10d$.

Energy changes

Energy is needed to raise the temperature of a solid, to melt it, to heat the liquid and to boil it. Where does this energy go to? It is worth taking a close look at a single change of state and thinking about what is happening on the molecular scale.

Figure 12.14a shows a suitable arrangement. A test-tube containing octadecanoic acid (a white, waxy substance at room temperature) is warmed in a water bath. At 80 °C, the substance is a clear liquid. The tube is then placed in a rack and allowed to cool. Its temperature is monitored, either with a thermometer or with a temperature probe and data-logger. *Figure 12.14b* shows typical results.

The temperature drops rapidly at first, then more slowly as it approaches room temperature. The important section of the graph is in the region BC. Here, the temperature remains steady for some time. The clear liquid is gradually returning to its white, waxy solid state. It is essential to note that heat is still being lost even though the temperature is not decreasing. When no liquid remains, the temperature starts to drop again.

From the graph, we can deduce the melting point of octadecanoic acid. This is a technique used to help identify substances by finding their melting points.

Heating ice

In some ways, it is easier to think of this experiment in reverse. What happens when we heat a substance?

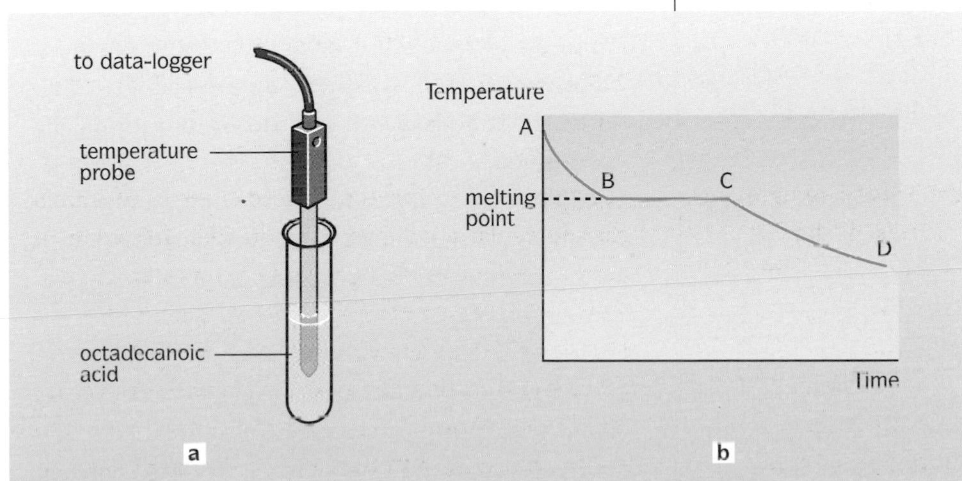

● ***Figure 12.14*** **a** Apparatus for obtaining a cooling curve, and **b** typical results.

Imagine taking some ice from the deep freeze. Put the ice in a well-insulated container and heat it at a steady rate. Its temperature will rise; eventually we will have a container of steam. *Figure 12.15* shows the results we might expect if we could carry out this idealised experiment. We will consider the different sections of this graph in some detail, in order to see

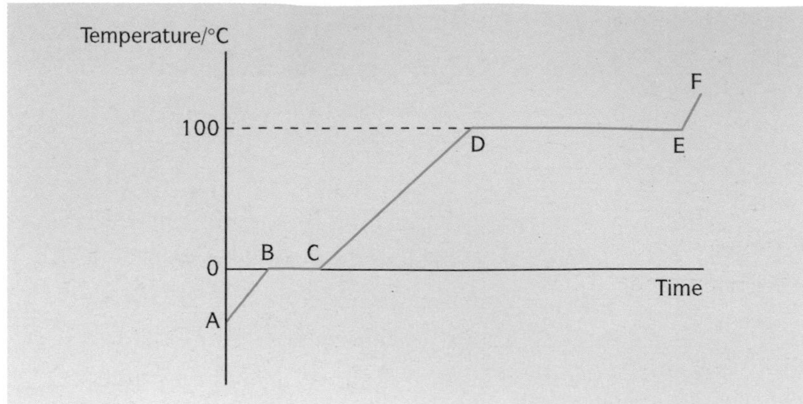

● ***Figure 12.15*** A temperature–time graph for water, heated at a steady rate.

where the energy is going at each stage. (Remember that we are putting energy in at a steady rate.) We need to think about the kinetic and potential energies of the molecules. If they move around more freely and faster, their kinetic energy has increased; if they break free of their neighbours and become more disordered, their potential energy has increased.

- *Section AB*
  The ice starts below 0 °C; its temperature rises. The molecules gain energy and vibrate more and more. Their kinetic energy is increasing.
- *Section BC*
  The ice melts at 0 °C. The molecules become more disordered. Their potential energy is increasing.
- *Section CD*
  The ice has become water. Its temperature rises towards 100 °C. The molecules move increasingly rapidly. Their kinetic energy is increasing.
- *Section DE*
  The water is boiling. The molecules are becoming completely separate from one another. Their movement becomes very disorderly. Their potential energy is increasing.
- *Section EF*
  The steam is being heated above 100 °C. The molecules move even faster. Their kinetic energy is increasing.

From this analysis, you should realise that a change of state involves the following: there must be an input of energy; the temperature does not change; the molecules are breaking free of one another; their potential energy is increasing.

In between the changes of state, the input of energy raises the temperature of the substance; the molecules move faster; their kinetic energy is increasing.

The hardest point to appreciate is that you can put energy into the system without its temperature rising. This happens during any change of state; the energy goes to breaking the bonds between neighbouring molecules.

It may help to think of temperature as a measure of the average kinetic energy of the molecules. When you put a thermometer in some water to measure its temperature, the water molecules collide with the thermometer and share their kinetic energy with it. At a change of state, there is no change in kinetic energy, so there is no change in temperature.

Notice that melting the ice (section BC) takes much less energy than boiling the same amount of water (section DE). This is because, when a solid melts, the molecules are still bonded to most of their immediate neighbours. When a liquid boils, each molecule breaks free of all of its neighbours. Melting may involve the breaking of one or two bonds per molecule, whereas boiling involves breaking eight or nine.

Evaporation

A liquid does not have to boil to change into a gas. A puddle of rain-water dries up without having to be heated to 100 °C. When a liquid changes to a gas without boiling, we call this **evaporation**. The gas formed is called a **vapour** – this is the term used to describe a gas below its boiling point.

Any liquid has some vapour associated with it. If we think about the microscopic picture of this, we can see why *(figure 12.16)*. Within the liquid, molecules are moving about. Some move faster than others, and can break free from the bulk of the liquid. They form the vapour above the liquid. Some molecules from the vapour may come back into contact with the surface of the liquid, and return to the liquid. However, there is a net outflow of energetic molecules from the liquid, and eventually it will evaporate away completely.

You may have had your skin swabbed with alcohol or ether before an injection. You will have noticed how cold your skin becomes as the volatile liquid evaporates. Similarly, you can become very cold if you get wet and stand around in a windy place. This cooling of a liquid is a very important aspect of evaporation.

When a liquid evaporates, it is the most energetic molecules that are most likely to escape. This leaves molecules with a below average kinetic energy. Since temperature is a measure of the average kinetic energy of the molecules, it follows that the temperature of the evaporating liquid must fall.

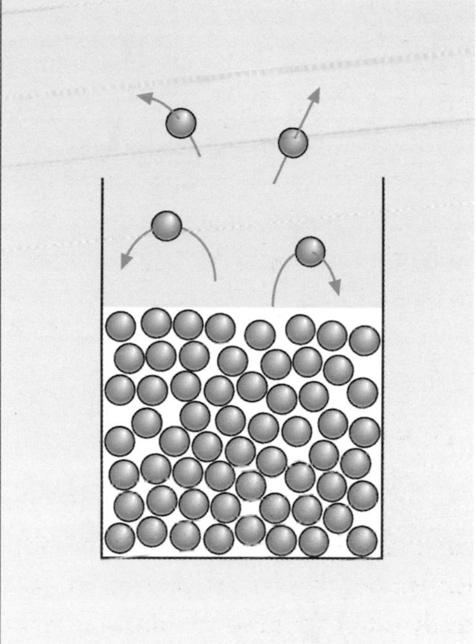

● **Figure 12.16** Fast-moving molecules leave the surface of a liquid.

SAQ 12.8

Use the kinetic model of matter to explain the following:

a If you leave a pan of water on the stove for a long time, it does not all boil away as soon as the temperature reaches 100 °C.

b It takes less energy to melt a 1 kg block of ice at 0 °C than to boil away 1 kg of water at 100 °C.

c When a dog is overheated, it pants. (Don't try to explain this to the dog!)

Calculating energy changes

So far, we have considered the effects of heating a substance in qualitative terms, and we have given an explanation in terms of a kinetic model of matter. Now we will look at the amount of energy needed to change the temperature of something, and to produce a change of state.

Specific heat capacity

If we heat some matter so that its temperature rises, the amount of energy we must supply depends on three things: the mass m of the material we are heating; the temperature rise $\Delta\theta$ we wish to achieve (Δ is Greek capital delta); and the material itself. Some materials are easier to heat than others – it takes more energy to raise the temperature of 1 kg of water by 1 °C than to raise the temperature of 1 kg of alcohol by the same amount.

We can represent this in an equation. The amount of energy ΔQ that must be supplied is given by

$$\Delta Q = mc\Delta\theta$$

where c is the specific heat capacity of the material. Rearranging this equation gives $c = \Delta Q/m\Delta\theta$. Hence the **specific heat capacity** of a substance is the amount of energy required to raise the temperature of 1 kg of the substance by 1 °C (or by 1 K). (The word 'specific' here means 'per unit mass', i.e. per kg.) From this form of the equation, you should be able to see that the units of c are $\mathrm{J\,kg^{-1}\,°C^{-1}}$ (or $\mathrm{J\,kg^{-1}\,K^{-1}}$). *Table 12.2* shows some values of specific heat capacity.

Specific heat capacity is related to the gradient of the sloping sections of the graph shown earlier in *figure 12.15*. The steeper the gradient, the faster the substance heats up, and hence the lower its specific heat capacity must be.

Substance	$c/\mathrm{J\,kg^{-1}\,°C^{-1}}$
aluminium	880
copper	380
lead	126
glass	500–680
ice	2100
water	4180
sea-water	3950
ethanol	2500
mercury	140

● **Table 12.2** Values of specific heat capacity c measured at 0 °C

Specific latent heat

In a similar way, we can think about the amount of energy we must supply to melt or boil a substance. In this case, we do not need to concern ourselves with temperature rise, since the temperature stays constant during a change of state. We can write an equation for the energy ΔQ that must be supplied to melt or boil a mass m of a substance:

$$\Delta Q = mL$$

Here L is the specific latent heat of the substance. Rearranging gives $L = \Delta Q/m$. Hence the **specific latent heat** of a substance is the energy that must be supplied to change the state of 1 kg of the substance. For melting, you may see this called the specific latent heat of fusion.

The word 'latent' means 'hidden', and refers to the fact that, when you melt something, its temperature does not rise and the heat that you have put in seems to have disappeared. *Table 12.3* shows some values of specific latent heat.

We shall now give two worked examples. In these, values for c and L are taken from *tables 12.2* and *12.3*.

1 When 26 400 J of energy are supplied to a 2 kg block of aluminium, its temperature rises from 20 °C to 35 °C. Find the specific heat capacity of aluminium.

We are going to use the equation $c = \Delta Q/m\Delta\theta$. We need to write down the quantities that we know:

$$\Delta Q = 26\,400\,\text{J}$$
$$m = 2\,\text{kg}$$
$$\Delta\theta = (35\text{–}20)\,°\text{C} = 15\,°\text{C}$$

Substance	*Melting* L/J kg^{-1}	*Boiling* L/J kg^{-1}
ice, water	334 000	2 260 000
ethanol	110 000	840 000
benzene	127 000	394 000
mercury	69 000	1 100 000
aluminium	412 000	
iron	270 000	
copper	205 000	
lead	25 000	

● ***Table 12.3*** Values of specific latent heat

Substituting gives

$$c = 26\,400\,\text{J}/(2\,\text{kg} \times 15\,°\text{C}) = 880\,\text{J}\,\text{kg}^{-1}\,°\text{C}^{-1}$$

2 How much energy must be supplied to change 2.0 kg of ice at −10 °C to steam at 100 °C?

Here we have four separate calculations to perform, corresponding to raising the temperature of the ice to 0 °C, melting it, heating the water to 100 °C, and boiling the water. You should be able to identify the four terms in the equation that follows:

$$\begin{aligned}\Delta Q &= 2\,\text{kg} \times 2100\,\text{J}\,\text{kg}^{-1}\,°\text{C}^{-1} \times 10\,°\text{C}\\ &\quad + 2\,\text{kg} \times 334\,000\,\text{J}\,\text{kg}^{-1}\\ &\quad + 2\,\text{kg} \times 4180\,\text{J}\,\text{kg}^{-1}\,°\text{C}^{-1} \times 100\,°\text{C}\\ &\quad + 2\,\text{kg} \times 2\,260\,000\,\text{J}\,\text{kg}^{-1}\\ &= 42\,000\,\text{J} + 668\,000\,\text{J} + 836\,000\,\text{J}\\ &\quad + 4\,520\,000\,\text{J} = 6\,066\,000\,\text{J}\end{aligned}$$

Notice that three-quarters of the energy is required to boil the water when it has reached 100 °C.

Ice, water, steam

Water is an unusual substance. We have already noted that it expands when it freezes – that is why ice floats on water. It also has an unusually high specific heat capacity. This means that water heats up and cools down relatively slowly. This makes water very suitable for the liquid in central heating systems.

Another consequence is that the sea cools down relatively slowly in the winter, compared to the land. Also it warms up relatively slowly in the summer. In the British Isles, we are surrounded by the sea, which helps to keep us warm in the winter and cool in the summer. In central Europe, far from the sea, temperatures fall more dramatically in the winter and rise higher in the summer. This is the origin of the difference between a maritime climate and a continental climate. If the sea was made of alcohol, the British climate would vary more between the seasons. You can probably imagine some other important consequences.

You will need to use data from *tables 12.2* and *12.3* above to answer SAQs 12.9 to 12.12.

SAQ 12.9

How much energy must be supplied to raise the temperature of 5 kg of water from 20 °C to 100 °C?

SAQ 12.10

Which requires more energy, heating a 2 kg block of lead by 30 °C, or heating a 4 kg block of copper by 5 °C?

SAQ 12.11

A well-insulated 1 kg block of iron is heated using a 50 W heater for 5 min. Its temperature rises from 22 °C to 55 °C. Find the specific heat capacity of iron.

SAQ 12.12

A 10 g block of ice at 0 °C is put into a glass containing 100 g of water at 20 °C. How much energy is taken in by the ice in melting? What will the temperature of the water be, once the ice has all melted?

SUMMARY

- Matter can exist in three phases, solid, liquid and gas, characterised by the spacing, ordering and motion of the molecules.
- The kinetic model of matter allows us to explain macroscopic properties (e.g. density, pressure, specific heat and latent heat) in terms of the behaviour of molecules.
- Evidence for the kinetic model comes from observations of Brownian motion.
- Changes of state can also be described in terms of changes in the spacing, ordering and motion of molecules.
- The pressure in a fluid is given by $p = \rho g h$.
- The specific heat capacity c of a substance is the energy required to raise the temperature of 1 kg by 1 °C.
- The energy transferred in raising the temperature of a substance is given by $\Delta Q = mc\Delta\theta$.
- The specific latent heat L of a substance is the energy required to change the state of 1 kg of the substance.
- The energy transferred in changing the state of a substance is given by $\Delta Q = mL$.

Deforming solids

By the end of this chapter you should be able to:

1. appreciate that deformation is caused by a force and can be tensile (stretching) or compressive (squashing);
2. describe the behaviour of springs in terms of load, extension, the spring constant and Hooke's law;
3. define and use the terms *stress*, *strain* and the *Young modulus*;
4. describe an experiment to determine the Young modulus of a metal in the form of a wire;
5. distinguish between elastic and plastic deformation of a material;
6. demonstrate knowledge of the force–extension graphs for typical ductile, brittle and polymeric materials, including an understanding of ultimate tensile stress;
7. distinguish between the structures of crystalline and non-crystalline solids;
8. deduce the strain energy in a deformed material from the area under the force–extension graph.

● ***Figure 13.1*** The stiffness of rubber is a crucial factor in bungee jumping.

Stretching a spring

Springs are usually made of metal. They help us to have a comfortable ride in a car, and they contribute to a good night's sleep. They can be made of materials other than metals – plastic, rubber, or even glass. Wood is a springy material, because trees must be able to bend in a high wind.

A force is needed to change the shape of a spring. If the spring is being squashed and shortened, we say that the force is **compressive**. More usually, we are concerned with stretching a spring, in which case the force is described as **tensile** *(figure 13.2)*.

It is simple to investigate the stiffness of a spring. The spring hangs freely with the top end clamped firmly *(figure 13.3)*. A load is added and gradually increased. For each value of the load, the extension of the spring is measured. (Note that it is

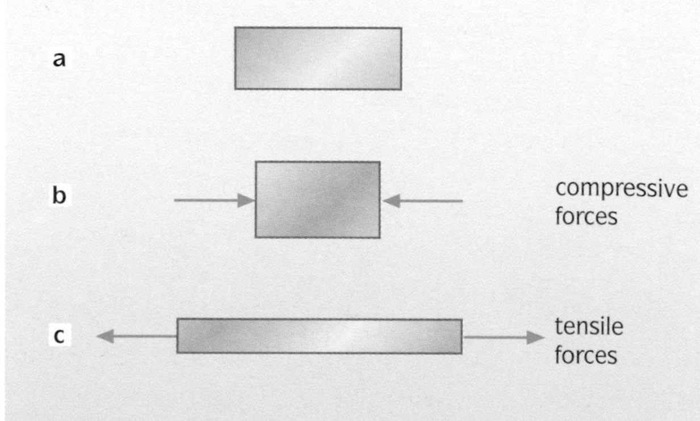

● ***Figure 13.2*** The effects of compressive and tensile forces.

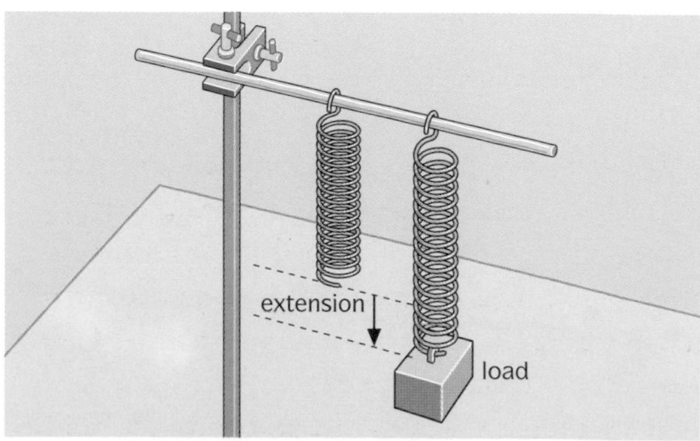

● ***Figure 13.3*** Stretching a spring.

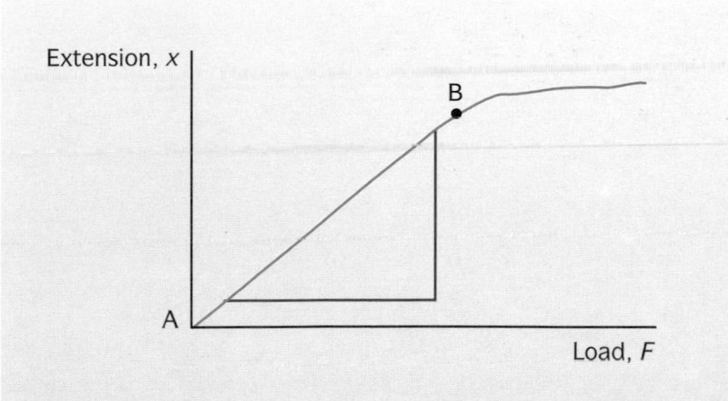

● ***Figure 13.4*** Load–extension graph for a spring.

important to determine the increase in length, which we call the **extension.**) To calculate the stiffness of the spring, we draw a graph of load against extension *(figure 13.4).*

Hooke's law

The graph shown in *figure 13.4* has extension on the vertical axis, and load on the horizontal axis. This is the conventional way of plotting the results of this experiment, since we are changing the load and this results in a change in the extension. For a typical spring, the first section of this graph AB is a straight line passing through the origin. This tells us that the extension x is proportional to the load F. We can write this as an equation:

$$F = kx$$

where $k = F/x$ is the **spring constant** of the spring (sometimes called the spring's stiffness). This is the force per unit extension, or the force needed to extend the spring by one metre. We can find the spring constant from the gradient of section AB of the graph:

$$\text{spring constant } k = \frac{1}{\text{gradient}}$$

Beyond point B, the graph is no longer a straight line. This is probably because the spring has become permanently deformed; it has been stretched beyond its elastic limit. The meaning of the term *elastic limit* is discussed further in a later section of this chapter (page 113).

If a spring or anything else responds to a tensile force in the way shown in *figure 13.4*, we say that

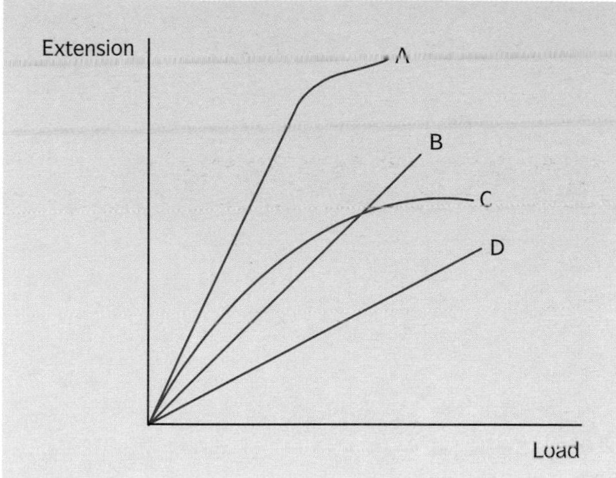

● ***Figure 13.5*** Load–extension graphs for four springs.

it obeys Hooke's law:

An object obeys **Hooke's law** if the extension produced in it is proportional to the load, provided the elastic limit is not exceeded.

SAQ 13.1

Figure 13.5 shows the load–extension graphs for four springs, A–D.

a Which spring has the greatest value of spring constant?

b Which is the least stiff?

c Which does not obey Hooke's law?

Investigating springs

Find two or three identical springs. You can combine springs in different ways *(figure 13.6)*: end-to-end (in series) and side-by-side (in parallel). You are going to measure the spring constant of a single spring, and of springs in series and in

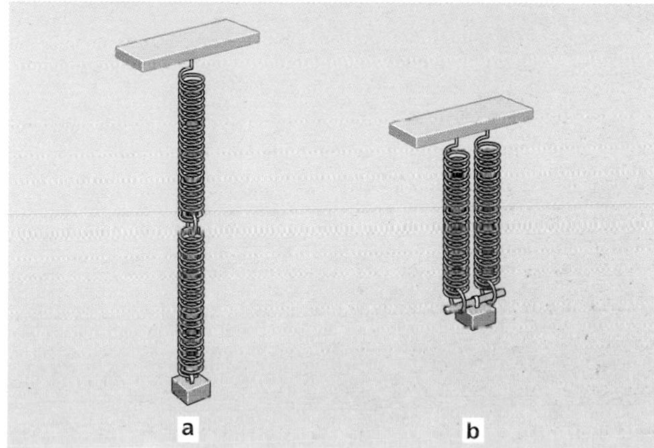

● ***Figure 13.6*** Two ways to combine two springs.

parallel. Before you do this, however, try to predict the outcome of your experiment:

- If the spring constant of a single spring is k, what will be the spring constant of two springs in series?
- And of two springs in parallel?

Make suitable measurements to check your predictions. You might extend your ideas to combinations of three or more springs.

Stretching materials

Because they are coiled, springs extend a lot for a small load. If you have a long piece of metal wire, it is possible to see it stretch, but this can take a large force. Materials scientists are often interested to find out about the characteristics of materials when large forces are applied to them. They may use large tensile testing machines capable of producing large compressive and tensile forces. One such machine is shown in *figure 13.7*.

When we measure the stiffness of a spring, we are only finding out about the stiffness of that particular spring. However, we can talk about the stiffness of particular materials. We might say, for example, that steel is stiffer than copper.

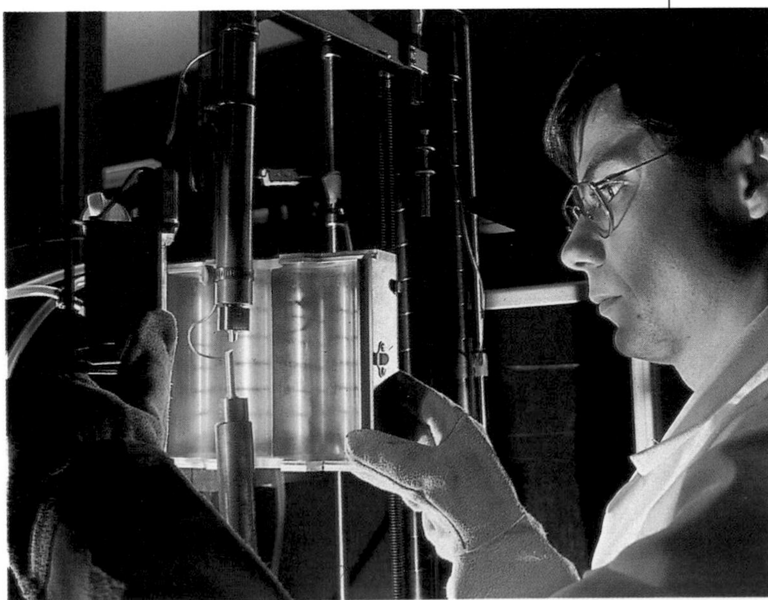

● ***Figure 13.7*** This tensile testing machine is being used to test the strength of a valve stem from a racing car engine.

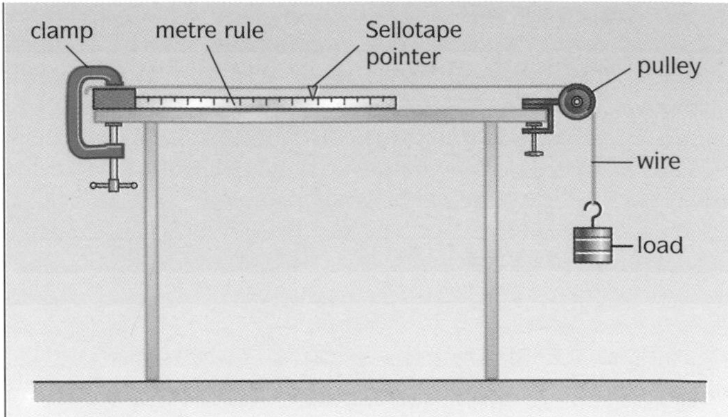

● ***Figure 13.8*** Stretching a wire in the laboratory.

Stress and strain

Figure 13.8 shows a simple way of measuring the stiffness of a wire in the laboratory. As the wire is stretched, the position of the Sellotape marker can be read from the scale on the bench.

Why do we use a long wire? Obviously, this is because a short wire would not stretch as much as a long one. We need to take account of this in our calculations, and we do this by calculating the strain produced by the load. The **strain** is the fractional increase in the length of the wire:

$$\text{strain} = \frac{\text{extension}}{\text{original length}}$$

Note that both extension and original length must be in the same units and so strain is a ratio, without units. Sometimes strain is given as a percentage.

Why do we use a thin wire? Obviously, this is because a thick wire would not stretch as much for the same force. Again, we need to take account of this in our calculations, and we do this by calculating the stress produced by the load. The **stress** is the load per unit cross-sectional area of the wire:

$$\text{stress} = \frac{\text{load}}{\text{cross-sectional area}}$$

Since load is in newtons and area in square metres, stress is similar to pressure, and has the same units: $\mathrm{N\,m^{-2}}$ or pascals, Pa. If you imagine compressing a bar of metal rather than stretching a wire, you will see why stress or pressure is the important quantity.

The Young modulus

We can now find the stiffness of the material we are stretching. Rather than calculating load/extension, we calculate the ratio of stress to strain. This quantity is called the **Young modulus** of the material:

$$\text{Young modulus} = \frac{\text{stress}}{\text{strain}}$$

The unit of the Young modulus is the same as for stress, $\mathrm{N\,m^{-2}}$ or Pa. In practice, values may be quoted in MPa or GPa (1 MPa = 10^6 Pa, 1 GPa = 10^9 Pa).

Usually, we plot a graph with stress on the vertical axis and strain on the horizontal axis (*figure 13.9*). This is the reverse of the spring graph (*figure 13.4*), where force is drawn on the horizontal axis; it is drawn like this so that the gradient is the Young modulus. It is important to consider only the first, straight section of the graph.

Table 13.1 gives some values of the Young modulus for different materials.

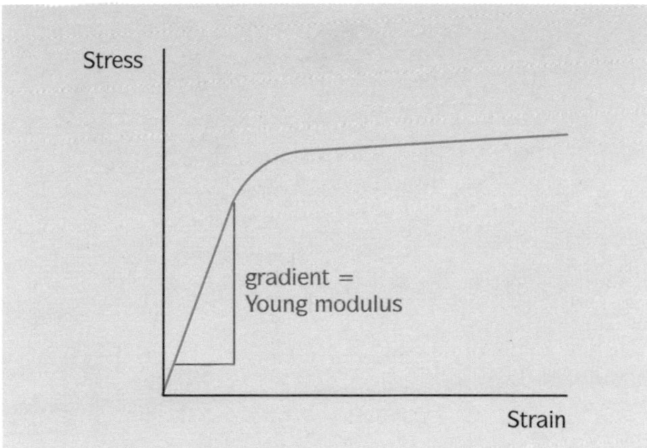

● ***Figure 13.9*** Stress–strain graph, and how to deduce the Young modulus.

Material	*Young modulus/GPa*
aluminium	70
brass	90–110
brick	7–20
concrete	40
copper	130
glass	70–80
iron (wrought)	200
lead	18
Perspex	3
polystyrene	2.7–4.2
rubber	0.01
steel	210
tin	50
wood	10 approx

● ***Table 13.1*** The Young modulus of various materials. Many of these values depend on the precise composition of the material concerned.

SAQ 13.2

List the metals in *table 13.1* from stiffest to least stiff.

SAQ 13.3

Which non-metal in the table is the stiffest?

SAQ 13.4

Figure 13.10 shows stress–strain graphs for two materials. Use the graphs to determine the Young modulus of each.

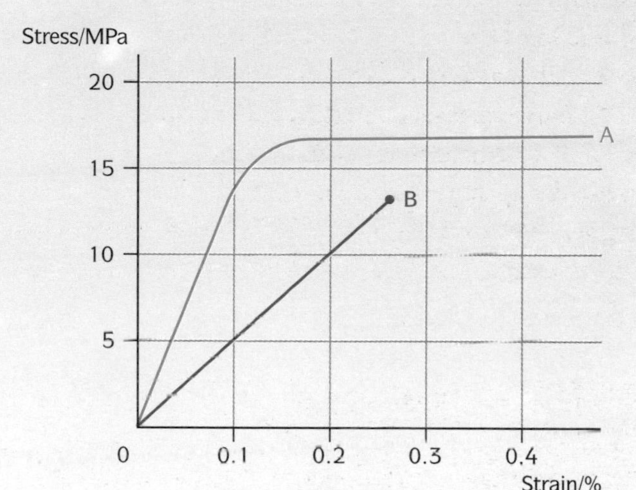

● ***Figure 13.10*** Stress–strain graphs for two different materials.

SAQ 13.5

A piece of steel wire, 200.0 cm long and having cross-sectional area 0.5 $\mathrm{mm^2}$, is stretched by a force of 50 N. Its new length is found to be 200.1 cm. Calculate the stress and strain, and the Young modulus of steel.

SAQ 13.6

By how much will a 1 m length of copper wire, diameter 1 mm, be stretched by a 10 N load? (Young modulus of copper = 130 GPa.)

Measuring the Young modulus

Metals are not very elastic. In practice, they can only be stretched by about 0.1% of their original length. Beyond this, they become permanently deformed. As a result, some careful thought must be given to getting results that are good enough to give an accurate value of the Young modulus.

First, the wire used must be long. The increase in length is proportional to the original length, and so a longer wire gives larger and more measurable extensions. Typically, extensions up to 1 mm must be measured for a wire of length 1 m. There are two possibilities: use a very long wire, or use a method that allows measurement of extensions that are a fraction of a millimetre.

Figure 13.11 shows an arrangement that incorporates a vernier scale, which can be read to 0.1 mm. One part of the scale (the vernier) is attached to the wire that is stretched; this moves past the scale on the fixed reference wire.

Secondly, the cross-sectional area of the wire must be known accurately. This is measured using a micrometer screw gauge, accurate to 0.01 mm.

Once the wire has been loaded in increasing steps, the load must be gradually decreased to ensure that there has been no permanent deformation of the wire.

Other materials such as glass and many plastics are also quite stiff, and so it is difficult to measure their Young modulus. Rubber is not as stiff, and strains of several hundred per cent can be achieved. However, the stress–strain graph for rubber is not a very straight line, and so the value of the Young modulus found is not very precise.

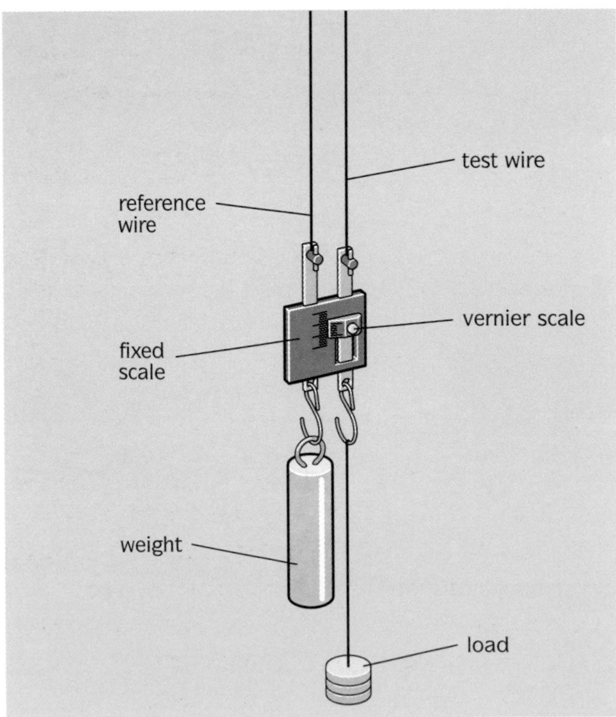

● ***Figure 13.11*** A more precise method for determining the Young modulus of a metal.

Describing deformation

The Young modulus of a material describes its stiffness. This only relates to the first, straight-line section of the stress–strain graph. In this region, the material is behaving in an elastic way, and the straight line means that the material obeys Hooke's law. However, if we continue to increase the load on the material, the graph may cease to be a straight line. *Figures 13.12–14* show stress–strain graphs for some typical materials, and we will discuss what these tell us in the paragraphs below.

- *Glass, cast iron (figure 13.12)*
  These materials behave in a similar way. If you increase the stress on them, they stretch slightly. However, there comes a point where the material suddenly breaks. Both glass and cast iron are **brittle**; if you apply a large stress, they shatter. They also show **elastic** behaviour up to the point where they break; if you apply a stress and then remove it, they return to their original length.

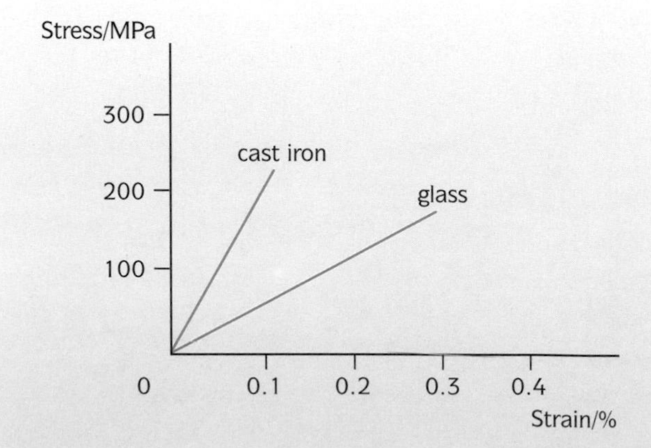

● ***Figure 13.12*** Stress–strain graphs for two brittle materials.

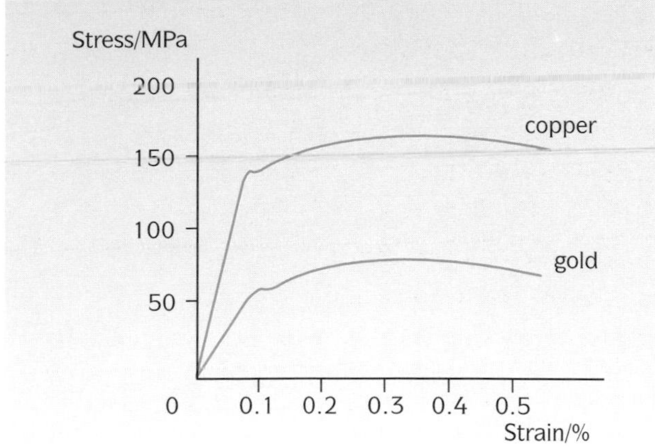

● ***Figure 13.13*** Stress–strain graphs for two ductile materials.

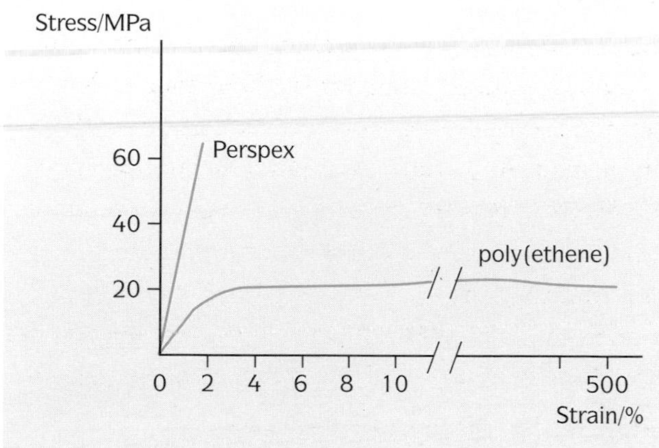

● ***Figure 13.14*** Stress–strain graphs for two polymeric materials.

- *Copper, gold (figure 13.13)*
  These materials show a different form of behaviour. If you have stretched a copper wire to determine its Young modulus, you will have noticed that, beyond a certain point, the wire stretches more and more and will not return to its original length when the load is removed. It has become permanently deformed. We describe this as **plastic** deformation. Copper and gold are both metals that can be shaped by stretching, rolling, hammering and squashing. This makes them very useful for making wires, jewellery, etc. They are described as **ductile** metals. (Pure iron is also a ductile metal. Cast iron has carbon in it – it's really a form of steel – and this changes its properties so that it is brittle.)
- *Poly(ethene), Perspex (figure 13.14)*
  Different polymers behave differently, depending on their molecular structure and their temperature. This graph shows two typical forms of stress–strain graph for polymers. Poly(ethene) is easy to deform, as you will know if you have ever tried to stretch a poly(ethene) bag. The material stretches (plastic deformation), and then eventually becomes much stiffer and snaps. This is rather like the behaviour of a ductile metal. Perspex behaves in a brittle way. It stretches elastically up to a point, and then it breaks. In practice, if Perspex is warmed slightly, it stops being brittle and can be formed into a desired shape.

To summarise, all materials show elastic behaviour up to the elastic limit; they return to their original length when the load is removed. Brittle materials break at the elastic limit. Ductile materials become permanently deformed if they are stretched beyond the elastic limit; they show plastic behaviour.

SAQ 13.7

Use the words *elastic*, *plastic*, *brittle* and *ductile* to say what the following observations tell you about the materials described.

a If you tap a cast iron bath gently with a hammer, the hammer bounces off. If you hit it hard, the bath shatters.

b Aluminium drinks cans are made by forcing a sheet of aluminium into a mould at high pressure.

c 'Silly putty' can be stretched to many times its original length if it is pulled gently and slowly. If it is pulled hard and rapidly, it snaps.

Stiffness and strength

It is easy to get these two terms confused. **Stiffness** (measured by the Young modulus) tells us about the elastic behaviour of a material. Most materials can be stretched elastically to a small degree. **Strength**, however, tells us about how much stress is needed to break the material. On a stress–strain graph *(figure 13.15)*, we look for the point at which the material breaks; the value of stress at this point is called the **ultimate tensile stress** of the

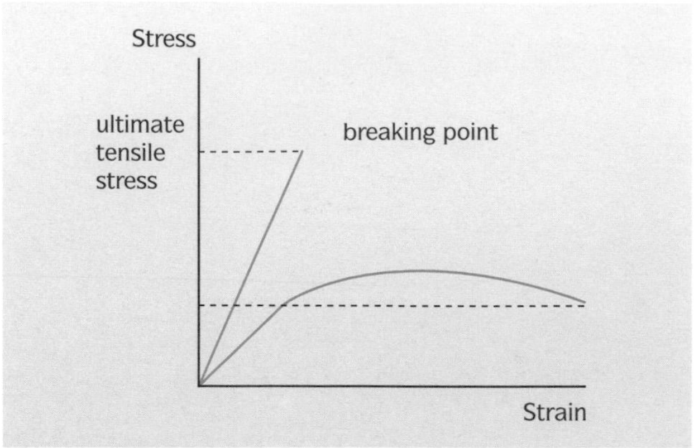

● **Figure 13.15** Defining the strength of a material.

material: *ultimate* because this is the end of the graph, *tensile* because the material is being stretched, and *stress* because we want to know the force that is required to break it.

SAQ 13.8

For each of the materials whose stress–strain graphs are shown in *figure 13.16*, deduce the values of the Young modulus and the ultimate tensile stress.

Explaining deformation

The behaviours of different materials under stress can be related to their underlying structures. The connection is rather complicated, and we will only consider an oversimplified picture here.

Many materials are **crystalline**. This means that the particles (atoms, ions or molecules) from which they are made are arranged in a regular way. Early evidence for this came from X-ray crystallography; nowadays, we have other techniques that allow us

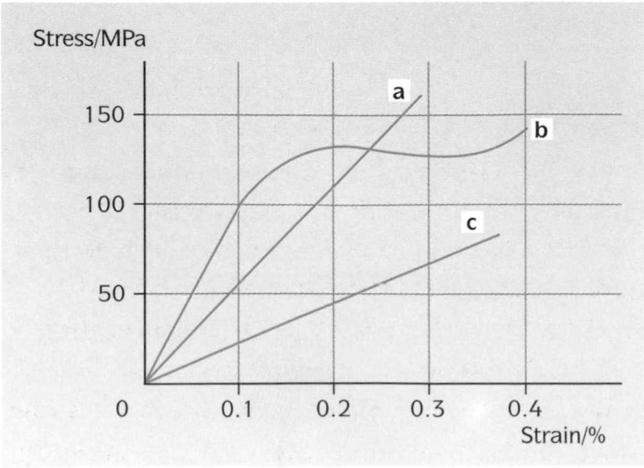

● **Figure 13.16** Stress–strain graphs for three materials.

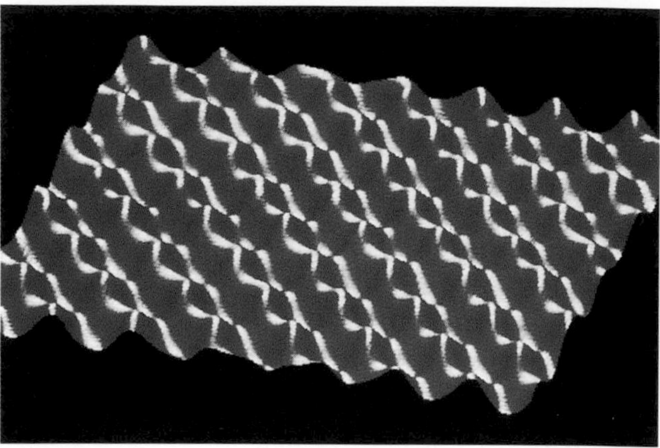

● **Figure 13.17** This image of atoms in graphite shows that, in this solid, they form a regular array.

to visualise the arrangement of particles; an example is shown in *figure 13.17*. You can see very clearly that these particles are arranged in regular rows. In a crystalline material, the particles are arranged in a giant three-dimensional array. Materials that have been found to be like this include metals and ionic substances such as sodium chloride. Sometimes this underlying structure is reflected in the macroscopic shape of crystals such as those shown in *figure 13.18*; very often, the underlying crystalline nature of a material is not at all obvious when we look at a piece of it – for example, it is not obvious that the atoms that make up a metal knife or fork are arranged in a uniform structure.

Other materials are **non-crystalline**. Their particles are arranged in a more random, jumbled kind of structure. Glass is often quoted as an example of this. Glass is a mixture of silica (silicon dioxide,

● **Figure 13.18** These crystals of rock salt have regular shapes, reflecting the regular arrangement of the particles of which they are made.

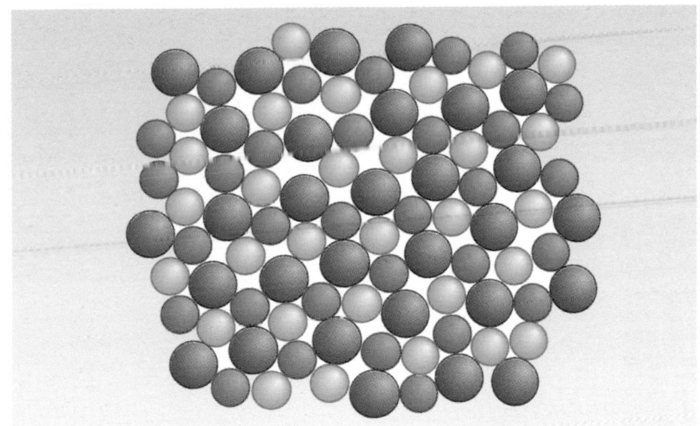

● *Figure 13.19* The particles of which glass is made form an irregular arrangement.

SiO_2) and other substances, and these atoms are packed together to form an **amorphous** structure *(figure 13.19)*. This picture is rather like that of the structure of a liquid; glass is like a liquid that has cooled down to become a solid without the atoms having been able to form into a regular pattern.

Polymers can have crystalline or amorphous structures. They are often a mixture of the two. Polymers are made of flexible, long-chain molecules, rather like cooked spaghetti. If you look at spaghetti on a plate, you will see that in some places the strands lie neatly side-by-side, and in other places they are tangled up. In a similar way, polymers have regions of crystalline order and regions of amorphous disorder *(figure 13.20)*.

How does this relate to how materials behave when they are stretched? In the elastic region, when the stress is low, the particles are pulled very slightly apart. When the stress is removed, they pull back together again *(figure 13.21a)*. In a brittle material,

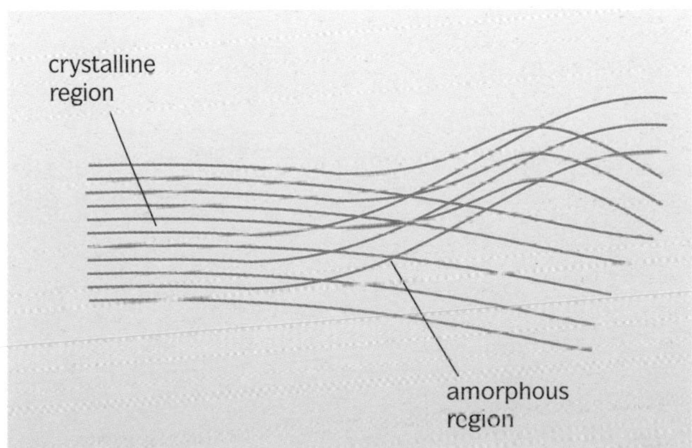

● *Figure 13.20* Long-chain polymer molecules tend to form partially ordered arrangements.

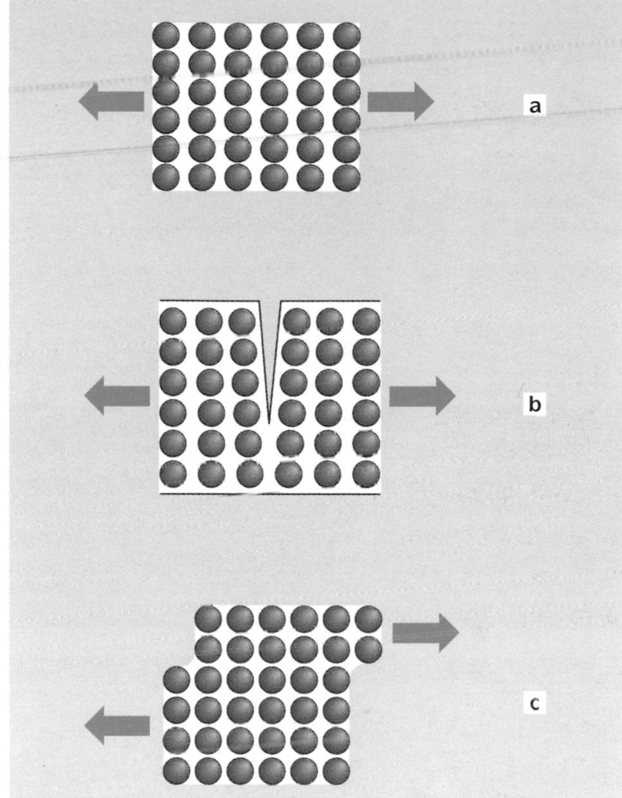

● *Figure 13.21* Three ways in which a material may behave under stress.

greater stresses pull the particles apart, and the material snaps *(figure 13.21b)*. In a ductile material, the particles start to slide over one another, and the material becomes permanently deformed *(figure 13.21c)*. This is particularly easy in metals, where all the atoms are identical. Ionic substances tend to be brittle because it is difficult for an ion to slide past another ion of the same charge.

Strain energy

Whenever you stretch a springy material, you are doing work. You will know this if you have ever used an exercise machine with springs intended to develop your muscles *(figure 13.22)*. Similarly, when you push down on the end of a springboard before diving, you are doing work. You transfer energy to the springboard, and you recover the energy when it pushes you up into the air.

We call the energy in a deformed solid the **strain energy**. If the material has been strained elastically (the elastic limit has not been exceeded), the

● ***Figure 13.22*** Eventually this athlete may have the strength to break the exercise machine.

energy can be recovered. If the material has been plastically deformed, some of the work done has gone into moving atoms past one another, and the energy cannot be recovered. (The material warms up slightly.) We can find out how much strain energy is involved from the force–extension graph, *figure 13.23*. We need to use the equation that defines the amount of work done:

work done = force × distance moved (in the direction of the force)

We consider first the portion of the graph where Hooke's law is obeyed, OA. The graph in this region is a straight line. The force gradually increases, and the extension increases in proportion. There are two ways to find the work done. First, we can think about the average force needed to produce an extension x. The average force is half the final force F, and so we can write

$$\text{strain energy} = \text{work done} = \tfrac{1}{2} \times \text{force} \times \text{extension} = \tfrac{1}{2}Fx$$

The other way to find the strain energy is to recognise that we can get the same answer by finding the area under the graph. The area shaded is a triangle whose area is $\frac{1}{2}$ × base × height, which again gives

$$\text{strain energy} = \tfrac{1}{2}Fx$$

In fact, this is true whatever the shape of the graph. The strain energy is always equal to the area under the force–extension graph. (Take care: here we are drawing the graph with extension on the horizontal axis.) If the graph is not a straight line, we cannot use the $\frac{1}{2}Fx$ formula, so we have to resort to counting squares or some other technique to find the answer.

We shall now do a worked example. *Figure 13.24* shows a simplified version of a force–extension graph for a piece of metal. Find the strain energy when the metal is stretched to its elastic limit and the work that must be done to break the metal.

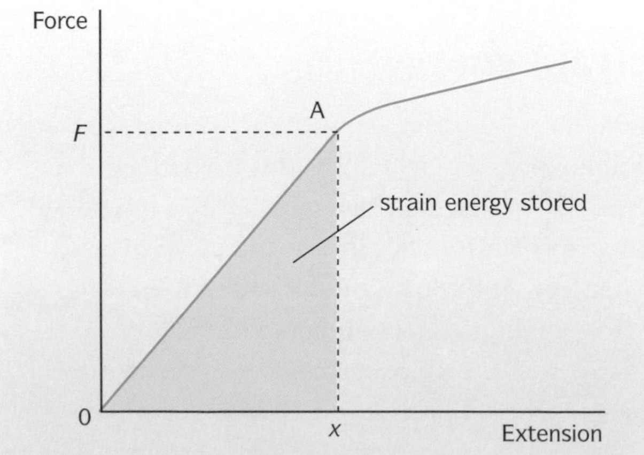

● ***Figure 13.23*** Strain energy is equal to the area under the force–extension graph.

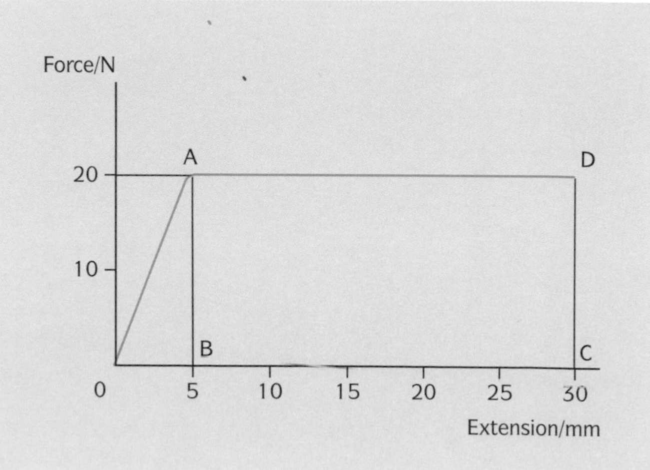

● ***Figure 13.24***

Here we need to find the area under the graph up to the elastic limit. The graph is a straight line up to $x = 5$ mm, $F = 20$ N, so the strain energy is the area of triangle OAB:

$$\text{strain energy} = \tfrac{1}{2}Fx = \tfrac{1}{2} \times 20\,\text{N} \times 5 \times 10^{-3}\,\text{m}$$
$$= 0.05\,\text{J}$$

Now we need to add on the area of the rectangle ABCD:

$$\text{work done} = 0.05\,\text{J} + 20\,\text{N} \times 25 \times 10^{-3}\,\text{m}$$
$$= 0.05\,\text{J} + 0.5\,\text{J} = 0.55\,\text{J}$$

SAQ 13.9

Estimate the strain energy stored when a diver presses the end of a springboard down a distance of 30 cm using a maximum force of 1500 N. Explain why your answer can only be an estimate.

SAQ 13.10

Figure 13.25 shows force–extension graphs for two pieces of polymer. For each of the following questions, explain how you deduce your answer from the graphs.

a Which has the greater stiffness?

b Which requires the greater force to break it?

c Which requires the greater amount of work to be done in order to break it?

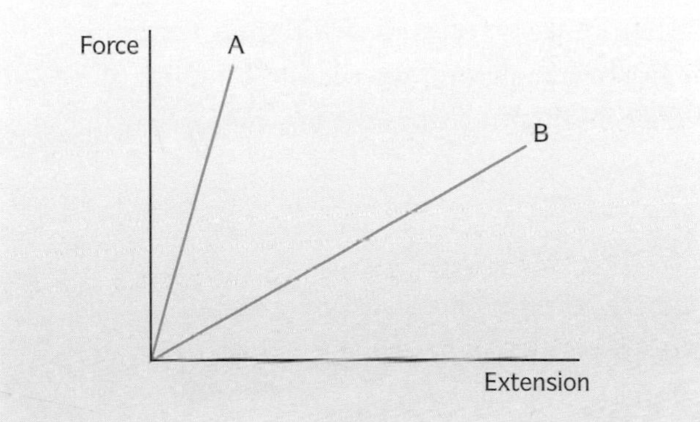

● ***Figure 13.25***

SUMMARY

- For a spring, a graph of load against extension is a straight line up to the elastic limit (Hooke's law).
- To describe the behaviour of a material under tensile and compressive forces, we have to draw a graph of stress against strain. The gradient of the initial linear section gives us the Young modulus, which tells us how stiff the material is.
- Beyond the elastic limit, brittle materials break.
- Ductile materials show plastic behaviour and become permanently deformed.
- The behaviour of a material can be related to its underlying crystalline or amorphous structure.
- The strain energy in a deformed material can be found from the area under the force–extension graph.

Ideal gases

By the end of this chapter you should be able to:

1 recall and use the equation of state for an ideal gas, $pV = nRT$;

2 understand the concept of an absolute scale of temperature;

3 recall the basic assumptions of the kinetic theory of gases;

4 explain how molecular movement causes the pressure exerted by a gas;

5 give a simple derivation of $p = \frac{1}{3}Nm\langle c^2\rangle/V$;

6 compare $pV = \frac{1}{3}Nm\langle c^2\rangle$ with $pV = nRT$ and hence deduce that the average kinetic energy of a molecule is proportional to T.

The gas laws and absolute zero

In chapter 12, we looked at the kinetic model of matter. This allows us to understand the macroscopic behaviour of matter (pressure, changes of state, etc.) in terms of the arrangement and motion of the microscopic particles of which matter is made. In this chapter, we will extend this study from qualitative descriptions to a more quantitative explanation of the behaviour of gases.

● ***Figure 14.1*** Hot air is less dense than cold air.

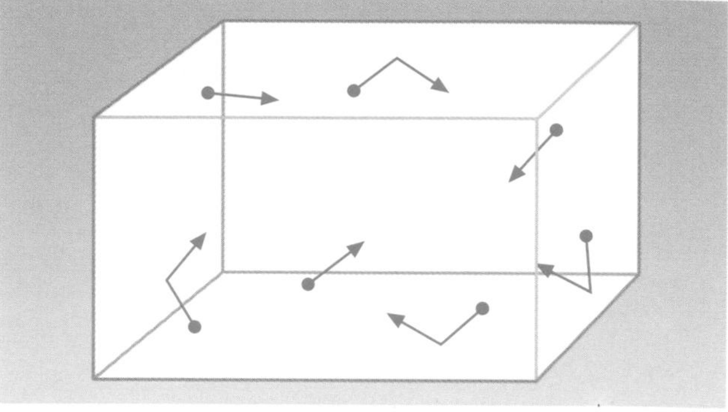

● ***Figure 14.2*** Between collisions, the molecules of a gas move rapidly in straight lines.

It is easier to develop a quantitative theory for gases than for solids and liquids because, in a gas, the particles of which it is composed are well separated. They collide with each other and with the walls of their container, but most of the time they are freely moving, and we can think of them as being small, hard spheres moving about rapidly in straight lines (*figure 14.2*).

Before we go on to develop this quantitative microscopic picture, we need to establish an equation that describes the macroscopic properties of gases.

Measuring a gas

We are going to picture a container of gas, such as the box shown in *figure 14.3*. There are four properties of this gas that we might measure: pressure, temperature, volume and mass.

- *Pressure*
  This is the force exerted per unit area by the gas on the walls of the container. It is measured in pascals, Pa ($1\,\text{Pa} = 1\,\text{N}\,\text{m}^{-2}$).
- *Temperature*
  This might be measured in °C, but in practice it is more useful to use the kelvin scale of

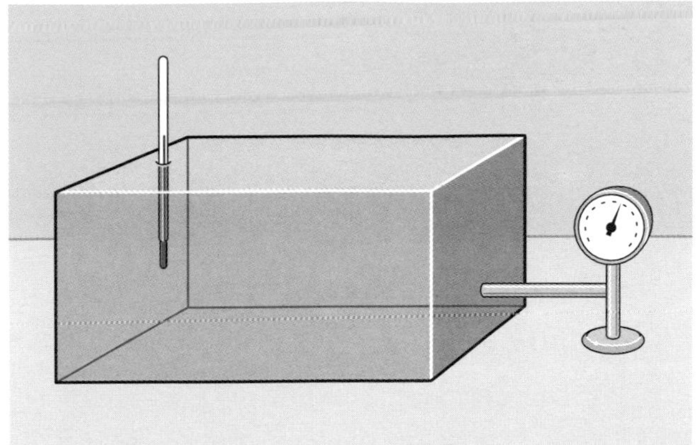

● ***Figure 14.3*** A gas has four measurable properties, which are all related to one another: pressure, temperature, volume and mass.

temperature. This scale starts at absolute zero, an idea that is discussed in detail below.

- *Volume*
  This is measured in m^3.
- *Mass*
  This is measured in g or kg. In practice, it is more useful to consider the **amount** of gas measured in moles.

One mole of any substance is equal to the relative molecular mass of the substance, measured in grams. (For example, one mole of oxygen O_2 has a mass of about 32 g.) A mole of any gas contains a standard number of molecules (the Avogadro number, 6.023×10^{23} molecules per mole, approximately). It turns out that, if we consider equal numbers of moles of two different gases under the same conditions, their properties are the same.

Boyle's law

This law relates the pressure and volume of a gas. If a gas is compressed (pressure increased), its volume decreases. Pressure p and volume V are inversely related. We can write **Boyle's law** as:

The volume of a fixed mass of gas is inversely proportional to its pressure, provided the temperature remains constant.

Note that this law relates two variables, pressure and volume, and it requires that the other two, mass and temperature, remain constant. If either changed as the pressure of the gas was changed, then the result would be different.

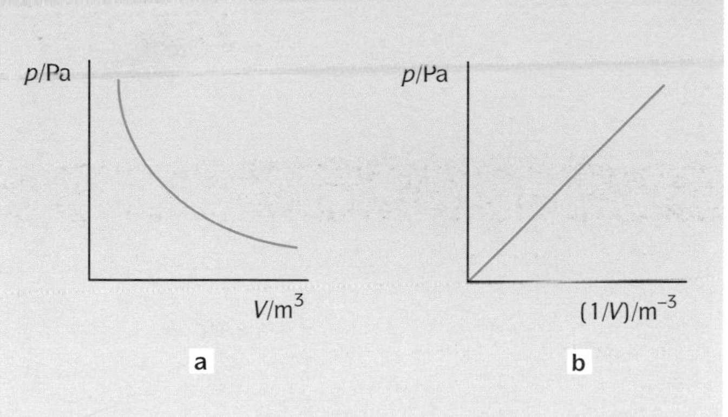

● ***Figure 14.4*** Graphical representations of the relationship between pressure and volume of a gas (Boyle's law).

This law can be written as either a proportionality or an equation:

$$p \propto 1/V \qquad \text{or} \qquad pV = \text{constant}$$

We can also represent Boyle's law as a graph, as shown in *figure 14.4*. A graph of p against $1/V$ is a straight line passing through the origin, showing direct proportionality.

Charles' law

This law describes how the volume of a gas depends on its temperature, and can be investigated using apparatus like that shown in *figure 14.5*.

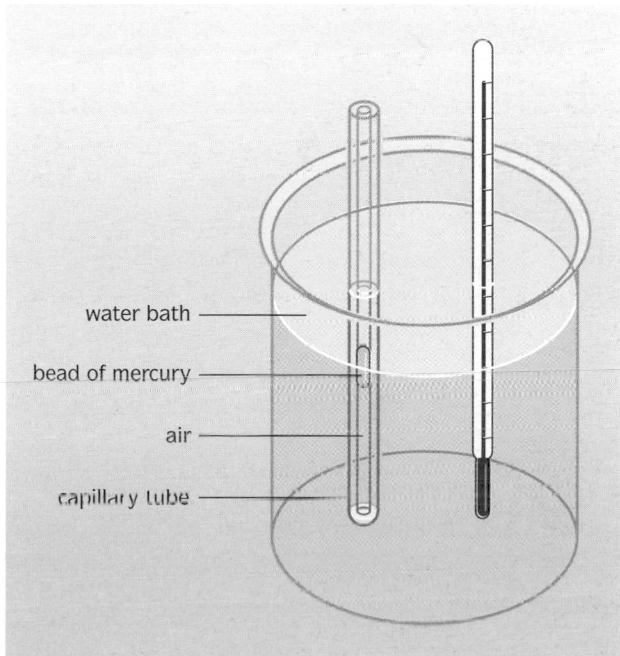

● ***Figure 14.5*** Apparatus for investigating Charles' law.

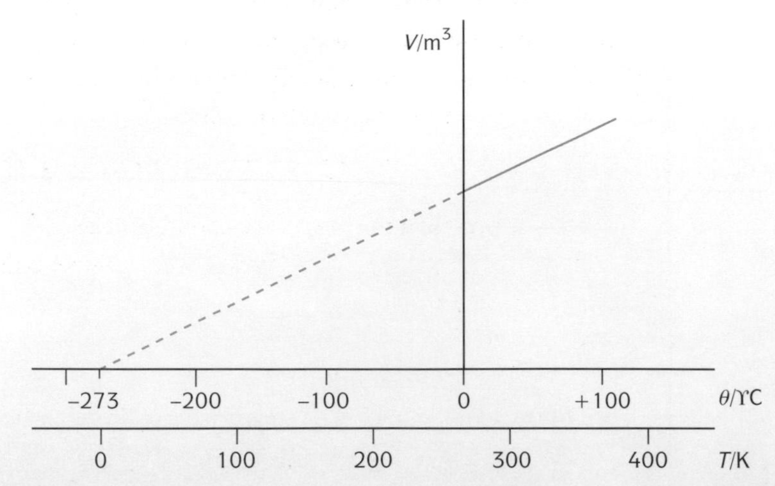

● ***Figure 14.6*** The volume of a gas increases as its temperature increases.

As the water bath is heated, the trapped air expands and its volume can be read from the scale. Notice that the pressure of the air remains at atmospheric pressure throughout. This arrangement can be used to find values of volume and temperature between 0 °C and 100 °C, and an idealised set of results are represented in *figure 14.6*.

This graph does not show that the volume of a gas is proportional to its temperature on the Celsius scale. If a gas contracted to zero volume at 0 °C, the atmosphere would condense on a cold day, and we would have a great deal of difficulty in breathing! However, the graph does show that there is a temperature at which the volume of a gas does, in principle, shrink to zero. This temperature is found by extrapolating the graph to zero volume (the dashed line), and it is roughly −273 °C. This is a fundamental temperature, below which it is impossible to go, and it is known as **absolute zero**.

Figure 14.6 also shows how we can renumber the temperature scale, starting at absolute zero, 0 K. Now 0 °C becomes 273.15 K and 100 °C becomes 373.15 K. This graph shows clearly that volume V of the gas is proportional to its absolute temperature, T (measured on the kelvin scale). We can write **Charles' law** as:

The volume of a fixed mass of gas is directly proportional to its absolute temperature, provided its pressure remains constant.

We can write this as a proportionality or as an equality:

$$V \propto T \qquad \text{or} \qquad V/T = \text{constant}$$

Note again that the other two variables, mass and pressure, must remain fixed for this law to hold.

The pressure law

This law describes how the pressure of a gas changes as the temperature changes. Again, we have to consider the absolute temperature of the gas. The relationship between pressure p and temperature T is shown as a graph in *figure 14.7*. Again, we have direct proportionality. We can write the **pressure law** as:

The pressure of a fixed mass of gas is directly proportional to its absolute temperature, provided its volume remains constant.

This can be written as:

$$p \propto T \qquad \text{or} \qquad p/T = \text{constant}$$

If we combine all three laws, we can arrive at a single equation for a fixed mass of gas:

$$\frac{pV}{T} = \text{constant}$$

This is useful because very often we have situations where all three variables, p, V and T, are changing at the same time. For example, if you increase the pressure on a gas, its volume will decrease and its temperature will increase.

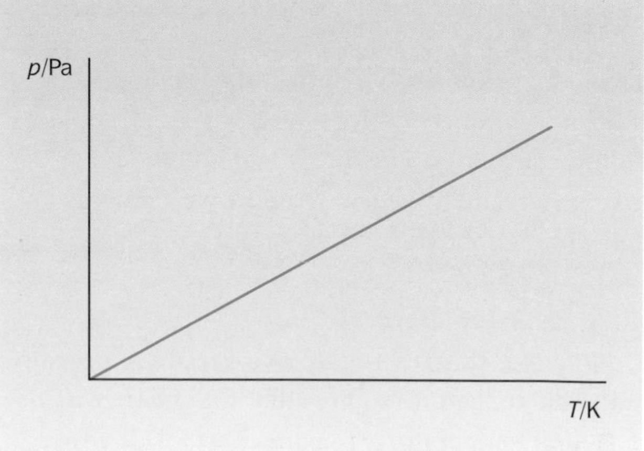

● ***Figure 14.7*** Graphical representation of the relationship between pressure and temperature for a gas.

The kelvin scale

The Celsius scale of temperature is based on the properties of water. It takes two fixed points, the melting point of pure ice and the boiling point of pure water, and divides the range between them into 100 equal intervals.

There is nothing intrinsically special about these two fixed points. In fact, both change if the pressure changes or if the water is impure. The kelvin scale is a better scale in that one of its fixed points, absolute zero, has a greater significance than either of the Celsius fixed points.

Absolute zero is a very significant temperature; we have arrived at it by considering the behaviour of gases, but its significance is greater than this. It is not possible to have a temperature lower than 0 K. Sometimes it is suggested that, at this temperature, matter has no energy left in it. This is not strictly true; it is more correct to say that, for any matter at absolute zero, it is impossible to *remove* any more energy from it.

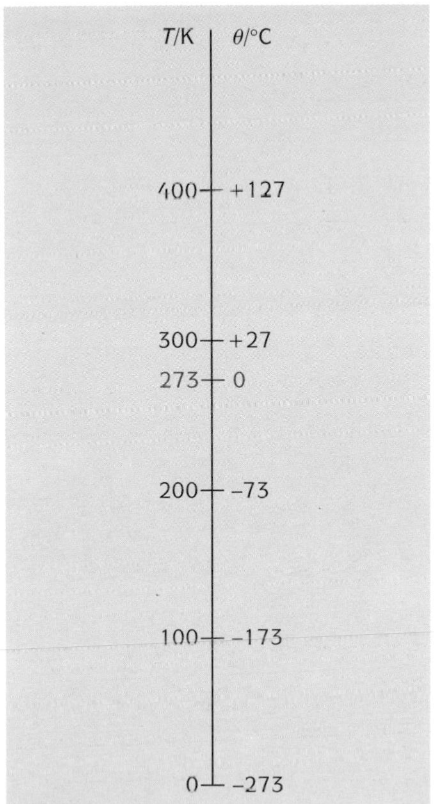

● ***Figure 14.8*** A conversion chart relating temperatures on the kelvin and Celsius scales.

We use different symbols to represent temperatures on these two scales: θ for the Celsius scale, and T for the kelvin scale. To convert between the two scales, we use these relationships:

$$\theta/°\mathrm{C} = T/\mathrm{K} - 273.15 \qquad T/\mathrm{K} = \theta/°\mathrm{C} + 273.15$$

For most practical purposes, we round off the conversion factor to 273 as shown in the conversion chart *(figure 14.8)*.

Ideal gases

The laws that we have considered above are based on experimental observations of gases such as air, helium, nitrogen, etc., at temperatures and pressures around room temperature and pressure. In practice, if we change to more extreme conditions, such as low temperatures or high pressures, gases start to deviate from these laws. For example, *figure 14.9* shows what happens when nitrogen is cooled down towards absolute zero. At first, the graph of volume against temperature follows a good straight line. However, as it approaches the temperature at which it condenses, it deviates from ideal behaviour, and at 77 K it condenses to become liquid nitrogen.

Thus we have to attach a proviso to the gas laws discussed above. We say that these laws apply to an ideal gas; when we are dealing with real gases, we have to be aware that their behaviour may be significantly different from that suggested by these laws.

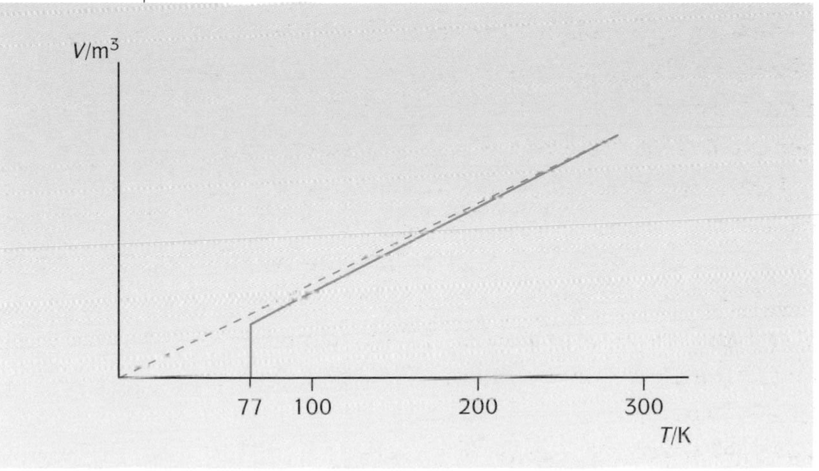

● ***Figure 14.9*** A real gas (in this case, nitrogen) deviates from the behaviour predicted by Charles' law at low temperatures.

An **ideal gas** is thus defined as one that obeys all three laws; in other words, pV/T = constant for a fixed mass of the gas.

SAQ 14.1

a Convert each of the following temperatures from the Celsius scale to the kelvin scale: 0°C, 20°C, 120°C, 500°C, −23°C, −200°C.

b Convert each of the following temperatures from the kelvin scale to the Celsius scale: 0K, 20K, 100K, 300K, 373K, 500K.

SAQ 14.2

Use the gas laws to explain the following observations:

a The pressure in a car tyre increases on a hot day.

b A toy balloon shrinks when placed in a fridge.

SAQ 14.3

The electrical resistance of a pure copper wire is mostly due to the vibrations of the copper atoms. *Table 14.1* shows how the resistance of a piece of copper wire is found to change as it is heated. Draw a graph to show these data, and use it to deduce a value for absolute zero. (Start the temperature scale of your graph at −300°C.) Explain why the resistance of copper should be zero at this temperature.

Temperature/°C	*Resistance*/Ω
10	3120
50	3600
75	3900
100	4200
150	4800
220	5640
260	6120

● ***Table 14.1*** Resistance of a copper wire

Equation of state

It is possible to write a single equation embodying all three gas laws, and taking into account the amount of gas being considered. For n moles of an ideal gas, we have

$$pV = nRT$$

This equation is known as the **equation of state** for an ideal gas; it is an equation that relates all of the four variable quantities that were discussed at the beginning of the previous section (page 118). The constant of proportionality R is called the **universal gas constant**, and its value is

$$R = 8.31\,\mathrm{J\,mol^{-1}\,K^{-1}}$$

Note that it doesn't matter what gas we are considering – it could be a very light gas like hydrogen, or a much heavier one like carbon dioxide. So long as it is behaving as an ideal gas, we can use the same equation of state with the same constant R.

Calculating n

Sometimes we know the mass of gas we are concerned with, and then we have to be able to find how many moles this represents. To do this, we use this relationship:

$$\text{number of moles} = \frac{\text{mass/g}}{\text{molar mass/g mol}^{-1}}$$

For example, how many moles are there in 1.6 kg of oxygen? Molar mass of oxygen = $32\,\mathrm{g\,mol^{-1}}$.
Number of moles = $1600\,\mathrm{g}/32\,\mathrm{g\,mol^{-1}}$ = 50 moles.

We shall now do two worked examples.

1 Find the volume occupied by 1 mole of an ideal gas at standard temperature and pressure.

Here we have the following values:

$$p = 1.013 \times 10^5\,\mathrm{Pa}$$
$$T = 273\,\mathrm{K}$$
$$n = 1$$

Substituting in the equation of state gives

$$V = nRT/p = 1 \times 8.31\,\mathrm{J\,mol^{-1}\,K^{-1}} \times 273\,\mathrm{K}/(1.013 \times 10^5\,\mathrm{Pa})$$
$$= 0.0224\,\mathrm{m^3}$$
$$= 22.4\,\mathrm{dm^3}$$

This value, the volume of one mole of gas at standard temperature and pressure, is well worth remembering. It is certainly known by all chemists.

2 A car tyre contains 0.02 m^3 of air at 27°C and at a pressure of 3×10^5 Pa. What is the mass of the air in the tyre? (Molar mass of air = 28.8 g.)

Here, we need first to calculate the number of moles of air using the equation of state.

$p = 3 \times 10^5\,\text{Pa}$
$V = 0.02\,\text{m}^3$
$T = 27°\text{C} = 300\,\text{K}$

So, from the equation of state:

$$n = pV/RT = \frac{3 \times 10^5\,\text{Pa} \times 0.02\,\text{m}^3}{8.31\,\text{J mol}^{-1}\text{K}^{-1} \times 300\,\text{K}} = 2.41\,\text{mol}$$

Now we can calculate the mass of air:

$$\text{mass} = \text{number of moles} \times \text{molar mass} = 2.41\,\text{mol} \times 28.8\,\text{g mol}^{-1} = 69.4\,\text{g}$$

SAQ 14.4

How many moles are there in 100 g of nitrogen? (Molar mass of N_2 = 28 g.) What volume does this mass occupy at standard temperature and pressure? (STP = 0°C, 1.013×10^5 Pa.)

SAQ 14.5

At what temperature would 1 kg of oxygen occupy 1 m^3 at a pressure of 10^5 Pa? (Molar mass of O_2 = 32 g.)

SAQ 14.6

A cylinder of hydrogen has a volume of 0.1 m^3. Its pressure is found to be 20 atmospheres at 20°C. What mass of hydrogen does it contain? If it was filled with oxygen instead to the same pressure, how much oxygen would it contain? (Molar mass of H_2 = 2 g, of O_2 = 32 g; 1 atmosphere = 10^5 Pa.)

Kinetic theory

The equation of state for an ideal gas relates four macroscopic properties of a gas – pressure, volume, temperature and amount of gas. The kinetic theory allows us to explain the properties of an ideal gas in terms of the behaviour of the microscopic particles (atoms or molecules) of which it is made. The rest of this chapter looks at how pressure and temperature relate to the motion of particles.

First, we need to establish the starting point of the kinetic theory. We picture a gas as being made up of a large number of fast-moving molecules (or atoms). They rush around in a rather haphazard way, colliding with one another and with the walls of their container. Collisions with the walls give rise to the pressure of the gas on the container; at higher temperatures, the molecules move faster.

There are four assumptions that form the basis of this simple version of the theory. These assumptions allow us to predict, for example, the pressure of the gas.

Assumptions

- The forces between molecules are negligible, except during collisions. (If the molecules attracted each other strongly, they would all tend to clump together in the middle of the container. The pressure would be lower at the walls than in the bulk of the gas.)
- The volume of the molecules themselves is small compared to the volume of the gas. (Remember that when a liquid boils and becomes a gas, its molecules become much farther apart. The air around us is about 99.9% empty space.)
- Most of the time, the molecules are moving in straight lines and at steady speeds. (The molecules collide with the walls of the container and with each other, but for most of the time they are moving with uniform velocities.)
- The collisions of molecules with each other and with the container are perfectly elastic. (Kinetic energy cannot be lost. It cannot become 'heat', since the 'heat' in a gas is simply the kinetic energy of the molecules.)

Calculating pressure

We start by picturing a single molecule in a cube-shaped box of side l (*figure 14.10*). This molecule has mass m, and is moving with speed c parallel to one side of the box (c is *not* the speed of light in this case). It rattles back and forth, colliding at regular intervals with the ends of the box and thereby contributing to the pressure of the gas. We are going to work out the pressure this one molecule exerts on

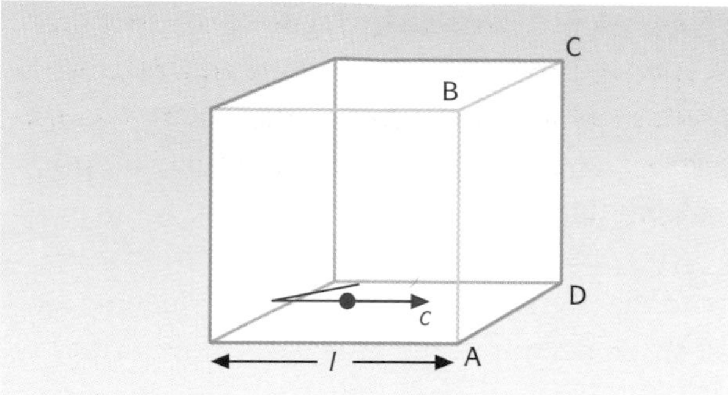

● **Figure 14.10** A single molecule moving in a box.

one end of the box, and then deduce the total pressure produced by all the molecules.

Consider a collision in which the molecule strikes side ABCD of the cube. It rebounds elastically in the opposite direction, so that its velocity is $-c$. Its momentum changes from mc to $-mc$. We can now find the change in momentum which results from a single collision:

$$\text{change of momentum} = -mc - (+mc) = -mc - mc = -2mc$$

Between consecutive collisions with side ABCD, the molecule travels a distance of $2l$ at speed c. Hence:

$$\text{time between collisions with side ABCD} = 2l/c$$

Now we can find the force that this one molecule exerts on side ABCD, using Newton's second law of motion. This says that the force produced is equal to the rate of change of momentum:

$$\text{force} = \frac{\text{change in momentum}}{\text{time taken}} = \frac{2mc}{2l/c} = \frac{mc^2}{l}$$

(We use $+2mc$ because now we are considering the force of the molecule on side ABCD; $-2mc$ is the change produced by the force of ABCD on the molecule. Recall Newton's third law of motion.)

The area of side ABCD is l^2. From the definition of pressure, we have:

$$\text{pressure} = \frac{\text{force}}{\text{area}} = \frac{mc^2/l}{l^2} = \frac{mc^2}{l^3}$$

In fact, we have not chosen a typical molecule, since this one is moving parallel to one side of the cube and only bouncing off two faces. A typical molecule will be moving at some angle in the box, tracing out a complicated path and bouncing off all six faces *(figure 14.11)*. Hence the force we calculated above is spread out over area $3l^2$, rather than l^2, and we have:

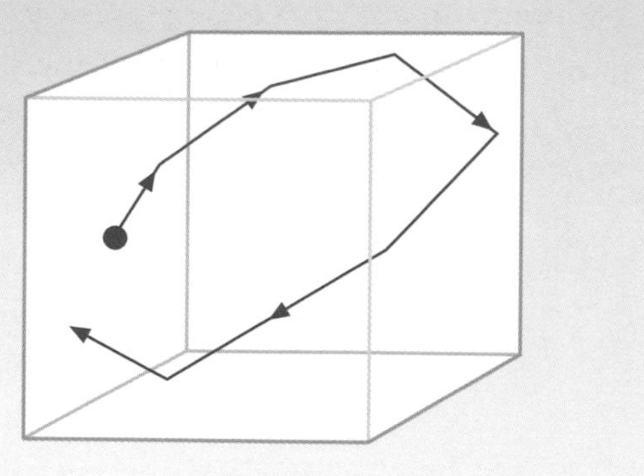

● **Figure 14.11** A typical molecule in a box collides with all six faces.

$$\text{pressure } p = \tfrac{1}{3}mc^2/l^3$$

Now we have to take account of the fact that there are a large number (N) of molecules in the box. Each has a different velocity, and each contributes to the pressure. We now imagine that they are all moving so that each contributes the same amount to the pressure, given by:

$$p = \tfrac{1}{3}m\langle c^2\rangle/l^3$$

where $\langle c^2\rangle$ is the average value of c^2 for all the molecules in the box. The total pressure of the gas in the box will thus be N times this amount:

$$p = \tfrac{1}{3}Nm\langle c^2\rangle/l^3$$

Finally, we can notice that l^3 is equal to the volume V of the cube, and so we can write

$$p = \tfrac{1}{3}Nm\langle c^2\rangle/V \qquad \text{or} \qquad pV = \tfrac{1}{3}Nm\langle c^2\rangle$$

A plausible equation?

It is worth thinking a little about whether the equation $p = \frac{1}{3}Nm\langle c^2\rangle/V$ seems to make sense. It should be clear to you that the pressure is proportional to the number of molecules, N. More molecules means greater pressure. Also, the greater the mass of each molecule, the greater the force it will exert during a collision.

The equation also suggests that pressure p is proportional to the average value of the speed squared. This is because, if a molecule is moving faster, not only does it strike the container harder, but it also strikes the container more often.

The equation suggests that pressure p is inversely proportional to the volume occupied by the gas. Here, we have deduced Boyle's law. If we think in terms of the kinetic model, we can see that if the gas occupies a larger volume, the molecules will spend more time in the bulk of the gas, and less time colliding with the walls. So the pressure will be lower.

These arguments should serve to convince you that the equation is plausible; this sort of argument cannot prove the equation.

SAQ 14.7

Check that the units on the left-hand side of the equation $p = \frac{1}{3}Nm\langle c^2\rangle/V$ are the same as those on the right-hand side.

SAQ 14.8

The quantity Nm is the total mass of the molecules of the gas, i.e. the mass of the gas. At room temperature, the density of air is about $1.29\,\mathrm{kg\,m^{-3}}$ at a pressure of $10^5\,\mathrm{Pa}$.

a Use these figures to deduce the value of $\langle c^2\rangle$ for air molecules at room temperature.

b Find a typical value for the speed of a molecule in the air by calculating $\sqrt{\langle c^2\rangle}$. How does this compare with the speed of sound in air, approximately $330\,\mathrm{m\,s^{-1}}$?

Temperature and molecular energy

We have now deduced an equation, $p = \frac{1}{3}Nm\langle c^2\rangle/V$, that relates two macroscopic quantities, the pressure and volume of a gas, to three microscopic quantities, the number, speed and mass of the molecules of which the gas is composed. Along the way, we have seen that this equation embodies Boyle's law.

Now we can go on to make more sense of this equation, by comparing it with the equation of state for an ideal gas. Here are the two equations, written so that both have the quantity pV on the left-hand side:

$$pV = \tfrac{1}{3}Nm\langle c^2\rangle$$
$$pV = nRT$$

Clearly, since the two left-hand sides are the same, the two right-hand sides must also be equal:

$$\tfrac{1}{3}Nm\langle c^2\rangle = nRT$$

We can use this equation to understand how the absolute temperature of the gas (a macroscopic property) is related to the mass and speed of the molecules. If we focus on the quantities of interest, we can see the following relationship:

$$m\langle c^2\rangle \propto T$$

It is easier to make sense of this if we write:

$$\tfrac{1}{2}m\langle c^2\rangle \propto T$$

The quantity $\frac{1}{2}m\langle c^2\rangle$ is the average kinetic energy of a molecule in the gas. This is proportional to the absolute temperature.

Increasing temperature

When we increase the temperature of a gas, we are giving it energy. The molecules of the gas move faster; they have more kinetic energy. We have now shown that, if we double the kinetic energy of the molecules, we double the absolute temperature of the gas.

To put this the other way round, when we measure the temperature of a gas, we are simply measuring the average kinetic energy of the molecules. The molecules collide with our thermometer, sharing their energy with it, and the result is that we know its temperature.

We conclude that the average kinetic energy of a molecule in an ideal gas is proportional to its absolute temperature. (We should really talk about translational kinetic energy. This is the energy that the molecule has because it is moving along; a

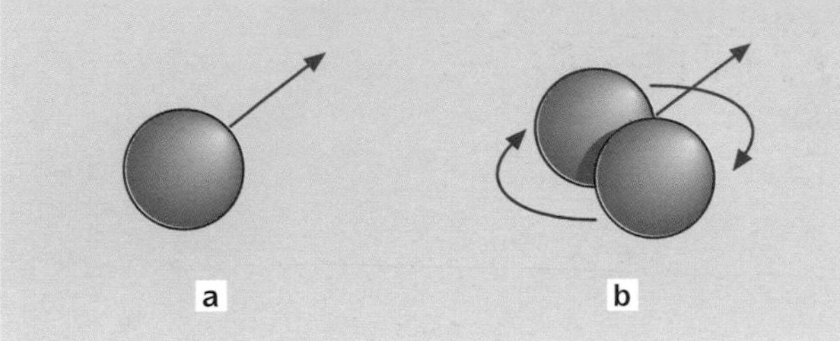

● ***Figure 14.12*** **a** A monatomic molecule can have translational kinetic energy. **b** A diatomic molecule can have both translational and rotational kinetic energy.

molecule made of two or more atoms may also spin or tumble around, and is then said to have rotational kinetic energy – see *figure 14.12*.)

SAQ 14.9

Show that, if the average speed of the molecules in a gas is doubled, the absolute temperature of the gas increases by a factor of 4.

SAQ 14.10

Air consists of molecules of oxygen and nitrogen. The nitrogen molecules have less mass than the oxygen molecules. In a particular sample of air, which would you expect to have the greater average speed? Explain your answer.

SUMMARY

- The gas laws are summarised in the equation of state for an ideal gas, $pV = nRT$. Temperature here must be measured on an absolute scale.
- The kinetic theory allows us to relate the macroscopic quantities of pressure, volume and temperature to the microscopic properties of the molecules that make up the gas.
- Pressure arises from collisions of molecules with the walls of the gas's container, and is given by $p = \frac{1}{3}Nm\langle c^2\rangle/V$.
- By comparing this equation with the equation of state, we find that the absolute temperature is proportional to the average translational kinetic energy of the molecules.

Thermodynamics

By the end of this chapter you should be able to:

1 derive, recall and use an expression for the work done by a gas that is expanding against a constant external pressure, $W = p\Delta V$;

2 be aware that the internal energy of a system is determined by the state of the system, and is the sum of the kinetic and potential energies of the molecules of the system;

3 recall the first law of thermodynamics expressed in terms of the change in internal energy ΔU, the heating of the system ΔQ and the work done on the system ΔW: $\Delta U = \Delta Q + \Delta W$.

Gases doing work

You can't get a good cup of tea at the top of Mount Everest. This is not simply because there are no cafés there; it's because of the problem of heating water to 100 °C. When you boil some water in a kettle, the steam that is produced has to escape. Steam is a gas, and it has to push aside the

● *Figure 15.1* Work must be done against atmospheric pressure in blowing up a balloon.

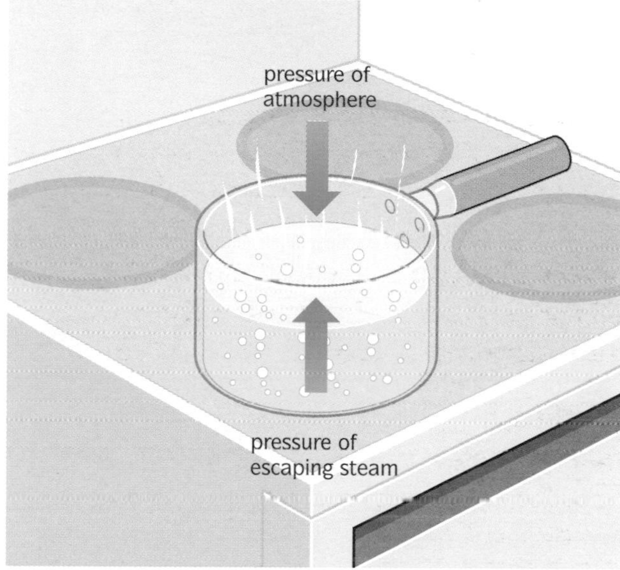

● *Figure 15.2* The pressure of the vapour escaping from water must equal atmospheric pressure if the water is to boil.

atmosphere, which is pressing down on the surface of the water *(figure 15.2)*. At normal atmospheric pressure (approximately 10^5 Pa), the water has to reach 100 °C before the steam can push the atmosphere aside and the water can boil steadily.

At the summit of Everest, the pressure of the atmosphere is much lower, only about one-third of the pressure at sea level. This makes it much easier for the steam to push the atmosphere aside, and the water boils at about 70 °C. Making tea with water at this temperature is like making tea with water from the hot tap; it is not hot enough to make a decent-tasting cup.

This may seem like a rather trivial example, but it illustrates the important idea that, when a gas expands against an external pressure, the gas has to do work.

SAQ 15.1

When you blow up a toy balloon, you have to do work. There are two things pushing back against the pressure of air in the balloon. What are they? Explain why it is easier to blow up a balloon in space, rather than at sea level.

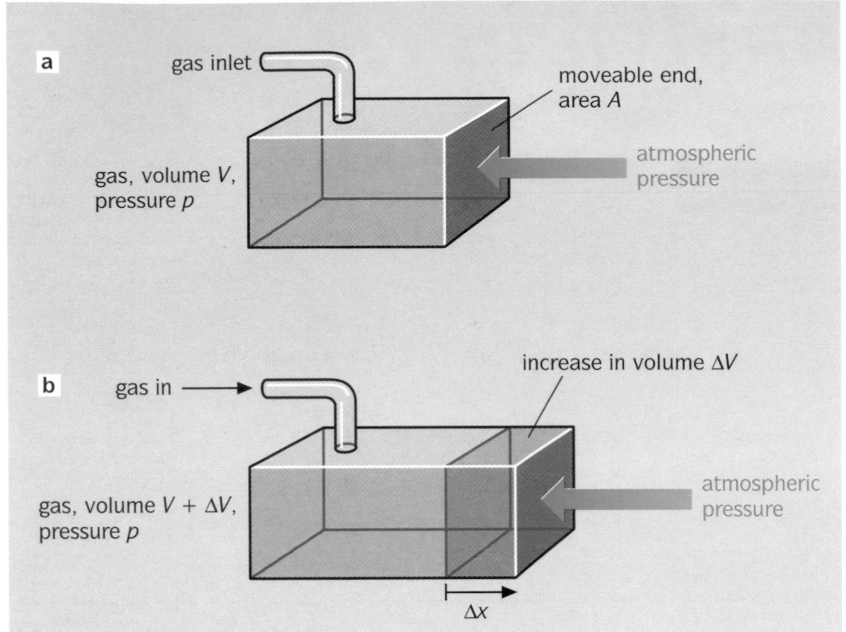

● ***Figure 15.3*** A gas expanding does work in pushing back the atmosphere.

Calculating work done

We can derive an expression for the work done by a gas as it expands if we consider a situation with simple geometry, as shown in *figure 15.3*. Here, some gas is contained in a rectangular box of volume V. One end of the box can slide along to keep the internal and external pressures the same. There is an external pressure p on the box, as shown in *figure 15.3a*. Now we imagine pushing more gas into the box, as in *figure 15.3b*. The gas in the box exerts a force F on the end of the box, which moves along a distance Δx. From the definition of work done (work done = force × distance moved in the direction of the force), we can find the work done by the gas against the external pressure:

$$\text{work done} = F \times \Delta x$$

From the definition of pressure (pressure = force/area), we can say that $F = p \times A$, and hence

$$\text{work done} = p \times A \times \Delta x$$

Now the quantity $A \times \Delta x$ is the increase in volume of the gas, which we write as ΔV. So now we can deduce:

$$\text{work done by the gas, } W = p\Delta V$$

This is a general expression for the work done by a gas expanding against a constant external pressure. We have deduced this expression for a rectangular container, but it is true for any shape. We can also apply it to a situation where a gas is compressed to a smaller volume by an external pressure:

$$\text{work done on the gas} = p\Delta V$$

Now we shall consider a worked example. A volume of $20\,\text{m}^3$ of nitrogen escapes from a gas cylinder. How much work is done by the gas against atmospheric pressure as it escapes? (Atmospheric pressure = 100 kPa.)

The volume of nitrogen has increased by $20\,\text{m}^3$ (measured at atmospheric pressure), so $\Delta V = 20\,\text{m}^3$. It is pushing against atmospheric pressure, so $p = 100\,\text{kPa} = 10^5\,\text{Pa}$. Now we can use $W = p\Delta V$:

$$\text{work done by the gas} = p\Delta V$$
$$= 10^5\,\text{Pa} \times 20\,\text{m}^3 = 2 \times 10^6\,\text{J}$$

The nitrogen does 2 MJ of work against the atmosphere.

Cooling down

If you have used a camping stove that works from a cylinder of propane or butane gas, you may have noticed that the cylinder gets quite cold during use. Water vapour tends to condense on the cold metal. Why does this happen?

If we think about the expanding nitrogen in the worked example above, we see that it does 2 MJ of work in expanding. It is transferring energy to the surrounding atmosphere, and so the energy of the nitrogen decreases. Its molecules move more slowly, and we observe this as a decrease in the temperature of the gas.

Similarly, as the camping gas expands out of the cylinder, it too must do work, and the temperature drops.

SAQ 15.2

As a toy balloon is blown up, the average pressure inside it is 110 kPa. If its final volume is 2 dm^3, how much work is done in blowing it up?

SAQ 15.3

When water boils to become steam at atmospheric pressure, its volume increases by a factor of 1750. How much work is done against atmospheric pressure (100 kPa) when 1 dm^3 of water is boiled completely to steam?

SAQ 15.4

A traditional school experiment involves evacuating a tin can. The can is crumpled by the pressure of the atmosphere. In one such demonstration, a 5 dm^3 oil can is used, and it is crushed by atmospheric pressure (10^5 Pa) until its volume is 20% of its original volume. How much work is done by the atmosphere in crumpling the can?

Internal energy

All matter is made up of particles, which we will refer to here as molecules. Matter can have energy. For example, if we lift up a stone, it has gravitational potential energy. If we throw it, it has kinetic energy. Kinetic and potential energy are the two general forms of energy. We consider the stone's potential and kinetic energies to be properties or attributes of the stone itself; we calculate their values (mgh and $\frac{1}{2}mv^2$) using the mass and speed of the stone.

● ***Figure 15.4*** Increasing the internal energy of a pebble.

Now think about another way in which we could increase the energy of the stone: we could heat it *(figure 15.4)*. Now where does the energy from the heater go? The stone's gravitational potential and kinetic energies do not increase; it is not higher or faster than before. The energy seems to have disappeared into the stone.

Of course, you already know the answer to this. The stone gets hotter, and that means that the molecules which make up the stone have more energy. They vibrate more and faster, and they move further apart. This energy of the molecules is known as the **internal energy** of the stone.

Molecular energy

In chapter 12, where we studied the phases of matter, we saw how solids, liquids and gases could be characterised by differences in the arrangement, order and motion of their molecules. We could equally have said that, in the three phases, the molecules have different amounts of kinetic and potential energies.

Now, it is a simple problem to find the internal energy of some matter. We add up the kinetic and potential energies associated with all the molecules in the matter.

For example, we consider the gas shown in *figure 15.5*. There are ten molecules in the box; each has kinetic and potential energy, and we can work out what all of these are and add them together. The principle at least is simple, and this example should serve to explain what we mean by the internal energy of a gas.

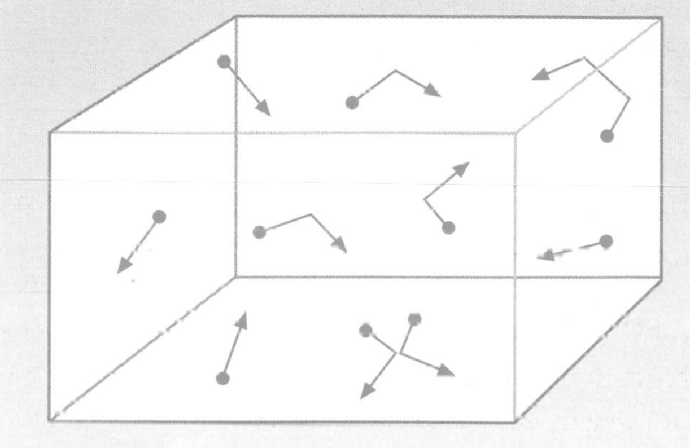

● ***Figure 15.5*** The molecules of a gas have both kinetic and potential energies.

Changing internal energy

There are two obvious ways in which we can increase the internal energy of some gas: we can heat it, or we can do work on it (compress it).

- *Heating a gas (figure 15.6a)*
  The walls of the container become hot, and so its molecules vibrate more vigorously. The molecules of the cool gas strike the walls, and bounce off faster. They have gained kinetic energy, and we say the temperature has risen.
- *Doing work on a gas (figure 15.6b)*
  In this case, a wall of the container is being pushed inwards. The molecules of the cool gas strike a moving wall, and bounce off faster. They have gained kinetic energy, and again the temperature has risen. This explains why a gas gets hotter when it is compressed. (We have already discussed why gases get cooler when they expand.)

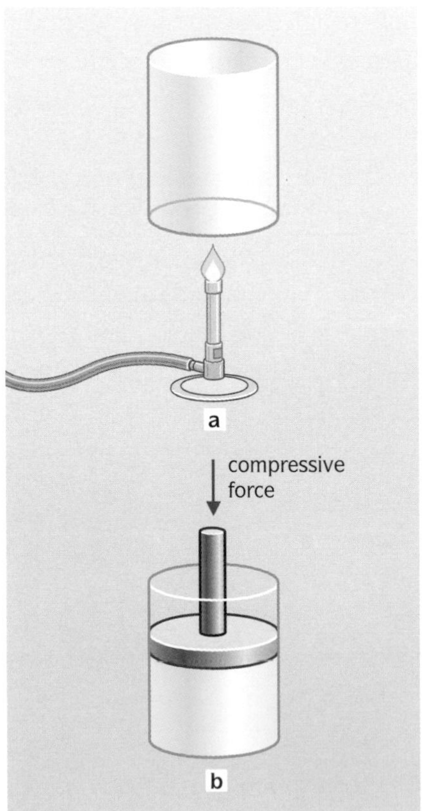

● **Figure 15.6** Two ways to increase the internal energy of a gas: **a** by heating it, and **b** by compressing it.

There are other ways in which the internal energy of a system can be increased; by passing an electric current through it, for example. However, doing work and heating are all we need to consider here.

The first law of thermodynamics

Thermodynamics means the study of energy changes. You already know the first law; it is simply the principle of conservation of energy. For the situation where a gas is being heated and compressed, two amounts of energy are being transferred in: some by heating ΔQ and some by doing work ΔW. The internal energy of the system increases by an amount ΔU, which is equal to the sum of the other two amounts:

$$\Delta U = \Delta Q + \Delta W$$

There is nothing very surprising about this equation, as long as you understand the terms being used. It may make more sense in words:

$$\text{gain in internal energy of system} = \text{energy transferred to system by heating} + \text{energy transferred to system by working}$$

Note that it is important to be clear about which way the energy is going. ΔQ and ΔW are both quantities of energy transferred into the system, so that both contribute to the increase in internal energy of the system. You may come across the same equation with minus signs, representing energy transferred out of the system.

● **Figure 15.7** The study of thermodynamics gave rise to the technology of steam power.

SAQ 15.5

A cylinder of air is heated by supplying it with 500 000 J of energy. At the same time, it expands and does 200 000 J of work against the external pressure. By how much does the internal energy of the air increase?

SAQ 15.6

The internal energy of the air in a balloon increases by 150 kJ when it is heated by 200 kJ of energy. Explain where the remaining 50 kJ has gone.

SUMMARY

- When a gas expands against an external pressure p, it does an amount of work $W = p\Delta V$, where ΔV is the increase in volume. This relationship follows from the definitions of work done and pressure.
- The internal energy of a system is the sum of the kinetic and potential energies of the molecules that make up the system.
- The first law of thermodynamics is a statement of the conservation of energy.
- The gain in internal energy of a system is equal to the sum of the amounts of energy transferred to the system by heating it and by doing work on it.

Thermal energy transfer

By the end of this chapter you should be able to:

1 appreciate that thermal energy is transferred from a region of higher temperature to a region of lower temperature;

2 appreciate that regions of equal temperature will be in thermal equilibrium;

3 describe mechanisms of thermal conduction (electron diffusion and lattice vibration) in crystalline materials;

4 describe convection, and explain the process as a consequence of change of density;

5 understand that bodies emit electromagnetic radiation at a rate that increases with increasing temperature;

6 describe and explain simple applications involving the transfer of energy by conduction, convection and radiation.

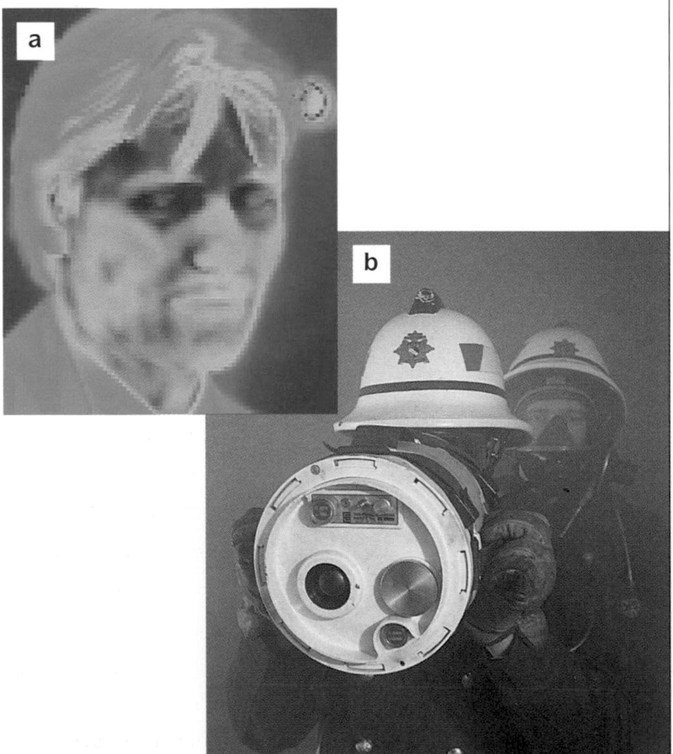

● ***Figure 16.1***

a A thermal image of a face. The red areas are the warmest, the blue areas are the coolest.

b The fire service uses thermal imaging cameras to locate trapped people.

Thermal conduction

Metals are good conductors of heat. You know this because, if you stand a metal teaspoon in a cup of hot tea, the end of the handle soon becomes hot. A plastic teaspoon would not conduct as well, so plastic is a good insulator. Why are metals good conductors, while plastics and many other materials are good insulators?

Metals are good at conducting both heat and electricity. The two mechanisms are similar; they both depend on the presence of free electrons in a metal.

Figure 16.2 shows a representation of a metal bar that is being heated at one end. The atoms at this end gain energy, and vibrate with increasing amplitude. The free electrons, which are moving about rapidly within the metal, gain some of this energy whenever they collide with a vibrating atom. When they reach the other end in the course of their random movement within the metal, they may collide with an atom and give up some of their energy. Thus the free electrons have helped to transfer energy from one end of the bar to the other.

Because the motion of the electrons in the metal is random, the conduction of heat depends on chance collisions between electrons and atoms. Overall, there is a net transfer of energy from the

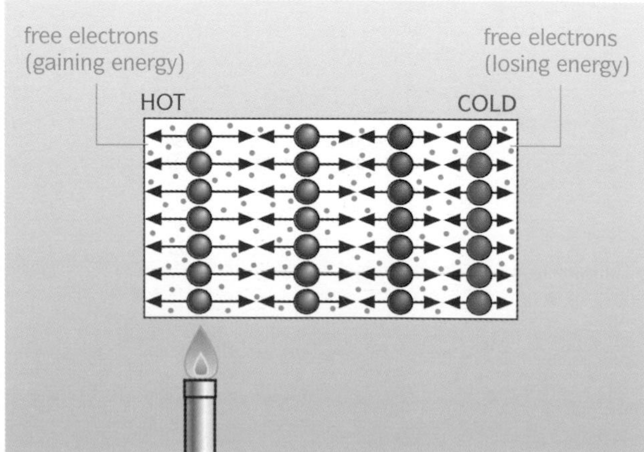

● ***Figure 16.2*** In metals, free electrons transport energy from hot regions to cooler regions.

hotter end to the colder end. This process is referred to as **electron diffusion.**

Conduction in insulators

Insulators do conduct heat, but not nearly as well as metals. A china cup, for example, is made of an insulating material, but it soon gets hot on the outside when it is filled with hot tea. If there are no free electrons in china, how can this happen?

Figure 16.3 illustrates the mechanism. We picture this bar of material as being made of a regular array or lattice of atoms. Again, one end of the bar is being heated. The atoms at this end vibrate with increasing amplitude; they collide with their neighbours, and share their energy. The neighbours collide with their neighbours, and so on. The energy is transferred gradually along the bar.

In general, this mechanism is much slower than the process of electron diffusion; an electron at one end of a piece of metal can be at the other end in a tiny fraction of a second. However, there is an interesting example of a non-metal that conducts heat very rapidly.

Diamond is a form of carbon, in which the atoms are bonded together very stiffly *(figure 16.4)*. A vibration of an atom at one point is very rapidly transferred from one atom to the next to the next, sharing the energy through the material. Diamond is the best thermal conductor of any material. (It is a very good electrical insulator, because it has virtually no free electrons.) So thermal conduction through insulating materials is

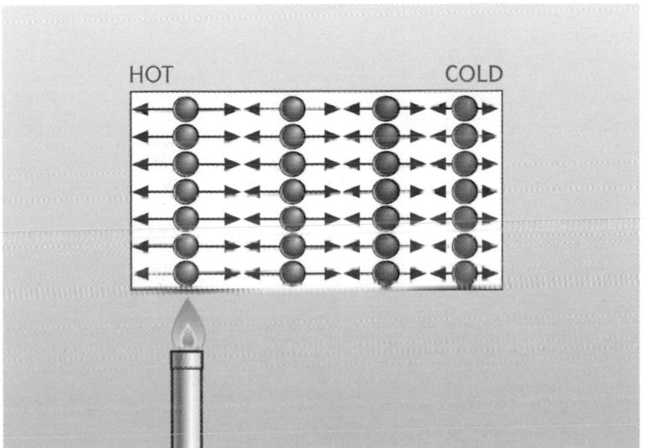

● ***Figure 16.3*** In non-metals, energy is transferred from hot regions to cooler regions by vibrations of atoms.

● ***Figure 16.4*** In diamond, carbon atoms are bonded tightly together in a tetrahedral (pyramidal) crystal structure. This is a model of the structure.

by means of **lattice vibration**; in metals, the process of electron diffusion dominates (though lattice vibration makes a small contribution).

Liquids, too, can conduct; liquid metals like mercury conduct very well. Gases, being mostly empty space, have neither free electrons nor a lattice to vibrate, and they are very poor conductors.

Feeling warm

If you look around the room in which you are at present, you can probably identify some materials that you could describe as 'warm', and others that are 'cold'. For example, wood seems warm to the touch, and clothes are generally made from warm materials. Metal objects such as chair legs and window frames seem cold to the touch.

When we touch something to find its temperature, we are using heat-sensitive nerve endings in our skin. We are really detecting the temperature of our skin. If we touch an insulating material like wood or plastic, our body heat warms it up, and it feels warm like our bodies. If we touch something made of metal, the heat from our fingers is conducted away, and our fingers become cold. This is what our nerves detect. So good insulators feel warm, and good conductors feel cold.

Diamond is an excellent thermal conductor, and this is made use of by jewellers. They touch a diamond against their upper lip, which is very sensitive to temperature. If it feels cold, the diamond is genuine, but if it feels warm, it is probably a paste fake. This is why diamonds are given the slang name of 'ice'.

● **Figure 16.5** Glider pilots rely on rising convection currents of warm air to give them extra lift.

From hot to cold

Heat flows from hot to cold. This is a rather crude way of describing **thermal energy transfer**. A better statement is that: thermal energy is transferred from a region of higher temperature to a region of lower temperature.

You should recall from our discussion of the idea of temperature in chapter 14 that 'a region of higher temperature' means a region where atoms have more kinetic energy, on average. The difference in kinetic energy between two regions is reduced as energy is shared between them. Conduction is one way in which this can happen (by electron diffusion or by lattice vibration). The remaining sections of this chapter look at two other mechanisms, convection and radiation.

Thermal equilibrium

Eventually, the temperature difference between the two regions may disappear. The two regions are at the same temperature, and we say that they are in **thermal equilibrium** with each other. There is no net flow of energy from one to the other. In fact, energy is constantly flowing, because there are still mobile electrons and lattice vibrations, but there is an overall balance of flow. Another word for balance is equilibrium.

SAQ 16.1

Use the ideas of electron diffusion and lattice vibrations to explain the following:

a All solids that are good conductors of electricity are also good thermal conductors.

b Not all good thermal conductors are good conductors of electricity.

c Gases are poor thermal conductors.

Convection

Glider pilots (*figure 16.5*) know that 'hot air rises'. This everyday statement is a useful way of remembering the basic idea of **convection.**

A glider pilot will look out for places where thermals (columns of warm air) are likely to be rising. The Sun shines on the ground, and reflected light, perhaps from a field of golden corn, warms the air. Air expands and becomes less dense when

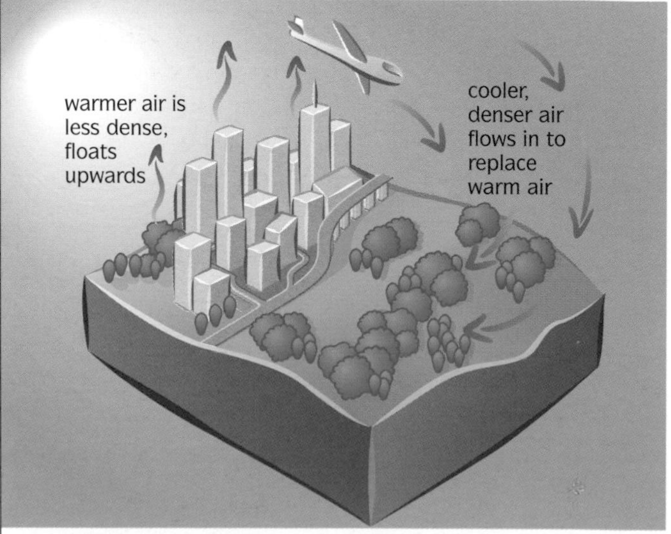

● **Figure 16.6** How a convection current arises on a sunny day.

it is warmed, and floats upwards in the same way that a less dense object like a cork floats on water, which is denser than cork. Cold air flows in to replace the warm air, and a convection current is established *(figure 16.6)*.

Fluid flow

Convection can be observed in any fluid; any substance that can flow, gas or liquid, is a fluid. The process relies on the fact that most fluids expand when they are heated. Expansion results in the same mass occupying a larger volume, and hence the density (= mass/volume) decreases. An electric kettle *(figure 16.7)* makes use of this; the heating element is at the bottom, and warm water rises to the top. Colder water sinks and flows in to replace the warm water, and is heated in turn. Eventually all of the water is hot.

SAQ 16.2

Domestic hot water tanks sometimes have two immersion heaters to heat the water. One is at the bottom, and the other is inserted half-way down *(figure 16.8)*. This second heater is intended to save energy and money for the home-owner.

Draw a diagram to show the convection current that will be established when the second heater is switched on, and explain why this can help to save energy.

SAQ 16.3

Water has a high specific heat capacity (see chapter 12). Consequently, on a hot day, the sea heats up more slowly than the land nearby. At night, the sea cools down more slowly than the land. Use the diagrams in *figure 16.9* to help you to explain why breezes tend to blow from land to sea in the morning, and from sea to land later in the day.

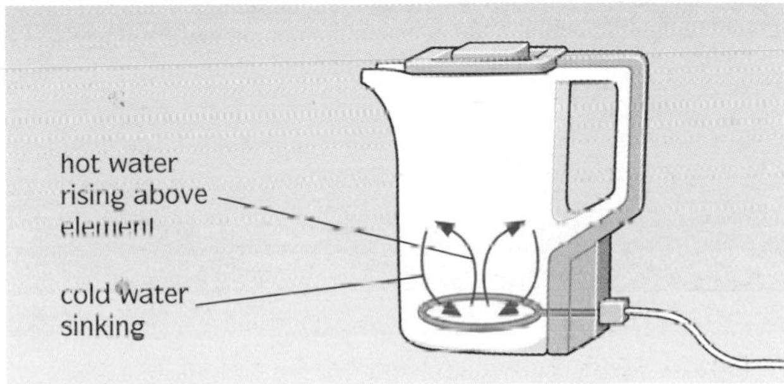

● **Figure 16.7** Convection currents in an electric kettle.

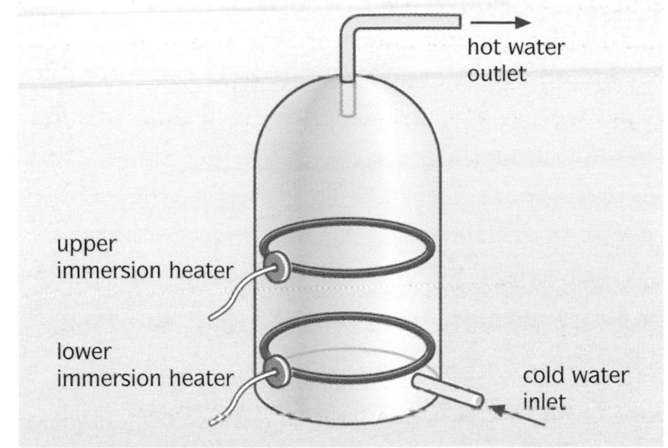

● **Figure 16.8** A hot water tank with two immersion heaters.

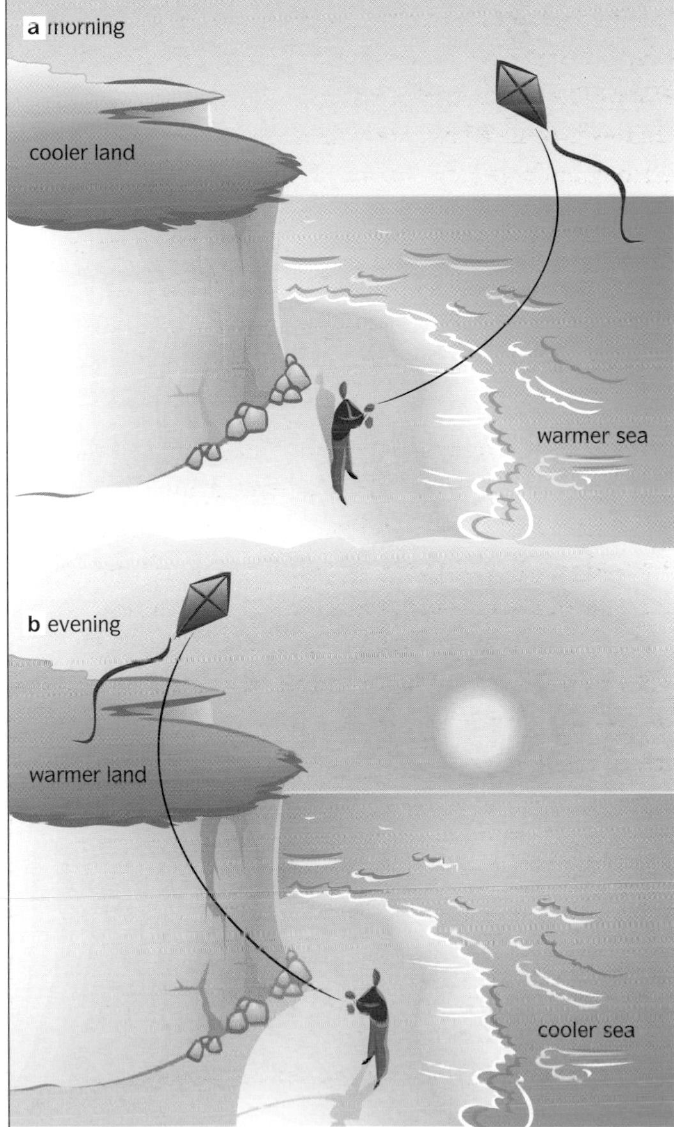

● **Figure 16.9** Why does the breeze blow in the other direction in the evening?

Radiation

We are all used to experiencing heat radiation when we sit near a glowing fire or in the Sun's hot rays. We are less familiar with the idea that we are all radiators of heat ourselves. The thermogram *(figure 16.10)* shows how a person looks when viewed with an infrared camera. Some parts of the body are hotter than others, and these show up as different colours in the image.

The infrared camera detects infrared radiation coming from the body. We are not normally conscious of this radiation, because the nerve endings in our skin are designed to detect things hotter (or colder) than ourselves.

In fact, every object that is hotter than absolute zero radiates infrared radiation. The hotter it is, the more radiation it emits, and the radiation is more energetic. (It has shorter wavelengths.) You can feel the radiation coming from a kettle containing boiling water, but you cannot see it. If a piece of metal is heated further, at about 500 °C it begins to glow a dull red colour. Then it glows orange, then yellow at about 800 °C, and finally white hot above 1000 °C. This is visible light radiation.

An object that is colder than its surroundings receives more radiation than it emits; its temperature will increase. An object that is warmer than its surroundings emits more radiation than it receives, and so it tends to cool down. Thus radiation is another mechanism that tends to bring objects into thermal equilibrium with surrounding objects.

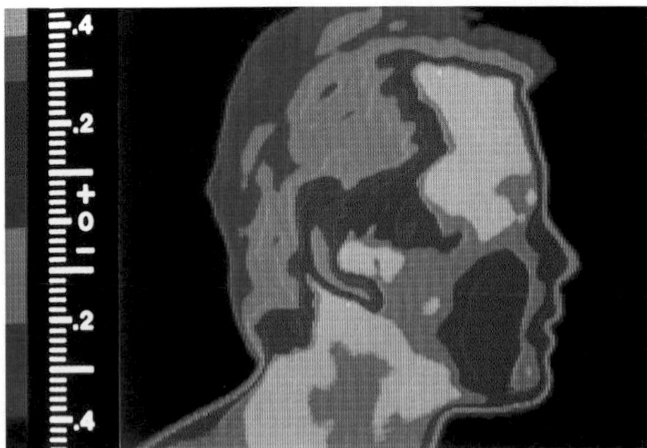

● ***Figure 16.10*** This thermogram of a human head was taken with a camera sensitive to infrared radiation. Different colours correspond to different temperatures.

Electromagnetic radiation and heat

Infrared radiation is part of the electromagnetic spectrum. It consists of electromagnetic waves whose wavelengths are longer than those of visible light. For very cold objects, the wavelengths may be very long, reaching into the microwave part of the spectrum.

Astronomers have found evidence of such microwave radiation pervading the Universe. This is called the microwave background, and is the remnant of radiation from the 'big bang', the giant explosion that is believed to have occurred at the beginning of time in the Universe. The wavelength distribution of the radiation corresponds to a temperature of just 2.7 K above absolute zero.

The infrared space telescope used to detect this radiation is shown in *figure 16.11*.

The fact that space is permeated by infrared radiation, and the fact that we can receive radiation from the Sun through space, shows that electromagnetic radiation can travel through a vacuum. Indeed, it travels faster through a vacuum than through any material, because there is no interaction with a material to slow it down.

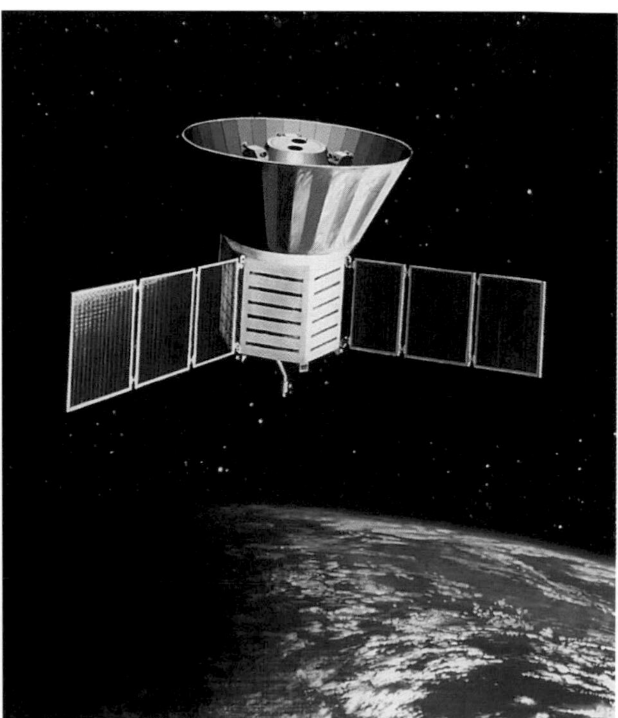

● ***Figure 16.11*** The COBE space satellite, used for investigating the background infrared radiation, left over from the 'big bang' at the origin of the Universe.

Good radiators

Some surfaces are better radiators of heat than others. Matt black surfaces are best; shiny metallic or white surfaces are worst.

Any surface that is a good radiator (emitter) of heat will also be a good absorber of heat. A poor radiator is a poor absorber, and so it is a good reflector.

In tropical countries, indigenous people often have dark skin. This enables their bodies to radiate away heat quickly, so that they do not overheat. If you do not want to absorb a lot of radiation from the Sun, then it is sensible to wear light-coloured clothing, which will reflect away visible light and infrared radiation.

Conduction, convection, radiation

It is worth comparing these three mechanisms of thermal energy transfer. In all three cases, there is a net flow of heat from a region of higher temperature to a region of lower temperature.

- *Conduction*
  Heat flows through a material without the material itself moving.
- *Convection*
  Heat is transported through a fluid material when the material itself moves.
- *Radiation*
  Heat is transferred by means of electromagnetic radiation, without the need of a material.

SAQ 16.4

Figure 16.12 shows three kettles. Explain the following features of their design by referring to conduction, convection and radiation as appropriate.

a The first kettle is made of metal, with an electric heating element inside. Why is it shiny all over? Why is its handle made of black plastic?

b The second kettle is heated on a gas stove. Why is its upper part shiny but its base dull? Why does it have a copper base?

c The third kettle is made of plastic. It has an electric heating element inside. Why is it white, rather than shiny?

● **Figure 16.12** Three kettles of different designs.

SAQ 16.5

Figure 16.13 shows a radiator and a convector heater, as used for domestic heating. Explain the features of their designs that make them good for this use. Are their names appropriate?

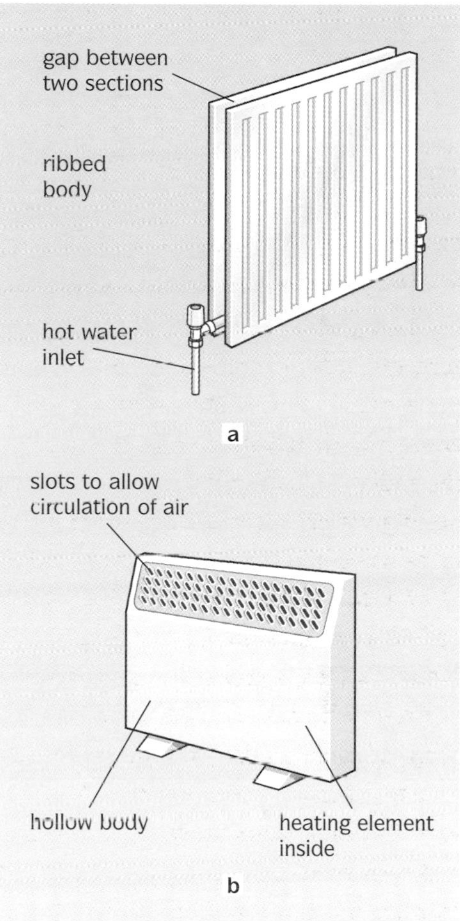

● **Figure 16.13** **a** A radiator and **b** a convector heater.

SAQ 16.6

Many houses have cavity walls. Most of the heat loss through such a wall is by convection in the air in the cavity, as shown in *figure 16.14a*. To reduce this, foam insulation is often inserted. This consists of a plastic or mineral material with many tiny bubbles of air inside (*figure 16.14b*). What effect will installing cavity foam insulation have on the rate of heat loss by **a** conduction, **b** convection, **c** radiation?

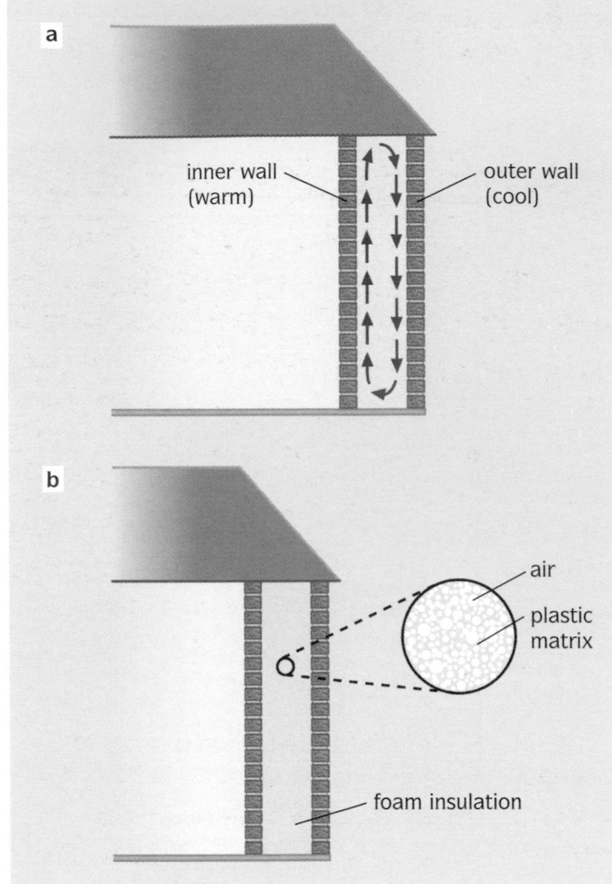

● **Figure 16.14** Foam insulation is designed to reduce heat loss through a cavity wall.

SAQ 16.7

Figure 16.15 shows an electronic component (a power transistor), fitted with a heat sink. The transistor gets very hot in use, and the heat sink helps to keep it cool. The sink is made of metal, and has several fins to increase its surface area. It is painted matt black. Explain how the different features of this design help to maximise heat loss from the transistor.

● **Figure 16.15** This transistor has a heat sink attached to help it to lose heat to the surroundings.

SAQ 16.8

A Thermos flask keeps cold things cold and hot things hot. *Figure 16.16* shows the design of a flask. Explain how the various features of its design help to slow down the rate at which the contents of the flask reach thermal equilibrium with their surroundings.

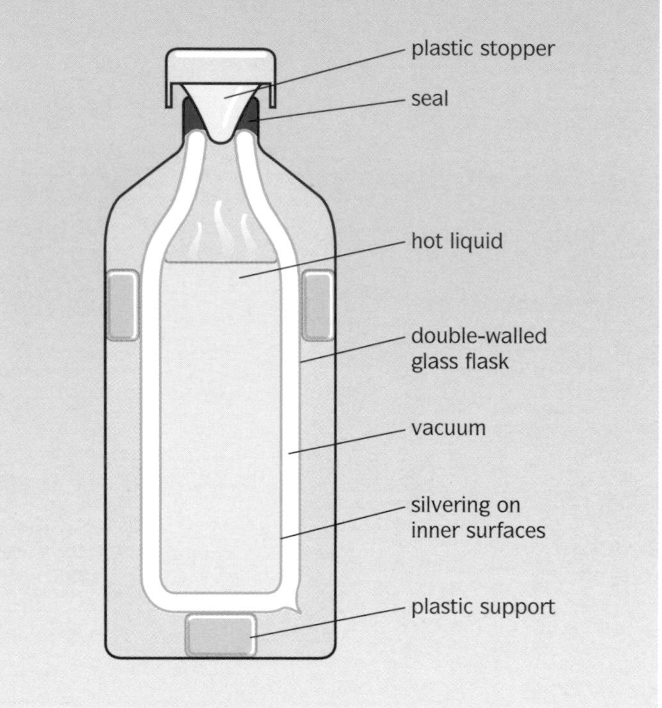

● **Figure 16.16** A Thermos flask keeps hot drinks hot (and cold drinks cold).

SUMMARY

- Thermal energy is transferred from regions of high temperature to regions of lower temperature.
- If two regions are at the same temperature, there is no heat transfer between them, and we say that they are in thermal equilibrium.
- There are three mechanisms of heat transfer: *conduction* (by electron diffusion and lattice vibrations); *convection* (by the movement of less dense fluid); *radiation* (by electromagnetic radiation, which increases with increasing temperature).
- Understanding these mechanisms allows us to control the rate of thermal energy transfer.

Quantum physics

By the end of this chapter you should be able to:

1. show an appreciation of the particulate nature of electromagnetic radiation;
2. recall and use $E = hf$;
3. describe the phenomenon of the photoelectric effect;
4. recall the significance of the threshold frequency;
5. explain why the maximum photoelectric energy is independent of intensity, and why the photoelectric current is proportional to intensity;
6. explain photoelectric phenomena in terms of photon energy and work function energy;
7. recall, use and explain the significance of $hf = \phi + \frac{1}{2}mv^2_{max}$;
8. appreciate that the photoelectric effect provides evidence for a particulate nature of electromagnetic radiation, while phenomena such as interference and diffraction provide evidence for a wave nature;
9. describe and interpret qualitatively the evidence provided by electron diffraction for the wave nature of particles;
10. recall and use the relation for the de Broglie wavelength $\lambda = h/p$;
11. understand the existence of discrete electron energy levels in isolated atoms and explain how this leads to spectral lines;
12. distinguish between emission and absorption line spectra;
13. recall and use the relation $hf = E_1 - E_2$.

Making macroscopic models

Science tries to explain a very complicated world. We are surrounded by very many objects, moving around, reacting together, breaking up, joining together, growing and shrinking. And there are many invisible things, too – radio waves, sounds, ionising radiation. If we are to make any sense of all this, we need to simplify it. We use models, in everyday life and in science, as a method of

● **Figure 17.1** An understanding of quantum mechanics has enabled physicists to develop many modern devices, such as the charge-coupled device (CCD), which is at the heart of this camcorder.

simplifying and making sense of everything we observe.

A model is a way of explaining something difficult in terms of something more familiar. For example, there are many models used to describe how the brain works *(figure 17.2)*. It's like a telephone exchange – nerves carry messages in and out

● **Figure 17.2** This seventeenth-century illustration shows a model of how a reflex reaction works. The man's toe gets hot, and this pulls a tiny thread attached to his brain. Spirit pours from the brain down the hollow tube, inflating the muscles in the leg, and causing the foot to withdraw. (From *Traité de l'Homme*, René Descartes, 1664.)

from various parts of the body. It's like a computer. It's like a library. The brain has something in common with all of these things, and yet it is different from them all. These are models, which have some use; but inevitably a model also has its limitations.

You have probably come across various models used to explain electricity. We cannot see electric current in a wire, so we find different ways of explaining what is going on. Current is like water flowing in a pipe. A circuit is like a central heating system. It's like a train carrying coal from mine to power station. And so on. All of these models conjure up some useful impressions of what electricity is, but none is perfect.

We can make a better model of electric current in a wire using the idea of electrons. Tiny charged particles are moving under the influence of an electric field. We can say how many there are, how fast they are moving, and we can describe the factors that affect their movement. This is a better model, but it is harder to understand because it is further from our everyday experience. We need to know about electric charge, atoms, and so on. Most people are happier with more concrete models; as your understanding of science develops, you accept more and more abstract models. Ultimately, you may have to accept a model that is purely mathematical – some equations that give the right answer.

In this chapter, we are going to look at two very powerful models – particles and waves. Remember that all models have their limitations. We are going to see what happens in situations where particle and wave models start to overlap, where both might be able to give explanations.

Particle models

In several earlier chapters, we have looked at the way in which particles behave. We picture particles as being objects that are hard, have mass and move about according to Newtonian mechanics *(figure 17.3)*. They have momentum and kinetic energy. When two particles collide, we can predict how they will move after the collision, based on knowledge of their masses and velocities before the collision. If you have played snooker or pool, you will have a pretty good picture of how particles behave.

Particles are a macroscopic model. Our ideas of particles come from what we observe on a macroscopic scale – when we are walking down the street, or observing the motion of stars and planets, or working with trolleys and balls in the laboratory. But what else can we use a particle model to explain?

The importance of particle models is that we can apply them to the microscopic world, and explain more phenomena.

Table 17.1 shows how, in particular areas of science, we can use a particle model to interpret and make predictions about macroscopic phenomena.

In chapter 14 we looked at the kinetic model of ideal gases. We picture gas molecules as small, hard

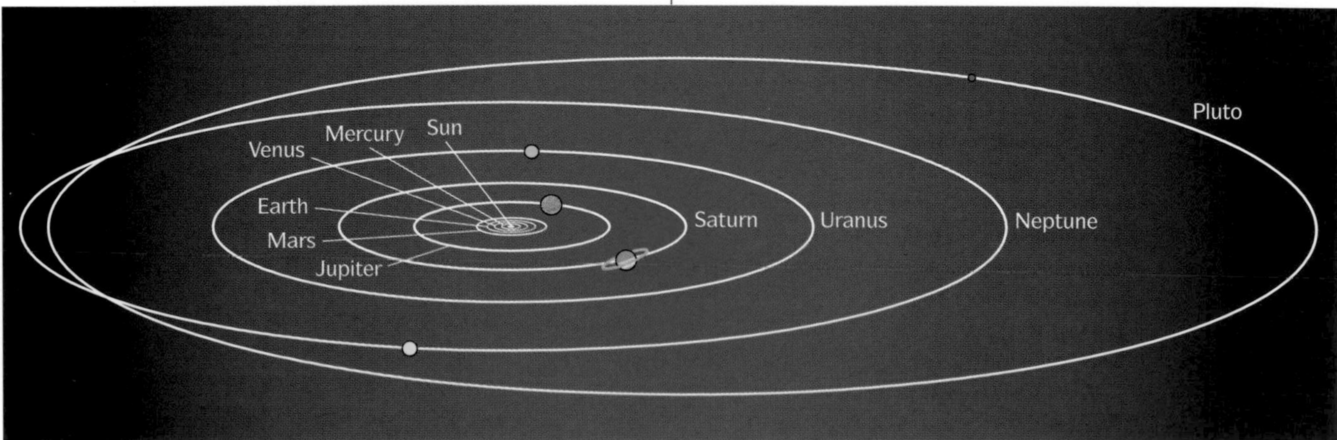

● ***Figure 17.3*** Classical mechanics based on Newton's laws of motion gave a very good description of the movement of planets in the Solar System.

Area	Model	Macroscopic phenomena
electricity	flow of electrons	current
gases	kinetic theory	the gas laws
solids	crystalline materials	mechanical properties
radioactivity	nuclear model of atom	decay, fission, fusion
chemistry	atomic structure	chemical reactions

● ***Table 17.1*** Particle models in science

particles, rushing around and bouncing off one another and their container. We can explain the macroscopic phenomena of pressure and temperature in terms of the masses and speeds of the microscopic particles. This is a very powerful model, which has been refined to explain many other aspects of the behaviour of gases.

Wave models

Waves are something that we see on the sea. There are tidal waves, and little ripples. Some waves have foamy tops, others are breaking on the beach.

Physicists have an idealised picture of a wave – it is shaped like a sine graph. You won't see any waves quite this shape on the sea. However, it is a useful picture, because it can be used to represent some simple phenomena. More complicated waves can be made up of several simple waves, and physicists can cope with the mathematics of sine waves. This is the principle of superposition, which we looked at in chapter 4.

Waves are a way in which energy is transferred from one place to another. In any wave, something is changing in a regular way, while energy is travelling along. In water waves, the surface of the water moves up and down periodically, and energy is transferred horizontally.

Table 17.2 shows some other phenomena that we explain in terms of waves.

The characteristic properties of waves are that they all show reflection, refraction, diffraction and interference. You have studied these phenomena in the *Foundation Physics* module, and in chapter 4. (Transverse waves also show polarisation.)

Since particle models can also explain reflection and refraction, it is diffraction and interference that we regard as the defining characteristics of waves. If we can show diffraction and interference, we know that we are dealing with waves *(figure 17.4)*. In the sections that follow, you will need to be familiar with these phenomena in particular.

Phenomena	Varying quantity
sound	pressure (or density)
light (and other electromagnetic waves)	electric and magnetic field strengths
waves on strings	displacement

● ***Table 17.2*** Wave models in science

● ***Figure 17.4*** A diffraction grating splits up light into its component colours and can produce dramatic effects in photographs.

Waves or particles?

Wave models and particle models are both very useful. They can explain a great many different observations. But which should we use in a particular situation? And what if both models seem to work when we are trying to explain something?

This is just the problem that physicists struggled with for over a century, in connection with light. Does light travel as a wave, or as particles?

For a long time, Newton's view prevailed – light travels as particles. He could use this model to explain both reflection and refraction. His model suggested that light travels faster in glass than in air. We now know that this is not the case, and this caused difficulties for the particle model. Young showed both diffraction and interference of light, and this convinced most people that light travels as waves.

In the rest of this chapter, we will look at particular situations where the wave model of electromagnetic radiation and the particle model of matter have run into difficulties, and discuss some of the ways in which physicists have tried to resolve these difficulties.

Electron waves

Electrons are particles. We can measure their charge and their mass. As far as we can tell, all electrons are identical.

We use the idea of electrons as particles to explain many phenomena – electric current, β-decay (beta decay), magnetic fields – and we use our understanding of electrons in many technologies – transistors, TV tubes, etc. *(figure 17.5)*.

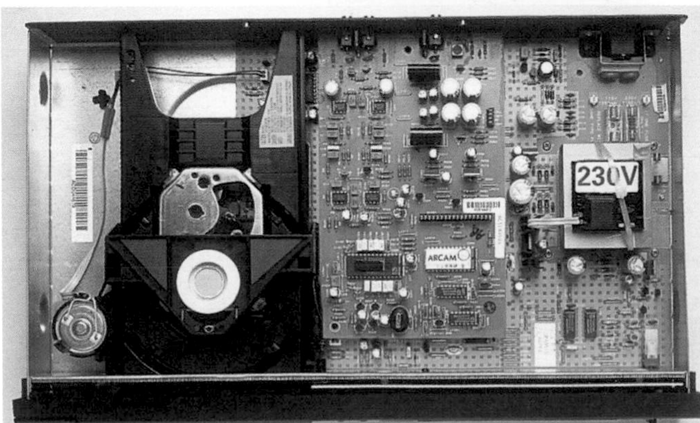

● ***Figure 17.5*** Electronic technology is the basis of many modern devices. The lower photograph shows the interior of a compact disc player.

Consequently, it is quite a surprise to find that there are situations where electrons appear to behave like waves. This is just what is observed when a beam of energetic electrons is used instead of a beam of light in a double-slit experiment.

Young's slits

One of the experiments that convinced nineteenth-century physicists that light is a wave was Young's double-slit experiment, discussed in chapter 4 (page 32). A beam of light is shone on a pair of parallel slits. Light spreads outwards (diffracts) from each slit into the space beyond; where light from the two slits overlaps, an interference pattern is formed.

We interpret these results using a wave model of light. At any point on the screen, light waves are arriving from each slit. Constructive and destructive interference result in this interference pattern.

The particle model of light cannot explain this pattern. If two particles of light arrived together, we would expect double the brightness. We cannot imagine two particles arriving together and cancelling each other out.

Electron diffraction

The surprising thing is that electrons show the same behaviour *(figure 17.6)*. A beam of electrons from an electron gun is shone on a double slit; beyond the slits is a screen coated with a phosphor, which produces a flash of light whenever an

● ***Figure 17.6*** When a beam of electrons passes through a graphite film, as in this vacuum tube, a diffraction pattern is seen on the screen.

electron strikes it. The photograph shows the resulting light and dark fringes.

This interference pattern seems to be clear evidence that electrons travel as waves. Indeed, we can measure the fringes and use the measurements to calculate the wavelength of the electrons, in the same way that the Young's slits experiment can be used to find the wavelength of light.

Surely, if we can measure the wavelength of something, it must be a wave? We have no trouble in accepting this for light or sound waves. Must we then accept that electrons travel as waves, and throw away all of our ideas of electrons as particles?

This is a difficult idea with which physicists have struggled for some time. This experiment shows that electrons appear to travel as waves. If we look a little more closely at the results of the experiment, we find something else even more surprising.

The phosphor screen gives a flash of light for each electron that hits it. These flashes build up to give the interference pattern *(figure 17.7)*. But if we see flashes at particular points on the screen, are we not seeing individual electrons – in other words, are we not observing particles?

It seems that the electrons leave the gun as particles, they pass through the slits as if they were waves, and they arrive at the screen as particles.

Another even more surprising result is found if we make the electron beam sufficiently weak that there is never more than one electron in the beam at a time. We still get a pattern of interference fringes. Each single electron seems to have passed as a wave through both slits, and then recombined on the other side to give a single flash at the screen.

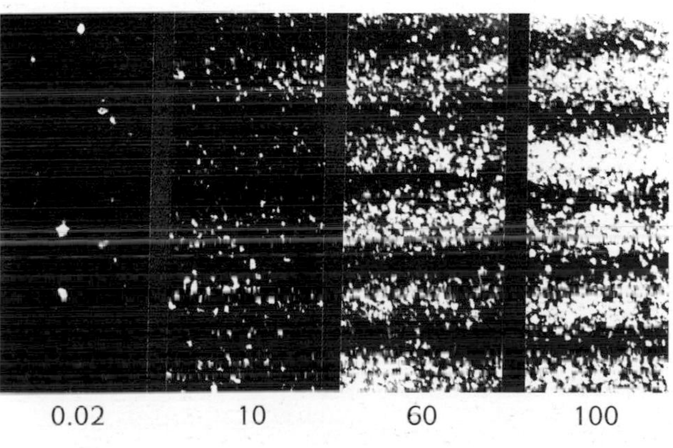

● ***Figure 17.7*** The speckled interference pattern shows that it arises from many electrons striking the screen.

At this point, you may want to know the answer to this puzzle. Are electrons particles, or are they waves? One answer, which you may have to be satisfied with at the moment, is that at times they behave like waves, and at other times they behave like particles. (Bear in mind that waves and particles are macroscopic ideas; we cannot see electrons, and so we can only compare their behaviour to waves and particles.)

Here are two rules that seem to describe the results of the double-slit experiment:

- When do electrons behave like waves? When they are going through slits.
- When do electrons behave like particles? When they interact with matter, for example when they arrive at the screen.

In a later section (page 152) we will discuss other ways in which these contradictory ideas might be reconciled. We will also see how particle properties (energy and momentum) and wave properties (wavelength and frequency) are related.

Investigating electron diffraction

If you have access to an electron diffraction tube *(figure 17.8)*, you can see for yourself how a beam of electrons is diffracted. The electron gun at one end of the tube produces a beam of electrons. By changing the voltage between the anode and the

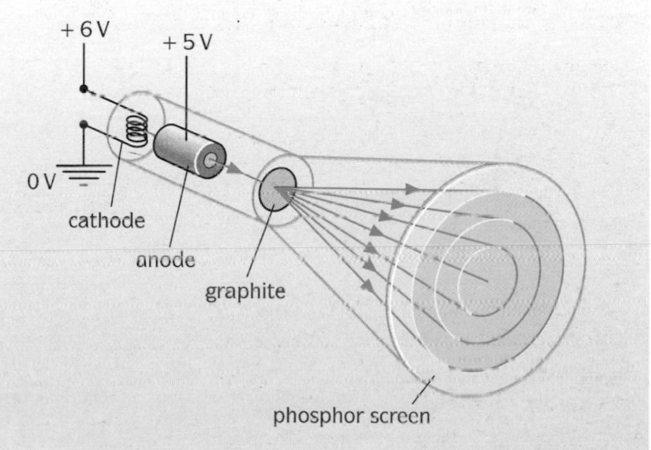

● ***Figure 17.8*** Electrons are accelerated from the cathode to the anode; they form a beam, which is diffracted as it passes through the graphite.

cathode, you can change the energy of the electrons, and hence their speed. The beam strikes a graphite target, and a diffraction pattern appears on the screen at the other end of the tube.

Graphite is a polycrystalline material. It is made up of many tiny crystals, each of which consists of large numbers of carbon atoms arranged in uniform planes. The planes of atoms are like a diffraction grating of many slits for the electrons, and the beam is diffracted onto the screen.

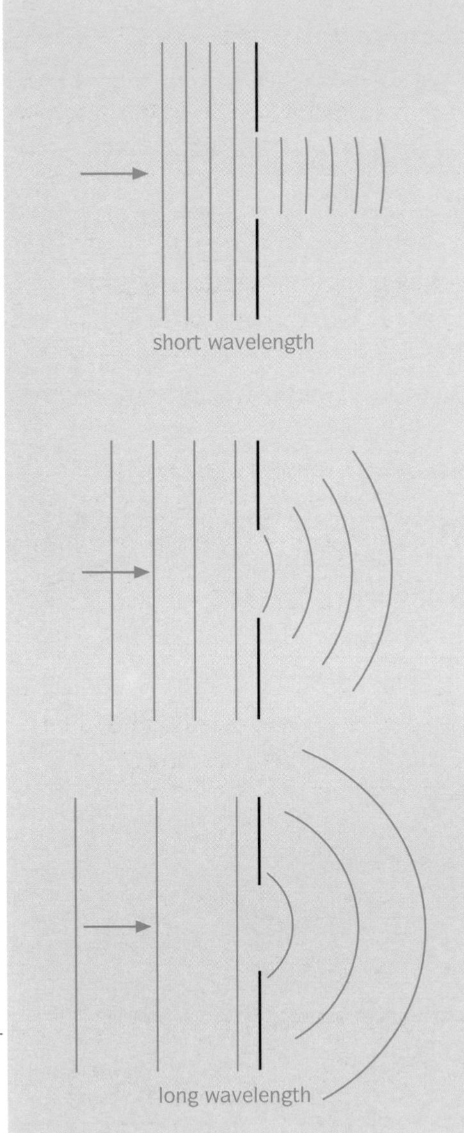

● ***Figure 17.9*** Waves of short (top) to long wavelength (bottom) are diffracted as they pass through a gap.

You can use the equipment to investigate how the wavelength of the electrons depends on their speed. Qualitatively, you should find that increasing the cathode–anode voltage makes the pattern shrink. The electrons have more energy (they are faster); the shrinking pattern shows that their wavelength has decreased.

You can find the wavelength λ (lambda) of the electrons by measuring the angle θ (theta) at which they are diffracted:

$$\lambda = 2d \sin \theta$$

where d is the spacing of the atomic planes of graphite.

You can find the speed of the electrons from the anode–cathode voltage V_{ac}. We have $W = QV = eV$. But $W = \frac{1}{2}mv^2$. So

$$\frac{1}{2}mv^2 = eV_{ac}$$

SAQ 17.1

The diagrams in *figure 17.9* show how waves are diffracted as they pass through a single slit. The waves have different wavelengths.

a What do the diagrams tell you about how the amount of diffraction depends on the wavelength of the waves?

b Draw a similar set of three diagrams. Show waves having the same wavelength in each diagram, but have gaps of different widths. Write a sentence to explain what your diagrams show.

SAQ 17.2

X-rays are used to find out about the spacings of atomic planes in crystalline materials.

a Describe how beams of electrons could be used for the same purpose.

b How might electron diffraction be used to identify a sample of a metal?

Particles of light

If electrons can behave as waves, can light behave as particles? The answer is yes, and you are probably already familiar with some of the evidence.

If you place a Geiger counter next to a source of γ-radiation (γ is Greek gamma), you will hear an irregular series of clicks. We say that the counter is detecting γ-rays. But γ-rays are part of the electromagnetic spectrum – they belong to the same family of waves as light, radio waves, X-rays, etc.

So, here are waves giving clicks, which are indistinguishable from the clicks given by α-particles and β-particles (α, β are Greek alpha, beta). We can conclude that γ-rays behave like particles when they interact with a Geiger counter.

This effect is most obvious with γ-rays, because they are at the most energetic end of the electromagnetic spectrum. It is harder to show the same effect for visible light.

Photons

The photoelectric effect, and Einstein's explanation of it, convinced physicists that light could behave as a stream of particles. Before we go on to look at this in detail, we need to see how to calculate the energy of photons.

Newton used the word *corpuscle* for the particles which he thought made up light. Nowadays, we call them **photons**, and we believe that all electromagnetic radiation consists of photons. Gamma photons (γ-photons) are the most energetic. The energy E of a photon is related to the frequency f of the radiation of which it is part:

$$E = hf \qquad \text{where} \qquad h = 6.63 \times 10^{-34}\,\text{J s}$$

This constant h is called the **Planck constant.** Its units are joule seconds (J s), but you may prefer to think of this as 'joules per hertz'. High-frequency radiation means high-energy photons.

Notice that this equation tells us the relationship between a particle property (the photon energy E) and a wave property (the frequency f). It is called the **Einstein relation,** and applies to all waves and all particles.

Since the frequency f and wavelength λ of a wave are related to the wave speed c by $c = f\lambda$, we can also write this equation as

$$E = \frac{hc}{\lambda}$$

Now we can work out the energy of a γ-photon. Gamma rays typically have frequencies greater than 10^{20} Hz. The energy of a γ-photon is therefore greater than $6.63 \times 10^{-34}\,\text{J s} \times 10^{20}\,\text{Hz} = 6.63 \times 10^{-14}\,\text{J}$, or about 10^{-13} J. This is a very small amount of energy on the human scale, so we don't notice the effects of individual γ-photons. (Some astronauts have reported seeing flashes of light as individual cosmic rays, high-energy γ-photons, have passed through their eyeballs.)

You will need these to answer the SAQs: speed of light in free space $c = 3 \times 10^8\,\text{m s}^{-1}$, Planck constant $h = 6.63 \times 10^{-34}\,\text{J s}$.

SAQ 17.3

Calculate the energy of a high-energy γ-photon, frequency 10^{26} Hz.

SAQ 17.4

Visible light has wavelengths in the range 400 nm to 700 nm. Calculate the energies of photons of red and violet light.

SAQ 17.5

To which region of the electromagnetic spectrum *(figure 17.10)* does each of the following photons belong: photon energy = 10^{-12} J, 10^{-15} J, 10^{-18} J, 10^{-20} J, 10^{-25} J?

SAQ 17.6

A 1 mW laser produces red light of wavelength 648 nm. How many photons does it produce per second?

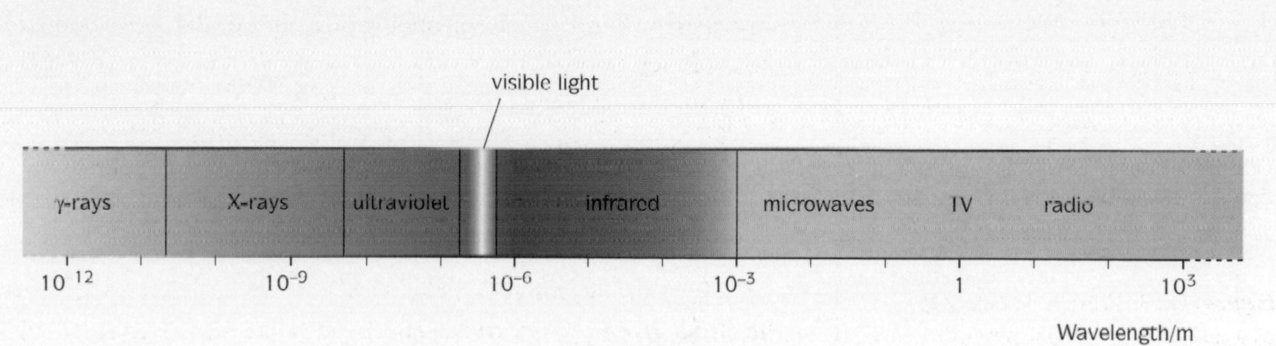

● ***Figure 17.10*** The electromagnetic spectrum.

The photoelectric effect

You can observe the photoelectric effect yourself by fixing a clean zinc plate to the top of a gold-leaf electroscope *(figure 17.11)*. Give the electroscope a negative charge, and the leaf deflects. Now shine light from a mercury lamp on the zinc, and the leaf gradually falls. Charging the electroscope gives it an excess of electrons. Somehow, the light from the mercury lamp helps the electrons to escape from the metal. The light causes electrons to move. (Hence the word 'photoelectric'.)

Placing the lamp closer causes the leaf to fall more rapidly – this is not very surprising. However, if you insert a sheet of glass between the lamp and the zinc, the light is no longer effective. The gold leaf does not fall. Glass absorbs ultraviolet radiation, and it is this component of the light that is effective.

If you try the experiment with a bright filament lamp, you will find it has no effect – it does not produce ultraviolet radiation. There is a minimum frequency that the light must have in order to release electrons from the metal. This is called the **threshold frequency**.

Physicists found it hard to explain why weak ultraviolet light could have an immediate effect on the electrons in the metal, but very bright light of lower frequency had no effect. They imagined light waves arriving at the metal, spread out over its surface, and they could not see how weak ultraviolet waves could be more effective than strong visible waves. Einstein came up with an explanation, based on the idea of light as photons.

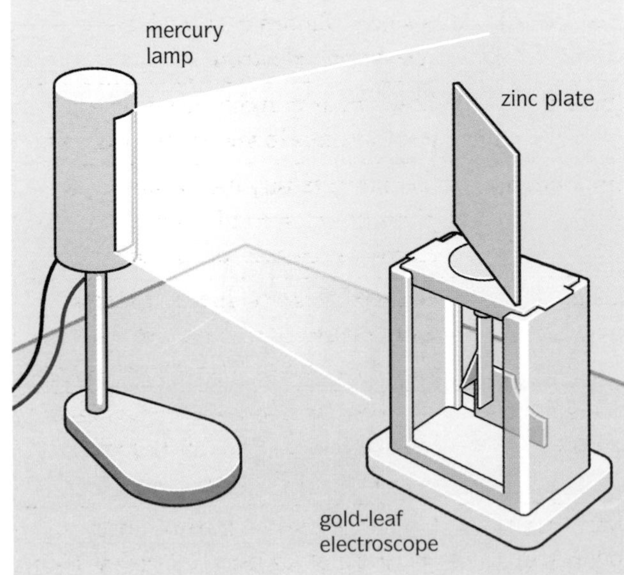

● **Figure 17.11** A simple way to observe the photoelectric effect.

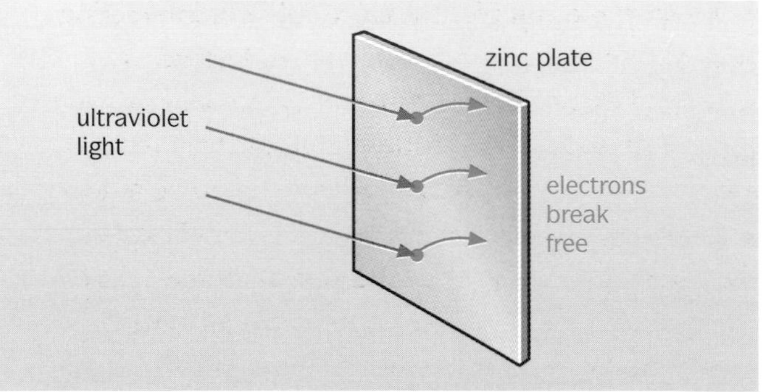

● **Figure 17.12** The photoelectric effect: when a photon of light strikes the metal plate, its energy may be sufficient to release an electron.

Einstein's explanation

Metals (such as zinc) have electrons that are not very tightly held within the metal. These are the conduction electrons, and they are free to move about within the metal. When photons of light strike the metal, some electrons break free *(figure 17.12)*. They only need a small amount of energy (about 10^{-19} J) to escape from the metal.

We can picture the electrons as being trapped in a potential energy 'well' *(figure 17.13)*. The most energetic electrons need to gain an amount of energy ϕ in order to escape.

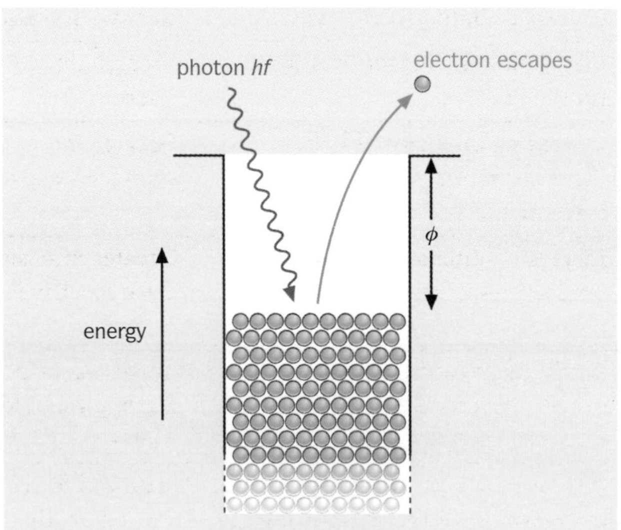

● **Figure 17.13** A single photon of light may release a single electron from a metal.

Einstein did not picture waves of light interacting with all of the electrons in the metal. Instead, he suggested that a single photon of light could provide the energy needed by an individual electron to escape. The photon energy would need to be at least as great as ϕ. By this means, Einstein could explain the threshold frequency. A photon of visible light has energy less than ϕ, so it cannot release an electron.

When a photon arrives at the metal plate, it may be captured by an electron. The electron gains all of the photon's energy, and the photon no longer exists. Some of the energy is needed for the electron to escape from the potential well; the rest is the electron's kinetic energy.

Now we can see that the photon model of light works because it pictures light as concentrated particles of energy, each one able to release an electron from the metal. The energy in light waves is too spread out to have the observed effect.

Further measurements showed that the electrons released had a range of kinetic energies up to some maximum value, E_{max}. These fastest-moving electrons are the ones which were least tightly held in the metal. Einstein produced an equation that related the value of E_{max} to the energy of the photon hf:

$$hf = \phi + E_{max} \quad \text{or} \quad hf = \phi + \tfrac{1}{2}mv^2_{max}$$

This equation can be understood as follows. We start with a photon of energy hf. It is absorbed by an electron. Some of the energy (ϕ) is used in escaping from the metal; the rest remains as kinetic energy of the electron.

If the photon is absorbed by an electron that is lower in the potential well, the electron will have less kinetic energy than E_{max} *(figure 17.14)*.

The quantity ϕ is called the **work function** of the metal. It is the minimum energy needed to

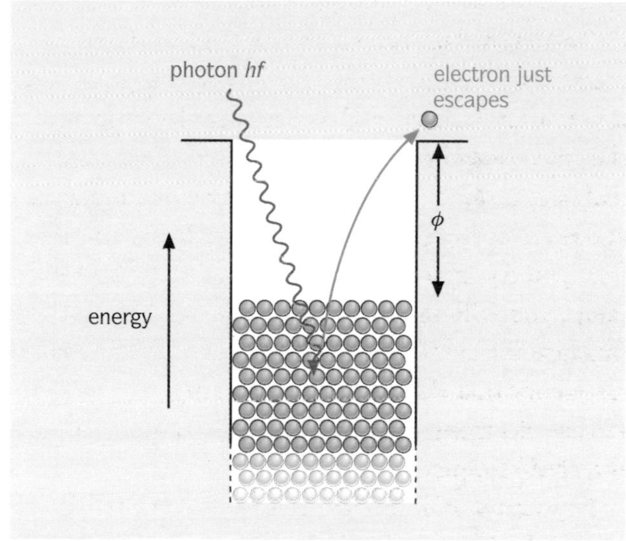

● ***Figure 17.14*** A more tightly bound electron needs more energy to release it from the metal.

Observation	*Wave model*	*Photon model*
Emission of electrons happens as soon as light shines on metal	Very intense light should be needed to have immediate effect	A single photon is enough to release one electron
Even weak (low-intensity) light is effective	Weak light waves should have no effect	Low-intensity light means fewer photons, not lower-energy photons
Increasing intensity of light increases rate at which electrons leave metal	Greater intensity means more energy, so more electrons released	Greater intensity means more photons per second, so more electrons released per second
Increasing intensity has no effect on energies of electrons	Greater intensity should mean electrons have more energy	Greater intensity does not mean more energetic photons, so electrons cannot have more energy
A minimum threshold frequency of light is needed	Low-frequency light should work; electrons would be released more slowly	A photon in a low-frequency light beam has energy that is too small to release an electron
Increasing frequency of light increases maximum kinetic energy of electrons	It should be increasing intensity, not frequency, that increases energy of electrons	Higher frequency means more energetic photons; so electrons gain more energy and can move faster

● ***Table 17.3*** The success of the photon model in explaining the photoelectric effect

remove an electron from the metal, and it is related to the threshold frequency f_0:

$$\phi = hf_0$$

Different metals have different threshold frequencies, and hence different work functions. For example, alkali metals such as sodium, potassium and rubidium have threshold frequencies in the visible spectrum. The conduction electrons in zinc are more tightly bound within the metal, and so its threshold frequency is in the ultraviolet.

Table 17.3 summarises the observations of the photoelectric effect, the problems a wave model of light has in explaining them, and how a photon model is more successful.

SAQ 17.7

Table 17.4 shows the work functions of several different metals.

a Which metal requires the highest frequency of light to release electrons?

b Which metal will release electrons when the lowest frequency of light is shone on it?

c What minimum frequency of light is needed for zinc to release electrons?

d What is the greatest wavelength of light that will release electrons from potassium?

Metal	*Work function* ϕ/J
caesium	3.0×10^{-19}
calcium	4.3×10^{-19}
gold	7.8×10^{-19}
potassium	3.2×10^{-19}
zinc	6.9×10^{-19}

● ***Table 17.4***

SAQ 17.8

Light of wavelength 2.4×10^{-7} m is shone on the surface of a metal whose work function is 2.8×10^{-19} J.

a What is the energy of an individual photon of this light?

b What is the maximum kinetic energy of electrons released from the metal?

c What is their maximum speed?

($h = 6.63 \times 10^{-34}$ J s; $c = 3.0 \times 10^{8}$ m s^{-1};
mass of electron $m_e = 9.11 \times 10^{-31}$ kg)

SAQ 17.9

When radiation of wavelength 2000 nm is shone on a metal surface, the greatest kinetic energy of the electrons released is found to be 4.0×10^{-20} J. What is the work function of the metal?

Light and atoms

In the mid-nineteenth century, scientists debated whether there were any limits to the questions that science could answer. It was suggested that scientists would never be able to discover what the stars were made of – they were too far away, and too hot. Within two years, however, the British astronomer William Huggins had shown that stars consisted of the same elements as all the familiar matter we know from the Earth. He did this by looking at the spectrum of light coming to us from the stars.

Line spectra

We rely a great deal on light to tell us about our surroundings. We have learnt, when young, to identify many different colours. Scientists take this further by analysing light, by breaking it up into a spectrum. You will be familiar with the ways in which this can be done, using a prism or a diffraction grating *(figure 17.15)*. The

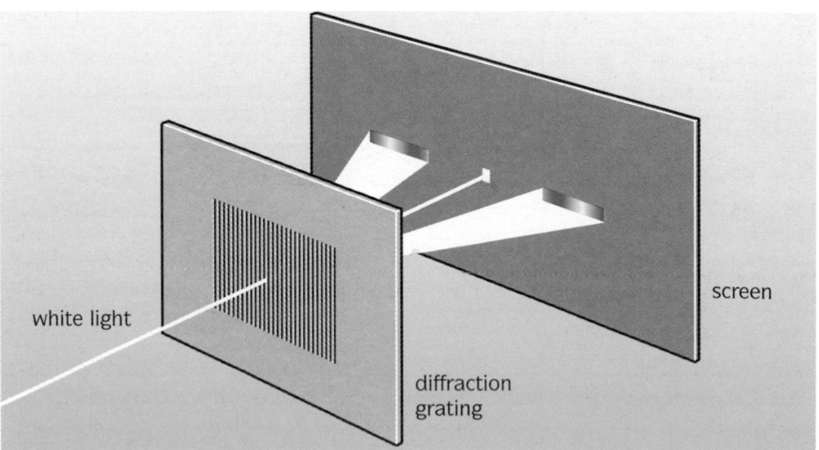

● ***Figure 17.15*** White light is split up into a continuous spectrum when it passes through a diffraction grating.

spectrum of white light shows that it consists of a range of wavelengths, from about 400 nm (violet) to about 750 nm (red), as in *figure 17.16a*.

It is more interesting to look at the spectrum from a hot gas. If you look at a lamp that contains a gas such as neon or sodium, you will see that only certain colours are present. If the source is narrow and it is viewed through a diffraction grating, a line spectrum is seen.

Figures 17.16b–d show the line spectra for several different elements. Because each element has a spectrum with a different collection of wavelengths, line spectra can be used to identify elements, and this is what Huggins did when he found out which elements are the most common in the stars.

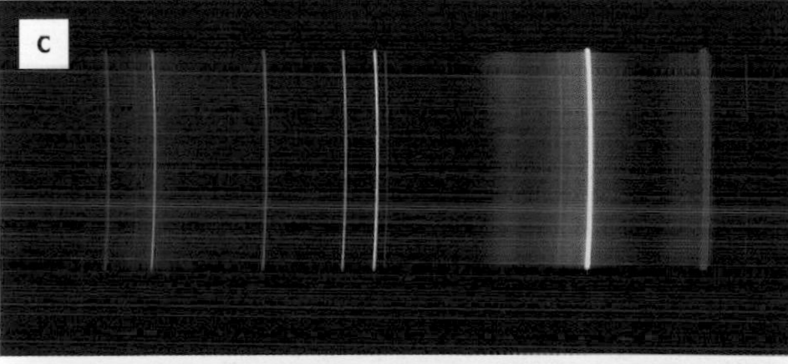

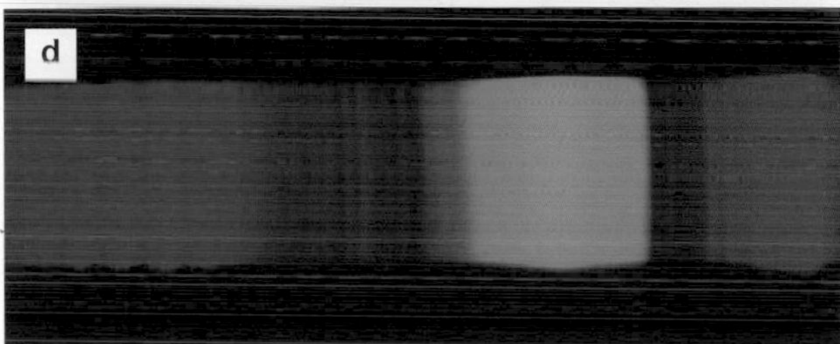

● ***Figure 17.16*** Spectra of **a** white light, and light from **b** mercury **c** helium and **d** copper.

● ***Figure 17.17*** An absorption spectrum formed when white light is passed through sodium vapour.

These spectra, which show the composition of light emitted by hot gases, are called **emission spectra**. There is another kind of spectrum, called an **absorption spectrum**, which is observed when white light is passed through a cool gas. After the light has passed through a diffraction grating (*figure 17.17*), the continuous white light spectrum is found to have black lines across it; certain wavelengths have been absorbed as the white light passed through the gas.

Absorption spectra are found when the light from stars is analysed; the interior of the star is very hot, and emits white light having all wavelengths in the visible range. However, this light has to pass through the cooler outer layers of the star, and certain wavelengths are absorbed. *Figure 17.18* shows the spectrum for the Sun.

Explaining line spectra

From the discussion above, we can see that the atoms of a given element (e.g. hydrogen) can only emit or absorb light of certain wavelengths.

Different elements emit and absorb different

● ***Figure 17.18*** The temperature of a star can be determined by observing its spectrum.

wavelengths. How can this be? To understand this, we need to establish two points:

- First, as with the photoelectric effect, we are dealing with light interacting with matter, so we need to consider light as consisting of photons; for light of a single wavelength λ, each photon has frequency f and energy hf.
- Secondly, when light falls on matter, it is the electrons that absorb the energy. When the electrons lose energy, light is emitted.

What, then, does the appearance of line spectra tell us about electrons in atoms? They can only absorb or emit photons of certain energies; from this we deduce that electrons in atoms can themselves only have certain fixed values of energy. You have probably come across this idea before, and it may not seem particularly odd, but it seemed very odd to scientists a hundred years ago.

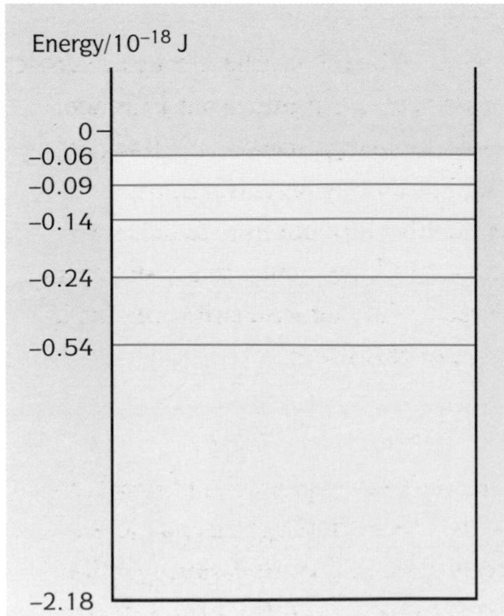

● ***Figure 17.19*** The energy level diagram for hydrogen.

Figure 17.19 shows diagrammatically the permitted energy levels for a hydrogen atom. An electron in a hydrogen atom can have only one of these values of energy; we say that its energy is quantised. This is one of the most important results of quantum theory.

Now we can explain what happens when an atom emits light. One of its electrons falls from a high energy level to a lower one *(figure 17.20a)*. It emits a single photon of light, and the energy of this photon is exactly equal to the energy difference between the two levels. If the electron falls from a higher level, it emits a more energetic photon. This explains why only certain energies (certain wavelengths) are present in the line emission spectrum of a hot gas. Different elements have different line spectra because they have different spacings in their 'ladders' of energy levels. (It is not within the scope of this book to discuss why this is; each element's energy level diagram can be worked out from the element's spectrum.)

Similarly, we can explain the origin of line absorption spectra. White light consists of photons of many different energies. For a photon to be absorbed, it must have exactly the right energy to lift an electron from one energy level to another *(figure 17.20b)*. If its energy is too little or too great, it will not be absorbed.

Photon energies

When an electron changes its energy from one level E_1 to another E_2, it either emits or absorbs a single photon. The energy of the photon hf is simply equal to the difference in energies between the two levels:

$$hf = E_1 - E_2$$

Referring back to the energy level diagram for hydrogen *(figure 17.19)*, you can see that, if an electron falls from the second level to

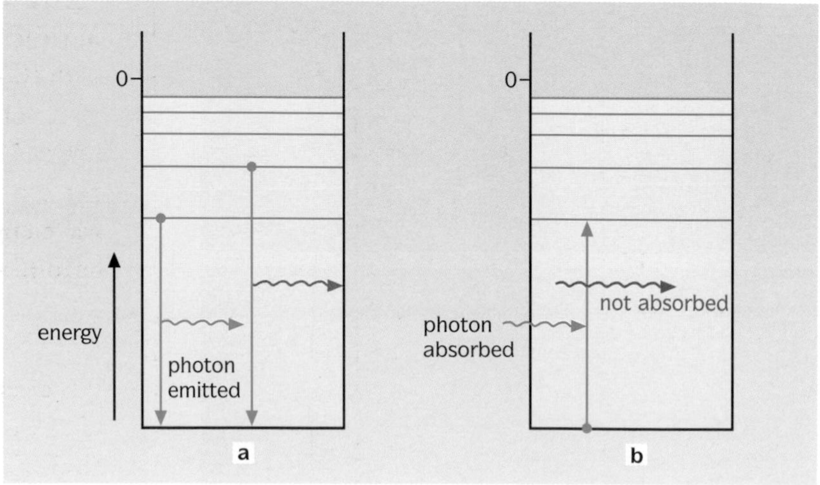

● ***Figure 17.20*** **a** When an electron drops to a lower energy level, it emits a single photon. **b** A photon must have just the right energy if it is to be absorbed by an electron.

the lowest level, it will emit a photon of energy

$$hf = [(-0.54) - (-2.18)] \times 10^{-18}\,\text{J}$$
$$= 1.64 \times 10^{-18}\,\text{J}$$

We can calculate the frequency and wavelength of this photon:

$$f = E/h = 1.64 \times 10^{-18}\,\text{J}/(6.63 \times 10^{-34}\,\text{J s})$$
$$= 2.47 \times 10^{15}\,\text{Hz}$$

$$\lambda = c/f = 3 \times 10^{8}\,\text{m s}^{-1}/(2.47 \times 10^{15}\,\text{Hz}$$
$$= 1.21 \times 10^{-7}\,\text{m} = 121\,\text{nm}$$

This is a wavelength in the ultraviolet region of the electromagnetic spectrum.

SAQ 17.10

Figure 17.21 shows part of the energy level diagram of an imaginary atom. The arrows represent three transitions between energy levels. Calculate the energy, frequency and wavelength of the photon absorbed or emitted during each of these transitions. In each case, say whether the photon would contribute to an emission or an absorption spectrum.

SAQ 17.11

Figure 17.22 shows another energy level diagram. Which of the following photon energies could be absorbed by such an atom: 6×10^{-18} J, 8×10^{-18} J, 14×10^{-18} J, 20×10^{-18} J, 25×10^{-18} J, 30×10^{-18} J?

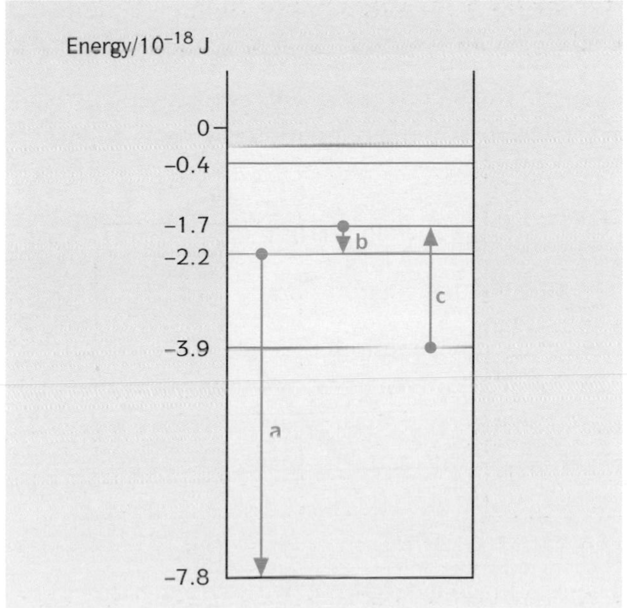

● ***Figure 17.21*** An atomic energy level diagram, showing three electron transitions between levels.

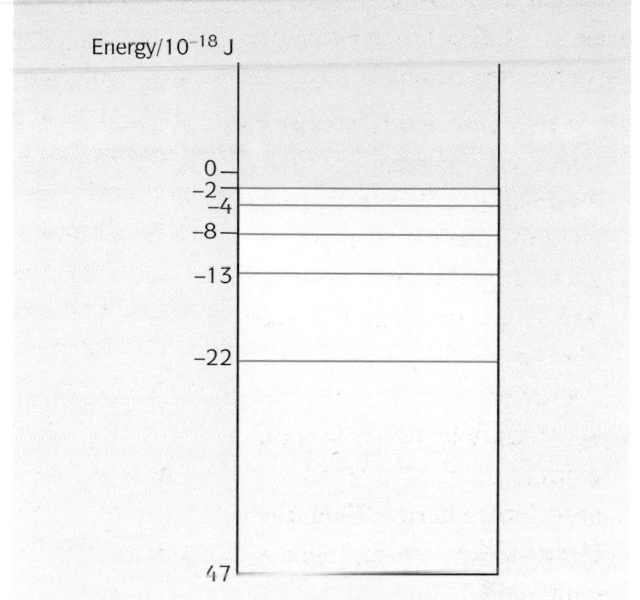

● ***Figure 17.22*** An atomic energy level diagram.

Isolated atoms

So far, we have only discussed the spectra of light from hot gases. In a gas, the atoms are relatively far apart (see chapter 12), so they do not interact with one another very much. As a consequence, they give relatively simple line spectra. Similar spectra can be obtained from some gemstones and coloured glass. In these, the basic material is clear and colourless, but it gains its colour from impurity atoms, which are well separated from one another within the material.

In a solid or liquid, however, the atoms are close together. The electrons from one atom interact with those of neighbouring atoms. This has the effect of altering the energy level diagram, which becomes much more complicated. The corresponding spectra have many, many different wavelengths present; further discussion of this is beyond the scope of this book.

Light: waves or particles?

It is clear that, in order to explain the photoelectric effect, we must use the idea of light as particles. Similarly, photons explain the appearance of line spectra. However, to explain diffraction, interference and polarisation of light, we must use the wave model. How can we sort out this dilemma?

We have to conclude that sometimes light shows wave-like behaviour; at other times it behaves as particles. In particular, when light is absorbed by a metal surface, it behaves as particles. Individual photons are absorbed by individual electrons in the metal. In a similar way, when a Geiger counter detects γ-radiation, we hear individual γ-photons being absorbed in the tube.

In the next section, we will draw together all of these ideas about waves and particles.

Waves, particles and people

Sometimes we have to explain the behaviour of light using a wave model, and sometimes using a particle model. Similarly, sometimes electrons behave as particles, and sometimes as waves. This is called **wave–particle duality**. No-one can be entirely happy with this situation, and physicists have spent a lot of time trying to sort out this dilemma.

First, we should remind ourselves that waves and particles are macroscopic phenomena. We are using these models to describe microscopic phenomena, and we should not be surprised that they do not work perfectly. But it is still difficult to explain why one model works well in one situation, and the other in another situation.

We should not try to imagine 'waves of matter' or 'particulate waves'; these do not give a true representation of what we observe. However, we can make things more acceptable by giving rules, which tell us when to use the particle model and when to use the wave model. Then, at least, we can solve problems, which is what we really require of physics.

Rules for light

- We use the *particle model* for light when light interacts with matter.

  Examples include the photoelectric effect (page 146) and emission and absorption of light by atoms (line spectra) (page 149).

- We use the *wave model* for light when the wavelength of the light is comparable to the dimensions of any object with which it interacts.

  Examples include diffraction by a single slit, double slit or diffraction grating, and subsequent interference. (The wavelength of visible light is of the order of 10^{-6} m, and so a slit of width 10^{-6} m has the greatest effect.)

These rules apply to all types of electromagnetic radiation.

Rules for matter

The *same* rules apply to matter as for light. To understand how to apply them, we need to say what we mean by the wavelength of something such as an electron, which we normally think of as a particle. (We have already seen on page 142 that electrons can be diffracted, and that we can therefore measure their wavelength.)

In 1924, de Broglie proposed that, just as light has a dual nature, so might all particles. He suggested that the wavelength λ of a particle was related to its momentum p by the equation:

$$\lambda = \frac{h}{p}$$

This says that the wavelength is inversely proportional to the particle's momentum, and the constant of proportionality is the Planck constant. Notice that, like the equation $E = hf$, this equation tells us how to translate between a wave property (λ) and a particle property (p).

We can now work out the wavelength of an electron, if we know its speed. For example, we can calculate λ for an electron moving at $10^7\,\text{m s}^{-1}$:

$$\lambda = \frac{h}{p} = \frac{h}{mv} = \frac{6.63 \times 10^{-34}\,\text{J s}}{9.11 \times 10^{-31}\,\text{kg} \times 10^7\,\text{m s}^{-1}}$$

$$= 7.3 \times 10^{-11}\,\text{m}$$

Hence the wavelength of this fast-moving electron is about 10^{-10} m, roughly the same size as the spacing between atoms in a solid. This is why electrons are diffracted by planes of atoms.

Human waves

The relationship proposed by de Broglie applies to all matter. Since people are made of matter, we can apply it to them.

The wavelength of a person of mass 66 kg running at $10\,\mathrm{m\,s^{-1}}$ is given by $\lambda = h/mv = 6.6 \times 10^{-34}\,\mathrm{J\,s} / (66\,\mathrm{kg} \times 10\,\mathrm{m\,s^{-1}}) = 10^{-36}\,\mathrm{m}$. This is a very small wavelength, much smaller than any gap the person is likely to try to squeeze through. For this reason, we do not use the wave model to describe the behaviour of people; we get much better results by regarding people as large particles.

This may seem like a rather silly example, but it shows why we do not often observe matter behaving as waves in everyday life; the corresponding wavelengths are too small. The example also shows the process we must go through when trying to decide whether to use the wave model or the particle model. We calculate the wavelength of a particle; if it is comparable to the width of any gap or obstacle, we use the wave model.

You will need the following information in answering the SAQ: Planck constant $h = 6.63 \times 10^{-34}\,\mathrm{J\,s}$, speed of light in free space $c = 3 \times 10^{8}\,\mathrm{m\,s^{-1}}$, speed of sound in air $= 330\,\mathrm{m\,s^{-1}}$ and mass of electron $= 9.11 \times 10^{-31}\,\mathrm{kg}$.

SAQ 17.12

For each situation described below, state whether the wave model or the particle model applies. Give calculations to support your answer.

a A person (mass 50 kg) walks at $3\,\mathrm{m\,s^{-1}}$ through a doorway 0.8 m wide. A laser beam of wavelength 650 nm and a sound of frequency 300 Hz also go through the doorway.

b A beam of electrons, each of momentum $10^{-18}\,\mathrm{kg\,m\,s^{-1}}$, passes atomic nuclei, diameter $10^{-15}\,\mathrm{m}$.

c A bullet of mass 25 g and travelling at $600\,\mathrm{m\,s^{-1}}$ strikes a target 20 cm across.

d Radio signals of frequency 6000 kHz pass between blocks of flats 80 m apart.

e A beam of electrons, accelerated to a speed of $10^{6}\,\mathrm{m\,s^{-1}}$, is directed on to an optical diffraction grating having 300 000 lines per metre.

f Light of wavelength 400 nm falls on photographic paper. (Energy needed to activate photographic emulsion $= 10^{-20}\,\mathrm{J}$.)

g A beam of neutrons, each of mass $1.8 \times 10^{-28}\,\mathrm{kg}$ and moving at $10^{7}\,\mathrm{m\,s^{-1}}$, is directed at a crystal whose lattice spacing is $8 \times 10^{-10}\,\mathrm{m}$.

SUMMARY

- Both electromagnetic radiation and matter exhibit wave–particle duality; that is, they show both wave-like and particle-like behaviours, depending on the circumstances.
- Electron diffraction is an example of a phenomenon explained in terms of the wave-like behaviour of matter.
- The photoelectric effect and line spectra are phenomena explained in terms of the particle-like behaviour of electromagnetic radiation.
- For light of frequency f, photons have energy hf, where h is the Planck constant.
- In the photoelectric effect, light falling on a metal surface may cause electrons to be ejected.
- A photon of light whose frequency equals the threshold frequency has just enough energy to release a weakly bound electron. A more energetic photon may release a faster-moving electron.
- Line spectra arise for isolated atoms. An electron moves from a higher energy level to a lower one, and the difference in energy is emitted as a single photon.

Nuclear physics

By the end of this chapter you should be able to:

1 represent simple nuclear reactions by nuclear equations;

2 appreciate that nucleon number, proton number and (energy plus mass) are all conserved in nuclear processes;

3 appreciate the association between energy and mass as represented by $E = mc^2$;

4 illustrate graphically the variation of binding energy per nucleon with nucleon number;

5 describe the relevance of binding energy per nucleon to nuclear fusion and nuclear fission.

Nuclear processes

From your study of atomic structure in the *Foundation Physics* module, you will be familiar with the 'nuclear model' of atoms, as shown in *figure 18.2*. Every atom has a central nucleus, surrounded by orbital electrons. The nucleus consists of protons and neutrons, and has most of the atom's mass and all of the positive charge. The electrons have very little mass; their negative charge exactly balances the positive charge of the protons in the nucleus.

● ***Figure 18.1*** Our understanding of nuclear physics has proved to be a mixed blessing. Nuclear weapons have dominated global politics for much of the twentieth century.

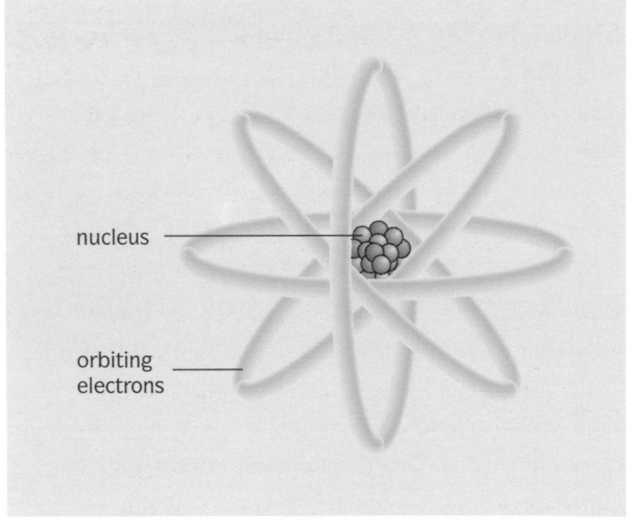

● ***Figure 18.2*** The 'nuclear model' of the atom has been successful in describing many aspects of the behaviour of matter on the atomic scale.

Remember that the nucleus is very tiny compared to the atom as a whole; its diameter is typically 10^{-15} m, while the atom's diameter is 10^{-10} m. On the scale of *figure 18.2*, the nucleus is really too small to see.

You should also be familiar with the notation used to represent different nuclei. Here are the symbols for two nuclides, both isotopes of carbon:

$${}^{12}_{6}\mathrm{C} \qquad {}^{14}_{6}\mathrm{C}$$

The upper number is the nucleon number or mass number A, and tells us the number of protons and neutrons; the lower number is the proton number Z. The general symbol for a nuclide X is

$${}^{A}_{Z}\mathrm{X}$$

In this section, we will look at how we can use the nuclear model to picture the nuclear processes of fission and fusion, and how we can represent these processes by balanced nuclear equations.

Nuclear fission

In Nature, we find nuclei with proton numbers up to $Z = 92$ (uranium). However, the most massive of these, beyond $Z = 83$, are unstable, and are gradually decaying away. In chapter 19, we will look in more detail at the nature of this radioactive decay.

However, there is another way in which massive, unstable nuclei such as uranium and plutonium ($Z = 94$) can become more stable. They can split apart into two more stable fragments; this process is called **nuclear fission.** Usually, fission occurs when a neutron collides with a large, unstable nucleus *(figure 18.3)*. The neutron is absorbed, making the nucleus even more unstable, and the nucleus then splits into two. Several neutrons are also released. (These neutrons may go on to cause the fission of other large nuclei. A chain reaction is set up; use is made of this in nuclear power stations and in nuclear explosions.)

We can represent nuclear fission by nuclear equations. Here is the equation for the fission shown in *figure 18.3*:

$${}^{1}_{0}\text{n} + {}^{235}_{92}\text{U} \rightarrow {}^{92}_{36}\text{Kr} + {}^{141}_{56}\text{Ba} + 3\,{}^{1}_{0}\text{n}$$

In words, this says that a single neutron ${}^{1}_{0}\text{n}$ collides with a uranium nucleus ${}^{235}_{92}\text{U}$. Fission occurs, resulting in isotopes of krypton and barium, and three neutrons are also released. (A neutron is represented by ${}^{1}_{0}\text{n}$. A proton is shown as ${}^{1}_{1}\text{p}$ or ${}^{1}_{1}\text{H}$.)

For this equation to be balanced, we require that both the proton number and the nucleon number are conserved; that is, the total number of protons (representing positive charge) must be the same on both sides of the equation, because we cannot create or destroy charge in a nuclear reaction. Similarly, the total number of nucleons (representing mass) must be the same on both sides. We can check like this:

- for Z $\quad 92 + 0 = 36 + 56 + 3 \times 0$
- for A $\quad 235 + 1 = 92 + 141 + 3 \times 1$

SAQ 18.1

Show that the following equation is correctly balanced.

$${}^{235}_{92}\text{U} + {}^{1}_{0}\text{n} \rightarrow {}^{138}_{54}\text{Xe} + {}^{95}_{38}\text{Sr} + 3\,{}^{1}_{0}\text{n}$$

SAQ 18.2

In a nuclear fission event, the large nucleus usually splits into two unequal fragments; sometimes two neutrons are released, sometimes three or four. Complete the following equations by ensuring that both proton number and nucleon number are conserved. (In **b**, you may have to use the Periodic Table or a list of the elements to help you identify the missing element.)

a ${}^{239}_{94}\text{Pu} + {}^{1}_{0}\text{n} \rightarrow {}^{145}_{56}\text{Ba} + {}^{93}_{36}\text{Sr} + ?$

b ${}^{239}_{94}\text{Pu} + {}^{1}_{0}\text{n} \rightarrow {}^{147}_{58}\text{Ce} + ? + 3\,{}^{1}_{0}\text{n}$

SAQ 18.3

A light nucleus can become unstable if it is bombarded with nuclear radiation. Complete the equation below to find the particle released when a nucleus of ${}^{14}_{7}\text{N}$ captures an α-particle ${}^{4}_{2}\text{He}$:

$${}^{14}_{7}\text{N} + {}^{4}_{2}\text{He} \rightarrow {}^{17}_{8}\text{O} + ?$$

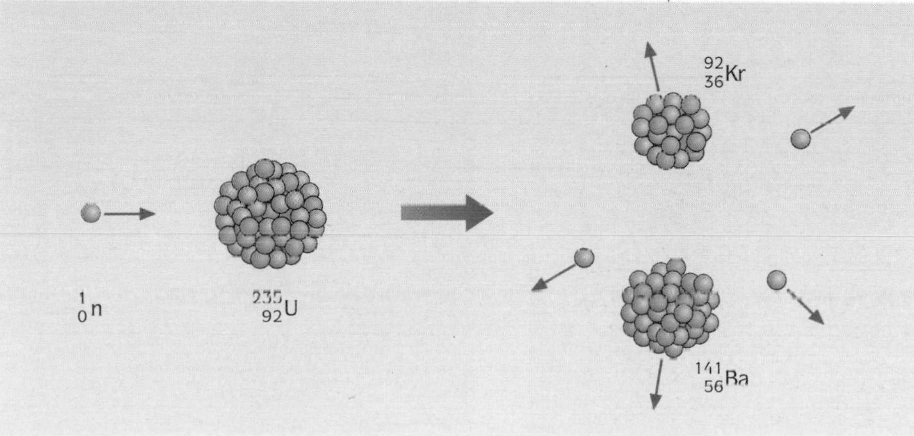

● ***Figure 18.3*** In stimulated nuclear fission, a neutron collides with a uranium nucleus, causing it to become unstable, so that it splits into two large fragments. More neutrons are released.

Nuclear fusion

Massive nuclei tend to be unstable, and they can become more stable through the process of fission. In a similar way, light nuclei can become more stable by joining together in the process of **nuclear fusion.** As a general rule, middle-sized nuclei tend to be the most stable. This will be discussed in more detail in the next section.

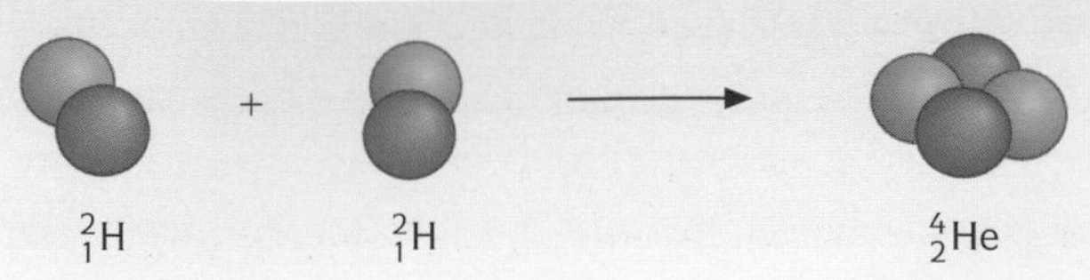

● ***Figure 18.4*** In nuclear fusion, two light nuclei join together to make a more stable nucleus.

Figure 18.4 shows two light nuclei, both isotopes of hydrogen, fusing to form a helium nucleus. The equation for this is:

$$^2_1\text{H} + ^2_1\text{H} \rightarrow ^4_2\text{He}$$

Note that, as before, both Z and A are conserved.

Often in fusion reactions, the result is not a single particle, but two or more. The reaction shown in the equation above can have an alternative outcome:

$$^2_1\text{H} + ^2_1\text{H} \rightarrow ^3_1\text{H} + ^1_1\text{H}$$

In the process of nuclear fusion, light nuclei are becoming more stable. Energy is released. This is the source of energy that keeps stars (such as the Sun) shining for billions of years. It is also hoped that one day we will be able to have fusion reactors for generating electricity. Prototype reactors, such as the Joint European Torus at Culham in Oxfordshire *(figure 18.5)*, suggest that controllable fusion reactions may one day be within our technological grasp.

SAQ 18.4

Complete the following equation for a fusion reaction in which three particles result:

$$^3_2\text{He} + ^3_2\text{He} \rightarrow ^4_2\text{He} + ?$$

SAQ 18.5

In one of the fusion reactions that occur in the Sun, the most stable isotope of carbon, $^{12}_{6}$C, is formed from the fusion of a proton with a nucleus of an isotope of nitrogen, $^{15}_{7}$N. Write a balanced equation for this reaction. What other new element is formed?

Explaining fission and fusion

In both fission and fusion, unstable nuclei have become more stable. Energy is released. In order to explain these processes, we need to be able to say where this energy comes from. One answer lies in the origins of the nuclei we are considering. Take, for example, uranium. The Earth's crust contains uranium. In some places, it is sufficiently concentrated to make it worth while extracting it for use as the fuel in fission reactors *(figure 18.6)*. This uranium has been part of the Earth since it was formed, 4500 million years ago.

The Earth formed from a swirling cloud of dust and gas, at the same time that the Sun itself was forming. These materials condensed under the

● ***Figure 18.5*** The JET torus at the Culham Laboratory in Oxfordshire is a European experiment to solve some of the problems associated with maintaining controlled nuclear fusion as a source of energy.

● ***Figure 18.6*** Uranium, the fuel for nuclear reactors, comes from mines like the Ranger mine in Australia.

force of gravitational attraction. But where did they come from in the first place? It is believed that heavy elements (such as uranium) were formed in a supernova. At some time in the distant past, an ageing star collapsed and then blew itself apart in an explosion of awesome scale. At the very high temperatures that resulted, there was sufficient energy available for light nuclei to fuse to form the heaviest nuclei, which we now find if we dig in the Earth's crust. It is this energy, from an ancient stellar explosion, that is released when a large nucleus undergoes fission.

Mass and energy

We can extend this explanation by asking: How can we calculate the amount of energy released in fission or fusion? To find the answer to this, we need to think first about the masses of the particles involved.

We will start by considering a stable nucleus, ${}^{12}_{6}C$. This consists of six protons and six neutrons. Fortunately for us, because we have a lot of this form of carbon in our bodies, this is a very stable nuclide. This means that the nucleons are bound tightly together. It takes a lot of energy to pull them apart.

Figure 18.7 shows the results of an imaginary experiment in which we have done just that. On the left-hand side of the balance is a ${}^{12}_{6}C$ nucleus. On the right-hand side are six protons and six neutrons, the result of dismantling the nucleus. The surprising thing is that the balance is tipped to the right. The separate nucleons have more mass than the nucleus itself. This means that the law of conservation of mass has been broken. We have violated a fundamental law of Nature, something that was held to be true for hundreds of years. How can this be?

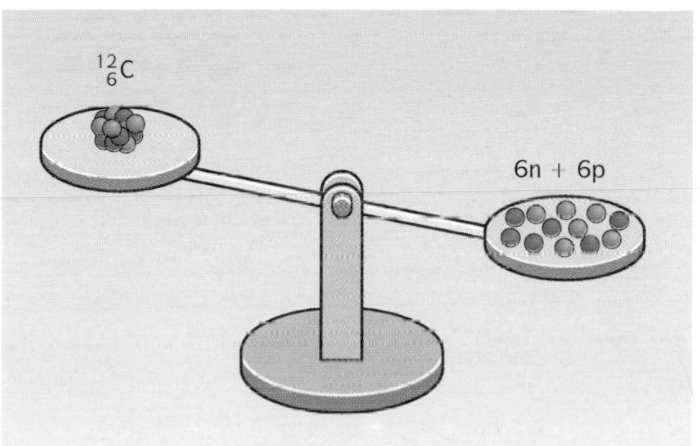

● ***Figure 18.7*** The mass of a nucleus is less than the total mass of its component protons and neutrons.

Notice that, in dismantling the ${}^{12}_{6}C$ nucleus, we have had to do work. The nucleons attract one another with nuclear forces, and these are strong enough to make the nucleus very stable. So we have put energy in to the system to pull the nucleus apart. Where has this energy gone?

At the same time, we have the mystery of the appearing mass. There is more mass when we have pulled the nucleons apart than when they are bound together.

You probably already know that these two problems, disappearing energy and appearing mass, can be solved together. We say that 'energy has turned into mass'. If we let the separate protons and neutrons recombine to make a ${}^{12}_{6}C$ nucleus, the extra mass will disappear and the missing energy will be released. This mass–energy conversion explains where the energy comes from in nuclear fusion.

A better way to express this is to treat mass and energy as aspects of the same thing. Rather than having separate laws of conservation of mass and energy, we can combine these two. The total amount of mass and energy together in a system is constant. There may be conversions from one to the other, but the total amount of mass plus energy remains constant.

Einstein's equation

If we are saying that the total amount of (mass plus energy) in a closed system remains constant, we need to know how to add mass (in kg) to energy (in J). Albert Einstein produced his famous equation, which allows us to do this. The energy E equivalent to mass m is given by

$$E = mc^2$$

where c is the speed of light in free space. The value of c is approximately $3 \times 10^8\,\mathrm{m\,s^{-1}}$, but its precise value has been fixed as

$$c = 299\,792\,458\,\mathrm{m\,s^{-1}}$$

Particle	Relative mass	Mass/10^{-27} kg
^1_1p	1.007 276	1.672 623
^1_0n	1.008 665	1.674 929
$^{12}_6C$	12.000 000	19.926 483

● ***Table 18.1*** Masses of some particles

Now if we know the total mass of particles before a nuclear reaction, and their total mass after the reaction, we can work out how much energy is released. *Table 18.1* gives the relative masses of the particles shown in *figure 18.7*. (These are measured on a standard scale where the mass of $^{12}_6C$ is defined as 12 exactly.) The masses are also given in kg.

The first thing to notice about these data is that, although the relative mass of $^{12}_6C$ is precisely 12, the mass of an individual proton or neutron is slightly more than 1. So the total mass of six protons and six neutrons is clearly greater than the mass of $^{12}_6C$.

Secondly, notice that the masses are not much greater than 1. Nuclear masses are measured to a high degree of precision, often to seven or eight significant figures, because it is the small differences *between* values that are important.

We can use the mass values in kg to calculate the mass that 'disappears' when nucleons combine to form a nucleus. So for our particles in *figure 18.7*:

$$\text{mass before} = (6 \times 1.672\,623 + 6 \times 1.674\,929) \times 10^{-27}\,\text{kg} = 20.085\,312 \times 10^{-27}\,\text{kg}$$

$$\text{mass after} = 19.926\,483 \times 10^{-27}\,\text{kg}$$

$$\text{mass difference} = (20.085\,312 - 19.926\,483) \times 10^{-27}\,\text{kg} = 0.158\,829 \times 10^{-27}\,\text{kg}$$

Thus there is a very small loss of mass when the nucleons combine to form the nucleus. We can now use $E = mc^2$ to calculate the energy released:

$$E = mc^2 = 0.158\,829 \times 10^{-27}\,\text{kg} \times (2.997\,925 \times 10^8\,\text{m}\,\text{s}^{-1})^2 = 1.43 \times 10^{-11}\,\text{J}$$

This may seem like a small amount of energy, but it is a lot on the scale of an atom. For comparison, the amount of energy released in a chemical reaction involving a single carbon atom would typically be of the order of 10^{-18} J, more than a million times smaller.

SAQ 18.6

a Calculate the energy released if a ^4_2He nucleus is formed from separate protons and neutrons.

b Calculate also the energy released per nucleon.

Mass values are given in *table 18.2*.

SAQ 18.7

Use the relative mass values given in *table 18.3* to explain why the fusion reaction

$$^4_2He + ^4_2He \rightarrow ^8_4Be$$

is unlikely to occur, unless some extra source of energy is supplied.

Binding energy and stability

We can now begin to see why some nuclei are more stable than others. If a nucleus is formed from separate nucleons, energy is released. In order to pull the nucleus apart, energy must be put in; in other words, work must be done against the forces holding the nucleons together. The more energy involved in this, the more stable is the nucleus.

The energy needed to pull a nucleus apart into separate nucleons is called the **binding energy** of the nucleus. Take care: this is *not* energy stored in the nucleus; on the contrary, it is the energy that must be put in to the nucleus in order to pull it apart. In the example of $^{12}_6C$ discussed above, we calculated the binding energy from the mass difference between the mass of the $^{12}_6C$ nucleus and the masses of the separate protons and neutrons.

Particle	Mass/10^{-27} kg
^1_1p	1.672 623
^1_0n	1.674 929
^4_2He	6.644 661

● ***Table 18.2*** Masses of some particles

Particle	Relative mass
^4_2He	4.001 506
^8_4Be	8.003 111

● ***Table 18.3*** Relative masses of some particles

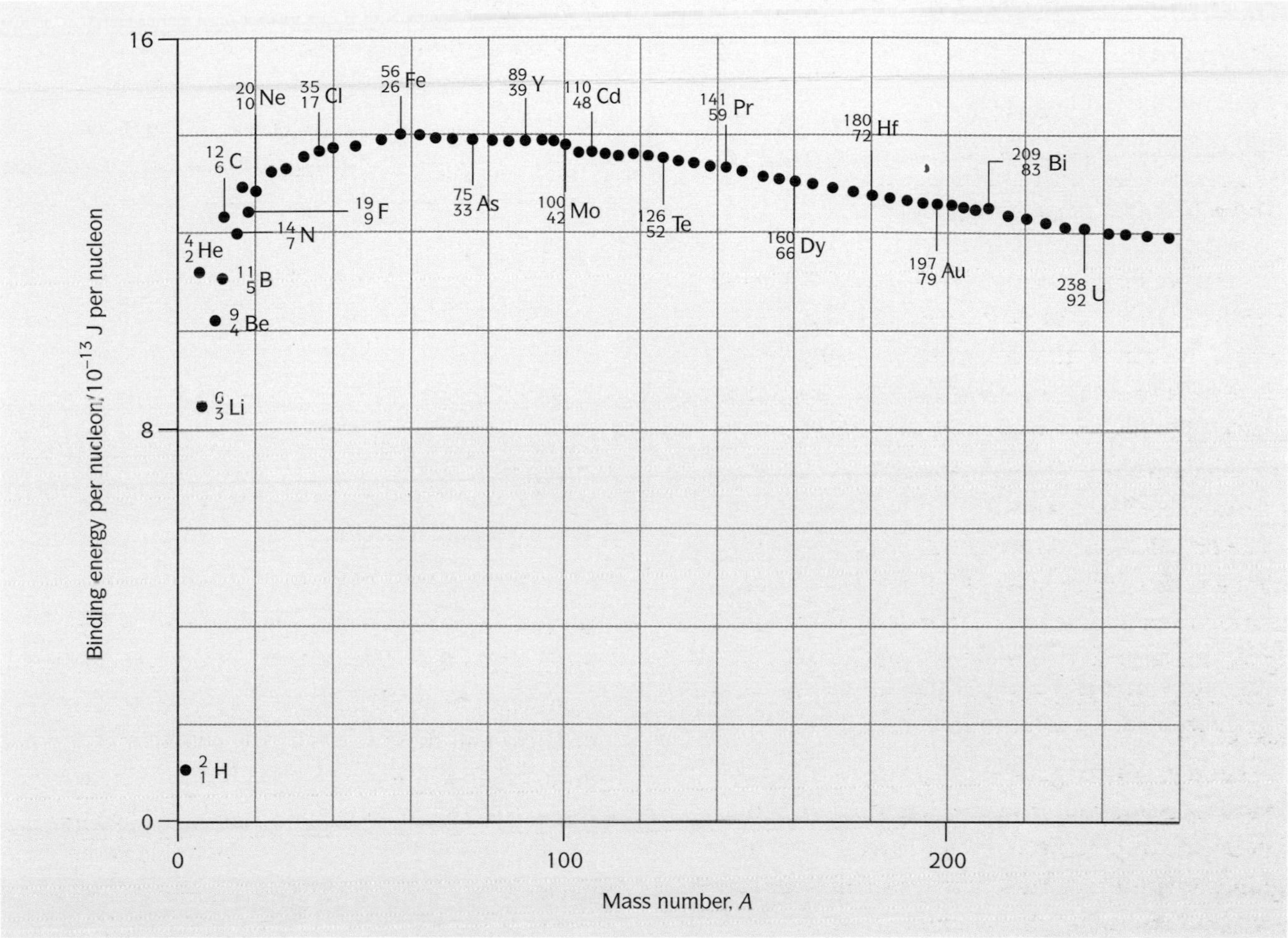

● ***Figure 18.8*** This graph shows the binding energy per nucleon for common nuclei. The nucleus becomes more stable as binding energy increases.

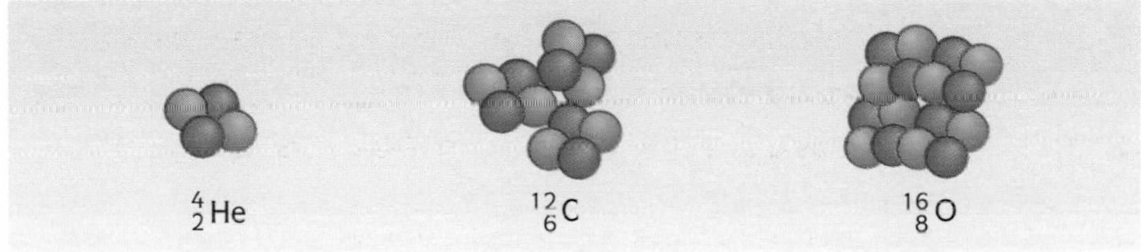

● ***Figure 18.9*** Light, stable nuclei are formed when α-particles are bound together.

In order to compare different nuclides, we need to consider the binding energy per nucleon. *Figure 18.8* shows the binding energy per nucleon for stable nuclei. This is a graph against A; the greater the value, the more tightly bound are the nucleons that make up the nucleus.

If you examine this graph, you will see that the general trend is for light nuclei to have low binding energies. For nuclides with $A >$ 20 approximately, there is not much variation in binding energy.

In fact, the greatest value of binding energy per nucleon is found for $^{56}_{26}$Fe. This isotope of iron requires the most energy per nucleon to dismantle it into separate nucleons.

Notice the anomalous position of $^4_2$He, which lies off the main curve of the graph. This nucleus (two protons and two neutrons, the same as an α-particle) is very stable. Other common stable nuclei include $^{12}_6$C and $^{16}_8$O, which can be thought of as three or four α-particles bound together *(figure 18.9)*.

Binding energy, fission and fusion

We can use the binding energy graph to help us decide which nuclear processes (fission, fusion, radioactive decay (chapter 19)) are likely to occur *(figure 18.10)*.

- *Fission*
  When a massive nucleus splits, it forms two smaller fragments. For uranium, we have $A = 235$, and the fragments have $A = 140$ and 95, typically. If we look at the binding energy curve, we see that these two products have greater binding energy than the original uranium nucleus. Hence, if the uranium nucleus splits in this way, energy will be released.
- *Fusion*
  In a similar way, if two light nuclei fuse, the final binding energy will be greater than the original value. There is a problem with the anomalous value for ${}^{4}_{2}\text{He}$. This makes it difficult for two of these nuclei to fuse; you worked this out from the particles' masses in SAQ 18.7.

SAQ 18.8

Use the binding energy graph to explain why fission is unlikely to occur with light nuclei ($A < 20$), and why fusion is unlikely to occur for heavier nuclei ($A > 40$).

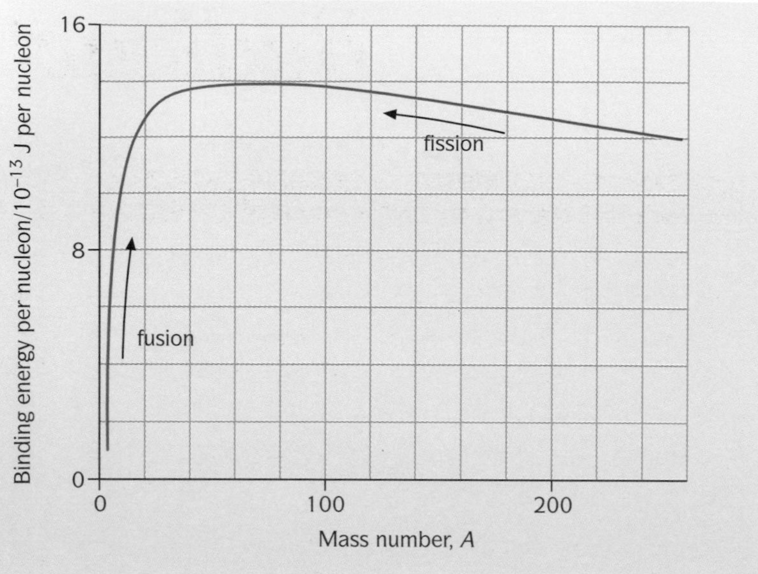

● ***Figure 18.10*** Both fusion and fission are processes that tend to increase the binding energy per nucleon of the particles involved.

SUMMARY

- Nuclear reactions can be represented by balanced nuclear equations. In any such reaction, the following quantities are conserved: proton number Z, nucleon number A, and (mass plus energy).
- In order to relate mass changes to energy changes, we use Einstein's equation $E = mc^2$.
- The binding energy of a nucleus tells us the energy required to break up the nucleus into separate nucleons.
- The binding energy per nucleon gives us an indication of the relative stability of different nuclides.
- The variation of binding energy per nucleon shows that energy is released when light nuclei undergo fusion and when heavier nuclei undergo fission, because these processes increase the binding energy per nucleon and hence result in more stable nuclides.

Radioactivity

By the end of this chapter you should be able to:

1 describe α-particles, β-particles and γ-rays as different types of ionising radiation;

2 distinguish between these types of radiation in terms of mass, charge, speed, penetrating properties and the effects of magnetic and electric fields;

3 describe experiments that illustrate their penetrating properties;

4 appreciate the spontaneous and random nature of nuclear decay, as shown by fluctuations in count rate;

5 define the terms *activity* and *decay constant*;

6 recall and use the decay law $A = \lambda N$;

7 recognise, use and represent graphically solutions of the decay law based on $x = x_0 e^{-\lambda t}$, where x may be activity A, number of undecayed particles N, or received count rate R;

8 define half-life $t_{1/2}$;

9 use the relation $\lambda = 0.693/t_{1/2}$.

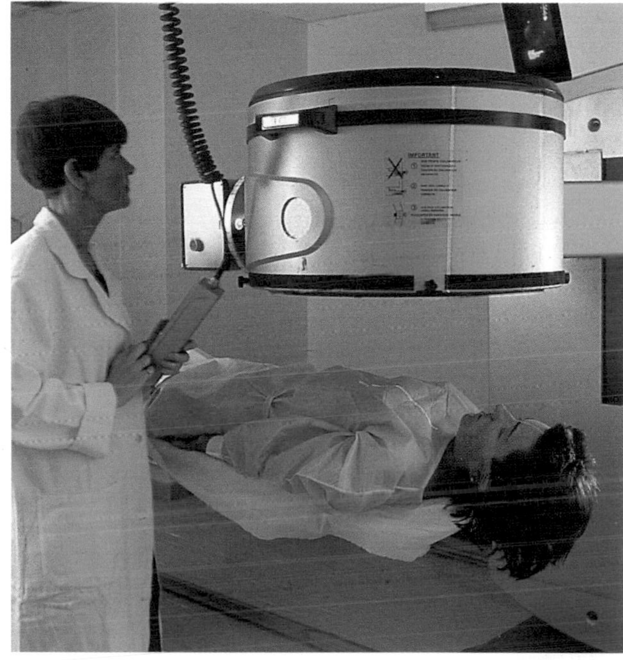

● ***Figure 19.1*** γ-rays at work. Here a patient is being prepared for a scan to check for cancer.

Ionising radiation

The three types of radiation, α, β and γ, that are emitted by radioactive materials are invisible. Although they are around us all the time, they were not discovered until 1896. In this section we will look at the properties of these kinds of radiation.

α, β and γ-radiation come from the nuclei of unstable atoms. Nuclei generally consist of protons and neutrons, and if the balance between these two types of particles is too far to one side, the nucleus may emit one or other kind of radiation as a way of achieving stability.

Table 19.1 shows the basic characteristics of the different types of radiation. *Table 19.2* is a reminder of the characteristics of protons,

Radiation	*Symbol*	*Mass* (relative to proton)	*Charge* (in terms of proton charge, $+e$)	*Speed*
alpha-particles	α, ${}^{4}_{2}\mathrm{He}$	4	$+2e$	'slow' ($10^6\,\mathrm{m\,s^{-1}}$)
beta-particles	β, β^-, e	1/1840	$-e$	'fast' ($10^8\,\mathrm{m\,s^{-1}}$)
gamma-rays	γ, hf	0	0	speed of light ($3\times10^8\,\mathrm{m\,s^{-1}}$)

● ***Table 19.1*** The nature of ionising radiation

Particle	*Symbol*	*Mass* (relative to proton)	*Charge* (in terms of proton charge, $+e$)
proton	${}^{1}_{1}\mathrm{p}$	1	$+e$
neutron	${}^{1}_{0}\mathrm{n}$	1	0
electron	${}^{0}_{-1}\mathrm{e}$	1/1840	$-e$

● ***Table 19.2*** The nature of subatomic particles

neutrons and electrons. (In these tables, masses are given relative to the mass of a proton; charge is measured in units of e, the electron charge.)

Note the following points:

- α and β are particles of matter, while a γ-ray is a form of electromagnetic radiation, similar to an X-ray but with a higher frequency.
- An α-particle consists of two protons and two neutrons, as in the nucleus of a helium atom. A β-particle is simply an electron.
- The mass of an α-particle is nearly 10 000 times that of a β-particle; a β-particle travels roughly 100 times faster than an α-particle.

Ionisation

Radiation affects the matter it passes through by causing ionisation. α and β-particles are fast-moving charged particles, and if they collide with or pass close to atoms, they may knock or drag electrons away from the atoms (*figure 19.2*). The resulting atoms are said to be **ionised**, and the process is called an ionising event. In the process, the radiation loses some of its energy. After many ionising events, the radiation loses all of its energy and no longer has any ionising effect.

α-radiation is the most strongly ionising, because it travels more slowly than β-radiation. This means that an α-particle interacts for longer with any atom which it passes, and so it is more likely to cause ionisation. β-particles are much lighter and faster, and so their effect is less. γ-radiation also causes ionisation, but not as strongly as α and β-particles, as γ-rays are not charged.

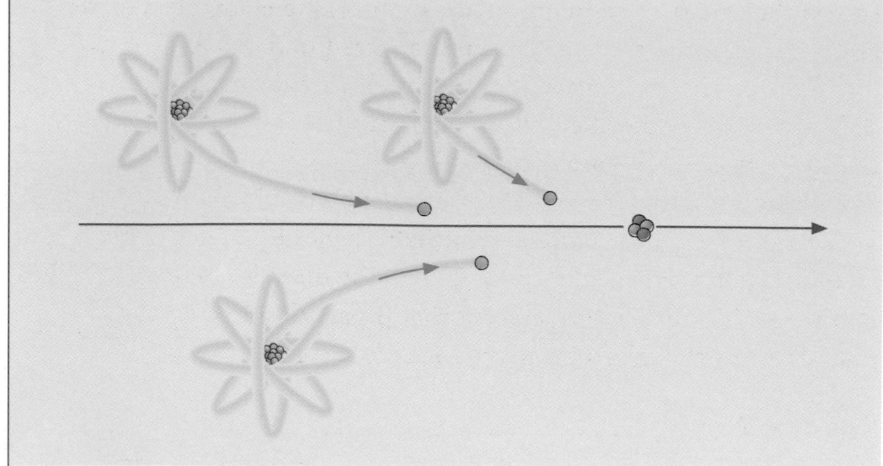

● ***Figure 19.2*** As an α-particle passes through a material, it causes ionisation of atoms.

SAQ 19.1

a Explain why you would expect β-particles to travel further through air than α-particles.

b Explain why you would expect β-particles to travel further through air than through metal.

Electric and magnetic fields

Because α, β and γ-radiations have different charges, they behave differently in electric and magnetic fields. This can be used to distinguish one kind of radiation from another.

Figure 19.3 shows the effect of an electric field. A mixture of α, β and γ-radiations is passing through the gap between two parallel

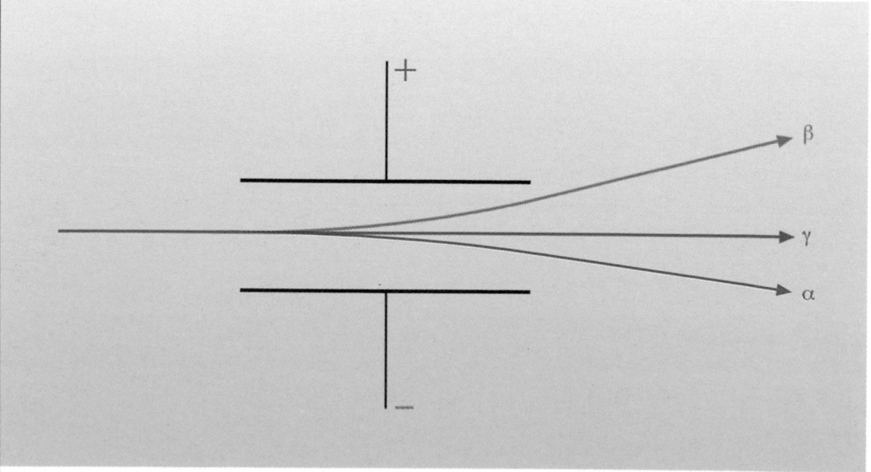

● ***Figure 19.3*** α, β and γ-radiations may be separated using an electric field.

plates; the electric field in this space is uniform (chapter 7). Since α and β-particles are charged, they are attracted to the plate that has the opposite charge to their own. β-particles are deflected more than α-particles, since their mass is so much less. γ-rays are undeflected since they are uncharged.

Figure 19.4 shows the effect of a magnetic field. In this case, the deflecting force on the particles is at right-angles to their motion. Fleming's left-hand rule (chapter 8) gives the direction of the force on the moving particles; remember that β-particles moving to the right constitute an electric current towards the left.

SAQ 19.2

a Some radioactive substances emit α-particles having two different speeds. Draw a diagram similar to *figure 19.3* to show how these particles would move in a uniform electric field. Label your diagram to show the tracks of the faster and slower α-particles.

b A β-emitting radioactive substance usually emits β-particles with a range of speeds. Add to the diagram you drew in **a** to show how these particles would behave in the uniform electric field.

● **Figure 19.5** α-particle tracks show up in this photograph of a cloud chamber. Notice that all the particles travel roughly the same distance through the air, indicating that they all have roughly the same energy.

Absorbing radiation

Safety note
When working with **radioactive sources**, it is essential to **follow the relevant safety regulations**, which your teacher will explain to you.

α-radiation

Because α-radiation is highly ionising, it cannot penetrate very far into matter. A cloud chamber can be used to show the tracks of α-particles in air *(figure 19.5)*; the tracks are very dense, because of the dense concentration of ions produced, and they extend for only a few centimetres into the air. By the time the α-particles have travelled this far, they have lost virtually all of their kinetic energy.

α-particles can also be detected by a solid-state detector, or by a Geiger tube with a thin end-window *(figure 19.6)*. By moving the source back and forth in front of the detector, it is simple to show that the particles only penetrate 5 or 6 cm of air. Similarly, with the source close to the detector, it can be shown that a single sheet of paper is adequate to absorb all of the α-radiation.

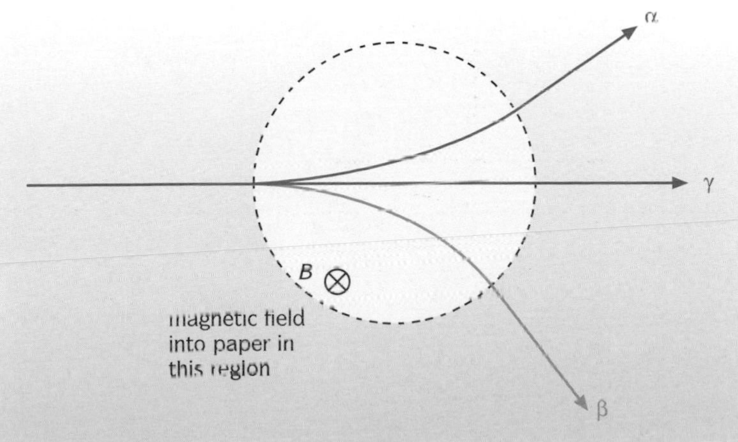

● **Figure 19.4** A magnetic field can also be used to separate α, β and γ-radiations.

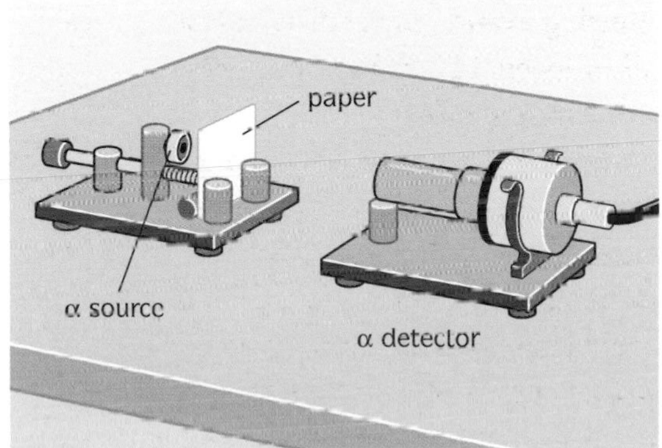

● **Figure 19.6** α-radiation can be absorbed by a single sheet of paper.

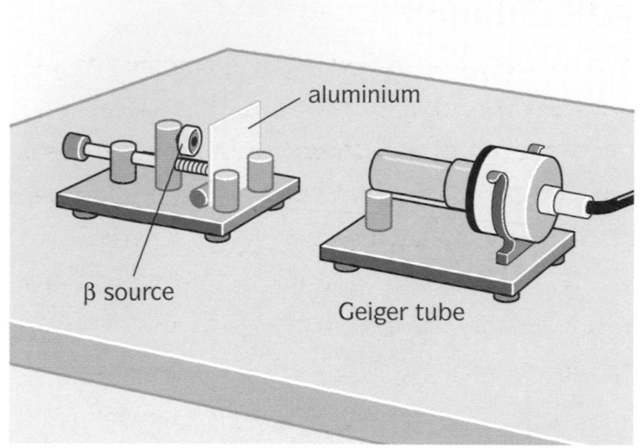

● **Figure 19.7** β-radiation passes readily through thin paper, but can be absorbed by a few millimetres of a light metal such as aluminium.

β-radiation

A Geiger tube can detect β-radiation. The source is placed close to the tube, and different materials are positioned between source and tube *(figure 19.7)*. Paper has little effect; a denser material such as aluminium or lead is a more effective absorber. A few millimetres of aluminium will completely absorb β-radiation.

γ-radiation

Since γ-radiation is the least strongly ionising, it is the most penetrating. Lead can be used to absorb γ-rays, as shown in *figure 19.8*. The intensity of the radiation decreases gradually as it passes through the lead; in principle, an infinite thickness of lead would be needed to absorb the radiation completely. (This is because a γ-photon must score

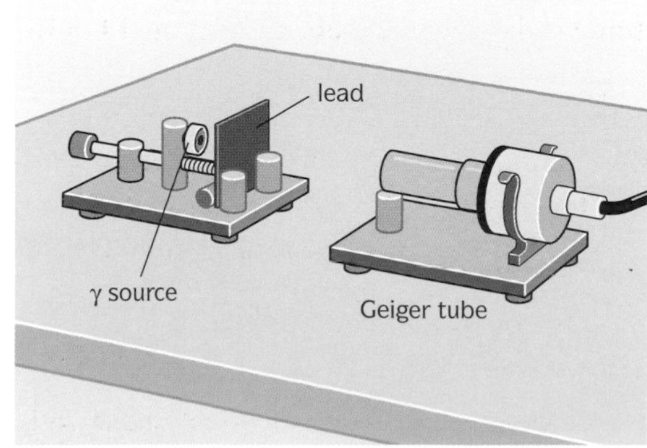

● **Figure 19.8** γ-rays are absorbed by lead, but a considerable thickness may be needed to reduce their intensity to background levels.

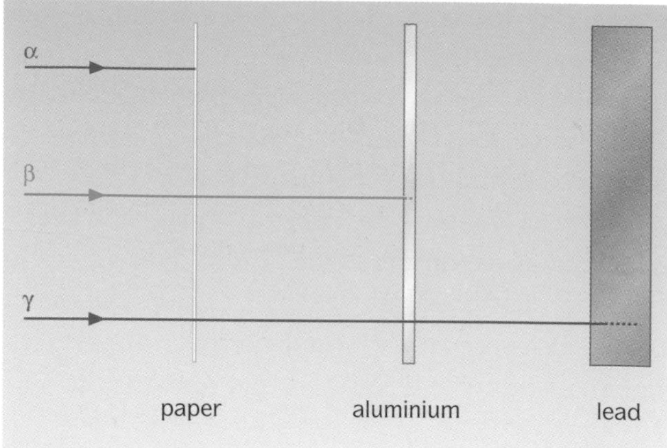

● **Figure 19.9** A summary of the penetrating powers of α, β and γ-radiations.

a 'direct hit' on the nucleus of a lead atom if it is to be absorbed. By the laws of chance, some photons travel a long way before scoring a bullseye.)

The different penetrating properties of α, β and γ-radiations are summarised in *figure 19.9*.

SAQ 19.3

Explain why the most strongly ionising radiation (α-particles) are the least penetrating, while the least ionising (γ-rays) are the most penetrating.

SAQ 19.4

A smoke detector *(figure 19.10)* uses a source of α-radiation to detect the presence of smoke in the air. Explain how the smoke detector works, and why an α source is more suitable for this than a β or γ source.

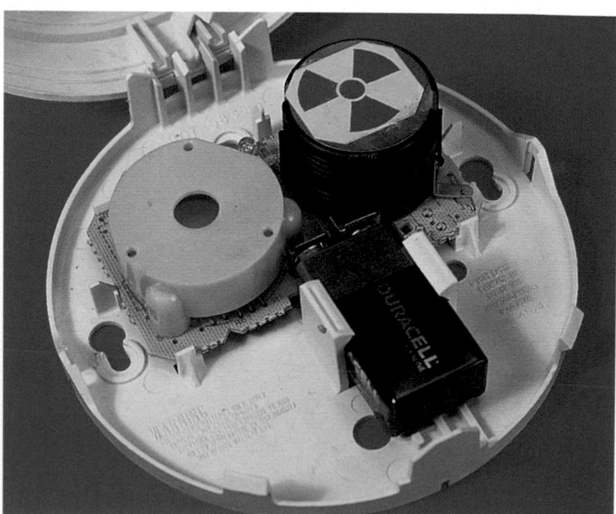

● **Figure 19.10** A smoke detector that uses the absorption of α-radiation as the principle of its operation.

Randomness and decay

Listen to a Geiger counter that is detecting the radiation from a weak source, so that the count rate is about one count per second. You will notice, of course, that the counts do not come regularly. The counter beeps or clicks in a random, irregular manner. If you try to predict when the next clicks will come, you are unlikely to be right.

You can see the same effect if you have a ratemeter, which can measure faster rates *(figure 19.11)*. The needle fluctuates up and down. Usually a ratemeter has a control for setting the 'time constant' – the time over which the meter averages out the fluctuations. Usually this can be set to 1 s or 5 s. The fluctuations are smoothed out more on the 5 s setting.

So it is apparent that radioactive decay is a random, irregular phenomenon. But is it completely unpredictable? Well, not really. We can measure the average rate of decay. We might measure the number of counts detected in 1000 s, and then calculate the average number per second. We cannot be sure about the average rate, either, because the number of counts in 1000 s will fluctuate, too. So all of our measurements of radioactive decay are inherently uncertain and imprecise.

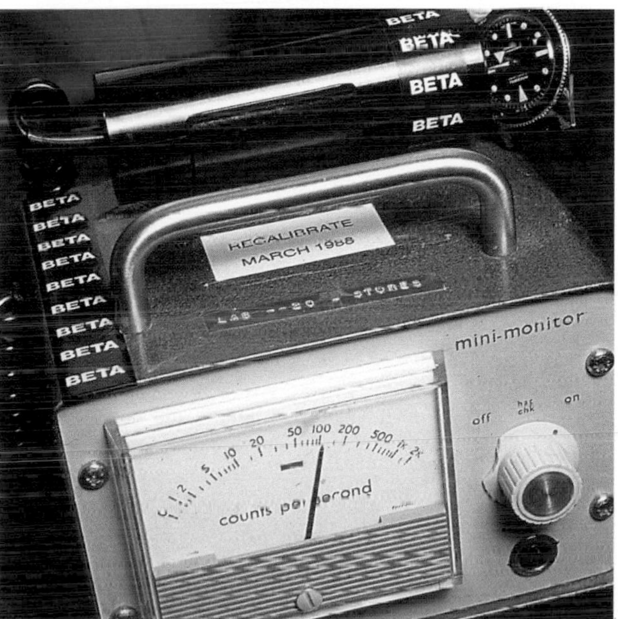

● ***Figure 19.11*** The time constant of this ratemeter can be adjusted to smooth out rapid fluctuations in the count rate.

Spontaneous decay

Radioactive decay occurs within the nucleus of an atom. A nucleus emits radiation, and the atom becomes an atom of a different substance. This is a spontaneous process, which means that we cannot predict, for a particular nucleus, when it will happen. If we sit and stare at an individual nucleus, we cannot see any change that will tell us that it is getting ready to decay. And if it doesn't decay in the first hour when we are watching it, we cannot say that it is any more likely to decay in the next hour.

This is slightly odd, because it goes against our everyday experience of the way things around us change. We observe things changing. They gradually age, die, rot away. But this is not how things are on the scale of atoms and nuclei. Many of the atoms of which we are made have existed for billions of years, and will still exist long after we are gone. The nucleus of an atom does not age.

If we look at a large number of atoms of a radioactive substance, we will see the nuclei gradually decay. However, we cannot predict when an individual nucleus will decay. Each nucleus 'makes up its own mind' when to decay, independently from its neighbours. This is because neighbouring nuclei do not interact with one another (unlike neighbouring atoms). The nucleus is a tiny fraction of the size of the atom, and the nuclear forces do not extend very far outside the nucleus. So one nucleus cannot affect a neighbouring nucleus by means of the nuclear force. Being inside a nucleus is a bit like living in a detached house in the middle of nowhere; you can just see out into the garden, but everything is darkness beyond, and the next house is 1000 km away.

The fact that individual nuclei decay spontaneously, and independently of their neighbours, accounts for the random pattern of clicks that we hear from a Geiger counter and the fluctuations of the needle on the ratemeter dial.

Decay constant

Because we cannot say when individual nuclei will decay, we have to start thinking about large numbers of nuclei. Then we can talk about the average number of nuclei that we expect to decay in a particular time interval; in other words, we can find out the average decay rate. Although we cannot make predictions for individual nuclei, we can say that certain nuclei are more likely to decay than others. For example, a nucleus of carbon-12 is stable; carbon-14 decays gradually over thousands of years; carbon-15 nuclei last, on average, a few seconds.

So, because of the spontaneous nature of radioactive decay, we have to make measurements on large numbers of nuclei and then calculate averages. One quantity we can determine is the probability that an individual nucleus will decay in a particular time interval. For example, suppose we observe one million nuclei of a particular radio-isotope. After one hour, 200 000 have decayed. Then the probability that an individual nucleus will decay in 1 h is 0.2 or 20%, since 20% of the nuclei have decayed in this time. (Of course, this is only an approximate value, since we might repeat the experiment and find that only 199 000 decay. The more times we repeat the experiment, the more accurate our answer will be.)

The probability that an individual nucleus will decay in a particular time interval is called the **decay constant**, symbol λ (lambda). For the example above, we have:

$$\text{decay constant } \lambda = 0.2\,\text{h}^{-1}$$

Note that, because we are measuring the probability of decay in a particular time interval, λ has units of h^{-1} (or s^{-1}, day^{-1}, year^{-1}, etc.).

Activity

The **activity** A of a radioactive sample is the rate at which nuclei decay. Activity is measured in decays per second (or h^{-1}, day^{-1}, etc.). An activity of one decay per second is one becquerel (1 Bq):

$$1\,\text{Bq} = 1\,\text{s}^{-1}$$

Clearly, the activity of a sample depends on the decay constant λ of the radio-isotope under consideration. The greater the decay constant (the probability that an individual nucleus decays in a particular time interval), the greater is the activity of the sample. It also depends on the size of the sample. For a sample of N undecayed nuclei, we have

$$A = \lambda N$$

We shall now look at an example. A sample consists of 1000 undecayed nuclei of a nuclide whose decay constant is $0.2\,\text{s}^{-1}$. What would the activity of this sample be? What would you expect its activity to be after 1 s?

Since activity $A = \lambda N$, we have

$$A = 0.2\,\text{s}^{-1} \times 1000 = 200\,\text{s}^{-1}, \text{ or } 200\,\text{Bq}$$

After 1 s, we might expect 800 nuclei to remain undecayed. The activity of the sample would then be

$$A = 0.2\,\text{s}^{-1} \times 800 = 160\,\text{Bq}$$

(In fact, it would be slightly higher than this. Since the rate of decay decreases with time all the time, less than 200 nuclei would decay during the first second.)

Count rate

Although we are often interested in finding the activity of a sample of radioactive material, we cannot usually measure this directly. This is because we cannot easily detect all of the radiation emitted. Some will escape past our detectors, and some may be absorbed within the sample itself. So our measurements give a received count rate R that is significantly lower than the activity A. If we know how efficient our detecting system is, we can deduce A from R.

SAQ 19.5

A sample of carbon-15 initially contains 500 000 undecayed nuclei. If the decay constant for this isotope of carbon is $0.30\,\text{s}^{-1}$, what is the initial activity of the sample?

SAQ 19.6

A piece of radium gives a received count rate of 20 counts per minute in a detector whose efficiency is known to be 10%. If the sample contains 1.5×10^9 atoms, what is the decay constant of this form of radium?

SAQ 19.7

A radioactive sample is known to emit α, β and γ-radiation. Suggest **four** reasons why the count rate measured by a Geiger counter placed next to this sample would be lower than the activity of the sample.

Decay graphs and equations

Radioactive substances gradually diminish as time goes by. The atomic nuclei emit radiation and become different substances. The pattern of radioactive decay is an example of a very important pattern found in many different situations, a pattern called exponential decay. *Figure 19.12* shows the decay graphs for three different radio-isotopes, each with a different rate of decay.

Although the three graphs look different, they all have something in common – their shape. They are curved lines having a special property. If you know what is meant by the half-life of a radio-isotope, then you will understand what is special about the shape of these curves. The half-life $t_{1/2}$ of a radio-isotope is the average time taken for half of a sample to decay *(figure 19.13)*. It takes the same amount of time again for half of the remainder to decay, and a third half-life for half of the new remainder to decay.

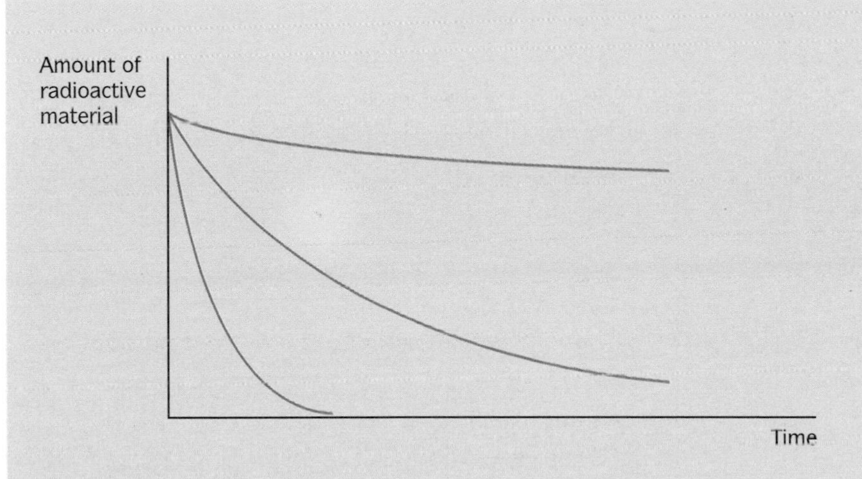

● ***Figure 19.12*** Some radioactive materials decay faster than others.

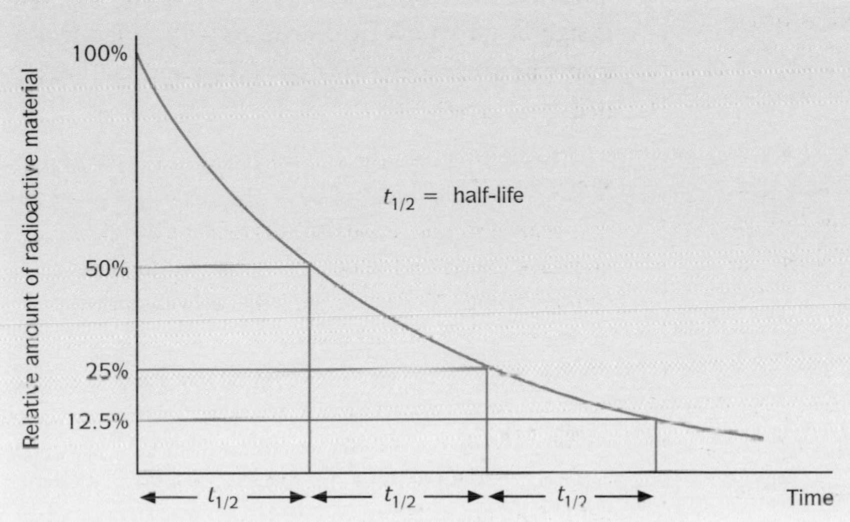

● ***Figure 19.13*** All radioactive decay graphs have the same characteristic shape.

In principle, the graph never reaches zero; it just gets closer and closer. (In practice, when only a few undecayed nuclei remain, it will cease to be a smooth curve and will eventually reach zero.) We use the idea of half-life, because we cannot say when a sample will have completely decayed.

Measuring half-life

If you are to measure the half-life of a radioactive substance in the laboratory, you need to choose something that will not decay too quickly or too slowly. In practice, the most suitable radio-isotope is protactinium-234, which decays by emitting β-radiation. This is produced in a bottle containing uranium *(figure 19.14)*. By shaking the bottle, you can separate the protactinium into the top layer of solvent in the bottle. The Geiger counter allows you to measure the decay of the protactinium.

After recording suitable measurements over a period of a few minutes, you can then draw a graph, and use it to find the half-life of protactinium-234.

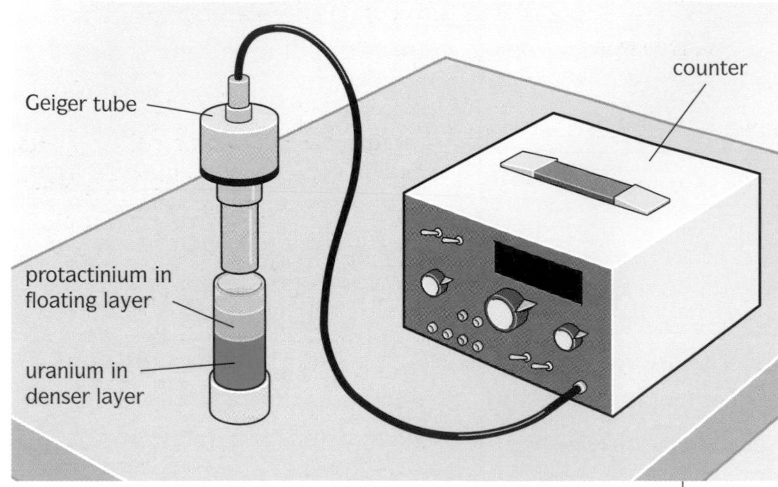

● ***Figure 19.14*** Practical arrangement for observing the decay of protactinium-234.

Mathematical decay

We can write an equation to represent this graph. If we start with N_0 undecayed nuclei, then the number N that remain undecayed after time t is given by

$$N = N_0 e^{-\lambda t} \qquad [\text{or} \qquad N = N_0 \exp(-\lambda t)]$$

In this equation, λ is the decay constant as before. Note that you must take care with units. If λ is in s^{-1}, t must be in s.

The symbol e represents the number e = 2.71828..., a special number in the same way that π (pi) is a special number. You will need to be able to use the e^x key on your calculator to solve problems involving e.

Usually, we measure the count rate R rather than the number of undecayed nuclei. This also decreases as the substance decays, and we can write

$$R = R_0 e^{-\lambda t}$$

Similarly, the activity of the sample decreases exponentially:

$$A = A_0 e^{-\lambda t}$$

We shall now work through some examples.

1 Suppose we start an experiment with 1000 undecayed nuclei of a radio-isotope for which $\lambda = 0.02\,s^{-1}$. How many will remain undecayed after 20 s?

In this case, we have $N_0 = 1000$, $\lambda = 0.02\,s^{-1}$ and $t = 20$ s. Substituting in the equation gives

$$N = 1000\,e^{(-0.02 \times 20)}$$

Calculating the expression in brackets first gives

$$N = 1000\,e^{-0.4}$$

Using the e^x key and multiplying by 1000 gives

$$N = 670$$

(This answer has been rounded off to the nearest whole number, because we cannot have a fraction of a nucleus. In practice, we would expect the number of undecayed nuclei after 20 s to be close to this answer.)

2 A sample initially contains 1000 undecayed nuclei of an isotope whose decay constant $\lambda = 0.1\,min^{-1}$. Draw a graph to show how the sample will decay over a period of 10 min.

The equation for this decay is $N = 1000\,e^{-0.1t}$. Calculating values of N at intervals of 1 min gives the table below, and the graph is shown in *figure 19.15*.

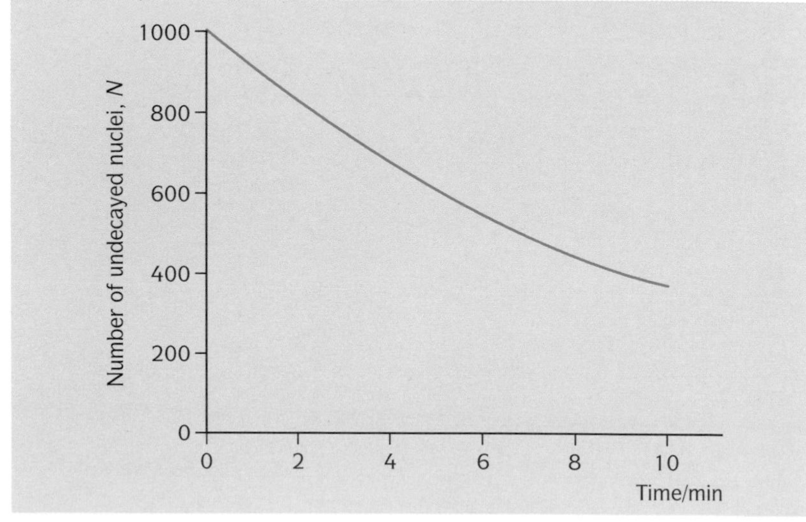

● ***Figure 19.15*** Radioactive decay graph for the second worked example.

t/min	0	1	2	3	4	5	6	7	8	9	10
N	1000	905	819	741	670	607	549	497	449	407	368

SAQ 19.8

The radio-isotope nitrogen-13 has a half-life of 10.0 min. A sample initially contains 1000 undecayed nuclei.

a Write down an equation to show how the number undecayed N depends on time t.

b How many will remain after 10 min, and after 20 min?

c How many will decay during the first 30 min?

SAQ 19.9

A sample of a radio-isotope, for which $\lambda = 0.1\,s^{-1}$, contains 5000 undecayed nuclei at the start of an experiment.

a How many will remain after 50 s?

b What will its activity be after 50 s?

SAQ 19.10

The value of λ for protactinium-234 is $9.63 \times 10^{-3}\,s^{-1}$. The table shows the number of undecayed nuclei, N, in a sample.

time/s	0	20	40	60	80	100	120	140
N	400	330						

Copy and complete the table. Draw a graph, and use it to find the half-life of protactinium-234.

SAQ 19.11

Carbon-14 is the radio-isotope used by archaeologists for radiocarbon dating of dead organic matter. Its value of λ is $1.21 \times 10^{-4}\,year^{-1}$. In laboratory tests, a sample of fresh material gives a count rate of $200\,min^{-1}$. Calculate how this rate will decrease over a period of 10 000 years. Draw a graph, and use it to determine the age of a sample that gives a count rate of $116\,min^{-1}$.

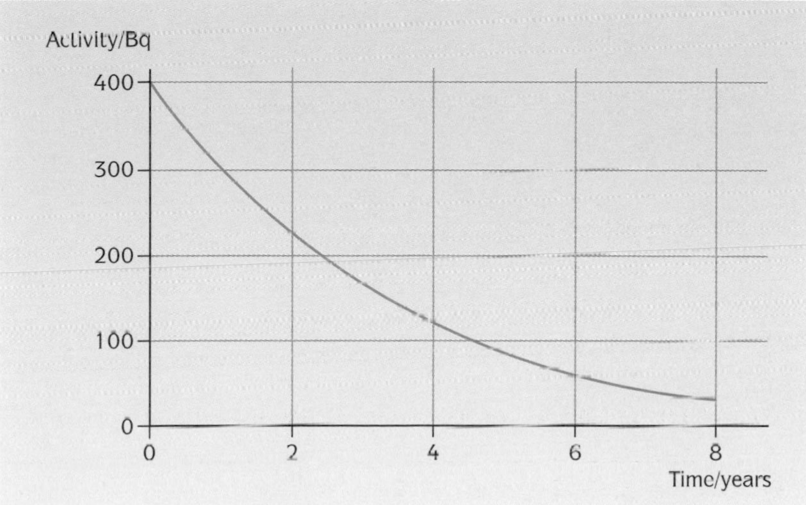

● ***Figure 19.16*** Decay graph for a radio-isotope of caesium.

Decay constant and half-life

A radio-isotope that decays rapidly has a short half-life $t_{1/2}$. Its decay constant must be high, since the probability of an individual nucleus decaying must be high. Hence there is a connection between half-life and decay constant. They are inversely related:

$$\lambda = \frac{0.693}{t_{1/2}}$$

(The constant 0.693 comes into this because $e^{-0.693} = 1/2$, approximately.)

Thus if we know either $t_{1/2}$ or λ, we can calculate the other. For a nuclide with a very long half-life, we might not wish to sit around waiting to measure the half-life; it is easier to determine λ by measuring the activity (and using $A = \lambda N$), and then deduce $t_{1/2}$.

Note that the units of λ and $t_{1/2}$ must be compatible; for example, λ in s^{-1} and $t_{1/2}$ in s.

SAQ 19.12

Figure 19.16 shows the decay of a radio-isotope of caesium, $^{134}_{55}Cs$. Use the graph to determine the half-life of this nuclide, and hence find the decay constant.

SAQ 19.13

The decay constant of a particular radio-isotope is known to be $3 \times 10^{-4}\,s^{-1}$. After how long will the activity of a sample of this substance decrease to one-eighth of its initial value?

SUMMARY

- There are three types of ionising radiation produced by radioactive substances, α- and β-particles and γ-rays.
- The most strongly ionising, and hence the least penetrating, is α. The least strongly ionising is γ.
- Their different charges, masses and speeds can be distinguished by the effect of an electric or magnetic field.
- Nuclear decay is a spontaneous and random process. This unpredictability means that count rates tend to fluctuate, and we have to measure average quantities.
- The half-life $t_{1/2}$ of a nuclide is the average time taken for half of the nuclei in a sample to decay.
- The decay constant λ is the probability that an individual nucleus will decay in a particular time interval.
- These two quantities are related by $\lambda = 0.693/t_{1/2}$.
- We can represent the exponential decrease of a quantity by an equation of the form $x = x_0 e^{-\lambda t}$, where x can be activity A, received count rate R, or number of undecayed nuclei N.

Answers to self-assessment questions

The answers are sometimes given to more significant figures than are allowed by the data, to assist with checking.

Chapter 1

1.1 a $29.9\,\mathrm{km\,s^{-1}}$ b $465\,\mathrm{m\,s^{-1}}$

c $86.4\,\mathrm{min}$

1.2 Speed does not change.

1.3 a $0\,\mathrm{m\,s^{-1}}$ b $0.4\,\mathrm{m\,s^{-1}}$

1.4 a Gravitational pull of Earth on Moon.

b Frictional force of road on wheels.

c Tension in string supporting the pendulum.

1.5 No frictional force between wheels and road. If driver turns steering wheel, car will carry straight on.

1.6 Speed and kinetic energy are scalar quantities; the others are all vectors. Speed is constant; velocity has constant magnitude but direction is changing (it is tangential to the circle); kinetic energy is constant; momentum has constant magnitude but direction is changing (tangential to the circle); centripetal force has constant magnitude but direction is changing (radial force); centripetal acceleration behaves in the same way as centripetal force.

1.7 $84.6\,\mathrm{min}$

1.8 $3.5\,\mathrm{m\,s^{-1}}$

End-of-chapter questions

1 a $184\,\mathrm{kN}$ b $7.71\,\mathrm{km\,s^{-1}}$

c $5500\,\mathrm{s}$ d 15.7 times

2 a $9.4\,\mathrm{m\,s^{-1}}$ b $177\,\mathrm{m\,s^{-2}}$

c $88\,\mathrm{N}$

3 a $24.3\,\mathrm{km\,s^{-1}}$ b $2.6 \times 10^{-3}\,\mathrm{m\,s^{-2}}$

c $1.6 \times 10^{21}\,\mathrm{N}$

Chapter 2

2.1 $6.67 \times 10^{-9}\,\mathrm{N}$

2.2 $10^{-6}\,\mathrm{N}$. Weight greater than this by factor of 10^{9}.

2.3 $9.86\,\mathrm{m\,s^{-2}}$

2.4 $73\,\mathrm{m}$

2.5 a $980\,\mathrm{J}$, $44.3\,\mathrm{m\,s^{-1}}$

b $62.5\,\mathrm{MJ}$, $54.1\,\mathrm{MJ}$, $8.4\,\mathrm{MJ}$, $4100\,\mathrm{m\,s^{-1}}$

c $9.8\,\mathrm{MJ}$, $4430\,\mathrm{m\,s^{-1}}$. The values differ because the equation $E_p = mgh$ works on the assumption that g is constant, but in this case the distance involved is large enough for g to change.

Box questions on measuring *G*

A $6.67 \times 10^{-9}\,\mathrm{N}$

B Lead is very dense, so for a manageable size of apparatus it will give the largest possible gravitational force.

C $1.69 \times 10^{-6}\,\mathrm{N}$

D 6×10^{-8} degrees

E In Cavendish's apparatus, the force between the masses is not balancing the weight of the sphere, so it can provide much more sensitive measurements than the 'pendulum' apparatus.

F So that the gravitational force on one small sphere would arise from the attraction of the large sphere next to it, and there would be little attraction due to the other large sphere.

G Cavendish's experiment can be used to determine a value for G. Then this can be used in Newton's equation for the gravitational force to estimate the mass of the Earth. So in effect it is 'weighing' the Earth.

Box questions on trip to Jupiter

A $62.5\,\mathrm{MJ\,kg^{-1}}$

B $1900\,\mathrm{MJ\,kg^{-1}}$, $27.2\,\mathrm{N\,kg^{-1}}$

C The more fuel that is carried, the greater the mass of the spacecraft at launch, and so more energy is required for the journey.

D Need $62.5\,\mathrm{MJ\,kg^{-1}}$ to get clear of Earth, so only hydrogen is suitable.

E $130\,\mathrm{MJ\,kg^{-1}}$

F Hydrogen.

G No. The return journey would be impossible, because the energy required to launch from Jupiter exceeds that of any of the fuels listed.

H $11.2\,\mathrm{km\,s^{-1}}$, $2.4\,\mathrm{km\,s^{-1}}$, $62\,\mathrm{km\,s^{-1}}$

I The escape velocity for the Moon is of the order of magnitude of the average velocity of gas particles, so gases can escape from the Moon.

J The average velocity of hydrogen and helium molecules exceeds that of the Earth's escape velocity, so these gases are present only sparingly in the atmosphere.

K Lots of hydrogen! (And other, heavier gases.)

End-of-chapter questions

1 Earth is slightly 'squashed' (diameter from pole to pole is less than that across the equator). You will weigh more at the North Pole. Scales do not measure mass, but weight. However, differences in weight are too subtle for insensitive bathroom scales to detect.

2 3.1 N (or 0.3 kg on scales). Measurable with bathroom scales, though hard to achieve accuracy.

3 $1.6\,\mathrm{N\,kg^{-1}}$, $272\,\mathrm{N\,kg^{-1}}$. Only a very thin atmosphere on the Moon because the gases can escape the weak gravity.

4 $2.8 \times 10^{-3}\,\mathrm{N\,kg^{-1}}$, $2.1 \times 10^{20}\,\mathrm{N}$, $2.8 \times 10^{-3}\,\mathrm{m\,s^{-2}}$

5 $25.0\,\mathrm{N\,kg^{-1}}$

6 Field strength due to Sun at Earth
$= 5.93\,\mathrm{mN\,kg^{-1}}$
Field strength due to Moon at Earth
$= 0.0342\,\mathrm{mN\,kg^{-1}}$
So the Sun exerts a greater pull per kilogram on sea-water.

7 $1.7 \times 10^{-8}\,\mathrm{N}$, $5.3 \times 10^{-8}\,\mathrm{N}$

8 Closer to the Moon. The point will be $3.42 \times 10^{5}\,\mathrm{km}$ from the centre of the Earth.

Chapter 3

3.1 *Free:* pendulum in clock; cymbal *after* being struck.
Forced: wing beat of mosquito; shaking of building *during* earthquake.

3.2 Curved.

3.3 10 cm, 120 ms, 8.3 Hz

3.4 **a** 20 cm **b** 0.4 s **c** 2.5 Hz
d -11 cm **e** $0\,\mathrm{cm\,s^{-1}}$ **f** $310\,\mathrm{cm\,s^{-1}}$

3.5 **a** 0.5

b Different frequencies means that the term *phase difference* is meaningless.

3.6 See *figure*.

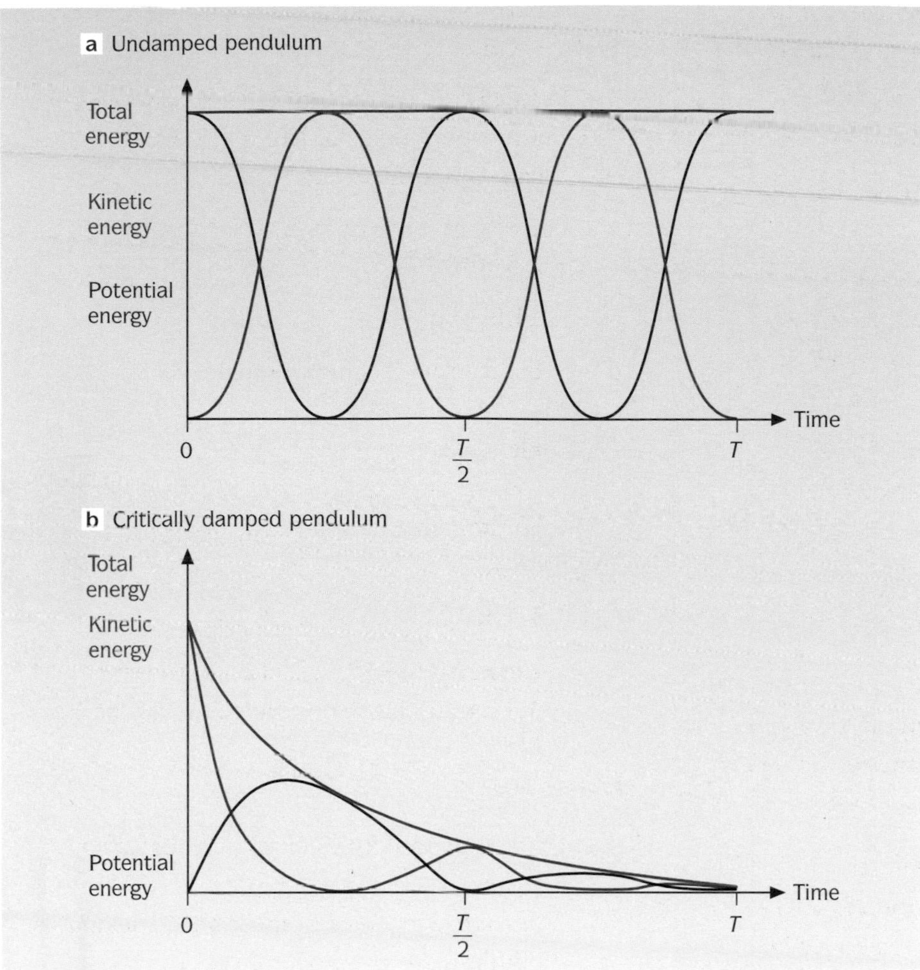

● ***Answer for*** SAQ 3.6

3.7 Useful and problematic examples of resonance:

Example	*Useful/problem?*	*What is resonating?*
Buildings in earthquake	Problem	Mechanical structure forced by energy from waves of earthquake
Components in engines	Problem	At certain rates of rotation, parts of an engine may resonate mechanically; the resonance is driven by the energy output of the engine. This can lead to components cracking or disintegrating, with dangerous consequences
Positive feedback in amplification systems (gives high-pitched squealing sound)	Problem	Microphone held too close to loudspeaker that is emitting waves of the same frequency as the microphone is tuned to, so the waves from the loudspeaker force the amplifier to resonate
Tuned radio	Useful	Electric signal in circuit forced by incoming radio waves
Microwave cooker	Useful	Water molecules forced by microwaves
Magnetic resonance in atoms	Useful	Nuclei in atoms behave as magnets; they can be made to resonate by electromagnetic waves. Each nucleus resonates at a different frequency, so the structures of molecules can be determined

Chapter 4

4.1 a 15 cm, 4 cm

b 20 cm, 2 cm

4.2 See *figure*.

4.3 Two loudspeakers with slightly different frequencies might start off in step, but they would soon go out of step. The interference at a particular point might be constructive at first, but would become destructive.

4.4 The intensity would increase.

4.5 See *figure*.

4.6 a See *figure*.

b 28 mm

4.7 In both cases, waves are reflected (by the metal sheet or by the water). The outgoing and reflected waves interfere to produce a standing wave pattern.

4.8 a Much easier to detect where sound falls to zero than where sound is a maximum.

b Increases accuracy – if the wavelength is short it is difficult to measure just one wavelength.

4.9 13.3 cm, 330 $m\,s^{-1}$

4.10 The grid spacing is much smaller than the wavelength of the microwaves, so the waves do not pass through. However, the wavelength of light is much smaller, so it can pass through unaffected.

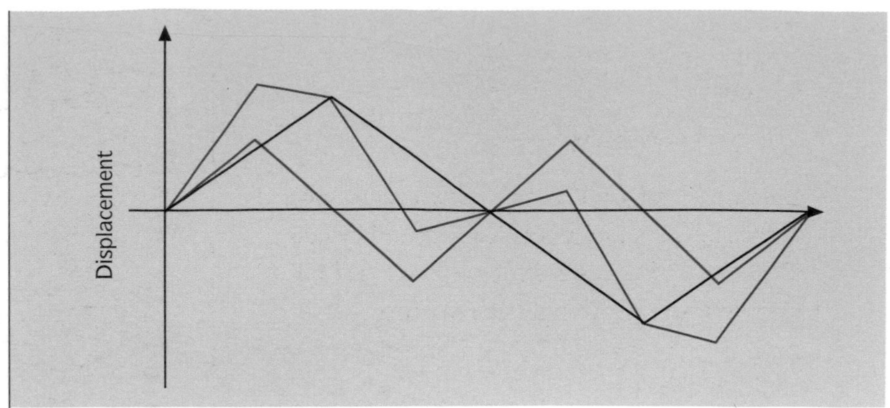

● ***Answer for*** SAQ 4.2

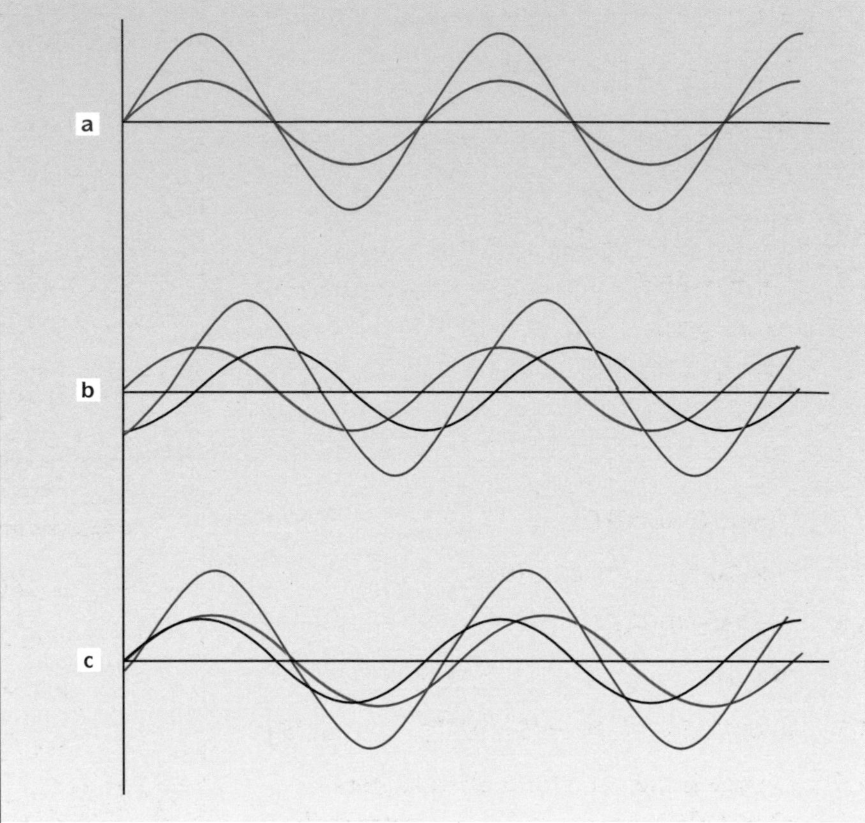

● ***Answer for*** SAQ 4.5

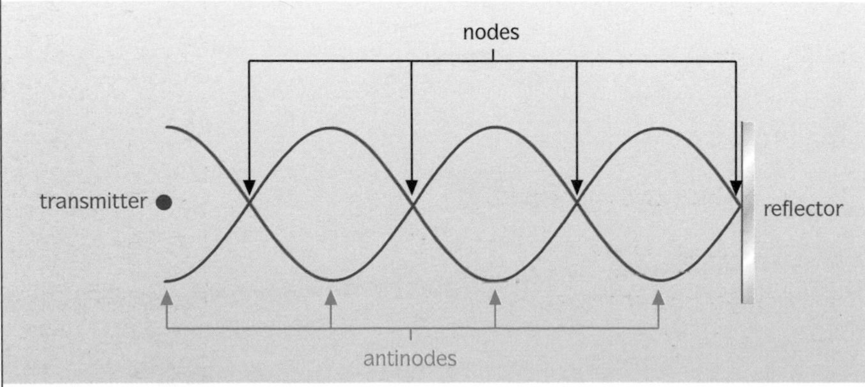

● ***Answer for*** SAQ 4.6a

Chapter 5

5.1 6 J, 5 kJ

5.2 120 C, 1440 J, 24 W

5.3 Chemical energy of battery changes to electrical energy, so current flows round circuit ($P = VI$). Electrons collide with atoms in resistors producing heat energy (power dissipated = I^2R). In 2 Ω resistor, power dissipated = 18 W; in 4 Ω, power = 9 W.

5.4 0.5 A

5.5 a 0.125 A, 2.5 V, 0.5 V

b 0.33 A, 1.67 V, 1.33 V

5.6 2.5 A

5.7 0.71 Ω

5.8 1.5 V, 0.5 Ω (approx.)

5.9 8 V, 4 Ω, 16 W

5.10 0 V to 8.3 V

5.11 6 V, 12 V

Chapter 6

6.1 3000 μC, 0.003 C

6.2 2×10^{-6} F, 2 μF, 2×10^{6} pF

6.3 0.05 A (50 mA)

6.4 800 μF

6.5 a 0.0625 J b 6.25×10^{-8} J c 5.29 J

6.6 Charge is the same for both capacitors (2×10^{4} C). Energy stored is greater in the 100 μF capacitor (4×10^{6} J compared to 2×10^{6} J).

6.7 a 0.72 J b 0.02 s

Chapter 7

7.1 a Positive charges repelling.

c Negative charges.

b Opposite charges.

7.2 See *figure*.

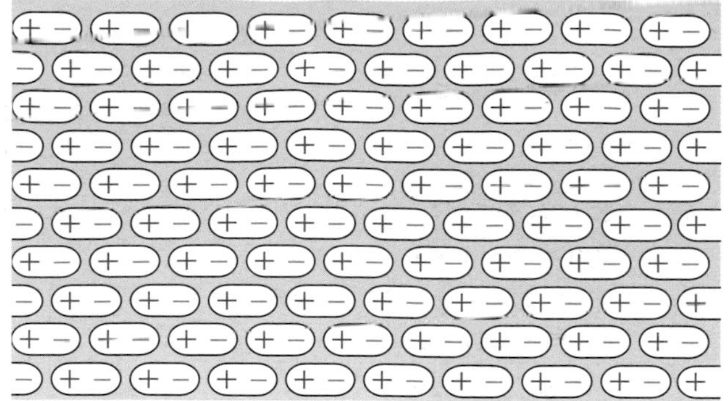

● **Answer for** SAQ 7.2

7.3 See *figure*.

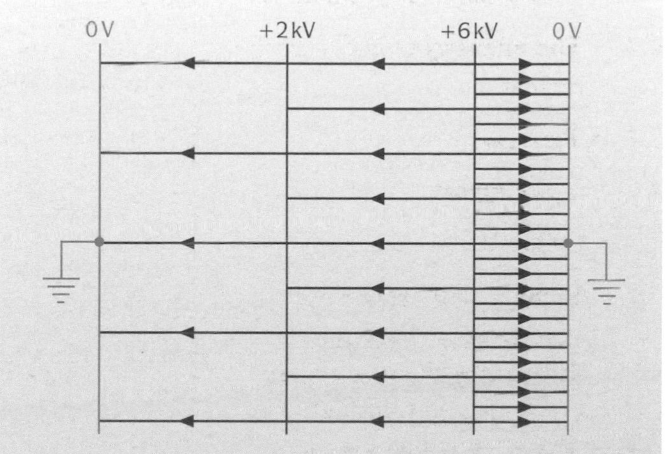

● **Answer for** SAQ 7.3

7.4 a 160 000 V b 0.08 mm c 400 MV

7.5 50 kV m^{-1} (50 kN C^{-1}), 100 kN

7.6 8.8×10^{17} m s^{-2}

7.7 See *figure*.

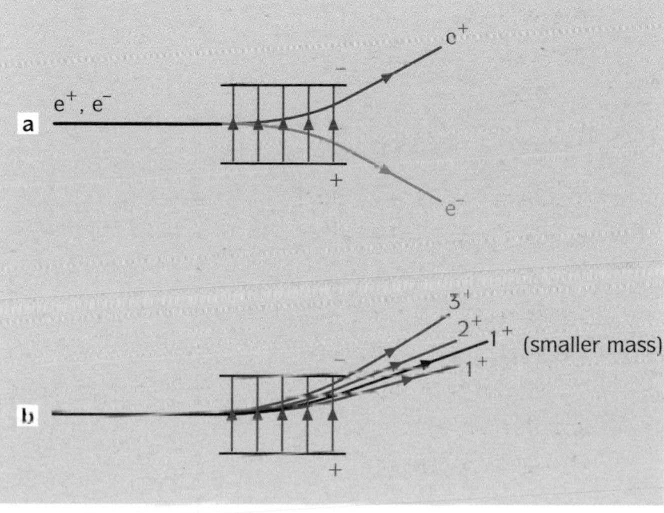

● **Answer for** SAQ 7.7

7.8 230 N, 1.9×10^{-34} N. This answer tells us that gravity is nowhere near enough to balance the electric repulsion. Therefore, some other force must hold the protons together (in fact, it is the *strong nuclear force*, but we do not need to cover it in this module).

7.9 6.0×10^{-7} N, 3.7×10^{12} V m^{-1}, 1.6×10^{21} V m^{-1}

7.10 1.8×10^{-5} C

Box questions on measuring *e*

A Charge on droplet must be negative.

B 180 V cm^{-1}

C 5.78×10^{-15} N

D 5.78×10^{-15} N

E -3.2×10^{-19} C

F β-radiation must be adding negative charge to the droplet. (You could argue that it is somehow reducing the mass, but this is less plausible and is not the correct interpretation.)

G 120 V

Box questions on comprehension

A See *figure*.

● ***Answer for*** box question A

B Field strongest near church tower (field lines and equipotential lines closer together).

C Lightning is more likely to strike the tower.

D See *figure*.

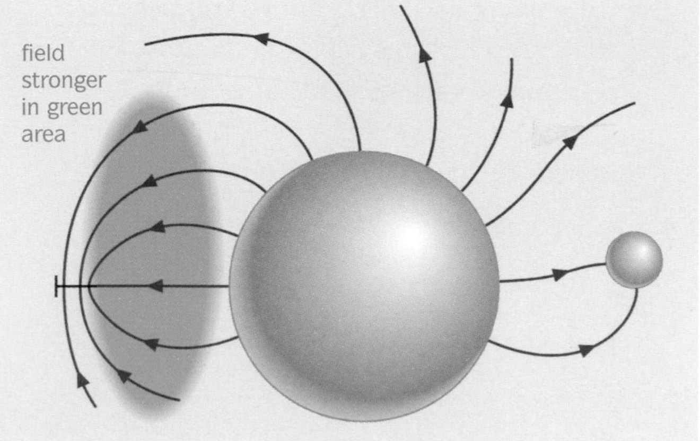

● ***Answer for*** box question D

End-of-chapter questions

1 **a** 0 J, 2 kJ, 1 kJ, 1.5 kJ

b 0 J, 4 kJ, 2 kJ, 3 kJ

2 1.1×10^{-6} C, 50 kV

3 **a** 800 kV

b For higher voltage, dome needs to be larger.

4 **a** 5 kJ, 2.5 kJ, 0 J, −5 kJ

b −5 kJ, −2.5 kJ, 0 J, +5 kJ

c 10 kJ, 5 kJ, 0 J, −10 kJ

Chapter 8

8.1 See *figure*.

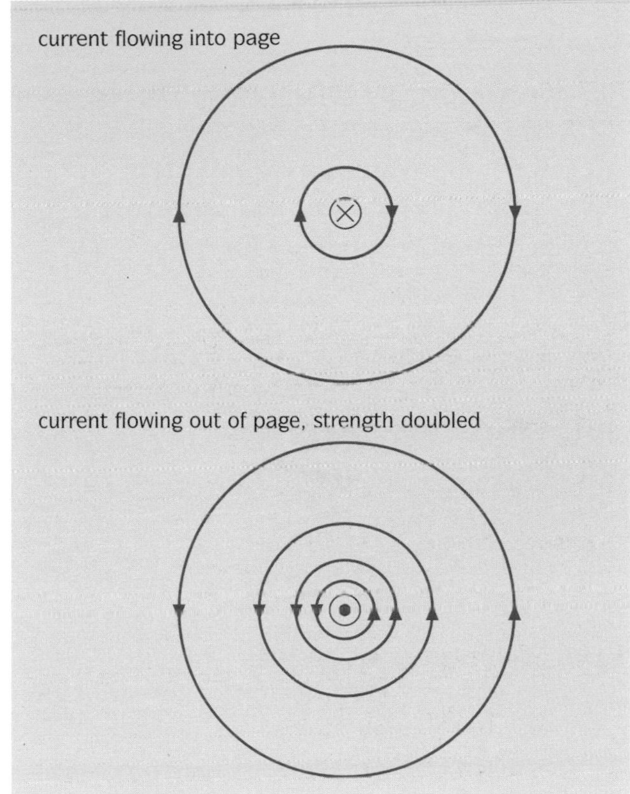

● **Answer for** SAQ 8.1

8.2 See *figure*.

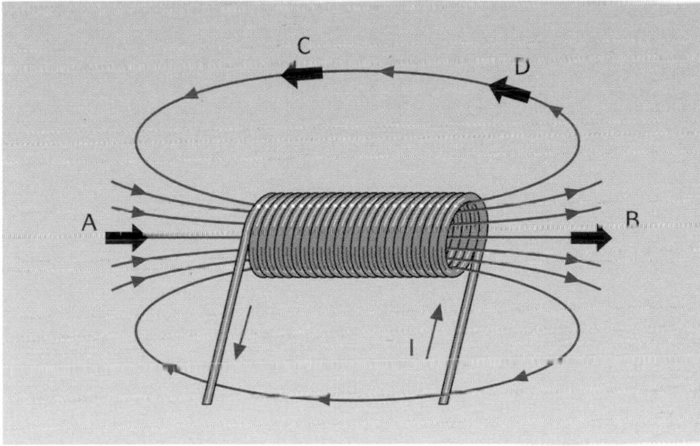

● **Answer for** SAQ 8.2

8.3 a Repel.

b Attract.

8.4 a No force.

b Force in to page.

c Force down.

8.5 See *figure*.

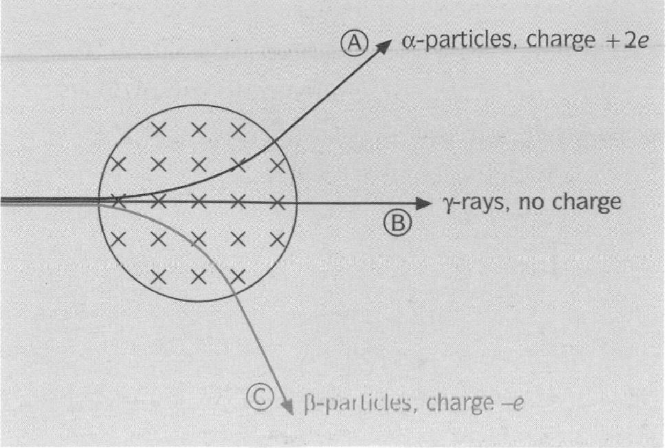

● **Answer for** SAQ 8.5

Chapter 9

9.1 a Section of wire in field moves down.

b Tilts down.

c Will try to move horizontally, *in to* horse-shoe.

d No movement.

9.2 7.8×10^{-3} T

9.3 a 0.375 N b 0.265 N c 0 N

9.4 a 2 N

b Pivot along one edge.

c More power by: increasing current, increasing number of turns in coil, increasing length of side in field, pivoting by centre of coil and have magnets either side, having magnets all round the circle through which the coil turns, increasing field strength.

9.5 a 8×10^{-14} N b 5.66×10^{-14} N

9.6 a Circular path will have smaller radius.

b Electrons will circle in the opposite direction.

c Circular path will have larger radius.

d Electrons will spiral around field lines because they will have a constant component of velocity in the direction of the field lines.

9.7 See *figure*.

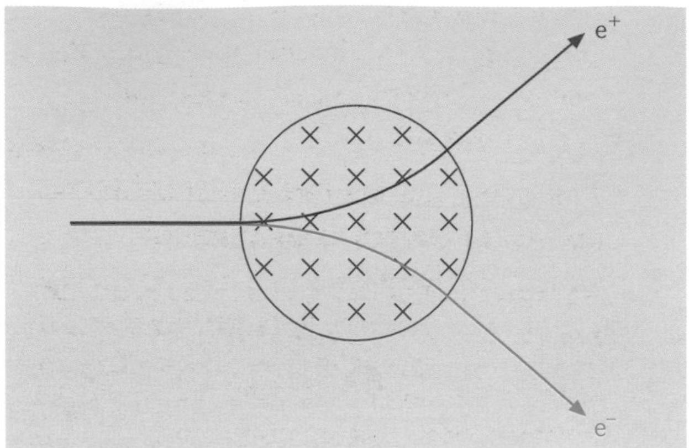

● ***Answer for*** SAQ 9.7

9.8 10^{-5}T

9.9 5.0×10^{-4}T

9.10 7.5×10^{-3}T

9.11 At the centre, flux is produced by coils to left and right. At the end, flux is due to coils to one side only. (Imagine cutting a long solenoid in half. The middle now becomes the ends of two solenoids, and the field for each is halved.)

9.12 5.1×10^{-3}N. They will repel each other.

9.13 Both forces are the same, equal and opposite (both forces depend on both I_1 and I_2 in the same way).

9.14 Coils will attract each other. If both currents reversed, they will still attract.

9.15 As; $kg\,m^2A^{-1}s^{-3}$; $kg^{-1}m^{-2}A^2s^4$; $m^2kg\,A^{-1}s^{-2}$.

End-of-chapter question

1 **a** 1.6×10^{-16}J, $1.87 \times 10^7\,m\,s^{-1}$

b $10\,000\,V\,m^{-1}$, 1.6×10^{-15}N

c No field in horizontal plane. 5.35×10^{-9}s.

d $1.76 \times 10^{15}\,m\,s^{-2}$, $9.4 \times 10^6\,m\,s^{-1}$

e 26.7 degrees

f 25.1 cm

g Deflection decreased; deflection increased.

h 5.35×10^{-4} T, in to page.

Chapter 10

10.1 Wire or coil cuts magnetic flux, driven by the pedals via the chain. Cut flux means current generated in wire to light the lamps.

10.2 Stronger magnet means more flux and more flux linkage, so larger e.m.f.
Faster movement means more flux cut/linked per second and more current generated, so larger e.m.f.

10.3 A→B, C→D. So Y is positive.

10.4 Left wingtip positive. It is negative in the Southern Hemisphere because the field direction is reversed.

10.5 Cutting much less flux. Only small components cut due to slight curvature at edges of field, rather than all the parallel flux in the space between the magnets.

10.6 Frequency determined by speed of rotation (so to keep constant, must be geared). E.m.f. affected by magnet strength, number of turns in coil, size of coil. Would normally be affected by speed of rotation, but in this case that has to be fixed.

Chapter 11

11.1 2.25×10^{-5}Wb

11.2 1.45×10^7Wb

11.3 2.0×10^{-3}T, 3.9×10^{-6}Wb

11.4 0.54 Wb

11.5 6 mV

11.6 0.6 V

11.7 0.4 T

11.8 **a** Stop pushing implies no flux is cut, so no current is generated. Therefore, no magnetic poles are formed and no work is done; there is no movement.

b Pull away implies that flux is cut, but near end to magnet becomes a S pole, so the poles attract each other, and work has to be done to pull magnet and coil apart.

11.9 See *figure*.

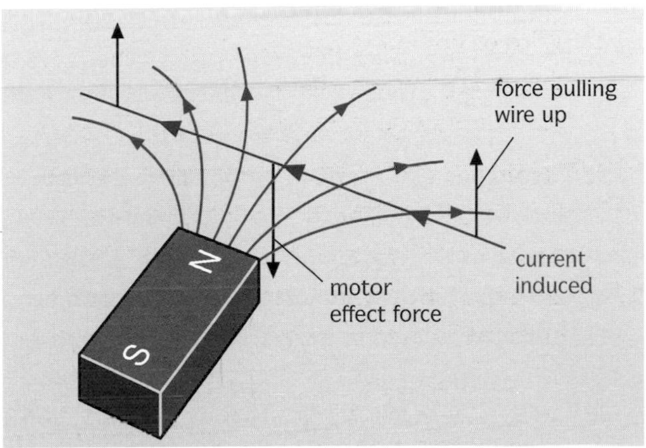

● *Answer for* SAQ 11.9

11.10 a Flux linkage, flux cut as magnet moves, so there is an induced e.m.f.

b No flux cut inside coil, the motion is parallel to the field.

c Magnet leaves coil, flux lines cut again, but e.m.f. is in reverse (negative) direction because current has to flow the other way (Lenz's law). Peak e.m.f. greater because magnet moving faster (acceleration due to gravity), the flux is cut at a faster rate and the e.m.f. is proportional to the rate at which the flux is cut. Also, faster movement means it takes less time to complete the section.

11.11 Have to do work against motor effect force from induced current when lights are on.

11.12 For direct current supply, flux lines constant means no e.m.f. induced.

11.13 See *figure*.

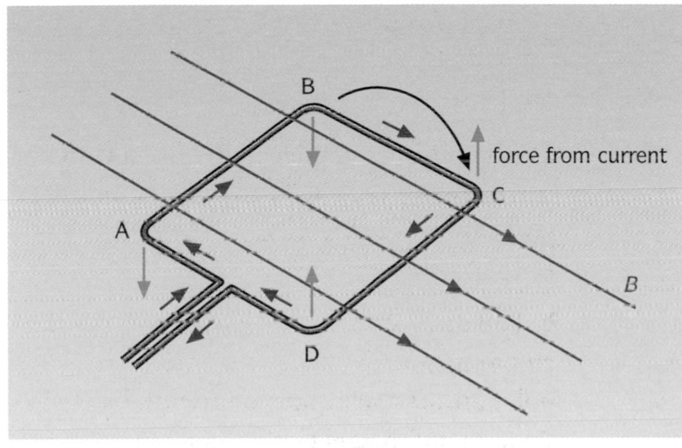

● *Answer for* SAQ 11.13

11.14 Alternating current. Usually, a bar magnet rotates inside a fixed coil. As the N pole passes one side of the coil, the current flows one way. Then the S pole passes, and the current reverses.

11.15 B greater means flux greater means $d\Phi/dt$ greater if same rate of movement.

A greater means flux greater means $d\Phi/dt$ greater if same rate of movement.

N greater means flux greater means $d\Phi/dt$ greater if same rate of movement.

ω greater means rate of cutting flux greater means $d\Phi/dt$ greater.

Chapter 12

12.1 Solid: well ordered, small spacing, no motion except lattice vibrations.
Liquid: less well ordered, small spacing but some gaps, motion fairly slow.
Gas: no order, large spacing, much fast and random motion.

12.2 a Metals are more dense.

b $(0.21 \times 1.43 + 0.79 \times 1.25)\,\text{kg}\,\text{m}^{-3} = 1.29\,\text{kg}\,\text{m}^{-3}$

c See *figure*.

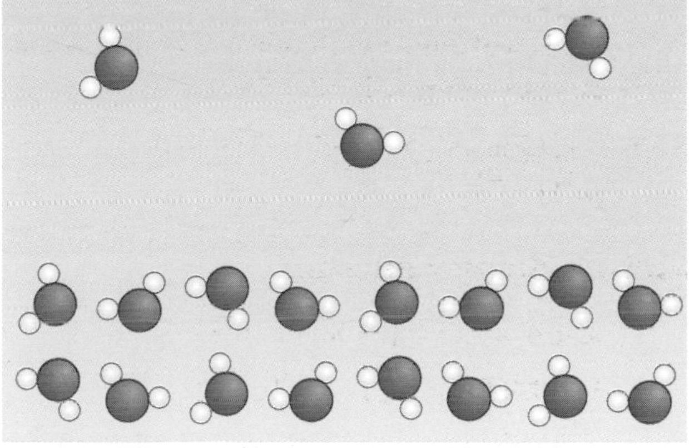

● *Answer for* SAQ 12.2c

12.3 $\frac{1}{2}MV^2 = \frac{1}{2}mv^2$

So

$$\frac{M}{m} = \frac{v^2}{V^2} = \left(\frac{v}{V}\right)^2$$

So $M \ll m$ implies that $v \gg V$.

12.4 2000 N, 5000 N, 10 000 N

12.5 a 7900 m

b Less dense the higher you go means that the height is underestimated.

c Not enough air pressure for there to be sufficient oxygen to breathe.

12.6 7350 Pa, 22.5 kPa

12.7 Upthrust on first box = upthrust on second box = 2450 N

12.8 a Takes energy (implying work and time) to separate all the molecules to form steam.

b Much greater energy required to separate all the molecules (to form gas) than to create some disorder but not separate (to form liquid).

c Speeds up evaporation from its tongue. Energy required for evaporation means that it cools down.

12.9 1.67 MJ

12.10 Copper (just)

12.11 455 $\mathrm{J\,kg^{-1}\,°C^{-1}}$

12.12 12 °C

Chapter 13

13.1 a D b A c C

13.2 Metals from most to least stiff:

	Metal	*Y*/GPa
Most stiff	steel	210
	iron (wrought)	200
	copper	130
	brass	90–110
	aluminium	70
	tin	50
Least stiff	lead	18

13.3 Stiffest non-metal is glass (*Y*=70–80 GPa).

13.4 12.5 GPa, 5.0 GPa

13.5 100 MPa, 0.05%, 200 GPa

13.6 0.10 mm

13.7 a Small loads, iron bath is elastic. Large loads, the cast iron is brittle and breaks.

b At high pressure (load) the aluminium undergoes plastic deformation: it is ductile.

c Small loads and slowly, plastic deformation. Large loads and rapidly, brittle.

13.8 a 50 GPa, 150 MPa b 100 GPa, 125 MPa

c 20 GPa, 70 MPa

13.9 225 J

13.10 a A has greater stiffness (less extension per unit force).

b A requires greater force to break (line continues to higher force value).

c B requires greater amount of work done to break (larger area under graph).

Chapter 14

14.1 a 273 K, 293 K, 393 K, 773 K, 250 K, 73 K

b −273 °C, −253 °C, −173 °C, 27 °C, 100 °C, 227 °C

14.2 a With *V* fixed, if *T* increases, so does *p* (because *pV*/*T* is constant).

b With *p* fixed, if *T* decreases, so does *V*.

14.3 See *figure*.

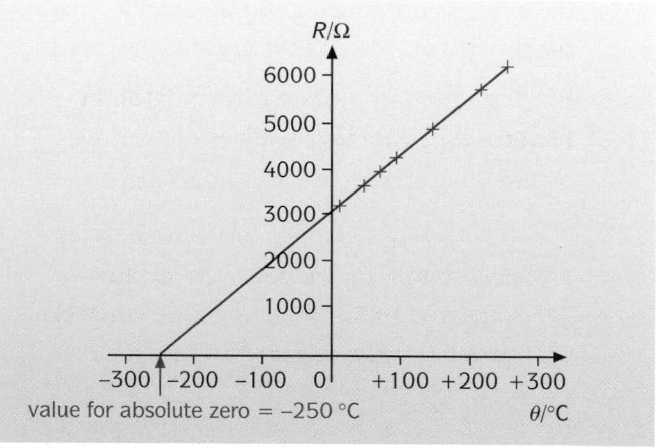

● ***Answer for*** SAQ 14.3

14.4 3.57 mol, 80 $\mathrm{dm^3}$

14.5 385 K (= 112 °C)

14.6 164 g, 2.63 kg

14.7 $p = \frac{F}{A} = \frac{ma}{A}$

Put in SI units for *m*, *a* and *A* to give units for *p*, $\mathrm{kg\,m^{-1}\,s^{-2}}$.

Similarly for right-hand side of equation, units are $kg\,m^{-1}\,s^{-2}$

14.8 a $2.3 \times 10^5\,m^2\,s^{-2}$

b $480\,m\,s^{-1}$, which is 50% greater than speed of sound in air.

14.9 Temperature is proportional to (average speed)^2. So if average speed doubles, temperature increases by a factor $2^2 = 4$.

14.10 Mass smaller means that average speed must be greater to keep average kinetic energy and hence temperature the same. So nitrogen speed is greater than oxygen speed.

Chapter 15

15.1 Two factors: tension in balloon, and air pressure on outside. In space there is no air pressure (though in fact to blow up a balloon you need air to breathe, so in a spaceship there is air pressure, though it may be less than on the ground).

15.2 220 J

15.3 175 kJ

15.4 400 J

15.5 300 kJ

15.6 Air does 50 kJ of work against tension in balloon and external pressure.

Chapter 16

16.1 a Good conductor of electricity means there are many mobile electrons, so they can also conduct thermal energy well.

b Good thermal conduction can be achieved by lattice vibrations rather than by electrons, but this process cannot make good electrical conduction.

c In a gas, there are few mobile electrons and no lattice vibrations.

16.2 See *figure*. Only water in the top half of the tank is heated. The water below the heater remains cold, as it does not become involved in the convection current.

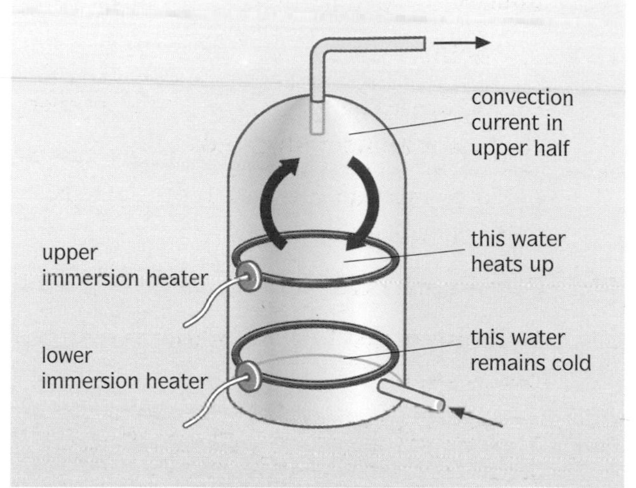

● ***Answer for*** SAQ 16.2

16.3 See *figure*.

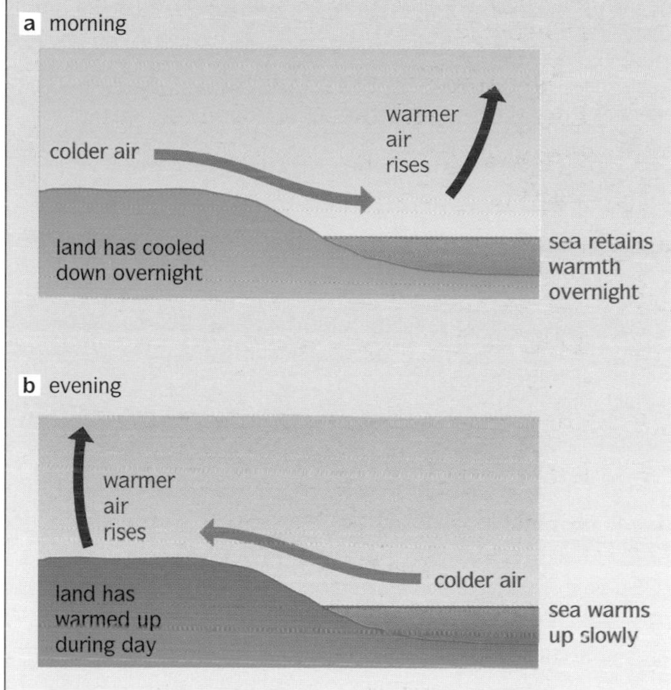

● ***Answer for*** SAQ 16.3

16.4 a Shiny to reflect and contain heat. Plastic is a poor conductor of heat so the handle stays cool.

b Dull base helps to absorb the heat from below. Shiny elsewhere to contain the heat once it is in the kettle. Copper is a good thermal conductor.

c Plastic is a poor conductor anyway, so this contains the heat. Difficult to get very shiny plastic!

16.5 Radiator: ribbed body increases surface area so it radiates more heat. Gap between sections sets up convection current. So the name is half right.
Convector: hollow body and air circulation set up convection current, so the name is quite right.

16.6 a Increases conduction, though not by a lot.

b Greatly reduces convection.

c Little change to radiation.

16.7 Metal: good thermal conductor. Matt and black surface: good radiator. Fins increase surface area, so increase radiation. Shape helps to establish convection currents.

16.8 Plastic stopper is a poor conductor. Also interrupts convection currents. Double wall with vacuum reduces conduction. Silvering reduces radiation. Plastic supports reduce conduction to casing. All these factors reduce heat loss (or heat gain).

Chapter 17

17.1 a Longer wavelength means greater diffraction.

b Smaller gap means greater diffraction. See *figure*.

17.2 a Electrons can behave as waves so they can be diffracted by spaces between atoms.

b Each metal has a different lattice structure, so that it will produce a different diffraction pattern.

17.3 6.63×10^{-8} J

17.4 2.8×10^{-19} J, 5.0×10^{-19} J

17.5 γ-ray, X-ray, ultraviolet, infrared, radio (VHF)

17.6 3.3×10^{15}

17.7 a Gold | b Caesium

c 1.04×10^{15} Hz | d 620 nm

17.8 a 8.3×10^{-19} J | b 5.5×10^{-19} J

c $1.1 \times 10^{6}\,\mathrm{m\,s^{-1}}$

17.9 5.9×10^{-20} J

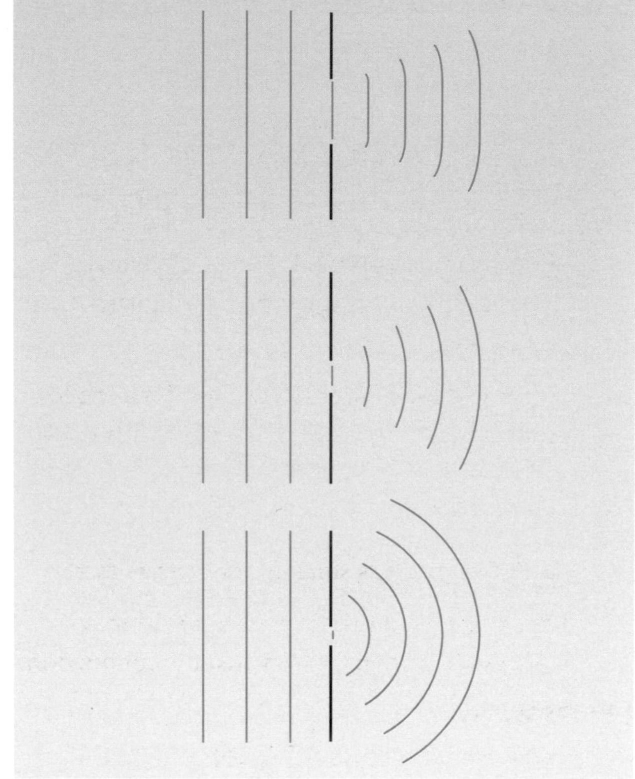

● ***Answer for*** SAQ 17.1b

17.10 a 5.6×10^{-18} J, 8.4×10^{15} Hz, 3.6×10^{-8} m

b 0.5×10^{-18} J, 7.5×10^{14} Hz, 4.0×10^{-7} m

c 2.2×10^{-18} J, 3.3×10^{15} Hz, 9.0×10^{-8} m

17.11 6×10^{-18} J, 8×10^{-18} J, 14×10^{-18} J, 20×10^{-18} J, 25×10^{-18} J correspond to differences between energy levels, so they can all be absorbed. 30×10^{-18} J does not correspond to a difference between energy levels and so cannot be absorbed.

17.12 a Particle model for person and for laser, wave model for sound.

b Wave model. | c Particle model.

d Wave model. | e Particle model.

f Wave model. | g Particle model.

Chapter 18

18.1 $^{235}_{92}\mathrm{U} + ^{1}_{0}\mathrm{n} \rightarrow ^{138}_{54}\mathrm{Xe} + ^{95}_{38}\mathrm{Sr} + 3\,^{1}_{0}\mathrm{n}$

For A $235 + 1 = 138 + 95 + (3 \times 1)$ is correct

For Z $92 + 0 = 54 + 38 + (3 \times 0)$ is correct

18.2 a 2^1_0n b $^{90}_{36}Kr$

18.3 ^1_1H

18.4 2^1_1H

18.5 $^{15}_{7}N + ^1_1H \rightarrow ^{12}_{6}C + ^4_2He$

18.6 a 4.5×10^{-12} J b 1.1×10^{-12} J

18.7 Energy released = -1.0×10^{-4} relative mass units, so energy is required rather than given out.

18.8 Fission for $A<20$ unlikely since forming less stable nuclei; similarly for fusion with $A>40$.

Chapter 19

19.1 a A β-particle is smaller and travels faster.

b Air is much less dense, also metal may 'poach' β-particles (electrons) for conduction.

19.2 See *figure*.

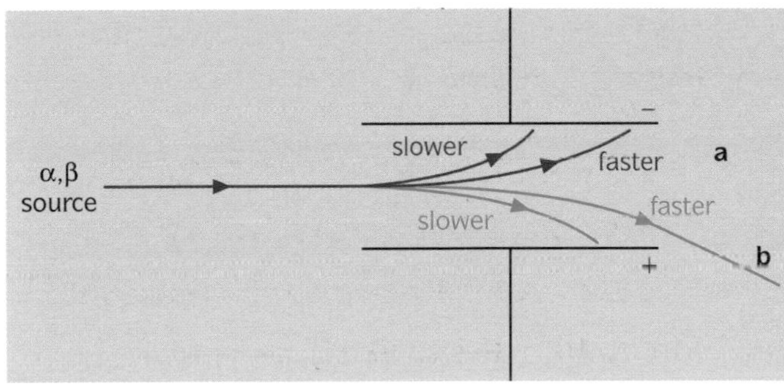

● **Answer for** SAQ 19.2

19.3 Most strongly ionising implies many more collisions occur, so there is greater loss of momentum and therefore less penetration.

19.4 The α-particles are detected by an electronic circuit. When smoke enters the device, the α-particles are absorbed. The circuit then switches on the alarm. Alpha radiation is most suitable because it is the most strongly ionising and so it is more likely to be absorbed by smoke.

19.5 150000 s^{-1}

19.6 2.2×10^{-9} s^{-1}

19.7 Count rate less than activity because:
(i) γ-rays not always detected (weakly ionising);
(ii) counter inefficient;
(iii) some radiation absorbed within sample before reaching detector;
(iv) detector is directional, so some radiation will move away from detector rather than towards it.

19.8 a $N = N_0 e^{-\lambda t}$ b 500, 250 c 875

19.9 a 34 b 3.4 s^{-1}

19.10 See *figure*. Half-life is 72 s.

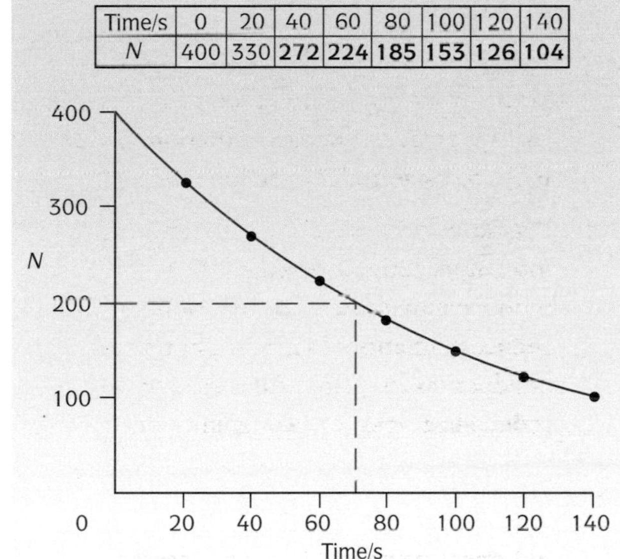

Time/s	0	20	40	60	80	100	120	140
N	400	330	272	224	185	153	126	104

● **Answer for** SAQ 19.10

19.11 See *figure*. Rate becomes 60 min^{-1}. Age will be 1500 years.

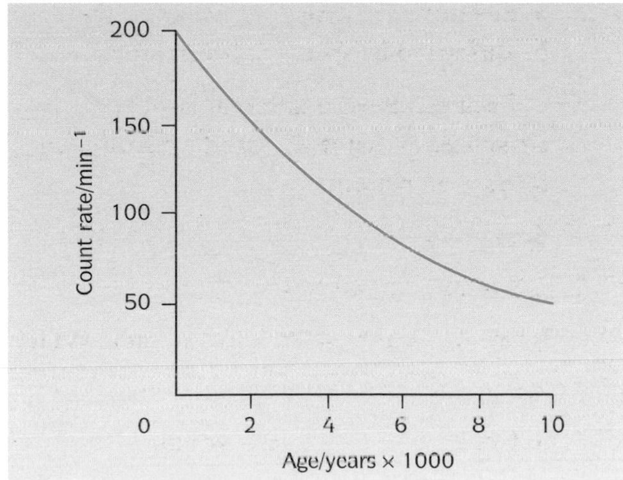

● **Answer for** SAQ 19.11

19.12 2.3 years, 0.30 $year^{-1}$

19.13 6900 s

Index (Numbers in italics refer to figures.)